HISTORY FROM THE HEART

[Plate 1]
ILLINOIS STATE QUILT
106" x 85"
Suzanne Hamer, Delores Jacobs, Roslyn
    Swanstrom and others
St. Charles, Kane County, Illinois, 1987

The State Quilt that is displayed in the Executive Mansion in Springfield was completed by more than eighty volunteers from the Prairie Star Quilt Guild and the Illinois Fox Valley Embroiderers' Guild. The scenes surrounding the State Capitol include Mann Chapel, 1857, Rossville; Murray House, 1842, Naperville; McDonough County Court House, 1869, Macomb; Ellwood House, 1879, DeKalb; Frank Lloyd Wright House and Studio, 1889, Oak Park; Lemuel Milk Carriage House, 1861, Kankakee; Grosse Point Lighthouse, 1873, Evanston; Old State Capitol, 1839, Springfield; Bloom Township High School, 1931, Chicago Heights; Executive Mansion, 1855, Springfield; Museum of Science and Industry, 1893, Chicago; Lyman Trumbull House, 1849, Alton; John Deere Blacksmith Shop, 1837, Grand Detour; Fort de Chartres, 1756, Prairie du Rocher; David Davis Mansion, 1869, Bloomington; Kimball House, 1890, Chicago; the Chicago skyline; and, the Great Seal of the State of Illinois that was adopted in 1818 and altered in 1868.

According to Resolution No. 772, adopted by the Illinois Senate and signed by senate president Philip J. Rock on February 25, 1988, the project participants contributed "something of lasting value to the State" and the senate expressed its appreciation for "the production of this future State heirloom."

Photo by Douglas Marvin

History from the Heart

Quilt Paths Across Illinois

E. Duane Elbert

E. Duane Elbert
& Rachel Kamm Elbert

Rachel Kamm Elbert

Based on findings of the
Illinois Quilt Research Project
Cheryl Kennedy, Project Director

Rutledge Hill Press
Nashville, Tennessee

Published in Nashville, Tennessee, by Rutledge Hill Press, Inc.
211 Seventh Avenue North, Nashville, Tennessee 37219

Typography by D&T/Bailey, Inc., Nashville, Tennessee
Design by Harriette Bateman

Library of Congress Cataloging-in-Publication Data

Elbert, E. Duane, 1935–
    History from the heart : quilt paths aross Illinois / E. Duane
Elbert & Rachel Kamm Elbert.
    p.   cm.
    Includes bibliographical references and index.
    ISBN 1-55853-155-6
    1. Quilting — Illinois — History. 2. Quilts — Illinois I. Elbert,
Rachel Kamm, 1935–   . II. Title.
TT835.E464   1993
746.9′7′09773 — dc20   93-17384
                                          CIP

Printed in Hong Kong
1 2 3 4 5 6 7 8 — 98 97 96 95 94 93

To All
Who Made the
Illinois Quilt Research Project
Possible

Executive Mansion
Springfield, Illinois 62701

April 14, 1993

Dear Friends of Illinois Quilts,

The Illinois Quilt Research Project has increased our
awareness of our state's heritage by helping us share our
treasures with each other. I am pleased that you will be able to
study and enjoy the symbols decorating a quilt that was made for
the Executive Mansion.

The quilt is made entirely of silk and depicts the Illinois
State Capitol bordered by eighteen Illinois structures which are
all on the National Register of Historic Places. Surrounding the
State Capitol is a design using the state tree, the White Oak;
the state flower, the violet; the state insect, the Monarch
butterfly; and the state bird, the cardinal. The quilt was sewn
in 1987 by seventy-eight volunteers who spent more than 4,000
hours completing the project. The quilt is currently part of the
decor of the Bartles Suite in the Executive Mansion. We are
proud to be able to enjoy its beauty and uniqueness in our home.

I am sure you will join the Governor and me in extending our
thanks to the hundreds of volunteers across the state who helped
make this book a success. Their efforts have increased our
understanding of the artistic and historic contributions made by
Illinois quilters and quilt collectors. I hope that <u>History From
the Heart</u> will encourage many others to discover and preserve the
heritage that is stitched into their quilts.

Warm wishes,

Brenda Edgar

Brenda Edgar
FIRST LADY

CONTENTS

ILLUSTRATIONS

Lura Lynn Ryan
912 South Greenwood Avenue
Kankakee, Illinois 60901

Dear Quilt Enthusiast,

Family history and tradition are integral parts of the American quilt making, quilt using and quilt preserving process. The stories recorded by the Illinois Quilt Research Project clearly indicate that our state is no exception. In addition to being a very practical bedcovering, quilts are also a folk art form that successfully carry family stories from generation to generation. While it is important to view the beauty in each quilt, it is also essential to remember the maker, to consider the era in which it was made and to recall its passage through time.

I am glad I was able to participate in this volunteer undertaking that has touched so many lives in Illinois. The project offered each one of us the opportunity to preserve a truly personal link that can bridge the gap between the past and the future.

My sincere thanks and congratulations to Cheryl Kennedy and the numerous others who so freely dedicated their expertise and untold hours in making this project a resounding success.

Sincerely,

Lura Lynn Ryan

PREFACE

Our roots extend deeply into the black soil of Central Illinois, intertwine with the fibers of many quilts, and are nurtured by the heritage of our native state. The Frontispiece quilt summarizes the proud record of Illinois by recalling the contributions of ordinary people, the state's historic sites, and its heroic figures. It is a reminder that our heritage can be found in a quilt as well as in a library or an archive, and that is a message we want to share with others.

Over the years we slowly learned that quilts are far more than pieces of colorful cloth stitched together in pleasing patterns. Each quilt is a chronicle of the past, for it retains the marks of its historical period. These properly recorded textile documents offer historians a rich source for material culture research; they are heritage and art rolled into one. Quilts record stories that are written with a needle rather than a pen. Our journey on the quilt paths of Illinois helped us discover a history that was written from the heart.

Quilts have always been a part of our lives, and our memorable ones range from childhood treasures to gifts from our mothers. It is difficult for us to imagine what life would be like without quilts. After our marriage, we didn't discuss whether we would make a quilt but rather how soon we could find the time to work on one. Our unplanned transition from using, to making, to collecting, to researching quilts was gradual and uneventful. The more we learned, the more we appreciated; the more we understood, the more we realized additional study was needed. An Old Testament writer encouraged us to "Read the history books and see—for we were born yesterday and know so little; our days here on earth are as transient as shadows. But the wisdom of the past will teach you. The experience of others will speak to you. . . ." (*The Living Bible,* Job, 8:8–11).

We certainly have benefitted from the accumulated wisdom of the past in the field of quilt history, and the experiences of others have indeed spoken clearly to us. We are indebted to the many people who previously traveled our national quilt paths, especially those active contemporary researchers who have worked so diligently to make quilt history a viable and respected part of the material culture field.

Our thanks is also due to the Illinois Quilt Research Project board members and the many dedicated volunteers—who worked long and hard to amass the data base and whose efforts continually sustained the Project. The documentation for any factual material relating to a quilt but not footnoted in the text will be found in the Project file for that quilt. We also wish to express our appreciation to the Early American Museum for providing work space and hosting Project meetings; to Tim Talbott and Marie Rieber for their research assistance; to Marianna Munyer and Nancy Curran for carefully reading the completed manuscript; to the Illinois State Historical Library, the University of Illinois Library, the Illinois State Library, and Springfield's Lincoln Library for the use of their collections; to Vic Stanis who shared her research library; and to Will and Evelyn Zehr for fantastic photography.

A special note of appreciation is reserved for a core of hardworking friends who provided exceptional assistance. It was a delight to have the able editorial expertise of Evelyn Taylor. No matter how many times we rewrote a chapter, she was always ready to read it again. The willingness of Al and Char Koelling to share their extensive experience, knowledge, and research is as memorable as is their cooperation and friendship. It is impossible to exaggerate the contribution of Cheryl Kennedy. She was always able to provide wisdom, encouragement, and a helping hand whenever we really needed it. Cheryl's leadership and support made our travels over the quilt paths of Illinois a pleasant and memorable experience.

Through personal experience, we know that an appreciation for the past and a love of history often begins at home. Our parents shared with us a desire for education, a broad interest in everyday life, and a strong reverence for family heritage. Without the valuable legacy of Raymond John (1900–1987) and Irene Shaffer Kamm (1903–1986); and Elmer Daniel (1906–1962) and Blanche Funkhouser Elbert (1907–1990) this book could not have been undertaken. It was, however, only with the patience and understanding of Edward Daniel-Kamm Elbert and Erik Dieter-Roeder Elbert that it has been completed. Over the years, it was the encouragement and co-operation of our family that made it possible for us to travel, to study, and ultimately to turn a dream into reality.

History From The Heart is the culmination of a lifelong attempt to combine our interest in material culture—the "things" of history—with the methodology of the research historian. Over the past eighteen years, our interpretations have been encouraged, enriched, and constructively challenged by students in the Eastern Illinois University graduate program in Historical Administration. We hope this book and the work of the Illinois Quilt Research Project will encourage them and many others— beginners, experienced collectors, and advanced professionals, whether a museum curator or an academic historian—to place quilts within a context and to study them as historical documents.

— Duane and Rachel Elbert

Woodford Farm
March 5, 1993

ACKNOWLEDGMENTS

The Illinois Quilt Research Project is co-sponsored by the Land of Lincoln Quilters Association and the Early American Museum of The Champaign County Forest Preserve District.

Project/Museum Director: Cheryl Kennedy
Authors: E. Duane Elbert and Rachel Kamm Elbert
Photographers: Wilmer Zehr and Evelyn Zehr

Project Board and Staff:
Judy Ash
June Briner
Dorothy Buerkle
Donna Dorr
Edith Erzen
Lesley Gray
Louise Guymon
Otto Haack

Edith Idleman
Alfred and Charlene Koelling
Debbie Langendorf
Phyllis Norton
Esther Raiha
Victorena Stanis
Tim and Mary Talbott
Ruth Ann Thompson

Our heartfelt thanks to all of the project consultants, Quilt Day organizers, volunteers, and participants we met on our quilt paths across Illinois.

Project support:
   Land of Lincoln Quilters Association
   Early American Museum
   Illinois Arts Council
   National Quilt Association
   Quilt Day Hosts and Sponsors
   All who became Friends of IQRP

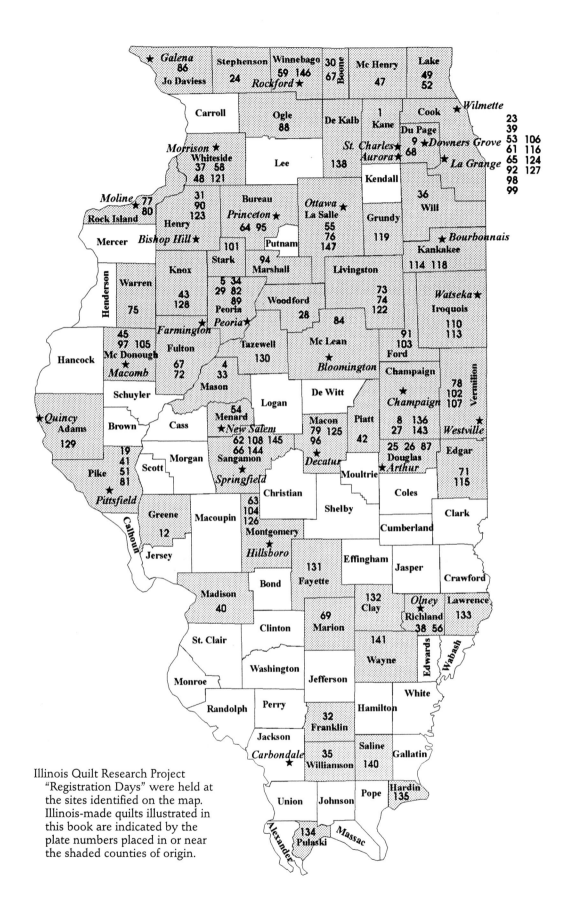

Galena ★
86
Jo Daviess
Stephenson
24
Winnebago
59 146
Rockford ★
30
67
Boone
Mc Henry
47
Lake
49
52

Carroll
Ogle
88
De Kalb
1
Kane
St. Charles ★
Aurora ★
68
Cook
Du Page
9 ★ Downers Grove
★ La Grange
Wilmette ★
23
39
53 106
61 116
65 124
92 127
98
99

Morrison ★
Whiteside
37 58
48 121
Lee
138
Kendall
Will
36
★ Bourbonnais

Moline ★ 77
80
Rock Island
Henry
31
90
123
Bureau
Princeton ★
64 95
Ottawa ★
La Salle
55
76
147
Grundy
119
Kankakee
114 118

Mercer
Bishop Hill ★
101
Putnam
94
Marshall
Livingston
73
74
122
Watseka ★
Iroquois
110
113

Henderson
Warren
75
Knox
43
128
Stark
5 34
29 82
89
Peoria
Woodford
28
84
91
103
Ford

Quincy ★
Adams
129
Hancock
McDonough ★
Macomb
45
97 105
Fulton
67
72
4
33
Mason
Farmington ★
Peoria ★
Tazewell
130
Mc Lean
Bloomington ★
Champaign
Champaign ★
78
102
107
Vermilion

Schuyler
Logan
De Witt
8 136
27 143
Westville ★

Brown
Cass
Menard
54
★ New Salem
62 108 145
66 144
Sangamon
Springfield ★
Macon
79 125
96
Decatur ★
Piatt
42
25 26 87
Douglas
★ Arthur
Edgar
71
115

Pike
19
41
51
81
Scott
Morgan
Moultrie
Coles
Clark

Pittsfield ★
Greene
12
Macoupin
Christian
63
104
126
Montgomery
★
Hillsboro ★
Shelby
Cumberland

Calhoun
Jersey
Madison
40
Bond
131
Fayette
Effingham
Jasper
Crawford

Clinton
69
Marion
132
Clay
Olney ★
Richland
38 56
Lawrence
133

St. Clair
Washington
Jefferson
141
Wayne
Edwards
Wabash

Monroe
Randolph
Perry
32
Franklin
Hamilton
White

Jackson
Carbondale ★
35
Williamson
Saline
140
Gallatin

Union
Johnson
Pope
Hardin
135

Alexander
Pulaski
134
Massac

Illinois Quilt Research Project
"Registration Days" were held at
the sites identified on the map.
Illinois-made quilts illustrated in
this book are indicated by the
plate numbers placed in or near
the shaded counties of origin.

HISTORY FROM THE HEART

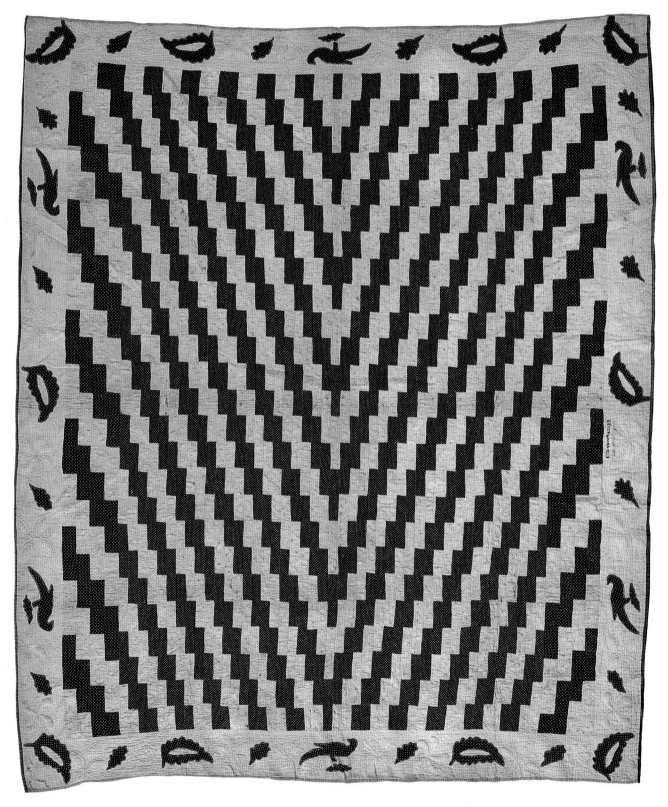

[Plate 2]
PHILADELPHIA BRICK
91″ x 79″

Mrs. Purdy, dates unknown
Philadelphia, Pennsylvania, 1813
Collection of Gladys Skinner Bunting

SHARING OUR HERITAGE: USING QUILTS AS A LINK TO THE PAST

Gonna take a sentimental journey,
Gonna set my heart at ease,
Gonna make a sentimental journey
To renew old memories.
—Bud Green, Les Brown, and Ben Homer,
  "Sentimental Journey," 1944

Interested in excitement and adventure? Then travel the quilt paths of Illinois in search of history's hidden treasures. It is a journey that begins right at home, for history deals with more than the long ago and far away. History is also the story of you, and it "can be satisfying to feel oneself part of something larger and more lasting than the moment, something that stretches both backward and forward in time."[1]

The new social history focuses on the everyday things around us, such as family, community, and quilts, involving the use of artifacts in addition to traditional historical research documents. It prefers to look at history from the bottom up. Thus, ordinary quilts become important materials linking the present to the past. They can uncover our own personal histories.[2] Authors recognized this long ago, and American literature contains quilt-related stories that involve the reader through the use of familiar subjects.[3] Children's literature has recently experienced an increase in the number of stories involving the making or use of a quilt. Thus America's late-twentieth-century fascination with quilts and quilting has at last reached another market.

Many people consider history an academic subject that is limited to stories of the rich and famous and that does not include us. The very word *history* is ominous. Becoming a part of history implies something reserved for noteworthy events. While that is true, there is more. Some historians realize that "a good understanding of the past, whether designated memory or history, needs to take into account nearby as well as national and international developments."[4] Few of us are ever directly involved in front-page events, and yet momentous incidents like the outbreak of war affect our everyday lives. This big picture provides the context in which we live.

Today we increasingly realize the importance of another kind of history.[5] It is much more personal, and it touches us in our homes, in our families, and in the objects of everyday life. David Russo, in his pioneering study *Families and Communities,* points out that "to shift our focus from *Americans in the aggregate* to *Americans as an individual* is to move from one end of the historical spectrum to the other. There is one connecting link, however: both involve 'persons.'"[6] All we have to do is find the correct path that will enable us to link the

object—quilts—with the people. When Judy Garland walked through the Land of Oz she followed the Yellow Brick Road. Here we begin our trek over the quilt paths of Illinois by following the "Philadelphia Brick Pavement."

How could one more appropriately begin the search for history in Illinois quilts than to follow a traveling document that started its own journey in the City of Brotherly Love where the word *Illinois* first gained widespread recognition among the English colonists? After the French and Indian War, a group of colonial Pennsylvania traders sought to profit economically through western land speculation. In 1766 several wealthy Philadelphians, including the prominent firm of Baynton, Wharton & Morgan, formed the Illinois Company. They requested a 1.2-million-acre land grant from the Crown as compensation for losses suffered during the war. Despite the support of Benjamin Franklin, who worked for the group while in London, the venture was lost as the colonies moved toward independence.[7]

A few decades later, a Philadelphia Brick quilt (sometimes called Philadelphia Pavement) left its Pennsylvania home with Eliza

Purdy as she headed west on horseback. Her mother and grandmother had made this unusual quilt and had marked its date. Eliza took it with her as she rode to Ohio for her 1813 wedding to Caleb Houston. The quilt's top and back are cotton, and the blue print of the back is brought to the front for binding. There is a wool batt with a linen towcloth covering. The border has appliquéd blue calico birds and leaves attached with buttonhole stitching of indigo-dyed linen thread.[8] Quilting stitches (7–8 per inch) are in double lines, clamshell, feather, and leaf motifs. The original ink inscription documenting her name and the year 1813 is now barely legible. About 1895 the present owner's aunt, Lucy Fleming Williams, embroidered a duplicate inscription above the original. The quilt had "hard use and was wearing out"; so the owner's great-grandmother reinforced the back in the 1890s by adding a large piece of blue checked print.

Since the quilt is owned in an Illinois county originally populated by many transplanted Pennsylvanians, it would be easy to assume the Houstons moved there directly from Ohio, but the assumption is incorrect. In fact, they never lived in Illinois. Nevertheless, the quilt path followed by Eliza Purdy's Philadelphia Brick clearly illustrates how a quilt's story preserves family history, how it makes the family much more aware of the need to share their heritage, and how a bride's "good" quilt was actually considered utilitarian by later generations. Regrettably, the owner never learned the names of her ancestors who made the quilt, but she does know how it got to Illinois.

Eliza Purdy Houston's daughter Emily married Newton Blair and left Ohio for Kansas before the Civil War. Their daughter Helen married K. G. Fleming, a Civil War veteran, in Solomon, Kansas, and her daughter Grace married C. D. Skinner at Solomon in 1898. The Skinners moved on to Colorado where Gladys

was born in 1903. In 1925 she arrived in Urbana to attend the University of Illinois, and three years later she married a fellow public-school teacher, Robert W. Bunting. Although the quilt has deteriorated through use, it is now being carefully preserved. Its unique design and unusual history make it an important part of Illinois' quilt heritage.

The Search for an Illinois Heritage

Unfortunately, not everyone recognizes the historic value of quilts. Some families would destroy a "worn-out old quilt" because it no longer has utility or monetary value. On the other hand, connoisseurs often acquire quilts solely on the basis of completeness, rarity, or artistic quality with little or no interest in preserving history.[9] Both of these approaches place our heritage at risk.

History slips away whenever we disregard potential storytellers. Countless unquilted tops and thousands of pieced, appliquéd, and embroidered blocks abound in the nation's attics and antique shops. Certainly, as historical documents they rarely speak to their incompleteness except when the blocks are obviously so irregular in size and shape no one could successfully join them into an acceptable quilt. Like many whole quilts, these fragments are frequently devoid of context and do not provide us with answers about who made them and when. Perhaps a balance can be reached if quilts and incomplete quilt projects are related to the families of their origin.

Oral tradition may indicate that illness, the birth of children, loss of a husband or lover, or the maker's untimely death intervened. Only by investigating the vagaries of everyday life in nineteenth- and

[Plate 3]
Collage of quilt blocks
Private Collections

twentieth-century America will the historical detective determine the facts as fully as possible and thus add to social history. It is extremely important to understand the various contexts in which these textiles were created, used, and preserved.

Each of the 15,808 quilts registered in the Illinois Quilt Research Project can offer the researcher at least one form of documentary evidence. Mrs. Horn's quilt is a good research document because it tells an important story about the impact the sewing machine made in quilt construction. Others send messages regarding favored types and pattern popularity, changing color preferences, and variations in acceptable sizes by period and/or region within the state. Every quilt reveals information about some aspect of fabric preference and use, about the historical evolution of textile manufacturing, and the use of handwork versus the sewing machine in construction technique.[12] In all periods there are also quilts

[Plate 4]
VASE OF FLOWERS APPLIQUÉ
76" x 77"

Mrs. Horn, dates unknown
Mason City, Mason County, Illinois,
   circa 1865
Collection of Suetta Martin

Shortly after the invention of the sewing machine, women learned that geometric patterns could easily be pieced by machine. For the most part, however, in the late nineteenth century, quilting was still done by hand. Mrs. Horn had a sewing machine, and perhaps she wanted to show her friends and relatives the machine's time-saving capabilities. She appliquéd her quilt top by hand, using a reverse blanket stitch over the raw edges of the cotton appliqués; and she hand-embroidered the stems and details on the flowers. However, she chose to quilt it by machine in an allover-grid pattern. It is the earliest machine quilting registered in the Project. The front and the back are both cotton, as is the thin batting.

Although a machinemade quilt might not be highly regarded by some today, it must be remembered that when few women owned an expensive sewing machine, the ability to create a useful masterpiece quickly could have been the envy of the neighborhood. Few women were able to do it, however, and perhaps no more than 10 percent of all 1865–1900 era quilts are machine quilted.[10]

like that of Leah Thornburgh (Plate 33) which provide readily accessible historical data written directly onto the bedcovering. Most, however, do not reveal their information so easily. Thus, maintaining a written history is important.

History textbooks will generally mention Elias Howe's invention of the sewing machine, but they rarely offer a general perspective from which to view the changes sewing machines brought to our ancestors' daily lives at home.[13] Most texts simply do not provide the tools that a family or a community needs for sharing a continuing tradition. By evaluating past experiences and renewing old memories, people learn who they are. Nearby history, including the study of quilts and other pieces of material culture, offers the historical researcher many problem-solving opportunities.[14]

A successful detective clearly understands the objective. Thus a humanities sleuth carefully investigates all the physical evidence and formulates sound open-ended, open-minded questions. Only when we know what we are looking for can we search for every clue and fit together as many pieces of the puzzle as possible. Contemplation, re-evaluation, and challenge must be integral parts of this process; thoroughness helps researchers understand each story more completely; adding the human element brings history to life. Quilts are a connecting link to the past, for they provide tangible evidence of the lives of real people.[15]

Every quilt has a story to tell, although some are easier to converse with than others. We often find that conversation is freer, more animated, and less superficial when we speak with a good friend or a relative than when we casually talk with a total stranger. Don't let your precious objects be strangers to

I. M. SINGER & CO.'S
NEW INVENTION
TRANSVERSE SHUTTLE
Letter A Sewing Machine

For Families and Light Manufacturing Purposes.

Also, Machines for Manufacturing BOOTS, SHOES, and
GARMENTS of every description. constantly on hand.

Western Office 140 Lake St., Chicago.

A. W. HARRIS, Agent.

Commission Agents wanted.

[Figure 1]
Sewing machine advertisement
West Urbana, Illinois, *Central Illinois
Gazette,* March 9, 1858

One historian called the sewing machine "the most significant domestic labor-saving device in the late nineteenth century." Sewing machine sales increased when Edward Clark of the Singer Company revolutionized merchandising by introducing installment payments and the trade-in allowance. Advertisements abound in Illinois newspapers, and the evidence of machine piecing found in Project registrations indicates a willingness on the part of women to use the machine to produce attractive quilts.[11]

your family. Make sure your heirs and your possessions are on speaking terms. Do not assume everyone knows about your ancestors and the legacy that connects them with specific possessions. Provide written stories for the benefit of future generations. If your heirs actually do not wish to keep the article and therefore donate it to a museum, the curator and the educator will bless you for providing the provenance. It is very difficult to attach the reality of everyday life to an inanimate object without the facts.[16]

As long as a quilt remains in the family, it is presumed that the knowledge about it can be passed from one generation to another. However, the success of oral transmission depends upon the tradition bearer accurately remembering and conveying the information. It also assumes the receiver is interested enough to listen carefully and over the years to recall completely the shared details. There always is the possibility that important facts can be lost by accident or that anecdotal myths might be added.[17]

Once the information chain is broken, later generations can do little to regain the lost knowledge. The complaint is often heard that a relative did not share information

more fully or, more frequently, regret is expressed that the person who now owns the quilt did not listen more carefully or ask more questions before the tradition bearer died. Multiple copies of written documentation provide the most accurate transmission of family history from one generation to another. This also encourages each generation to add its own written association with the object before passing it to the next owner.

Good advice all too often falls on deaf ears. The inability of many owners to tell about their quilts was one of the most painful experiences of the Project. "How I wish we had been more interested before it was too late!" wrote one quilt owner. Another correspondent, unable to answer all the research questions, explained her lack of information by stating, "I only remember the quilt folded up in a closet and my mother showing it to us kids one day. She said it wasn't to be used because it belonged to her great-grandparents. I don't know why, maybe it was just supposed to be handed down from generation to generation." Such laments were common.

In the minds of some of the Project's founding mothers, this erosion

of family heritage symbolizes our diverse and mobile society as well as a rapidly decaying community structure. They sensed a need to create an atmosphere of appreciation for quilts that went beyond the field of folk art. There was a desire to find the stories relating to state, local, and especially family history that had been stitched into the calico. Quilts, after all, are not merely warm bedcoverings or a colorful home decoration; they are also family history lessons. The Project would offer a wonderful opportunity to help "future generations to understand how we live, what is important to us, and why."[18]

Self-esteem begins with an understanding of who we are and how we fit into our nation, state, community, and family. Why not begin that search for a unifying identity with a universally treasured cultural artifact—a quilt!

[Plate 5]
GEM OF THE PRAIRIE
111" x 71"

Peoria Area Stitchers Guild Quilt Group
Peoria, Peoria County, Illinois, 1985
Collection of Gems of the Peoria NQA
    Chapter

The Peoria group is one of many Illinois
quilt guilds that actively supported the
Project. Its quilt, a kaleidoscope of life in
Illinois, includes an Amish farm as well
as the state's oldest Catholic church.
The native Illinois wildflowers are also
part of the quilt, and corn—a gift of the
Native Americans and a major economic
resource for the state's farmers—is another motif found in the quilting.

The Gem of the Prairie quilt top is cotton and polished cotton embellished by
metallic braid, ribbon, beads, and polished stone; the back is the same green
cotton as the front. The group selected a
polyester batting and used handmade
straight-cut green cotton for the binding.
It is applied by machine on the front and
by hand on the back. Construction of
the top is by machine and by hand. The
quilting stitches (8–10 per inch) are in
outline, in-the-ditch, and in parallel
lines, and they also create corn stalks
and prairie grass in the large green areas
of the four corners.

The Illinois Quilt Research Project

From the very beginning, the Project's structure came through the
quilt guilds that were organized
across the state in the 1980s. In July
1985 the Decatur Quilters Guild
hosted a meeting to create a statewide quilters organization, and the
Land of Lincoln Quilters Association was formed. Some participants
shared their thoughts on the recently
completed Kentucky Quilt Project.
Discussion of an Illinois project
continued, and at a February 1986
meeting in Springfield, the Illinois
Quilt Research Project became a reality. Cheryl Kennedy, director of
the Early American Museum in Mahomet, was elected project director.
In August 1987 a meeting with the
Indiana Project director in Indianapolis provided much needed or-
ganizational assistance.

Working through the local guilds
and the Congress of Illinois Historical Societies and Museums, Cheryl
Kennedy began setting up sites for
future quilt registration days. Becoming "deluged with letters of
support and interest" and also receiving some financial assistance,
she began scheduling registration
sites from downstate to the Chicago metropolitan area. As local
support committees organized, the
state group established the guidelines that would ultimately dictate
the Project's results.

The committee first needed to
decide what information would be
required about each quilt registered. Other state projects shared
their registration forms, and the Illinois committee members chose the
most pertinent features. They also
decided to register any antique or
contemporary quilt, quilt top, or

[Plate 6]
HMONG QUILT
91" x 72"

Maker unknown, dates unknown
Thailand, 1984
Collection of Edith Idleman

The Illinois Project was not limited to quilts made in the United States. A number of quilted textiles, including one reportedly removed from the palace of Egypt's King Farouk, were brought in to be registered. They represent the diversity of quilts now owned by residents of the Prairie State.

Hmong quilts attracted a wide market in the United States as a result of the Vietnam War. The Hmong were an independent agrarian tribe living in the mountainous borderland between China and Laos. Caught in the midst of the Southeast Asian conflict, they supported the American soldiers and were thus marked for annihilation by the North Vietnamese and their allies. Survivors sought refuge in Thailand, and many subsequently migrated to the United States. Hmong refugees in Thailand made this appliqué piece.

The Hmong have adapted their traditional Pa Ndau needlework, which includes appliqué, reverse appliqué, and embroidery, to the American quilt form. The quilts have become a source of much-needed income for the refugees.

The top and back are both cotton. There is no batt, and it is not quilted. The binding is front brought to the back. The piece is constructed entirely by hand, and the top and back are linked together by reverse appliqué and by appliqué on appliqué.

As the Hmong change their colors and designs in order to sell their work, they are losing important features of an ancient culture. School and television distract the teenagers, and older women now find the demanding work too time consuming. One researcher predicted that in fifty years the true Hmong works will be seen only in museums.

quiltlike comforter completed before 1950 regardless of the area of origin as long as it was owned by an Illinois resident, or an Illinois-made quilt currently owned out of state. The group arranged to deposit the completed forms and pictures with the Illinois State Museum where the collection would become accessible for research.

The Project's broad scope for collecting information enabled Illinois owners to register several Hmong quilts. A new collecting field, these textile documents recall our diplomatic and military involvement in Southeast Asia. As an immigrant community undergoes Americanization, its work changes in response to cross-cultural encounters and marketplace pressures. Thus, Hmong products have already become a part of the state's quilt history.[19]

The Project recorded all quilts regardless of age, including those just recently completed. By accepting contemporary quilts, the committee wished to encourage intergenerational dialogue between younger quilt owners and their quilting mothers and grandmothers while the older generations were still living. The Project committee thought a cut-off date might discourage the participation of working quilters by indirectly implying that present-day quilting was unimportant. Thus, a firm commitment to contemporary history was a priority from the beginning. The committee opted to paint a total picture on a large canvas rather than attempt to highlight only selected objects.

Once the committee completed its basic organization, it was time to begin doing the work. Networking with neighboring professionals eliminated reinventing the process. Therefore, training for the state committee was done by volunteers from the Indiana Project. Suellen Meyer from Missouri provided instruction on fabric dating, and several members attended sessions offered by Barbara Brackman of Kansas.

When it seemed as though all the pieces were in place, the first quilt registration day was announced for February 1988 in Decatur. The committee wondered if anyone would come. The hard-working volunteers completed 392 registrations in one day and felt no more than that would ever show up again. Little did they know! Cheryl Kennedy worked closely with local organizers to establish thirty different site days and with the office of then lieutenant governor, George Ryan, to generate publicity. The combined efforts contributed a final tally of 15,808 completed registrations over the course of the project.[20]

Each site day presented unique problems, but over the months the established pattern was fine tuned. The form was modified after the first few quilt days to adjust slightly the location of questions on the sheet. Forms were distributed in advance to save time at the registration location. To reduce misunderstanding due to the use of terminology unfamiliar to the general public, "quilt documentation days" became "quilt registration days" and "quilt documentation" was changed to "physical analysis."

Still, there were problems. The public response was usually much larger than anticipated, and processing the quilts often took longer than expected. The weather could be uncooperative; a camera could malfunction; a few registrants failed to understand why it took so long; the volunteers sometimes got very tired; and several quilt owners occasionally felt their quilts would not be considered for the book if they did not go through physical analysis. It sometimes took a while to reestablish one's perspective on the project's goals and to regain a sense of accomplishment and humor.

Almost three and one-half years elapsed between the first registration day at Decatur and the thirtieth, held at Macomb. By that time, the work was routine for the seasoned volunteers. Macomb was a typical registration site, but somehow it also was different. Underneath the tiredness and the frustration there always was the exhilaration of seeing an ever-flowing stream of quilts.

It was a pleasant June night as we headed west across the flat prairie farmlands of central Illinois. Our goal was to make the three and one-half hour drive to Macomb during the cooler part of the day. Even the motel mattress felt good after a full day of work followed by a long drive. The parish hall of the Methodist Church was dark and empty when we arrived there early the next morning. Within a few minutes, a carload of familiar faces appeared, and then another. The local volunteers found the light switches; out came the set-up floor plan; the now-familiar boxes of table coverings, tape, white gloves, and photography equipment were unpacked; and an experienced organization wheeled into action. The set-up ended none too soon, for the waiting area filled rapidly with boxes and pillowcases bulging with quilts. By the time the project boss-of-the-day gave the signal, everyone was at his or her assigned station and ready to go.

The next day the equipment was taken down for the last time. That did not, however, mean the work was done. Piles of data are lifeless without analysis and worthless unless they can be shared with the public. Committee members and volunteers tabulated statistics and pored through the forms and slides. Approximately a thousand quilts were chosen and sent to the authors, who worked with their outline to make the final selections.

The committee invited the finalists to four professional photography sites. Despite the winter schedule, the weather cooperated; but not all the quilts arrived. Some addresses were not current; some

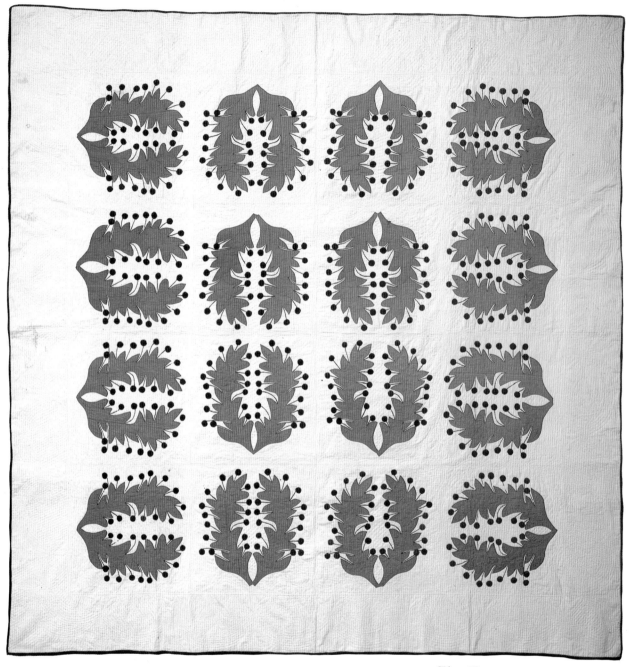

[Plate 7]
LEAVES AND CHERRIES
103" x 103"

Mary Elizabeth Byrod, 1838–1929
Halifax, Dauphin County, Pennsylvania,
  circa 1850
Collection of the Illinois State Museum

The quilt top, back, and handmade
straight-cut binding are cotton. The
leaves are appliquéd; the cherries are
stuffed; and the stems are embroidered
in wool. All the work is done by hand.
The quilting stitches (8 per inch) can be
found in heart, leaf, swag, tassel, braid,
parallel lines, and outline motifs.

[Figure 2]
"A Quilting Party in Western Virginia"
Gleason's Pictorial Drawing Room
Companion
Boston, Massachusetts, October 21,
1854, p. 249

The nineteenth-century caption editor may have unwittingly described twentieth-century Illinois when he wrote: "The expressive countenances of the group are full of meaning, and the various relationships each sustains to the others will readily suggest themselves to the observer. Age and infancy, youth and maturity are here delineated, ease and awkwardness, roughness and gentle refinement, just such a heterogeneous compound of life, as such social gatherings are composed of. There is something unique and peculiar in the countenances of the various actors in the scene."[23] There is also "something unique and peculiar" about each quilt, quiltmaker, and quilt owner. Nevertheless, despite our heterogeneous diversity, a shared bond connects us one to another as we take our place around society's quilting frame.

owners were in Florida for the winter; several did not wish to make a long trip; and a few decided not to have their quilts in the book. Fortunately, 80 percent graciously showed up at the appointed time and place, delighted with the opportunity to help the project once again. The loss of the others, however, left gaping holes in the book's outline. Fortunately there were preselected alternates, and additional contacts filled a fifth photography day to assure a well-rounded selection for book and lecture illustrations.

Sharing the Connection

The committee's determination to share its findings is the heart of the Illinois Quilt Research Project. Much has been learned by studying other projects, and it is our hope that fellow quilt students across the nation may profit from the Illinois Project report. Sharing information

about the Mary Elizabeth Byrod quilt is one small example. When the family moved to Illinois in the nineteenth century, they brought with them an unusual Leaves and Cherries quilt. One might indeed be tempted to term it unique had not Jeannette Lasansky pictured two similar quilts.[21] Without the Union County Historical Society's Oral Traditions Project we would not have been able to place this quilt in its original context. We now know it is not one of a kind, and we hope the Pennsylvania researchers discover that a Keystone State textile document is on file in Illinois.

The Project, like a quilt, is a way to share the past with the present and the future. One portion of the work will be shared through this publication; a second part will be available to the public as a traveling exhibit; and it is hoped the data base will be used for many years by other researchers. By reporting our findings, we share the spirit of Illinois quilts with our fellow Prairie State residents and reach out to a much broader public beyond the state boundaries.

[Plate 8]
QUILT PATHS ACROSS ILLINOIS
76" x 65"

Illini Country Stitchers,
Champaign, Champaign County,
    Illinois, 1990
Collection of M. Kathleen Edwards

Families from every part of the state
brought their precious textile treasures
to registration days. Their paths are recalled in the design of a quilt named to
commemorate the Illinois Quilt Research Project. The pieced bedcovering
has a cotton top and back. It is bound by
a cotton bias-pieced fabric and is applied
by both machine and by hand. The
quilting is by machine. The quilt was
raffled as a money-raising effort to help
finance the Project.

From the beginning, the Illinois Quilt Research Project was committed to seeing quilts as far more than the sum of colorful cloth bits stitched together in pleasing patterns. Quilts have the ability to make connections. They can link us together in families and communities, and they can overcome distinctions within a diverse society. They are a chronicle of our individual, family, and national pasts as much as any document ever written. Properly recorded, quilts can tell the researcher about America's industrial growth, expanding transportation system, migration patterns, economic swings, artistic trends, national moods, and particularly the changing role of women in American life.[22] Whether the stitches are large and awkward or small and neat, these fragile records can emotionally, as well as graphically, bind us together while opening a window of understanding on the past and offering a treasure to future generations. Quilts are history; they are the quiet, personal statements of our nation's unsung heroines and heroes.

Each piece of the past tells a story that broadens our awareness of the state's shared history, reveals the strength of its geographic diversity and cultural unity, and provides the continuity that links the past to the present. Quilts contain volumes of cultural information about the times in which they were created and the circumstances in which they were used. Each one can tell us about the lives of the people associated with it. Whether a quilt is created for utility or beauty and made out of love or sheer necessity, it retains the indelible marks of its maker and its historical period. Preserved like a letter or a photograph, it can help those who want to read artifacts understand our heritage better.

Many of the antique quilts we study today originally brought family and community together around the quilting frame. Their generative powers have not diminished over the decades, and they still draw us together as families and communities. The shared values of quilts, which are deeply embedded in tradition, memory, and history, remain a compelling link to the past. The Illinois Quilt Research Project heightened heritage awareness, generated greater individual involvement with family and community, and encouraged participants to see everyday household artifacts as valuable cultural documents.

As our readers make their nostalgic journey through old memories, they will visit the closets, chests, attics, walls, and beds of Illinois. Eight years ago several volunteer surveyors began mapping the state's patchwork wilderness, eventually creating a series of quilt paths across Illinois. We sincerely hope this guidebook to their work will lead you to a better understanding of your own heritage.

[Plate 9]
MARINER'S COMPASS
73″ x 72″

Verdilla Frances Carpenter Zook,
   1848–1925
Naperville, DuPage County, Illinois,
   circa 1880
Collection of Rollin Taecker

Mrs. Zook's unusual all-cotton
handsewn quilt is both pieced and
painted. The handmade straight-cut
binding taken from a different printed
cotton than is used elsewhere on the
quilt is applied by hand. The quilting
(6 stitches per inch) is in cable and
concentric circle motifs. Some of the
fabrics are older than 1880.

WESTWARD, HO!
A NEW HOME IN ILLINOIS

The Promised Land always lies
on the other side of a wilderness.
—Havelock Ellis,
The Dance of Life, 1923

When Christopher Columbus sailed for the Orient in 1492, a mariner's compass pointed the way. The intricate design on the face of that instrument eventually became a well-known quilt pattern. Today the colorful motif that helped keep the great explorer on a westward course recalls the importance of travel and migration in the history of Illinois and of quilts.

The 1492 voyage made modern Illinois inevitable. Although geography temporarily delayed European expansion in the Mississippi Valley, it did not long isolate the state. Distance made travel difficult but not impossible. By 1673, sixty-five years after founding Quebec, the French knew that the Great Lakes system and its related rivers offered an extensive interior waterway. However, until the railroad-building era of the 1850s, Illinois was not easy to reach.

The emergence of modern Illinois was tied to the expansion of Europe's seventeenth-century marketplace into North America. It was only a matter of time until the pioneers' goal of economic and social mobility made the exploration of Illinois' natural resources became a means to that end. In an age devoid of road maps and scientific charts,

western travel involved many risks. A compass could be a traveler's best friend.

By the nineteenth century, a compass increasingly replaced reliance on the sun and stars. Its free-pivoting needle pointed to the magnetic north, day or night and in all kinds of weather. The compass was a common piece of travel equipment by the time settlement reached Illinois.

A Mariner's Compass Leads the Way

Successfully adapting the Mariner's Compass motif to a quilt requires technical ability equal to a navigator's skill.[1] Verdilla Zook's accurate design met that challenge, as she met many others during her lifetime. Born of Amish stock in Lancaster County, Pennsylvania, she moved to Naperville in the 1870s. The strong, sturdy, and industrious woman reared three of the eight children born to her. She spent her last twenty years as a widow, operating the local telephone switchboard from her home.

In 1903 Verdilla Zook's daughter Mary, a Naperville seamstress, mar-

ried a student at North Central College, and the couple moved to his farm home near Watertown, South Dakota. Verdilla died in Naperville in 1925, and the colorful bedcovering moved west to join her daughter. Following Mary Zook Taecker's death in 1951, the quilt passed to her daughter, Mabel Taecker. Mabel gave it to her brother Rollin when she entered a nursing home in 1985. He and his wife, Pat, who is a quilter, were thrilled to receive the quilt, for they appreciated the difficulty involved in piecing it.

Two years after his mother's death, Rollin's work enabled him to live in Naperville, her old hometown. Thus, sixty years after the quilt moved to South Dakota, the compass pointed east and the quilt came home to Illinois. More than a century after Verdilla completed this quilt, a proud family shared her Mariner's Compass with the Illinois Quilt Research Project. The twenty-four points she so carefully pieced will point the way as we travel the quilt paths of Illinois.

Those same twenty-four indicators also identify the various points from which settlers came as they followed their dreams. Migrants to Illinois from the East, South, Europe, and Africa, as well as their descendants, have contributed to the development of Illinois and the state's quilting tradition. In turn, their children and grandchildren have radiated in twenty-four directions to take their place in the life of the United States.

Verdilla Zook's family is an excellent example of mobility. Her persecuted Swiss–Amish ancestors sought religious freedom and economic opportunity in Pennsylvania. She and her family pursued the American dream to Illinois; her daughter followed it to South Dakota; and her grandchildren and great-grandchildren have scattered in twenty-four directions, achieving success in the nation's professional and corporate world. As we follow the quilt paths of Illinois, may the symbolism of her Mariner's Compass quilt be as inspirational to you as it has been to her family.

From Settlement to Statehood, 1673–1818

The first quilted object to enter Illinois is undocumented. In the spring of 1673 when French voyageurs descended the Mississippi and returned north via the Illinois River, they provided a link to European culture and fashion. Under the leadership of Louis Jolliet and Jacques Marquette, the expedition established an era of French control over the Illinois Country and the Illini Indians, which endured almost a century.

Father Marquette returned in 1674–75 to found the state's first Christian mission at present-day Utica. Robert Cavelier de la Salle and Henri de Tonti soon built Indian trading posts near Peoria and on Starved Rock. By the late 1690s the warring Fox tribes forced the Illini Confederation to abandon the Upper Illinois Valley and retreat to the river's mouth. On the Mississippi River's broad eastern floodplain the

[Figure 3]
Verdilla Frances Carpenter Zook
Born November 7, 1848, Loganville
    Township, Lancaster County,
    Pennsylvania
Died September 30, 1925, Naperville,
    DuPage County, Illinois

native peoples reestablished their villages. The French priests opened new missions at Cahokia and Kaskaskia in 1699 and 1703 and in so doing founded Illinois's oldest permanent settlements.

French families soon followed, and a viable agricultural community developed. The population remained small, but the French era left a permanent imprint. The flavor of Illinois's first ethnic enclave can be sampled today at such state-owned historic sites as Cahokia Courthouse, Fort de Chartres, and the Pierre Menard Home.

Although these early settlers must have known quilted clothing, if not bedding, during the Illinois Quilt Research Project no one registered a quilted textile artifact from the state's French era. Eighteenth-century petticoats, intended to be seen through a wide opening in the front of a skirt, were enhanced with quilting motifs of flowers, vines,

and large feathered leaves, designs that were later used on bed coverings. The garments' intricate quilting designs provided decorative elements as well as the securing technique.[2] Directions for making quilted petticoats from discarded silk dresses were still available in 1850.[3]

After the 1763 Treaty of Paris, which ended the French and Indian War, victorious England replaced France as the dominant power in Illinois. Great Britain's control, however, was short lived. Unrest was already apparent in British North America when English troops occupied Fort de Chartres in 1765, and the fort was abandoned a few years later. Rising defense costs forced England to ignore the frontier and focus on the rebellious coastal settlements. In an attempt to stimulate economic recovery and assert its authority over an expanding colonial area, Parliament passed a series of measures that laid the groundwork for the American Revolution.

Permanent American control of Illinois began with the peaceful capture of Kaskaskia by George Rogers Clark in 1778. Operating under commission from Governor Patrick Henry, Clark and his small band of Virginians occupied the area. In 1783 the Treaty of Paris ended the conflict, and the Mississippi River became the new nation's western boundary.

The treaty made Virginia a superpower. A 1609 grant to the Virginia Company had given that state the oldest claim to what is now West Virginia, Kentucky, Ohio, Indiana, Illinois, Michigan, Wisconsin, and part of Minnesota. Conflict arose between the "landless states" and those holding extensive western areas. Seven states eventually surrendered their over-mountain claims. Virginia's 1784 cession of its lands north of the Ohio River gave America's Confederation government an opportunity to create its own colonial policy.

[Figure 4]
Handmade nineteenth-century quilted
  petticoat.
Private collection

The nineteenth-century Pennsylvania
cotton sateen petticoat is hand quilted.
Its simple eleven-inch-high border design is created by a six-channel,
S-shaped tin template with parallel lines
three-fourths of an inch wide. The
upper part of the petticoat is quilted
(10 stitches per inch) in a clamshell
motif. A very thin wool batt is between
the sateen and the solid-color cotton
backing of the border and the printed
blue cotton under the remainder of the
skirt. The hem is bound by bringing the
front to the back and covering it with a
five-eighths-inch-wide corded black ribbon. All stitching is by hand.
    It is illustrated with a homespun,
handwoven, woolen dress. The
Hamilton County, Illinois, garment
dates from the early statehood period.
All stitching on it is by hand.

Congress soon passed two laws
that would be significant in Illinois
history. The Ordinance of 1785 provided for the survey and sale of
land. By creating the familiar mile-
square 640-acre sections, this act
left a permanent cultural imprint on
the landscape that when viewed
from the air often appears as a gi-
gantic patchwork quilt. Two years
later the Northwest Ordinance created a multistep system designed to
transform a frontier region into a
state with powers equal to the original thirteen.
    In addition, Article VI established
legal parameters that affected migration and influenced the state's
quiltmaking traditions. That article
prohibited slavery in the Northwest
Territory; and although criticized
by some settlers and often circum-
vented by the use of indentures, the
law eventually had its intended

effect. Fearing loss of their human
property, slaveowners avoided Illinois while Yankees and immigrants
arrived in increasing numbers.
    American government finally came
to Illinois in March 1790 when the
governor of the Northwest Territory,
Arthur St. Clair, arrived in Kaskaskia.
During his two-month visit, he
learned that conflicting land claims
dating from the French, English,
and Virginia periods created a legal
snarl that made the immediate survey of unoccupied land impossible.
The government's inability to sell
land and its failure to establish an
effective local government temporarily discouraged population
growth.
    Illinois' future began to look
brighter at the beginning of a new
century. As Ohio edged closer to
statehood, Congress created the Indiana Territory in 1800. Approx-

imately twenty-five hundred people
lived in the Illinois portion of this
new governmental unit. The number was about evenly divided between recently arrived Americans
and the remaining French.
    A rising population helped Illi-
nois become a separate territory in
1809. However, the shocking Fort
Dearborn massacre in 1812 discouraged further expansion until
after the War of 1812. When migration resumed in 1815, flatboats, keel-
boats, and some steamboats crowded
the Ohio River every summer. One
1818 traveler noted: "The numerous
companies of emigrants . . . might
appear, to those who have not wit-
nessed them almost incredible. But
there is scarce a day . . . but what
there is a greater or less number of
boats to be seen floating down its
gentle current, to some place of destination."4

Encouraged by this strong influx, the territorial legislature, meeting at Kaskaskia in December 1817 and January 1818, requested Congress to authorize statehood, called a constitutional convention, and ordered a special census. During the summer of 1818, the census takers found more than the required forty thousand people. On December 3, 1818, Illinois became the nation's twenty-first state. Because of its size and unique geographical position, Illinois soon became the terminal point for migration paths from many different parts of the United States and Europe. This diversity gave Illinois significant material culture resources for ideal quilt research.

Migration from the Upper South

The Upland South contributed the largest share of Illinois' earliest settlers, but migrants from the Middle Atlantic and New England states and Europe also moved into the southern portion of the state. Some migrants from Maryland, Virginia, and North Carolina went overland directly to the Ohio River. Others used that stream's southern tributaries, including the Kentucky, Tennessee, Cumberland, and Green rivers, to reach Illinois. Each of those routes became a path that brought the new settlers and their cultural heritage to the developing state of Illinois.

Many territorial and state officials—including such prominent figures as Ninian Edwards, Nathaniel Pope, Daniel Pope Cook, Shadrach Bond, and Edward Coles—were born in southern states. Like the population as a whole, the leadership represented the entire range of public opinion on slavery. Some proslavery settlers hoped to legalize the institution, but they were un-

successful during the 1818 constitutional convention. The last attempt to amend that document to legalize slavery failed in 1824.[5]

When Edward Coles, the state's second governor, left Charlottesville, Virginia, in 1819, he took with him the three families of black slaves he had inherited from his father. He brought them to Illinois to liberate them in a free state. The band headed west through the Valley of Virginia and into the Appalachian Mountains toward the headwaters of the Monongahela River. There they built flatboats on which to descend the river to Pittsburgh where it joins the Allegheny to form the Ohio River. Because of his antislavery political career, the history of Edward Coles, including his migration route, is well known.[6]

The Project's research base clearly indicates the same cannot be said for every family moving west. The route followed by Wesley and Ann Varner Spitler, who moved from Virginia to Indiana in 1835, is not recorded, but some of the quilts Ann brought with her on that trip survive, and they help each new generation relive her experience and preserve her history.

Many communities in the Valley of Virginia were populated by descendants of Germans who had emigrated into the British colonies through the port of Philadelphia. As the Pennsylvania backcountry filled with German adherents to the various Evangelical, Lutheran, and Reformed doctrines, with English Quakers and Scots–Irish Presbyterians, settlement pushed westward toward the Appalachian chain. Rather than cross the rugged mountain ridges, the forerunners of the frontier movement turned into the valley system and moved south—through Maryland's Hagerstown Valley and across the Potomac into the Shenandoah Valley, or the Valley of Virginia. There they found fertile soil, and their towns and farms,

[Figure 5]
Ann Varner Spitler
Born March 5, 1811, Luray, Page County,
   Virginia
Died January 29, 1879, Montrose,
   Effingham County, Illinois

intermittently sprinkled along the Great Wagon Road, flourished.[7]

David Varner, the son of German immigrants, and his wife, Barbara Hershberger, were part of that developing area. Their daughter Ann, born in 1811, married Wesley Spitler on September 19, 1833. He was a teacher, farmer, surveyor, and merchant. Two years later the Spitlers moved to what was then considered the "far west." As a surveyor in Virginia, Wesley had observed a lot of land, and he was impressed with the soil of newly opened northwestern Indiana. The family arrived about the time the last Indians left the area.

Wesley purchased a large tract of unbroken prairie and timber land near Rensselaer in sparsely settled Jasper County. According to his 1904 obituary, "Fruitful fields took the place of waiving [sic] prairie grass and a substantial home was the result. . . . For a number of years he was surveyor of Jasper County. He was also a member of the commission whose duty it was to set off the swamp land of his own

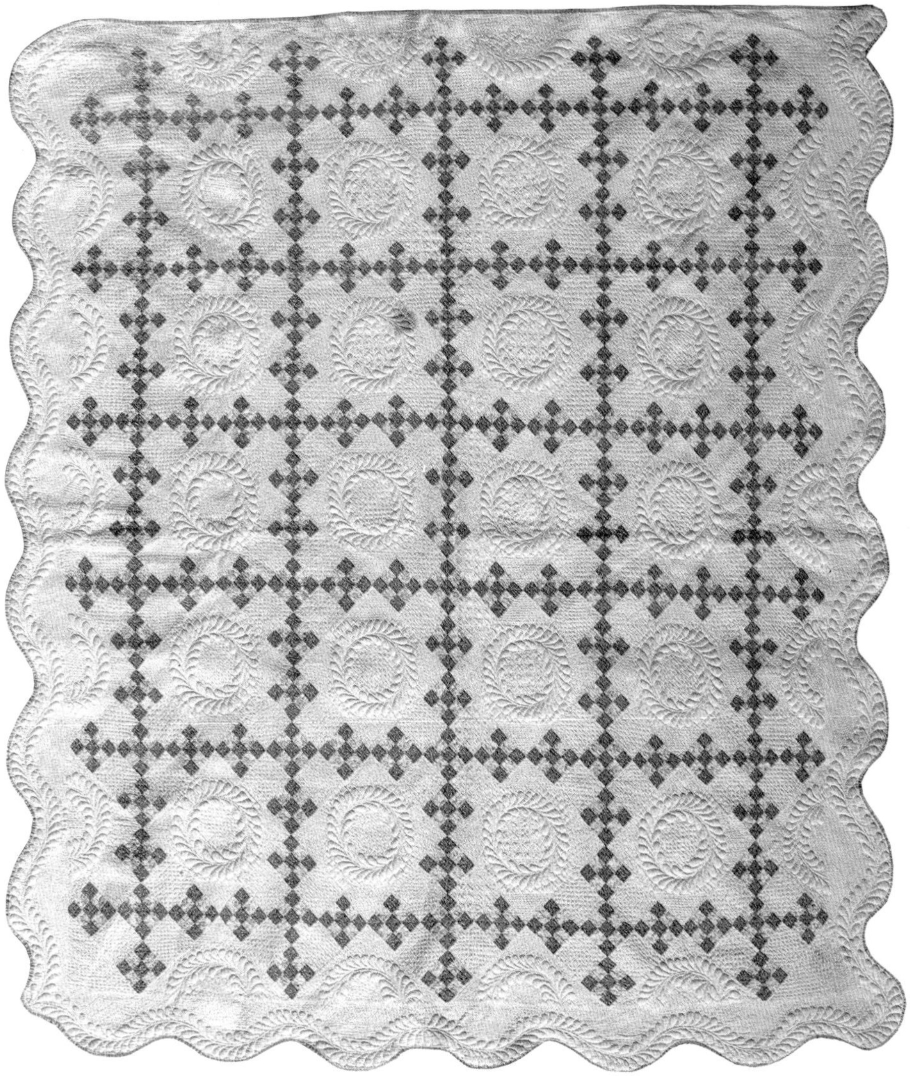

[Plate 10]
SINGLE IRISH CHAIN
84" x 75"

Ann Varner Spitler, 1811–1879
Luray, Page County, Virginia, circa 1840
Collection of Mildred Spitler Johnson

Ann's prized quilts went with her each time the family moved, and several are still owned by her family. A descendant also owns the chests that held her possessions on the wagon trip from Virginia to Indiana. The Single Irish Chain was her prized possession.[11] The top and back, as well as the batt, are cotton, and it is finished with a handmade straight-cut faded green cotton binding. The construction is entirely by hand, and each corner is uniquely shaped. Surely this is not an accident, but if it originally had symbolic value, it has been lost through time. The exquisite quilting (10–12 stitches per inch) forms grids, feathers, and parallel lines. There is stuffed work in the feather wreaths and the feathers in the border, with the holes through which Ann pushed the stuffing visible on the back.[12]

county and that of Newton County adjoining it."[8] Wesley, an active Democrat who named a son Andrew Jackson Spitler in 1837, was also elected school trustee. For some now forgotten reason, the Spitlers decided to leave Indiana at the end of the Civil War.

In 1865 Wesley, Ann, and their five surviving children joined the more than thirty thousand other Virginians then living in Illinois. They moved to Effingham, where "He and his sons at once entered into the merchandise business." The town incorporated as a city in 1867, and Spitler became one of the first four elected aldermen. The following year he paid $2,600 for a 200-acre farm near Montrose. David, Sara, and Mary remained in Effingham County while Abram became the senior partner in the Spitler, Noble & Co. insurance firm in Mattoon, and George became a builder of telegraph lines, a merchant, and a banker at Mt. Zion.[9]

When Ann died at their Montrose farm home in January 1879, Wesley wrote an obituary for *Signs,* a Baptist magazine they had read since 1835. He reported the skill of two physicians could not avert the death of his beloved wife, whom he characterized as "meek, gentle, and merciful." She died after suffering six days with acute bronchitis. Despite her pain, Wesley noted, "she never murmured, but leaned upon her heavenly Husband, as she had for many years, who, she always said, was the author and finisher of her faith. She could talk till within a few hours of her death, and seemed to have her senses as long as she had breath. . . . May God the Father enable all his children to live in peace, union and fellowship, is the prayer of a sinner saved by grace, I hope."[10] It was winter. Perhaps one of the many quilts she made during her lifetime was on her bed that day.

Wesley lived at Montrose for another quarter century. His ninety-two years between October 19, 1811, and May 8, 1904, spanned a successful career in three states and gave him a front row seat for the exciting events associated with the evolving nation. His obituary noted that one seldom lives long enough "to be accorded the honor of being a pioneer of two separate and distinct sections of [the] country."[13]

When Wesley and Ann Spitler headed to Indiana in 1835, they pushed farther than many other settlers. Most families moving north of the Ohio River sought the good land still available in the center of Indiana and Illinois. Perhaps the lower price was a factor, or maybe there was plenty of work for a surveyor as the government put vacated Indian lands on the market.

By the time the Spitlers settled in Indiana, the federal land office was doing a booming business in Shawneetown, Illinois. That Ohio River village became one of the state's most important early commercial centers. Farther on downstream at Cairo, the Ohio joins the Mississippi at a point as far south as the Virginia–North Carolina boundary. The state's extremely long north–south axis offers cultural and climatic diversity. In the early years geography made it easy for Southerners, particularly those living in Kentucky, to move into Illinois.

Migrants from the Southern Uplands, who composed a majority of the state's settlers from 1815 to 1830, came by land as well as by water. One writer observed families traveling in a "Tennessee wagon, that resembled a flatboat on wheels. . . . covered over with white sheeting . . . and . . . [containing an] enormous quantity of freight. . . . Women, children, beds, buckets, tubs, old fashioned chairs, including all the household furniture usually used by our log-cabin ancestors; [and] a chicken coop . . . tied on behind."[14]

There is no record of the route used by Sarah Vaughn Black's family when they moved to Morgan County after 1850. She was born in 1834 at Fairview, near Hopkinsville, Todd County, Kentucky. Like many other nineteenth-century young women, she pieced her quilt (in 1850 when she was sixteen years old) and brought it to Illinois with her. Her all-cotton quilt is worked entirely by hand and quilted (7 stitches per inch) in parallel lines and a leaf motif. As with most "good quilts," a lack of hard wear indicates the pride the owner and her family took in this quilt.

Many of those migrants from Kentucky and other slaveowning states were experienced frontiersmen, especially the small farmers, who were being driven out by the rapidly expanding plantation economy. They disliked competing with cheap slave labor; they opposed the laws that restricted voting to the wealthier landowners; and they resented the class distinctions created by slavery. The rising price of land created by the desire of slave owners to expand their holdings made it economically a good time to sell out and move north. All of those factors encouraged thousands of Southerners to cross the Ohio River and many of them came to Illinois.[15]

By 1860 about sixty thousand Kentuckians and forty thousand Tennesseans had spread themselves over a large part of southern

and west-central Illinois. They were heavily concentrated in areas with access to the southern-flowing Illinois rivers. They flocked to the river valleys; and when those had filled up by the time of statehood, they pushed into the adjacent wooded uplands. In the 1820s they were taking up land at the rate of 500,000 acres a year. By the 1830s, when migration from the South began to diminish, most of the wooded land of southern and west-central Illinois was occupied.[16]

Potential migrants were also strongly influenced by contact with family members already living in Illinois who could confirm or deny stories about such critical things as soil fertility, cost of land, and the usefulness of prairie land. Extant letters from a group of North Carolina German Lutherans moving to Hillsboro, Montgomery County, in the 1830s clearly indicate the value of personal testimony.

On "Eprile 11th 1830" Joseph Cress addressed a letter to "all our friends and relations." Obviously in response to an inquiry, he wrote: "[W]e ar veary glad to hear that you had not give out coming to see us and I think about the first of October wold be the best time to start and if you can git two hundred dollars take it along. You can git a hundred and sixty acres of first rate land . . . ."

On the same day, he wrote to his "Beluved friends Nicholas and Sophia" that he was well satisfied to be in Illinois:

> I think the gratest forchen that ever I made I mad by moovig. It casted me a heep tell I wase fixt and got hear but I dont mind all that. . . . I have know got two hundred and forty ecres of land, two cows and calfs and 14 head of hogs, 3 bed steds, a spining wheel, and what we need for the begaining [seasons?]. . . . You stated that I shold praise it to its oness value. I cannot praise it with pen and ink but if I cold stand with you face and face I cold tell you a heep about it.

[Plate 11]
SUNBURST
100" x 82"

Sarah C. Vaughn Black, 1834–1914
Fairview, Todd County, Kentucky, 1850
Collection of the Illinois State Museum

George E. Ludewick, another North Carolinian at Hillsboro, told his parents on June 23, 1832, "I like this country well, and I should like to stay." Six months later Daniel F. Ludewick also wrote home:

I must still say that I am satisfied as to my moving to this country. . . . I own three hundred and sixty acres of land, and that is good, and the money that it cost me would not have bought me 100 acres with you. I understand that Brother Nicholas has bought Michael Side's old place. I would all but laugh to see him plow them old wourn out red fields. . . . I will only say that if any of our old friends intend to come to this country that they can't come too quick, for land is taken up very fast and is valuable.[17]

The North Carolinians who moved to Montgomery County were the cutting edge of a new breed: the prairie farmers, the men who plowed the prairie sod. The earlier upland pioneers were the traditional self-sufficient hunter–farmer type. They were woodsmen more familiar with the ax, rifle, and hunting knife than with the plow. They faced an isolated frontier in Illinois as a previous generation of their family had done in Kentucky or Tennessee. Handmade textiles, another facet of their traditional self-sufficient existence, dominated the lives of their wives and daughters, and it is likely that most early nineteenth-century Illinois quilts were pieced of homespun linen or wool. One source noted that in 1810 Illinois had 12,000 people and 460 looms that produced 90,000 yards of cloth.[18]

One observer, who arrived in Madison County from Tennessee in 1817, noted: "The surrounding country . . . was quite sparsely settled, and destitute of any energy or enterprise among the people; their labors and attention being chiefly confined to the hunting of game . . . and tilling a small patch of corn for bread, relying on game for the remaining supplies of the table. The inhabitants were of the most generous and hospitable character, and were principally from the Southern States; harmony and the utmost good feeling prevailed throughout the country."[20] Economic and kinship ties kept many of these migrants facing toward their former homes.

The early Illinois economy was predominantly influenced by a geographical connection to the South. The state's southern-flowing waterways—the Wabash, Ohio, Mississippi, and Illinois rivers—offered farmers a convenient natural out-

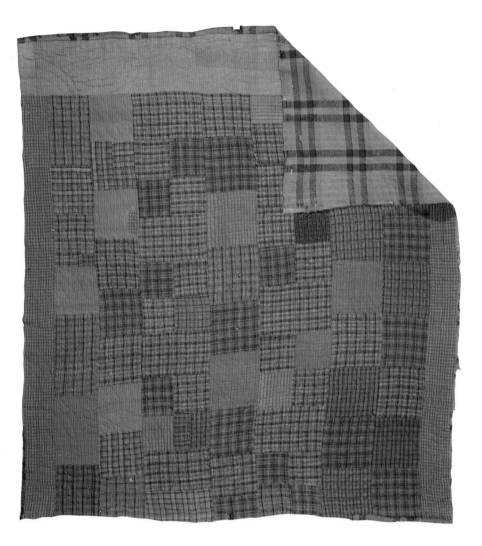

let. In the decades before the railroad provided access to eastern markets, the river trade created such a strong tie to the southern economy that sectional allegiance was seriously divided in Illinois on the eve of the Civil War. The state's earliest immigration left an important legacy, and the lower part of Illinois still retains its southern complexion.

The nation's decennial census, which began in 1790 and originally enumerated only the head of the family by name, began listing each individual and noting the place of birth in 1850. Analysis of this census information indicates that the state's southern-born population was most heavily concentrated in the southern and west-central counties. The natural water routes critically influenced the source areas of the Upland South migration and the eventual place of settlement in the Prairie State. It is not unusual for quilt registrants in southern and western Illinois to trace their family and quilt genealogies to a southern state. However, a thorough statistical analysis of the Illinois Quilt Research Project registration forms will probably indicate that the overall influence of southern quiltmakers on Illinois' quiltmaking tradition is slightly overshadowed by their Yankee and foreign-born counterparts.

[Plate 12]
ONE PATCH
80″ x 74″

Sally Kincaid Mitchell, 1819–1902
Greenfield, Greene County, Illinois,
   circa 1875
Collection of the Illinois State Museum

The Project registered no Illinois-made quilt pieced of handwoven fabrics that dated to the early nineteenth century. However, it is probable that the circa 1875 woolen pieced plaid quilt made by Sally Kincaid Mitchell of Greene County is very similar to the type that once dominated early Illinois. Composed of homespun and handwoven wool (quilted 3–4 stitches per inch), with wool batting, one side features plaids, stripes, and solids while the other is all plaid. The edge is bound by bringing the back to the front and stitching it by hand.[19]

Middle State Migration

Migration to Illinois from the Middle Atlantic states did not begin as early as it did from the South. Nevertheless, when people began moving west in the 1820s and 1830s from New York and New Jersey, they made an imprint upon Illinois' cultural heritage. The quilting contribution of Pennsylvania is particularly significant.

Current research, nationally and regionally based quilt collections, and the strong market for contemporary and antique quilts made in Pennsylvania attest to that state's long-standing leadership in the history and study of the American quilt. Thus, it is not surprising to find that the workmanship and creativity of Pennsylvania quilters is strongly represented in the Illinois Quilt Research Project data or to learn that many mid-nineteenth-century Illinois residents could trace their family to the Keystone State. Pennsylvanians wishing to move west enjoyed ready access to a road system leading to the western-flowing Ohio River and to the nation's first major "interstate highway."

A military road cut during the French and Indian War soon facilitated civilian travel across the state's ridge and valley system. In the early nineteenth century, the federal government widened, graded, and surfaced this highway with gravel to produce an all-weather route known as the National Road. It was also called the Cumberland Road because it originated in Cumberland, Maryland. By 1818 it had reached the Ohio River at Wheeling. Within a few years the federal and state governments pushed it westward, intent upon opening the interior lands to settlement and commerce. Extending from Wheeling to St. Louis, it remained a major route and in the twentieth century was replaced by U.S. 40, then by I–70. With access to the Ohio River and the National Road, Pennsylvanians moved west and brought quiltmaking traditions with them.

Pennsylvanians contributed significantly to the development of the Prairie State. The 1860 census recorded more than eighty thousand of them living in Illinois. There were major concentrations in Stephenson, Rock Island, Putnam, and Stark counties in northwestern Illinois as well as in Wabash County in the southeastern part of the state. Pennsylvanians were often the second dominant population group in other counties. Economic difficulties forced many Keystone State families to consider migration. Financial instability and unemployment distressed the manufacturing and laboring community, while the thin-soiled hillsides were hard to farm. In addition, flattering circulars touting the benefits of Illinois induced many to make the trip.[21]

Most pre-1850 Pennsylvania quilts can be traced to families who migrated from the British Isles. The Germans did not bring a quilting tradition with them to America, but they eventually acquired the technique from their English neighbors.[22] Weaving was a more important tradition than quilting to this group.[23] The first documented Pennsylvania German quilt is dated 1814. Other early Keystone State quilts indicate additional Pennsylvania German women accepted the quilting tradition by mid-century and actively pursued it in the years following the Civil War when handweaving declined in the face of competition with factory-made goods. According to Patricia Herr, a Lancaster County, Pennsylvania, needlework authority, the Germans had an affinity for "exuberant colors and bold motifs."[24]

Interviews with elderly quilters helped Jeannette Lasansky divide Pennsylvania quilts into the plainer

[Plate 13]
RED AND GREEN FLORAL APPLIQUÉ
87" x 72"

Probably M. Huber, dates unknown
Town unknown, probably Pennsylvania,
　circa 1865
Private collection

The unidentified M. Huber boldly appliquéd a German name on the bedcovering and utilized several classical Pennsylvania traits in creating what was surely a best quilt. These appliqué quilts were normally considered as show pieces and were rarely used. They were usually only taken out of storage and placed on a bed for an important occasion or for a special guest. The extensive wear on this quilt, which is probably due to repeated and over-zealous laundering techniques, is unusual on a quilt of this calibre. Perhaps the obvious neglect is the work of Huber's descendants who failed to appreciate the quiltmaker's diligent work, or it might have been sold at auction to someone who merely wanted a utilitarian bedcovering.

Huber selected the readily available mid-nineteenth century Pennsylvania appliqué colors: red and green with yellow for accent. These commercially produced cottons, which were available in the East by 1850, enabled quiltmakers to create an allover pattern with a definite color scheme.[26] Huber employed a bold scale in laying out the quadrant set and created a rectangular quilt by adding two partial blocks. The maker further enlarged the quilt by inserting a generous white sashing cut from the same cotton used for the top and the back of the quilt. The quilting pattern creates an overall grid (quilted 6 stitches per inch). Green piping enhances the red cotton binding on the top side. All the construction is by hand. A wide border contains an undulating vine border with yellow-centered red flowers. The one exception is a yellow flower with a red center, surely not a careless mistake. Regrettably, we can no longer ask the maker to share the secret with us, but contemporary theorists will offer a variety of undocumented "reasons."

pieced utilitarian types and "fancy work" appliqués. The quilt of the anonymous M. Huber is obviously a fancy effort going beyond a utilitarian cover. It is made with the familiar midcentury red, green, and yellow colors and bold naturalistic motifs so characteristic of the Pennsylvania Germans. According to one author, that ethnic group preferred vivid, contrasting colors, such as reds and greens. Their "love of color and active patterning . . . is evident in many of their decorative arts." They frequently used an undulating vine as a border and the "fully open . . . appliqué flowers were . . . Germanic designs that were used repeatedly by

nineteenth-century Pennsylvania German quilters."[25]

Jeannette Lasansky, a nationally recognized authority on Keystone State quilts, notes the Pennsylvania German appliqué work became "a formula with endless variation" based upon "formal busyness" and "restrained boldness." As the Germans migrated into Virginia and North Carolina, they took with them their "preference for bright, vivid, even gaudy color schemes."[27] Perhaps they brought it to Illinois also, but few Illinois-made quilts fitting this description were registered with the Illinois Quilt Research Project.

The growing number of Pennsylvania Germans in Illinois by the 1830s encouraged the Pennsylvania Lutheran Synod to take a strong interest in the state. John Heyer, a missionary pastor, left his congregation in Somerset on December 30, 1835, to tour the West. Because of muddy roads, he opted for a steamboat to Cincinnati. From there he traveled to Louisville and then to Corydon, Indiana, where he "proceeded mostly on by-roads, to shun the mud" and arrived at the Wabash River on January 23, 1836. He crossed to Mount Carmel on the Illinois side and found so many people from "Old Pennsylvania" that "he felt himself at home."[28]

During the 1840s many Pennsylvania Germans from Centre, Clinton, Union, and Lycoming counties settled in several Stephenson County townships near Freeport. One group attracted attention as it moved overland along a northern route in 1843. The Clarion, Pennsylvania, *Register* noted: "On Wednesday May 31, a company of about sixty emigrants passed through this place on their way . . . to Stephenson county, Illinois. They had fourteen wagons, each drawn by an elegant span of horses. . . . They were all from one neighborhood, had plenty of cash and appeared in fine spirits." Later the Michigan City, Indiana, *Gazette* noticed that on June 27, "Quite a caravan of the hardy sons of Pennsylvania passed through this city on their way to Stephenson county, Illinois. There were fourteen wagons and sixty-one persons."[29] One can only imagine how many Pennsylvania quilts were a part of the cultural treasures that filled those fourteen wagons.

Not everyone joined a caravan, and not all the Pennsylvanians moving to Illinois were Germans. The Alexander Thompson family of Greenspring (near Newville) in Newton Township, Cumberland County, decided to move by themselves. When they left on May 7, 1839, they were part of a stream of Scots–Irish Presbyterian farmers who continuously sought greater opportunities in the West.

Family tradition indicates that Thompson wished to acquire more land for "the boys," three sons ranging in age from eighteen to twenty-nine who headed west with the family. A fourth, thirty-two-year-old John, was already living in western Indiana when his eighty-year-old father wrote on September 27, 1838, to explain his relocation plan. John, along with his wife, Sarah, their two children, and the families of his two married sisters, Rachel Miller and Elizabeth Miller, were probably searching for a new permanent location. At the time they were living near Eugene in Vermilion County. His descendants have preserved a copy of his informative letter.

In the early phase of the Panic of 1837 — the worst depression the nation had experienced to that time — Alexander Thompson decided that if he could sell his farm for $7,000, he would move west. The year 1838 was disastrously dry.

[Figure 6]
Alexander Thompson home
Cumberland County, Pennsylvania
May 1899

> We have had a very long drouth [*sic*] from the middle of June till two days ago; we had no rain to wet the ground, more than to lay the dust, the ground is now wet plough deep; we are saving our grain, there is no pasture of any kind, we have been foddering our stock this two weeks; there has been no pasture for horses, cow, sheep, hog nor goose nor duck, they had all to be fed since the grasshoppers got scarce, they were very plenty this season in some places, did damage our grain; market is got high here, corn & rye will be worth at present from 80 to 90 cents per bushel owing to the corn crop missing, the rye crop being light also.

Having successfully sold his 185 acres for $39 per acre, the Thompson family prepared to head west the following spring. Payments would be made in installments — $4,000 down on April 1, 1839, with $1,000

> to be paid in one year in small notes bearing interest and the remaining 2215 Dollars to be paid in three annual equal payments. . . . So then we will now be making ready to push our fortune to the west if all goes well, we will start about the middle of May and will be with you perhaps the last of June if God grants us health and strength. . . . We will I think take two horses[,] wagons[,] and our Dearborn; whether that will be enough or not we can't tell till we get put; I suppose you can give us some information as you have went the road before us.

An undated clipping from a twentieth-century issue of the Albany, Illinois, *Review* reported Thompson brought "a number of pieces of furniture" which eventually became "treasures in the homes of his grandchildren." The pieces included a walnut table and a chest of drawers.

The Thompsons had easy access to the National Road, long a heavily used route to the frontier. Twenty years earlier a traveler had viewed the caravans and thought "Old America seems to be breaking up, and moving westward. . . . The number of emigrants who passed this way, was greater last year than in any preceding; and the present spring they are still more numerous than the last. Fourteen waggons [*sic*] yesterday, and thirteen today, have gone through this town."[30] It was still busy when the Thompsons moved to Illinois. *Niles' Weekly Register* noted: "The National Road has the whole season been blocked up with movers' wagons and from the representations, people enough have changed homes from the east to the west in 1839 to add another state to the national constellation had they all located in a single territory."[31]

[Figure 7]
Margaret Thompson Blean
Born May 8, 1819, Greenspring,
    Cumberland County, Pennsylvania
Died June 12, 1903, Albany, Whiteside
    County, Illinois

Without a breakdown, the large Conestoga wagons could travel up to fifteen miles a day, so the move from Pennsylvania to Illinois could take seven to nine weeks.

Although tradition indicates the family passed through Indianapolis where twenty-nine-year-old William became ill and died, a printed source claims his death occurred in Xenia, Ohio.[32] Since both sites were on the National Road, that route seems the likely one. The Thompson caravan, perhaps delayed by William's illness, probably did not arrive at John's Vermilion County, Indiana, home, about twenty miles southeast of Danville, Illinois, until August or September.

On September 9, 1839, Alexander appeared at Newport before the Vermilion County Circuit Court to apply for a Revolutionary War pension. Although Congress had passed a law providing for this in 1832, the elderly veteran had not previously collected any money

due him. Since he was eligible for $10 every six months, he claimed $170 back pay, which he could use to establish his family in their new western home.

Selecting a new home in the West was a problem. Obviously the family had been considering the Rock River Valley of northwestern Illinois, an area that was beginning to grow rapidly following the defeat of the Indians in the 1832 Black Hawk War. Thompson raised the subject with his son:

> When I wrote last I understood by Samuel Miller [Rachel's husband] that you had a notion to go to Rock River; I think in my letter I was in favor of you going there but since, I have heard that [the] Miami Indian Reserve will come into market this fall by government; It is said by all who have seen it, that it is preferable to almost any other place in Indiana; If you have not been to Rock River yet, you should think and inform yourself about this as you have a better opportunity of knowing about it than I can as you live near the place and likewise consult your friends on these particulars.

The Miami Reserve was about seventy miles northeast near Kokomo in present-day Howard and Tipton counties.

No extant documents indicate why the family left Indiana and settled in Whiteside County. Margaret's obituary notes that the family arrived in the county in the fall of 1839 and built a log cabin in Greenfield, now Newton, Township.[33] A local referendum in 1851 changed the name to commemorate the Pennsylvania township where the Thompson family had lived before coming to Illinois. Sixteen Thompson family members spent their first winter together in their one-room cabin. Alexander Thompson died September 25, 1840, less than a year after settling "his boys" on their new land in the West. The boys — both sons and sons-in-law — obviously liked their

[Plate 14]
MARGARET QUILT
112″ x 91″

Margaret Thompson Blean, 1819–1903
Greenspring, Cumberland County,
   Pennsylvania, 1839
Collection of Margaret F. Corney

new state, as their descendants are still there.

When the Thompsons left Pennsylvania, their twenty-one-year-old daughter, Margaret, brought along her new quilt. The red-and-white pieced cotton top, cotton back, and cotton batting are elaborately quilted (10 stitches per inch) in parallel lines and stipple, and each of the plain blocks features a different floral quilting design. The binding is back brought to front. All work is by hand. Tiny quilting stitches in a triangular white block adjacent to the border painstakingly record its origin: "Margaret Thompson Cumberland Cty, State of Penn Newton Township, Green Spring April 4, 1839." Known in the family as "the Margaret Quilt," it is passed to the oldest Margaret in each generation. When Margaret Thompson Blean died June 21, 1903, she was survived by her husband and four of their seven children.

"Aunt Margaret," as she was affectionately known throughout the Whiteside County area where she spent most of her long life, married Robert Clark Blean on July 3, 1845. A native of nearby Newville in Cumberland County, Pennsylvania, he surely knew Margaret before she moved to Illinois. "Uncle Robert's" obituary indicates "Blean came west to Illinois in 1843 and after remaining a short time returned to Pennsylvania," but he came back in the spring of 1845 "and has resided here continuously ever since."[34]

Like Alexander Thompson's family, Margaret Thompson Blean's quilt has remained in Illinois. Margaret Blean Wood owned it from the time her father died in 1906 until her own death in 1943. Her daughter Lida continued to live in the Wood home and kept the quilt as long as she was able. When she sold the house to move into a nursing home in 1966, the quilt passed to her sister, Leah Margaret Wood Finnicum, who kept it until she died in 1983. She had, however, lived with her daughter, the present owner,

[Plate 15]
Close-up of the documentation Margaret stitched into her quilt.

since 1971. Margaret Finnicum Corney, the fourth Margaret to cherish the quilt, intends to give it to her granddaughter, Anne Margaret.

Owned by a descendant, the Thompson quilt is accompanied by excellent research materials. The Beekman quilt also has an impressive file, but it has passed outside the family and the conclusions about the original owner and the quilt's migration to Illinois are somewhat tentative.

William Beekman's friendship quilt[35] is a significant document because through it historians may study several different segments of Illinois history. One of the very few Project quilts tracing its origin to an old-line Dutch colonial family, it also provides the researcher with an interesting look at early Illinois business practices.[36] Most importantly, however, it is the earliest friendship quilt

discovered in the Illinois Quilt Research Project, and the time and place of its origin provide a strong tie to the cultural pattern of a mid-nineteenth-century quilt fad.[37]

William T. Beekman of New Jersey was already living at Clary's Grove, near New Salem in Menard County, when the Thompsons headed for Illinois in 1839. Beekman was a carpenter and a wheelwright who "worked at his trade," according to the 1889 Menard County history. A church he built for the Clary's Grove Baptist congregation in 1845 remained in use until 1871. He later served two terms in the state legislature.[38]

Accompanying the Beekman quilt is an 1838 letter from his family in New Jersey, which implies he is no longer living near them. Initially this is puzzling, for the letter is written from Harlingen, New Jersey, and is addressed to William at Harlingen. One wonders why a letter that provides details about a marriage and two local deaths would be written to someone living nearby. Although the paper upon which the letter is written was folded, sealed, and ad-dressed, there is no indication of a postage charge.[39]

What evidence is found within the text? Sister Cornelia tells him to "Thank Grandpa for sending you these [I]nteligencers there is some good reading in them[.]" The letter is obviously part of a package, for she is also sending him a "bosom" [shirt?] she made. She has "another almost done but had not time to finish it." Although his location is not defined, there is ample evidence he is not living in New Jersey. "I must quit now but not before I tell you that if Ma had consented I would have come out with Miss Conover[.] I think I would like the travel[.]"

That there are no questions about his trip west and how he likes the area may indicate he has been there long enough to have already answered such queries. In typical nineteenth-century prose, his sister Sarah indicates there has been an extended absence. She hopes he will not interpret her "long unbroken silence to the want of that natural affection which ought to exist between a brother & sister rest assured my dear William tho I hav [sic] as it were remained in silence my Thoughts have often very oft been with you & often have I pictured in livelyest Imagination myself by your side enjoying the uninterrupted Enjoyment of a long & interesting conversation with you."

The letter from brother Benjamin refers to farming matters, and his report of the past growing season would indicate William has not been in New Jersey recently. Benjamin had a "midling good crop of rye and oats," but the corn "is all dride up for we have the greatest drouth here that we have ever known." His cryptic message, "Jim we live yet on the old long feald," is probably directed to the second brother in Illinois. He

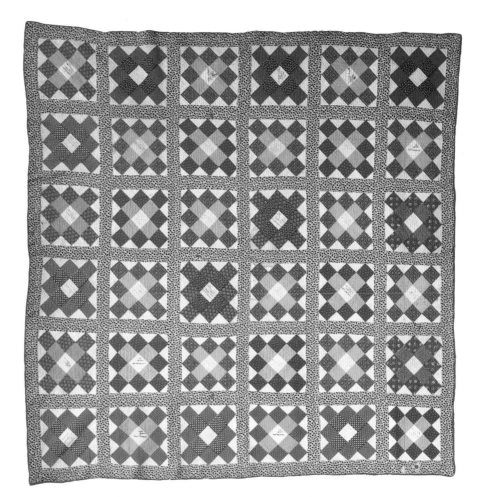

[Plate 16]
CHIMNEY SWEEP
88″ x 88″

Maker(s) unkown
Harlingen, Somerset County, New
   Jersey, 1850
Private collection

Since all the dated blocks in the New Jersey single-pattern friendship quilt bear the year 1850, it can be immediately assumed William did not bring it to Illinois with him in 1837. Why did he receive it in 1850? Perhaps he was home for a visit. The quilt was apparently made during a short period of time. Twenty-four of the thirty-six signed blocks are dated from March 10 to April 1, 1850, while eight are simply "1850" and four have no date at all. The identified towns include Harlingen, and the nearby Somerset County communities of Blawenburg, Rocky Hill, Griggstown, Milestone, New Brunswick, Somerville, Raritan, and North Branch.

The quilt is made of a surprising range of printed cotton fabrics within a limited color spectrum. Oddly enough, the sprinkling of blue patches stands out from the masses as boldly as a New Jersey Dutchman might have appeared on the Illinois frontier. Perhaps the unusual similarity of fabrics and large number of matching pieces, as well as the small range of dates, indicate the quilt was constructed of new fabric and on a demanding schedule. It is all cotton on the front and back, with a cotton batt. The binding is handmade, straight-cut solid red cotton applied by hand. All the piecing is by hand, and the quilting (8–9 stitches per inch) is in echo and parallel lines. It is an early example of a type of quilt that would remain popular in Illinois.

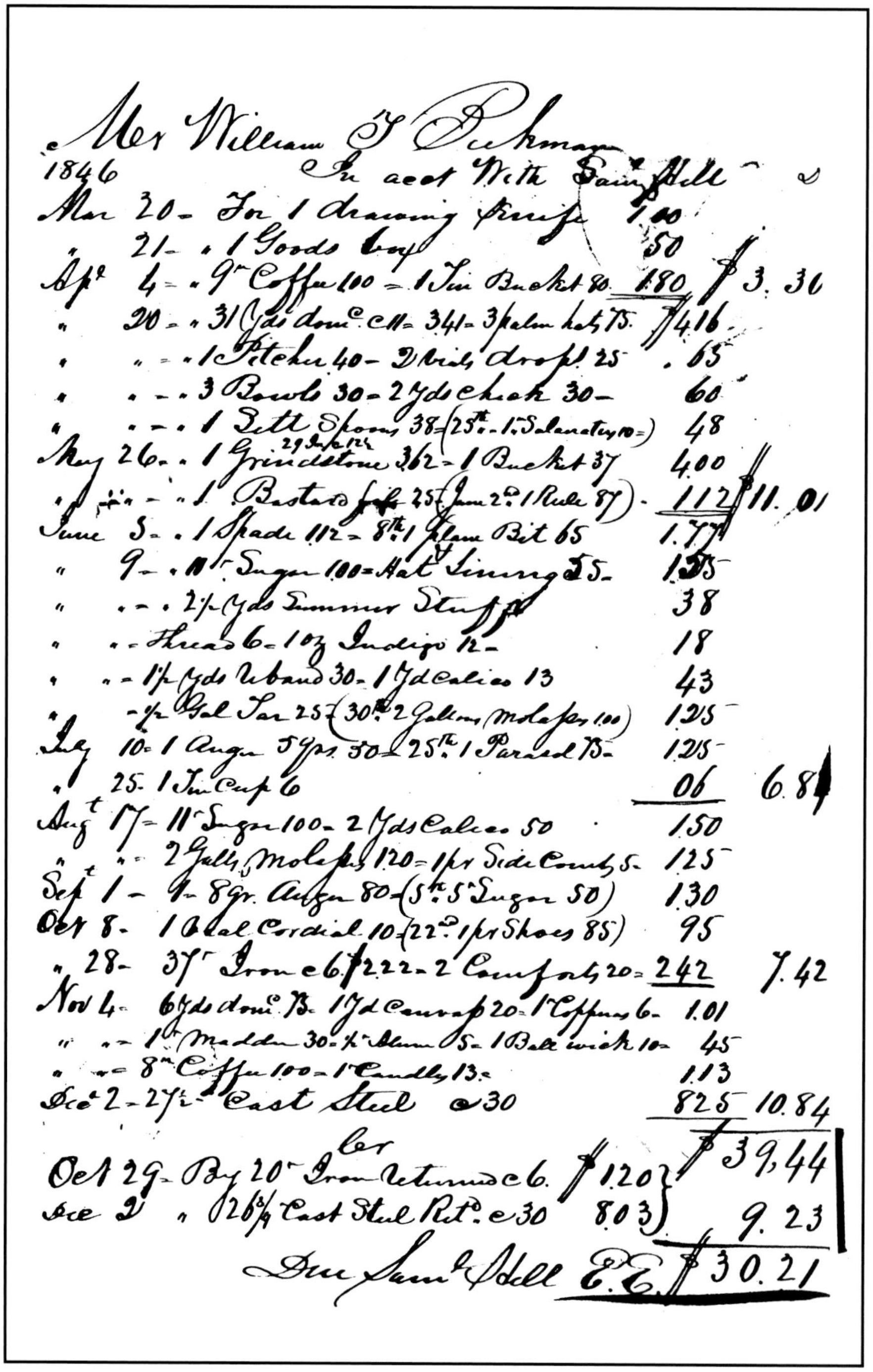

[Figure 8]

William T. Beekman's 1846 bill from Petersburg merchant Samuel Hill included textiles and related items such as domestic, summer stuff, thread, indigo dye, "riband," calico, comforts, canvas, copperas, madder, and alum. Hill tried to meet his customers' needs by stocking a variety of goods. During the year, Beekman made other purchases. While he never heard of a charge card, he was nevertheless very familiar with buying on credit. It was not unusual for such accounts to build for several years before being paid or written off as a bad debt.

notes that "Miss Conover aat [sic] dinner with us to day. . . . I leave all the rest for misses Conover to tell you." Perhaps she stopped by to visit his family before leaving for Illinois, and it was she who brought along the package and the unmailed letter.[40]

William Beekman, who was born February 23, 1815, in Somerville, Somerset County, New Jersey, moved to Menard County, Illinois, in 1837 and died at Petersburg on August 14, 1899. He arrived in the Sangamon Valley in time to have the opportunity to do business with Sam Hill, an Ohio-born merchant who opened a general store at New Salem in 1829 and relocated in Petersburg in 1839.[41]

Beekman regularly charged his purchases at Hill's store. In 1846 he received a bill that reveals the wide range of consumer goods available in Menard County in the 1840s before the arrival of railroads. Although none of the textiles in his 1850s friendship quilt came from Hill's store, the same kind of factory-made fabric used in it could have been purchased in Petersburg and many other seemingly isolated communities throughout rural Illinois.[42]

During the pre–Civil War period, New York experienced the same economic growing pains that plagued her neighboring states to the east and to the south. Rent remained high in rural and urban areas despite a decline in wages and agricultural prices. Population declined in many counties as the numbers moving west increased. Many of the farmers who chose not to move west switched from grain production—principally wheat—to dairying.

The completion of the Erie Canal encouraged many New Yorkers to move west with migration particularly strong in the 1840s and 1850s. By 1860 they were the dominant group in the northern third of Illinois. Although domestic migration from the Northeast to Illinois decreased as available land supplies

[Figure 9]
Abigail Safford Barrett
Born July 17, 1842, Essex, Essex County,
    New York
Died January 28, 1905, Fulton,
    Whiteside County, Illinois

dwindled, the movement never stopped completely during the nineteenth century. Newly developing agricultural or business opportunities continued to lure the young and ambitious following the Civil War. Henry Safford Barrett was one of the many New Yorkers who chose to begin life anew in Illinois.

Westport, Essex County, New York, is in the northeastern part of the state, on the western shore of Lake Champlain about 125 miles north of Albany. It was Barrett's birthplace in 1831. Young Henry was eighteen in 1849 when he struck out for western New York in search of employment. He worked for two years in Fulton, a small town between Syracuse and Oswego; and in the spring of 1851 he was caught up in the western fever and left for Illinois. He traveled by railroad and stagecoach to Chicago, Freeport, and Savanna. Upon arriving in Carroll County he learned that his luggage and money were missing. He found employment, and by the spring of 1857 he had saved enough money to buy a 320-acre farm in York Township of Carroll County.

He became ill shortly after his purchase, but he eventually managed to save one-half of the farm by selling the other 160 acres. He built a comfortable home on the property and in the fall of 1866 returned to his native state for a visit. At Essex, New York, on February 12, 1867, he married Abigail Emery Safford, a long-time friend, neighbor, and distant relative. The twenty-four-year-old bride was born in Essex. Aware that Abigail would soon be leaving for the West, her many friends and relatives dipped a pen into ink and signed the white center square of the Chimney Sweep pieced quilt blocks. It was one of the era's most popular friendship quilt patterns.[43] Abigail's quilt is all cotton in the top, back, and batt and is bound with handmade straight-cut cotton stitched

[Plate 17]
CHIMNEY SWEEP
85″ x 77″

Abigail Safford Barrett, 1842–1905
Westport, Essex County, New York,
    circa 1867
Collection of Jon Andrew Lockhart

by hand. The quilting (8 stitches per inch) is in parallel lines.

Henry and Abigail traveled west by wagon, bringing with them a load of furniture and household goods, including two quilts — a friendship quilt that was the treasured gift from their friends and a pieced yellow and white Delectable Mountains. The Barretts lived on the Carroll County farm until 1883 when Henry purchased 180 acres in Ustick Township of neighboring Whiteside County. While living there, they belonged to the Spring Valley Presbyterian Church where Henry served as an elder for several years. They remained in Ustick Township until moving into Fulton on June 1, 1899, where Henry died two years later.

Abigail lived until 1905. The family remembers her as a kind and gentle woman who was a good housekeeper and skilled in the sewing arts. The Barretts reared three children — their two daughters, Mabel and Cora, and an adopted son, Dwight Orion Barrett — and their descendants still live on the family farm. Today Abigail's quilts, her picture album, and a number of family books are preserved by the family as mementos of America's westward expansion and the role Henry and Abigail Barrett played in the development of Illinois' quilt history.

From Yankee Homespun to Cotton Prints

A major factor causing the exodus to the West was the economic climate of New England where the small, often unproductive farms could not compete with the inexpensive wheat coming east over the Erie Canal. Wool prices declined, and a constant influx of foreign labor kept wages low. Geography did not provide the Northeast with the naturally accessible routes available to other sections, and no easily traveled and inexpensive waterway connected the Hudson River to the Great Lakes before the Erie Canal opened in 1825. However, once completed, that facility became an overnight sensation and the mule-drawn barges carried thousands of homeseekers to the West. Governor DeWitt Clinton's "Big Ditch" drastically changed the future of Illinois as thrifty, hardworking Yankees filled up the northern and east-central portions of the state.

The completion of this route, which provided a water link from New York City through the Great Lakes to Chicago, opened a new marketplace for the agricultural surplus of Ohio; and the price of eastern wheat fell so drastically that small New England farmers could no longer survive economically. Some found employment in the proliferating textile mills, while those interested in farming or small business enterprises sought greener pastures on the frontier. New England suffered severe economic dislocation during the Panic of 1837, and the movement from rural New England reached flood stage by the 1840s.

This massive migration produced high concentrations of Yankees in the Midwest. Ohio's Western Reserve, southern Michigan, and northern Indiana attracted the earliest migrants. Illinois did not become a prime destination until the Black Hawk War

[Plate 18]
WHOLECLOTH QUILT
98″ x 90″

Sarah Petts Davis, dates unknown
Sandwich, Barnstable County,
    Massachusetts, circa 1832
Collection of the Illinois State Museum

eliminated the Indian threat in 1832. This also provided the opportunity to open a new commercial center at the mouth of the Chicago River in 1833. The 1860 census shows more than 120,000 New Yorkers and 50,000 New England Yankees living in the northern half of the state and in the east-central Grand Prairie area.

The Illinois State Museum's worsted homespun wool quilt is an example of the early-nineteenth-century wholecloth quilted bed-covering available for our examination today. The circa 1830s quilt came west with a family from Sandwich, Massachusetts, an ocean port at the northern base of Cape Cod. Made completely from materials normally produced on a New England farm, it exemplifies the principle of self-sufficiency and is historically significant as a typical textile that migrating Yankees brought to the frontier.[44]

Peter Cook, former head curator of the Bennington (Vermont) Museum, recently examined those New England bedcoverings. With tongue-in-cheek he proposed substituting "woolsey-woolsey" for what is often called linsey-woolsey. Ultimately, he uses the simple "wool bedquilt" as an appropriate professional term. He identified three general categories within this group: "the glazed solid-color calamanco that emphasizes the three-dimensional patterns reflected on its surface. A second form with the same stitching technique is a quilt without the glazed surface. A pieced quilt utilizing contrasting calamanco or unglazed solid-colored fabrics to form the quilt top is the third type."[45] The quilt made by Sarah Petts Davis falls into the second category.

During the early nineteenth century, the solid color wholecloth quilt "which could add a sense of formality and magnificence to a bedchamber," was commonplace in New England.[46] Very few are dated, and most have lost their prove-

nance. They are usually found with a different natural-dye color on each side. Sarah used worsted homespun wool for the top and the back of her quilt and placed wool between the layers as batting. She quilted the surface (7 stitches per inch) with feathers, flowers, and parallel lines.

In the absence of colorfully pieced or appliquéd designs, the maker of a wholecloth quilt must create visual impact by painstakingly stitching various motifs into an overall attractive pattern. Examination of such quilts reveals that fine needlework is not easily done when sewing through two pieces of homespun wool with a filling of even a thin woolen batting.

While these quilts appear durable and still can be found in the marketplace, it is also apparent that many more were created than what can be accounted for today. Many were probably attacked by moths, and it is possible that some later generations viewed these plain, warm coverings as expendable utilitarian objects rather than show quilts worthy of preservation. The surviving number of homespun quilts does not adequately indicate the original popularity of America's woolen bedquilts.[47]

The Album pieced quilt top belonging to the Winn family was begun by unidentified relatives still living in Sarah Converse Winn's native Arlington, Massachusetts. The family thinks that it might have been the work of the local Congregational church. After signing and dating each block, Julia Converse, daughter of Hannah Winn's brother, Joseph Converse, sent it to Illinois in 1880. At first glance the quilt is both puzzling and deceiving, with dates ranging from 1844 to 1912. However, the signatures having 1840 to 1880 dates on blocks made of fabrics from the 1870s refer to birth years or they memorialize deceased family members. Those

[Plate 19]
ALBUM BLOCK
79" x 79"

Harriet Ann Winn Penstone, 1843–1942
   and Sarah Louise Winn, 1839–1919
Arlington, Middlesex County,
   Massachusetts, 1880
   and Griggsville, Pike County, Illinois,
   1912
Collection of Sue Lightle

[Plate 20]
The presentation block is addressed to
"Dear Jennie" and is dated February 25,
1880.

with twentieth-century dates were added to the modified quilt top in Illinois before it was quilted.

When James Winn was born in Arlington, Massachusetts, on January 31, 1808, he was a seventh-generation descendant of Edward Winn, an Englishman who had settled at nearby Woburn in 1641. After James completed an apprenticeship to a groceryman in Boston's Quincy vegetable market, "the opportunities offered by the new and growing West" attracted him to Illinois. James moved to Griggsville in 1833, purchased forty acres of government land, and entered the pork-packing and shipping business. For several years he traded with Boston merchants by way of New Orleans. Once established, he sent for his bride-to-be. Hannah Converse, born at Arlington on February 7, 1811, arrived in the spring of 1836. They married at Griggsville on May 12. Between 1837 and 1856 Hannah

[Figure 10]
Sarah Louise Winn
Born July 1, 1839, Griggsville, Pike
County, Illinois
Died December 25, 1919, Griggsville,
Pike County, Illinois

There is yet another mystery. The blocks are now hand stitched to sashing that is uniform throughout the top. However, clearly visible rows of closely spaced small round holes beside many seams indicate that the Massachusetts-pieced blocks were originally joined by machine to each other or to another sashing and perhaps were aligned in a different configuration. The quilt is made entirely of cotton and edged by bringing the back to the front. This is the only part of the quilt sewn by machine. The quilting (6 stitches per inch) is in outline and parallel lines.

bore nine children. Although James died January 10, 1860, his wife lived until March 30, 1888.[48]

The Winns exchanged pictures and letters with their eastern relatives, and in 1880 members of the Winn and Converse families in Massachusetts sent an album quilt to Hannah Converse Winn's oldest daughter. Hannah Jane Winn (1837–1925), also known as Jennie, was an invalid for many years. For an unknown reason, the unfinished gift languished until 1912 when her un-

married sister, Sarah Louise (Aunt Lou), and one of her married sisters, Harriet Penstone, took the quilt apart, added more blocks, and quilted it. When the two unmarried sisters, Jennie and Sarah, died, Jennie Alice Leeds, Harriet's daughter and Jennie's namesake, inherited the quilt. Her daughter, Susan Alice Leeds Lightle, the present owner, believes the quilt was finished in 1912 when the latest dated blocks were added to it. There is a block with the name of her brother, Ralph Stratton Leeds. He was born in 1910, although his block is dated 1912. There is no block for his sister Sue who was born in 1914.

Because the blocks are pieced of so many different fabrics, the quilt provides an excellent resource for studying printed cotton textiles of the 1870s. It also documents the strong, enduring ties of kinship that bound together families long separated by the process of westward migration.

The Midwest Migration: From Ohio and Indiana to Illinois

American development of eastern Ohio was progressing by 1790, and that portion of the state was rapidly being settled when Ohio entered the Union in 1803.[49] Settlers from the Upland South, Pennsylvania, and New England made important contributions to the area, and by 1850 many of their sons and daughters had moved on to carve out a life for themselves in Illinois. The 1860 census indicates that Ohio-born settlers dominated east-central Illinois. On the eve of the Civil War, the more than 130,000 native Ohioans living in the Prairie State constituted the largest group of non-Illinois American-born people in the state's population.

Ohio experienced economic difficulties after the Panic of 1837, and by the 1840s many farmers realized that the glaciated northern portions of the state could out-produce the hilly unglaciated southern counties. Finding no room for expansion at home, many established families and young sons of Ohio pioneers, imbued with the idea of a better life in the West, headed for the unoccupied and less expensive land of Indiana and Illinois. Sometimes the family heritage quilt so prized by their heirs did not make that trek with them.

Ade and Rebecca Lowrey Law, the parents of ten children, left southeastern Ohio's Noble County for a new home east of Taylorville, Illinois. Because they traveled by rail, their 1857 trip was surely less tiring than the journey many earlier travelers had experienced. This marvelous technological innovation rapidly transformed the nation's transportation network and forever altered the migration process.

In a lengthy June 13, 1857, letter, later printed in a 1939 Taylorville *Courier,* Ade Law tells his daughter Susanna, who remained in Ohio with her husband, about the trip west and their new life in Illinois. They parted at Jonesville, Ohio, and he describes the family's excursion as

a very pleasant one. . . . We left Zanesville the next day at nine o'clock and got to Pana the day following at 10 o'clock making a ride of 25 hours. All the girls enjoyed theirselves first rate. Little Lydia was at home all the way while on the cars. She had something to say to almost all the persons on the train. She went where she pleased. The passengers took great delight in talking to her and they give her oranges, apples and sweet cakes, candy and nuts of different kinds—twice as much as she could eat.[50]

Ade had already written two letters that did not reach his Ohio relatives before he received the first

[Plate 21]
FLOWER APPLIQUÉ
82" x 81"

Susan Lowrey, dates unknown
Wayne Township, Noble County, Ohio,
  circa 1850
Collection of Letha Ransdell

letter from them. How did they know where to address the letter? He obviously knew the town to which they would be moving when he left Ohio. In his letter he reports he "planted thirty acres for George Law." A brother or a cousin was probably already living near Taylorville before Ade brought his family west.

His very lengthy letter is filled with praise for Christian County, and he is eager for Susanna and her husband, James Finley Riggs, to join them in Illinois. They never did. Writing, "We are well satisfied with the country," he continued:

> It certainly is the most delightful and loveliest and most handsomest country I ever saw. . . . the general yield of corn to the acre is 80 to 100 bushel. The average crop of wheat is 30 to 40 bushel per acre. Potatoes, turnips and vines of every kind yields at least double to what they do in Ohio. One man can tend 40 acres of corn himself alone with less labor then he can ten in Ohio. Here the land is level, smooth and light and rich as cream and not a stump or rock in one thousand acres. Here wheat and oats is harvested with machinery. Man's labor is comparatively light to what it is in Ohio and another advantage is a man has as much pasture that grows spontaneously on the prairie, half leg high, sufficient for the cattle on a thousand hills. He has not to provide this, it is free. Another advantage is, we have railways passing in every direction, all thru the country, making a market for every thing a man has to sell.

The Laws were becoming established in the area by renting a house or by living with someone else, for Ade reports "we go one and a half miles to our work." His sons helped out by working for others. "Wages is high. Ezra [age fifteen] is still working at $12.00 a month. Laban [older than Ezra] is helping the neighbors with their corn at $1.00 a day. He has worked twenty-eight days.

William and myself have plowed and planted fifty-five acres for ourselves. . . . We are now breaking up the sod for wheat. . . . I want to move and build on my own land before winter." He realized that the house would cost a little more to build than in Ohio because there was very little timber in the region. However, when he was done with the buildings and fencing he would have "a farm that is worth something. . . . for my part I am satisfied that it is the country for me and what few days I have to spend on earth let me spend them in Christian Co. Illinois."[51]

In 1867 Ezra married Dora F. Van Dillian, whose family had come to Christian County from Ohio in 1857 when she was seven years old. The Van Dillians did not use the railroad.

> Her parents, who were lured to the west by the government land opening, with several other families formed a caravan of three covered wagons and started west on the migration taking the Old National Pike as far as western Indiana, from there they blazed their own trail over the prairie bringing their horses and cattle with them . . . arriving some time in April 1857 locating . . . on a farm two miles south of Owaneco.[52]

Like the family to which it belonged, the quilt migrated from Ohio to Illinois. It did not, however, arrive in the 1850s. It was the work of Rebecca Lowrey Law's unmarried sister, Susan Lowrey, who remained in Ohio. Violet Ellen Law, Ade's unmarried daughter who was living with her sister, Catherine Law Hague, recorded in her notebook that on March 13, 1905, she received $108.19 from her Aunt Susan Lowrey's estate. It is assumed that Catherine received the quilt at the same time. It has remained in her family. The red, pink, and green appliqué with stuffed work represents a palette and genre typical of the time period. It is nicely quilted

(9 stitches per inch) in grid, outline, and closely spaced parallel lines.

By 1860 approximately 62,000 Hoosiers had moved from Indiana to Illinois. During the remaining decades of the nineteenth century, the Hoosiers continued to come, with some like the Hinds family bringing their quilts along on the journey. One of these textile documents participated in an unusual American history event, as we shall see.

An old adage declares that histories of wars are written by the victors. That is particularly true of the American Civil War. In a fiercely contested, long, bloody struggle, the industrialized North, blessed with abundant productive capacity, an excellent transportation system, and mechanized agriculture, slowly penetrated and wore down the poorly financed, less populated, agriculturally based South. While the Southern invasions of Maryland in 1862 and Pennsylvania in 1863 cannot be ignored, they do emerge as costly Northern victories balanced by the South's devastating losses. The July 1863 Confederate foray into southern Indiana was quite different.

General John Hunt Morgan's invasion of that northern state came as a surprise, and his daring raid frightened thousands of Hoosier civilians. After he and his 2,400 men crossed the Ohio River, word spread rapidly about the impending disaster, and the area went into a state of panic. The Confederate forces captured Corydon before swinging through Salem, Vienna, Lexington, Paris, Vernon, and Dupont, Indiana. They pressed on into Ohio trying to avoid pursuers and attempting to find a safe place to recross the river into Kentucky. They did not succeed. Morgan's capture is not the turning point in the Union's eventual defeat of the Confederacy, and more often than not the affair is omitted from history textbooks.[53]

It is not, however, forgotten in the annals of Indiana and of frightened

[Plate 22]
MEXICAN ROSE VARIATION
86″ x 82″

Sarah Isabel Herron Hinds, 1831–1898
Lexington, Scott County, Indiana,
   circa 1860
Collection of Jack A. Miller

Hoosier families such as that of Almon Hinds. Sarah Isabel Herron Hinds completed her appliqué quilt in a design similar to the Mexican Rose pattern. The nine blocks are neatly appliquéd with red and orange flowers tied together by green leafy stems, and the whole is framed by a floral bud and swag border in the same color cotton appliqué. The top, back, and batt are all made of cotton. The handmade straight-cut red cotton binding is stitched by hand on both the front and back. The quilting (8 stitches per inch) is found in feather motifs around each block, diagonal lines within the blocks, and outlines around the appliqués. There are also hearts.

Sarah was born April 4, 1831, at Lexington, Indiana, where she later married Almon D. Hinds. They were living in Lexington when word arrived of Morgan's approaching force. Fearing loss of their worldly goods to the marauding band, Almon hastily decided to bury their most valuable possessions. Sarah obviously considered that her recently completed quilt fit the description, and it went into the ground along with the silverware and jewelry. While in the ground rain water seeped through the protective covering, and it was stained.[54]

Despite the damage, Sarah continued to treasure her quilt until her death in Indiana in 1898. In 1894 her son, Walter Isaac Hinds, married a Macon County, Illinois, resident and moved to Decatur. Walter or his daughter Irene, who made many visits to her Indiana relatives, brought the quilt to Illinois. For more than 125 years, this Civil War survivor has proudly borne its battle scars and, as a firsthand witness, the quilt has offered each new owner a personal contact with an American tragedy. Today the Hoosier Civil War quilt resides in Illinois along with many other treasures migrants have brought from other states.

Although the quilts selected for illustration represent the major sources of domestic migration in early Illinois history, they are only a small sampling of the many early non-Illinois quilts registered by the Project. There are quilts to tell the story of family migrations from almost every state in the Union before 1850. Geography placed Illinois in the nation's heartland and blessed the Prairie State with a water network to the Ohio and Mississippi Valley states as well as to the Atlantic and the Gulf of Mexico. By the mid-nineteenth century that was supplemented with an expanding rail network that soon made Chicago the nation's transportation center. Illinois's access to national and international markets contributed to a rapidly rising population during the entire nineteenth century.

Shortly after Illinois entered the Union in 1818, the state attracted increasing attention from European travelers and colonizers. Within a short time, hundreds of foreign-born settlers joined their American neighbors in seeking a better life in Illinois. The Prairie State rapidly diversified and over the decades acquired a rich ethnic heritage.

Verdilla Zook's compass has accurately led us along the state's domestic quilt paths. We are confident her Mariner's Compass will faithfully guide us over those quilt paths that begin far across the ocean.

[Plate 23]
OF THEE I SING
72″ x 72″

Anne Stephens Marcisz, 1931–
LaGrange, Cook County, Illinois,
    1985–86
Collection of the maker

2

SINGING MISS LIBERTY'S PRAISES: THE QUILTS OF OUR IMMIGRANTS

Give me your tired, your poor,
Your huddled masses yearning to breathe free,
The wretched refuse of your teeming shore,
Send these, the homeless, tempest-tossed, to me:
I lift my lamp beside the golden door.
— Emma Lazarus,
"The New Colossus," 1883

The United States is indeed a nation of nations, and Illinois is a state of nations. Over the years, these newcomers to the Prairie State often met discrimination, and many battled poverty and illiteracy. Although change came slowly, a growing recognition of the state's diversity encourages present-day Illinoisans to celebrate ethnicity and share their cultural heritage. Perhaps no event in recent history highlighted this more than the Statue of Liberty centennial in 1986.

As part of that celebration, the Museum of American Folk Art sponsored a contest that attracted the attention of a LaGrange quilter. Anne Stephens Marcisz, who began sewing at age nine, joined a group quiltmaking effort in 1979 to celebrate the town's centennial. A few years and several quilt classes later, she designed, pieced, appliquéd, and quilted Of Thee I Sing as her entry in the museum's 1986

Great American Quilt Contest.[1]

The quiltmaker's creativity, technical skill, and attention to historical detail invite a thoughtful examination. Anne wanted to "show the spirit of the immigrants who came to America from all of the countries of the world and who courageously set out across the continent in search of liberty." As they followed their dream, "they established industries, farms, and cities. They built and fought for a nation founded on the great documents which guarantee liberty and freedom for all Americans."

Anne's quilt top is cotton with some cotton/polyester appliqués on the flags. The back is cotton, and the binding is handmade bias tape applied by hand. Most of the construction is by hand, but the long seams are by machine. The quilting (7–8 stitches per inch) is in outline, cable, and wave motifs. The quiltmaker's design places one of

America's most powerful symbols amidst the flags of our immigrants' homelands and successfully links a New-World craft tradition with its Old-World heritage.

Whether they stitched from necessity or the desire to create, thousands of foreign-born Illinoisans and their descendants contributed to the state's colorful quilt history. Countless registrations document the zeal with which these immigrants assimilated America's utilitarian art form into their cultural tradition.

For many of the tired, poor, and homeless, Miss Liberty's lamp of hope was a light that sped the needle as it joined different shapes, sizes, and colors into a historical mosaic. Illinois quilts reflect an important national tradition, an emergence of unity out of diversity. In Illinois *E. Pluribus Unum* is not only cast in metal and carved in stone, it is also stitched in cotton, wool, and silk.

The Illinois Germans

Foreign migration further diversified Illinois' domestic population. Unemployment, poverty, crop failure, political discrimination, and religious persecution encouraged Europeans to seek an improved life in the New World. German, Irish, and English immigrants were the most numerous by 1850. Twenty years later those groups remained dominant, as 15 percent of Illinois family heads were German, 9 percent Irish, and 8 percent English.[2]

Waves of European Germans supplemented the German-speaking settlers from Pennsylvania, North Carolina, and Ohio, and the group remained the state's top ethnic community at the turn of the century. Those *Auswanderers* created a serious depopulation problem for the Fatherland. During one three-year period in the early 1850s, more than one-half million Germans left for America—a loss of 1.5 percent of the population. Depopulation affected some provinces more than others. During the 1849–1856 period, the Rhenish Palatinate lost 10 percent of its population. During the nineteenth century, Illinois received a large portion of those German immigrants. In 1860 the 22,000 Germans in Chicago constituted 40 percent of the 54,000 foreign-born residents and 20 percent of the 109,000 total population of the city. On the eve of the Civil War, Illinois had 130,000 German-born residents, which represented approximately 7.5 percent of the state's population.[3]

When World War I began, ten million Americans had been born in Germany or were first-, second-, or third-generation German-Americans. One-tenth of those Germans and German-Americans lived in Illinois, where they often dominated rural areas and remained numerically important in Chicago, Peoria, Quincy,

Belleville, and many smaller centers. Adherence to the German language and culture was strong, but the German contribution to Illinois was suddenly obscured by wartime hysteria. Only in recent decades have a growing number of towns hosted German ethnic festivals.[4]

Caroline Crusius was seventeen years old when she married Frederick J. Koehler on September 10, 1816, in Wolfstein, Rhenish Bavaria. She was thirty-four years old and the mother of seven children when her husband, a butcher by trade, brought the family to America in 1833 "to seek their fortunes." Their initial American home was in Tiffin, Seneca County, Ohio. Then they moved to Fort Wayne, Indiana, in 1837, to Joliet, Illinois, in 1839, and to Stephenson County in 1841. When they settled on a farm in Section Four of Silver Creek Township at the east edge of Freeport, they were the parents of five boys and five girls. Frederick Koehler purchased twenty-seven acres from the federal government in 1843. He died October 2, 1846, and his wife remained on the farm until two years before her death.[5]

When Mrs. Koehler died in 1883, a local newspaper called her one of "the old pioneers of Stephenson County . . . one of the oldest of the old settlers, an honored, respected and well known personage."[7] When they arrived in 1841, the Koehlers joined a growing German community and they lived amid many Pennsylvania Germans who moved into the rich farmland around Freeport during the same time period. These Germans founded many Lutheran and German Reformed churches in Stephenson County. Mrs. Koehler attended a German Reformed church in Freeport.

Although Caroline's obituary provides important genealogical data, it leaves many questions unanswered. It does not tell us if she knew how to quilt as a child in Ger-

[Figure 11]
Caroline Crusius Koehler
Born July 31, 1799, Meisenheim,
    Rhenish Bavaria
Died November 17, 1883, Freeport,
    Stephenson County, Illinois

Caroline was sixty-nine years old when she stitched *1868* on her red, green, and orange appliqué flower quilt. The distinctive colors, boldly designed quadrant block style, and undulating floral vine border are important characteristics of the period.[6] The all-cotton quilt is constructed by hand, except for the binding, which is back brought to front and sewn by machine. The quilting (8 stitches per inch) is worked in outline, floral, and vine motifs.

many, if she acquired the skill after settling in Stephenson County, where she got the inspiration for this particular design, or (and perhaps this is the most significant question of all) what cultural interaction occurred between Mrs. Koehler and the Stephenson County Pennsylvania German community. If the history of this quilt did not link it specifically to a German immigrant, it would be easy to see it as the work of a Pennsylvania German quiltmaker.[8]

[Plate 24]
APPLIQUÉD FLOWERS
82" x 82"

Caroline Crusius Koehler, 1799–1883
Freeport, Stephenson County,
   Illinois, 1868
Collection of Mary Guentner

Perhaps the Koehler family did not come in search of religious freedom, but some Illinois Germans did. Many European Protestant reformers followed Martin Luther's example and put forth new theological ideas and practices that influenced portions of German-speaking Europe. Present-day denominations look back to founding fathers such as John Calvin, Ulrich Zwingli, Menno Simons, and Jacob Amman.

German immigration to Illinois encompassed the entire spectrum of the Fatherland's religious diversity. While Roman Catholic, Lutheran, Evangelical, and Reformed traditions dominate most Illinois German communities, other parts of the German religious heritage remain. The Amish, Mennonite, and Apostolic Christian traditions of the Anabaptist movement, as well as the Moravian and Brethren heritage, are present in scattered areas.

Under the leadership of Menno Simons, a Dutch priest, the Mennonites originated in the lower Rhine Valley as one branch of the sixteenth-century Anabaptist movement. Simons disagreed with Luther's retention of infant baptism, and the Anabaptists (rebaptizers) insisted upon adult baptism even if the individual had been baptized as a child. The movement spread up the river to Switzerland.

Amish Germans settled in several parts of Illinois, with one of the largest groups living in the Arthur area. Named for Jacob Amman, the Amish began as a splinter group of the Swiss Brethren Mennonites. Suffering from decades of persecution from Catholics and Lutherans, the non-liturgical, pacifist Amish and Mennonites eventually sought religious and economic refuge in William Penn's Peaceable Kingdom. [9]

The German migration to Pennsylvania that began in the late seventeenth century swelled to flood stage by the early eighteenth century. Thousands from the Rhine Valley crossed the Atlantic in fervent hope of greater economic opportunities in North America. The Anabaptists were a small part of this total migration, and the Amish represent a minority of the overall Anabaptist movement. Nevertheless, their dress codes and well-publicized rejection of worldly things such as electricity often give the impression to the outside world that this sect is the one and only Pennsylvania German group. That is far from true. [10]

German farmers hungry for fertile land in abundance headed for the unoccupied areas west of Philadelphia. Soon the German-speaking colonists dominated a settlement-region focused in Lancaster and adja-

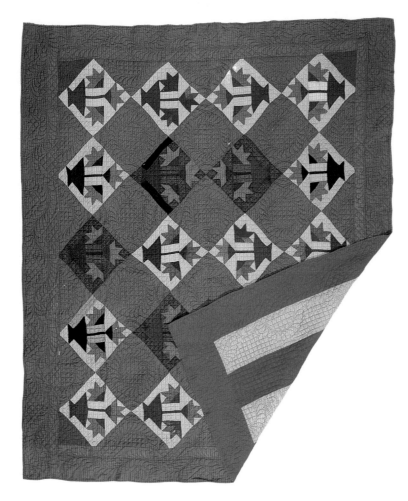

[Plate 25]
LILY BASKET
82″ x 70″

Magdalena Yoder, unknown dates
Arthur, Douglas County, Illinois,
    circa 1880
Collection of Ann Wasserman

Of the very few Amish quilts registered, Magdalena Yoder's cotton and wool Lily Basket with wide vertical bars on the back is an outstanding example. Both the top and the back are machine pieced from cotton and wool, with wool batting. The binding is handmade straight-cut cotton attached by machine and by hand. The quilting (8–9 stitches per inch) creates arcs, feathering, and a grid.

cent counties. For several decades at least the Amish within the German migration felt they were far enough away from the worldliness of Europe and Philadelphia to live their lives in relative isolation and enjoy the security of nearby lands available for their grandsons.

The belief in an abundant land supply was short lived. As immigration from the Fatherland continued unabated, the "plain Dutch" Amish and Mennonites followed their "fancy Dutch" neighbors, and they rapidly expanded into the adjacent Pennsylvania counties and eventually extended into Maryland and Virginia. Their first major transmontane colonial outreach was into Ohio during the first years of the nineteenth century.[11] Several decades later, they were scouting for land even farther west.

Arthur, located in east-central Illinois, is the center of a German-speaking Old Order Amish farming community. Toward the end of the Civil War, several Amish communities in the East were seeking inexpensive land for expansion. In 1864 Joel Beachy of Grantsville, Maryland, and Moses Yoder of Summit Mills, Pennsylvania, brought the search to the Midwest. They were on their way home after an unsuccessful trip through Wisconsin and Missouri when they stopped at Pana and then headed for Mattoon, Arcola, and Arthur.

The flat, swampy Grand Prairie area of east-central Illinois was just on the brink of development. The area, which suffered from inadequate natural drainage and a total lack of navigable waterways, began to grow after the Illinois Central Rail-

road linked Mattoon and Champaign to Chicago and the East Coast in the 1850s. Beachy and Yoder liked what they saw in Illinois, and on March 3, 1865, the Yoder, Miller, and Otto families arrived from Pennsylvania. Others soon joined them from Ohio, Indiana, and Iowa. Moses Yoder bought a 640-acre section of land from the railroad in the late 1860s for eight dollars an acre.[12]

Although well known throughout a wide area in Illinois, the Arthur Amish community is smaller and far less nationally recognized than its counterparts in Pennsylvania, Ohio, and Indiana.[13] Despite a self-imposed withdrawal from the world and the physical distance between the communities, lines of communication do exist. A remarkable similarity in patterns and color combinations are evidence that quilting traditions are obviously shared.

An unusually strong ethnic identity establishes the obvious cultural qualities one finds in Amish quilts. An accepted restrictive lifestyle defines what is and what is not permissible. Innovation is not encouraged, and change comes slowly. The differences between Pennsylvania and midwestern Amish quilts is attributable to geographic separation rather than evolutionary change. After carefully examining a number of Amish quilts and comparing them with known examples of non-Amish bedcoverings from the "English" community, it soon becomes apparent that the color palette is restricted and solid colors predominate and are preferred to prints; nonrepresentational geometric pieces are permitted, while representational appliqué is considered too worldly.

Western Amish quilts, such as the Lily Basket from the Arthur community, clearly indicate an increasing interaction with the "English" world. Ohio and Illinois Amish quilts differ significantly from those made in the Lancaster, Pennsylvania, area. Pennsylvania Amish quilts are generally square, use a central design, and have wide borders; those made early in the twentieth century are of wool, although other fabrics were used later. The midwestern Amish use a wider variety of colors, accept more traditional American pieced patterns, make rectangular quilts with smaller borders, and are not limited to the use of wool fabric. The prosperity of the Arthur Amish enabled them to develop fancier quilts that compared favorably with those of Holmes County, Ohio, and Lancaster County, Pennsylvania.[14]

The Nine Patch quilt of Lydia Otto Helmuth certainly exemplifies the preference of the Illinois Amish for block pattern quilts as compared to the central medallion type favored by many quilters from Lancaster County. Born on May 8, 1864, a daughter of Daniel and Barbara

Otto of Somerset County, Pennsylvania, Lydia was a member of the original Illinois Amish families. She made some of the seams with her mother's 1874 treadle sewing machine, which the family kept until selling it in 1981. The quilt was made for the marriage of her daughter Amanda, probably before that event took place. Amanda's sisters, aunts, and nieces would have all helped with the quilting.

It was customary for the Amish to cut up old clothes rather than buy special fabrics for quilting, but it is quite obvious the cotton sateen for the top was purchased especially for making this quilt. It was permissible in most Amish communities to use purchased fabric for the larger parts of the quilt, such as the back and the border, but the pieced

[Plate 26]
NINE PATCH
87" x 71"

Lydia Otto Helmuth, 1864–1930
Arthur, Douglas County, Illinois,
 circa 1910
Collection of Ervin Yoder

Amanda Helmuth Yoder recognized that this was meant to be a special quilt and used it only on her guest bed. The diagonal fading across the quilt indicates there was a sunny window in the guest bedroom. The back is cotton, and there is a wool batt. The binding is the back brought to the front and sewn by hand. The quilting (8 stitches per inch) employs floral, feather, and leafy scroll motifs.

portion itself was generally limited to leftover or recycled dress materials. Each Amish community set its own standards for what was allowable. Eve Granick's observation that "Fine quality fabrics were quite important in Arthur," is certainly demonstrated in the Helmuth quilt.[15] While Amish rules about using buggies and avoiding electricity are easily noticed, it is more difficult for an outsider to differentiate the subtleties of community codes regarding color choice in clothing, quilting, and interior decoration.

Quilts were an innovative bedcovering not widely used by any of the Pennsylvania Germans until the mid-nineteenth century. Thus it is not surprising that very few Amish quilts date before 1880, and in some Pennsylvania communities they are limited to variations of the Four Patch and Nine Patch, while acceptable colors are restricted to browns, blues, darker purples, blacks, darker greens, yellow ocher, and the darker reds. While it is not difficult to see some of that influence in this quilt, it is also apparent that the color palette is definitely that of Illinois rather than Pennsylvania. New styles inevitably grew out of interaction between the Amish and their "English" neighbors. Despite the restricted nature of this social interaction within the Douglas and Moultrie County areas, there still was more access to ideas outside the Amish circle in Illinois than there was in Pennsylvania.[16]

Mennonite quilts, like the Mennonite religion, can exhibit a strong relationship with the Amish. The theology and material culture of these two Germanic groups stem from the same sources, but over the years they moved in slightly different directions. The "horse and buggy Amish" of the Arthur area interact with "the world" as little as possible. The Old Order still adheres to a strict distinctive dress code and meets in members' homes

rather than a church sanctuary. The Mennonites, on the other hand, have preserved the essence of their theology and social cohesion within the broader framework of contemporary society. They drive cars, worship in churches, and dress tastefully without pursuing a strict policy.[17]

The East Bend Mennonite community near Fisher, the area in which the Yarn Starflower quilt originated, did not exist until the late 1880s. Founded near the Sangamon River in Champaign County's East Bend Township, it is situated in the heart of a rich prairie area that was not developed until the latter part of the nineteenth century. As Amish Mennonites from the Morton, Goodfield, and Hopedale area southeast of Peoria began looking for an agriculturally rich region in which to expand, this section of the Grand Prairie was just coming into its own. The land was fertile and reasonably priced, and local communities with transportation links to Champaign were emerging. Charles Stormer, the first Amish Mennonite to arrive here, in 1882 paid $27.50 an acre for land. Samuel S. Zehr's farm cost $18.75 an acre in 1891 when he purchased eighty acres for $1,500.

There were enough Mennonites to begin holding worship services in 1889, and a congregation was organized a year later. Peter Zehr, who had been ordained at Goodfield in 1883, moved to East Bend and was ordained bishop in 1893. According to the Illinois Mennonite authority Willard H. Smith, Zehr "was a sincere, kindly man with a motto which he had printed on cards to hand out to his friends declaring: 'I expect to travel through this world but once. Any good therefore that I can do, or any kindness I may be able to show any one, let me do it now. I shall not pass this way again.'"[18]

In the summer Katie spent her time gardening and canning, and during the winter her attention turned to indoor activities such as quilting. She would piece in the afternoons and evenings as time per-

[Figure 12]
Katie Zehr Cender
Born October 5, 1877, Morton, Tazewell County, Illinois
Died January 10, 1944, Fisher, Champaign County, Illinois

John Cender
Born August 26, 1877, Roanoke, Woodford County, Illinois
Died November 21, 1935, Fisher, Champaign County, Illinois

[Plate 27]
YARN STARFLOWER
88″ x 71″

Katie Zehr Cender, 1877–1944
Fisher, Champaign County, Illinois,
   circa 1900
Collection of Alva and Edna H. Cender

Katie Zehr was the daughter of Bishop
Peter and Barbara Heiser Zehr. She made
many quilts from leftover scraps, but the
amount of matching blue and black in
this example surely indicates a special
purchase of fabric to assure uniformity.
No two of the fifty-three starflowers are
exactly alike; the random use of some
colors and the abundance of others perhaps indicate that remnants and a
special purchase of yarn were required.
The nonmatching fabric swatches in the
border were removed from sample
books for men's suits. Loren Pfoff, of
Pfoff's General Store in Foosland, gave
her his discontinued sample books
when she traded her weekly accumula-
tion of chicken eggs for commodities the
family could not produce at home.

Katie's Yarn Starflower quilt is an excellent example of the great similarity in
color one finds in Amish and Mennonite
quilts of this period while at the same
time exhibiting the extent to which a
Mennonite quilter might go to adapt a
new technique. Katie's clipped yarn
chenille-type flowers were created with
the aid of a metal template. The wool,
cotton, and silk top is machine stitched
to a foundation fabric. The quilting (4
stitches per inch) ties it to a striped cotton flannel backing. There is no batting.
The wool bias binding is applied by
hand.

mitted, and occasionally her sisters,
Amelia Zehr Birkey and Lizzie Zehr
Cender, would join her for quilting.

In the spare time she found during any season of the year, Katie
enjoyed traditional late Victorian
pastimes. She covered cigar boxes,
also obtained from Pfoff's General
Store, with cloth and gave them as
gifts for handkerchiefs and trinkets.
After removing the suiting fabric swatches for quilting, Katie
converted the sample books into
scrapbooks. In them she combined
colorful calendar pictures with inspirational columns clipped from

periodicals such as *Capper's Farmer*
and the *Gospel Herald,* a Mennonite
weekly. Her quilts and handicrafts
are still appreciated by her family
today.

While examples of Amish and Mennonite quilts registered in the Project
are not numerous, there are enough
to provide a good cross section of
change over time. The somber-
colored woolen and cotton fabrics
selected by Magdalena Yoder in
1880 differ greatly from the gaily
figured cotton prints used by Anna
Ulrich fifty years later. There is also

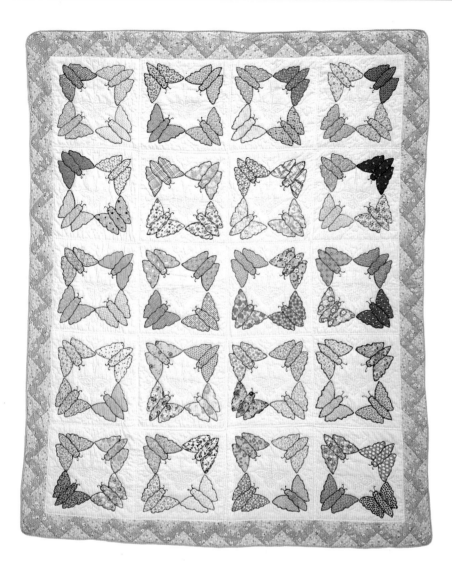

[Plate 28]
BUTTERFLIES
108″ x 67″

Anna Marie Reeser Ulrich, 1855–1941
Eureka, Woodford County, Illinois, 1929
Collection of Mary E. Gilkeson

Anna Ulrich's all-cotton quilt top was pieced and appliquéd in 1929 but not quilted until 1986. The batt is modern polyester, and it is bound with commercial bias tape that is stitched by machine on the front and finished by hand on the back. The blocks are pieced by hand and the appliquéd butterflies are attached with a buttonhole stitch. Anna's daughter, Viola A. Harnish, had the butterfly quilting pattern and did the marking while numerous friends and relatives helped do the quilting at the Mennonite Maple Lawn Nursing Home in Eureka. The quilting (8 stitches per inch) is in outline and butterfly motifs.

a contrast in the patterns between the highly stylized Lily Basket and the popular and overly commercialized Butterflies of the Depression era. The visual differences so clearly exhibited by these two quilts also represent the widening gulf between the rigidly enforced cultural isolation of the Amish and the evolving and more open relationship between the Mennonites and their "English" neighbors.

Anna's father, Christian Reeser, left his native Alsace in 1839 when he was twenty years old. From New Orleans, his port of arrival, he moved upstream to an Amish settlement in Butler County, Ohio, northwest of Cincinnati. About 1847 he joined a brother near Muncie, Indiana, where he married Barbara Zimmermann on April 25, 1852. Five years later they relocated to a farm in the Mackinaw River Valley near Congerville in Woodford County, Illinois. In 1867 he was ordained as a Mennonite preacher. Christian was interested in national and international events as well as in religion and he regularly read a German-language newspaper published in Allentown, Pennsylvania. He also voted regularly and supported each Democratic candidate from James Knox Polk in 1844 through James Cox in 1920, with the exceptions of the two times he voted for a Republican—Abraham Lincoln in 1860 and 1864.

Woodford County was one of the main Mennonite centers in Illinois when Reeser settled there in 1857. During his ministry, he served the Roanoke congregation north of Eureka as well as the Rock Creek congregation south of town. The nearby Partridge congregation near Metamora constructed the first Mennonite church in Illinois in 1854. Worshiping in a church was a new experience for the Illinois Mennonites. Since their faith was officially outlawed by most German provincial governments, they had been forced to worship in their homes. In America the conservative Amish continued to do so as a matter of faith and they follow the same practice today. Many small but significant differences distinguished the more conservative Amish and the increasingly moderate Mennonites, such as their manner of dress and the acceptance or rejection of such modern technology as photography, automobiles, electricity and, of course, the quilts produced by the two groups.[19]

In 1874 Christian's daughter, Anna Maria Reeser, married David Ulrich whose German Mennonite family also had settled in Woodford County. David and Anna lived near or in Eureka most of their lives with the exception of a short residency in Missouri early in the twentieth century. Anna Reeser Ulrich and her daughters were active quilters, usually having a quilt in a frame in the living room. The present Butterfly quilt owner remembers playing under the frame as a child and pouting when her mother, Viola A. Harnish, would not take her home when she wished to go.[20]

The present owner, a granddaughter of the maker, remembers growing up "down the block from my grandparents' retirement home in Eureka. I watched my grandmother piece and appliqué while sitting in her sewing rocker at a window in the living room. I remember her wearing the dresses of the black or the grey prints; and my Aunt Anna, who never married, lived there too. I recognize the prints of her dresses and aprons and, most significantly, I see pieces of my own childhood dresses."

It is important to notice the range of colors, fabrics, and patterns within this group of four Amish and Mennonite quilts. Contrast this group of quilts with the work of Caroline Koehler (Plate 24) and M. Huber (Plate 13). Doing so will help to define visually the different approaches to quilting between the Plain and Fancy Dutch in the late

nineteenth and early twentieth centuries (these Germans were called "dutch" through a mispronunciation of the word *Deutsch,* meaning "German").

Immigrants from the British Isles

From the founding of Jamestown, Virginia, in 1607 to the creation of Georgia in 1733, Great Britain played the major role in creating the United States of America. Although German, Dutch, French, and Scandinavian immigrants added cultural diversity to the colonial population, the dominance of English, Scots–Irish, Irish, and Welsh migrants insured that their English language, culture, economy, and political system would prevail.

After the Revolution, the migration from the British Isles, with the exception of Ireland, declined while the influx from continental Europe rose. Nevertheless, agricultural and industrial depression, heavy taxes, and poor wages continued to encourage migration. Decade after decade England provided a small contingent of emigrants for Illinois, and over the years England was the third largest contributor to the state's population. At midcentury there were several scattered concentrations, but Albion remained the most famous English community in early Illinois. That colony, founded in 1818 under the leadership of Morris Birkbeck and George Flowers, proved the usefulness of the Illinois prairie as agricultural land.[21]

English migration continued after the Civil War, and the arrival in 1888 of William and Harriet Cook is typical of a young couple seeking the American dream. They came to Peoria and soon settled near Mapleton, where Esther pieced and tied a Nine Patch wool comforter in 1888–1889.

William was born and raised in

[Figure 13]
Anna Marie Reeser Ulrich, seated right front center, with her husband, David Ulrich, and their children.
Born December 17, 1855, Muncie, Delaware County, Indiana
Died October 12, 1941, Eureka, Woodford County, Illinois

[Plate 29]
NINE PATCH COMFORTER
76" x 72"

Harriet Esther Stenning Cook,
    1856–1900
Mapleton, Peoria County, Illinois,
    1888–1889
Collection of Thelma L. Swarts Tuggle

Lincolnshire where his father was a farmer and part-time collier. As he grew up, he tired of life on the farm, and when he was twenty years old he went in search of work to Sheffield where his older sister, Lizzie, lived. He later became a porter in the Liverpool Workhouse Hospital. There he met Harriet Esther Stenning, who was to become a nurse when she completed her three-year nursing program on November 18, 1886. They married in May 1887 and soon left for America.

Since they had English friends living in Peoria County, that was their destination. They lived east of Mapleton in Hollis Township. Bill began farming and working part-time in the Kingston Mines coal field. A son, Thomas William, born August 29, 1889, died on September 25. During her pregnancy, Harriet

pieced a wool Nine Patch comforter top of mauve and light tan plaid set together with a wine-colored plaid. She filled it with a cotton batt, backed it with a plaid cotton flannel, and tied it with white wool yarn. The new wool comforter was destined to see much use over the next few years as three additional children joined the family: Lucy, October 18, 1890; Stenning, October 24, 1892; and, Laurence, February 4, 1896.

In 1888 the Cooks became friends with Mr. and Mrs. Walter S. Stewart, who lived a little north of them, southeast of Smithville. The land was rich and not as hilly as where the Cooks lived. The Stewarts, who had no children, wanted Bill, Harriet, and the children to move closer to them. While it would mean moving away from their English friends, it would also offer the Cooks better

farming land. By 1899–1900 Bill found a farm for rent in the area, and the family prepared to relocate.

March 1, 1900, was a miserably cold day with the temperature two degrees above zero. At least that was better than February 25 when it had been five below. It would be a long, miserable, nine-mile trek from their home of twelve years to the newly rented farm. Bill piled part of their belongings as high on his wagon as he could, and the remainder filled the Stewart's wagon. Although Harriet was suffering from a bad cold, she drove the children in the horse and buggy to their new home. The wool comforter covered them up to their chins, but they were still chilled to the bone.

Despite the weather, the move could not be delayed. By customary

[Figure 14]
Harriet Esther Stenning Cook
Born January 18, 1856, Sussex County,
  England
Died March 3, 1900, Smithville, Peoria
  County, Illinois

law the move must occur on or immediately before March 1, and the
moving plans must be coordinated
among all the concerned parties. By
that date the farmer would have the
previous year's crop out of the field
and to market, and it was not yet
time to begin spring plowing and
seeding. March, the first month of
the new year under the old calendar,
was long considered the time to settle up debts and settle down in a
new home.

The Cook family's dream of a
long and happy life on their new
farm was short lived. On the third
of March, Harriet died of pneu-
monia, and Bill was left to care for a
nine-year-old daughter and seven-
and four-year-old sons. With the
help of the Stewarts and a hired
housekeeper, Bill got through the
year; but when the crop was out of
the field in the fall, he made plans to
return to his parents in England.
The family, and the wool comforter,
left Peoria County in December
1900. Lucy would long remember
acquiring head lice on the trip and
the rough manner in which her

grandmother used "red percipity," a
poisonous mercury chloride powder,
as a disinfectant. It was not considered a sin to get lice, but it certainly
was one to keep them!

Less than a year after arriving
back in England, Bill left again for
America, leaving the children behind. Lucy later told her children
about the outdoor brick bake oven
in the back yard, going to school
and to church, and the severe pun-
ishments her brothers received for
even the slightest infractions. In
November 1903 Bill wrote that his
children should come home, and
preparations were hastily made.
Aunt Lizzie Cook Guy took the children and their baggage, including
the comforter, to Sheffield where,
knowing she would never see them
again, she had their picture taken.
Then she escorted them to Liverpool and placed them aboard a ship
bound for New York City. On the
ship all three slept in the same bunk
with their mother's comforter over
them. During the three-week voyage, they spent the Christmas and
New Year holidays on the ocean.

[Figure 15]
William Cook
Born May 11, 1863, Gosberton,
  Lincolnshire, England
Died February 17, 1933, Argenta, Macon
  County, Illinois
Pictured with his three children, Lucy,
  Stenning, and Laurence, during the
  summer of 1900. This was shortly
  after Harriet's death and before the
  family left for England.

Thirteen-year-old Lucy success-fully mothered her eleven- and seven-year-old brothers on the ship, through customs, across the city to the railroad, and on board a train for Illinois.

Bill, who was now remarried and living near Parnell in Dewitt County, was to pick them up in Farmer City. There was a snowstorm, and it was late in the evening of January 8, 1904, when the children got off the train. No one was there to meet them. The station agent was con-sidering taking them home with him for the night when Bill arrived in a horse-drawn wagon. He took them to a different home to meet their stepmother and her new baby boy.

Harriet's children went out on their own as soon as they were old enough to leave and find work. Lucy became a hired girl, and the boys found farm jobs as hired men. On August 17, 1911, Lucy married Francis Elmer Swarts and moved to Cisco, taking the twenty-two-year-old comforter with her.

Three of Lucy's seven children died in infancy. The survivors in-clude a daughter, Thelma Laverne Swarts, who recalls that the "com-forter was always brought out of the bedding box in the closet when it began to get chilly." Thelma also re-members that each spring all the bedding, including the quilts and comforters, were cleaned by fold-ing, placing each in warm water and soap suds, and gently pressing down with a "stomper" to force the soapy water through the fabric. They would then be rinsed at least twice and hung on the clothes line to dry in the sunshine.

Lucy Swarts permitted the chil-dren to use the comforter but ex-pected them to respect it. "You could put the comforter on the rug in front of the door on a hot summer night so you could get the breeze between the front door and the din-ing room door, but you had to be careful that you did not spill any-thing on it. It was understood that

the comforter was made by Grandma Cook." According to Thelma, "We and the comforter have been well cared for through many sicknesses, and it has kept five generations warm and comfortable and will do so for more, I am sure."

The stereotypical Illinois Irishman worked the Galena lead mines in the 1830s, helped build the Illinois–Michigan Canal in the 1840s, and constructed Illinois railroads in the 1850s. With much less fanfare, many also became agricultural laborers. Religious persecution, high rents, poor soil, and famine annually drove thousands of impoverished Irish farmers to the land of opportunity. The 1850 census recorded about 28,000 Irish in Illinois; the figure rose to over 87,000 by 1860. Many were Catholics from the southern portion of the island, but there were also Scots–Irish Protestants from North-ern Ireland, or Ulster. Both groups suffered the same economic and so-cial dislocation in the nineteenth cen-tury.[22]

Hannah Hutchinson learned to quilt as a girl in Ireland. As one of eight children, she grew to maturity on a small farm in a family of weavers who operated four looms in their small home. She later recalled that the family grew potatoes, cabbage, and turnips and drank buttermilk. Hannah not only helped in the home but "made her pin money," as she later said to her grandchildren, by hemming linen handkerchiefs for a factory.

The Hutchinson family migra-tion began when several of Han-nah's brothers came to Illinois to work on farms. Her parents and the remaining family members, includ-ing Hannah, joined them in north-ern Illinois in 1868. The family settled on a farm near the Boone–McHenry county line, and while Hannah was living there she care-fully selected a red and white calico with a tiny *H* pattern and pieced her Old Maid's Puzzle quilt. Hannah and her mother saved, washed, and

[Figure 16]
Lucy, Stenning, and Laurence Cook Liverpool, England, December 1903, just before returning home to Illinois.

[Plate 30]
OLD MAID'S PUZZLE
78″ x 75″

Hannah Hutchinson Davidson,
　1843–1939
Capron, Boone County, Illinois, 1875
Collection of William, Jr., and Selma
　Davidson

[Figure 17]
Hannah Hutchinson Davidson
Born September 15, 1843, County
　Armagh, Ireland
Died August 16, 1939, Chemung,
　McHenry County, Illinois

Thomas Davidson
Born April 9, 1846, County Armagh,
　Ireland
Died February 21, 1936, Chemung,
　McHenry County, Illinois

The Davidsons are pictured on the front
steps of their Illinois farm home.

cleaned the wool tags—portions of the fleece too soiled for her father to sell—for use in the batting. The cotton top and back that encase the wool are bound by handmade straight-cut cotton binding. The quilt pieces (7 stitches per inch) are handsewn.

The quilt was completed before Hannah's February 23, 1876, marriage to Thomas Davidson, who had arrived in Illinois from County Armagh in 1871. He worked on an aunt's farm in DeKalb County for two years to pay for his passage from Ireland to the United States. Then he worked as a hired man for several years in Boone County before marrying Hannah. She later told her family they started farming with $100, a team of horses, and the bed and bed tick given him by the lady on whose farm he had worked.

Hannah and Thomas were a hard-working couple who used their cows and hogs to pay for their first eighty-acre farm. She skimmed cream from the milk and churned butter for sale, and Thomas fed the buttermilk to his hogs before taking them to market. In 1890 they bought a two-hundred-acre farm near Chemung in McHenry County. Thomas moved his wife and three young sons into the big brick house and expanded their dairy operation. The family still manages a dairy herd on their centennial farm.

No matter where Hannah Davidson lived, her "good" red and white quilt was never used. The maker's granddaughter, Hannah Ames, recalled that "when I was a girl, it was packed away in a trunk of linens. When my sister and I would ask to see it, she would spread it on her bed to admire and to air it. She would tell us about making it. Then we would refold it with its tag 'for the boy,' my brother." It was the

[Plate 31]
MISSOURI PUZZLE
81" x 63"

Betsy Britta Ersdotter Lindstrum,
    1827–1887
Bishop Hill, Henry County, Illinois,
    circa 1880
Collection of the Bishop Hill Heritage
    Association

only pieced quilt Grandma Hannah had, and for young Hannah "it started a lifelong interest in quilts."

When the elder Hannah was seventy-five years old, living with Thomas in a part of the old brick home, she began raising her second family. Her three grandchildren, ranging in age from eleven months to four and one-half years, lost their mother to appendicitis. Hannah Ames remembers that all of her grandmother's beds had handmade quilts "but," she added, "these everyday quilts were whole cloth or 'strippies,' with flour sack backings and old blankets or worn materials for fillers. The quilting designs were all alike—allover lines an inch apart" in a zigzag streak-of-lightning motif.[23]

The McHenry County farm Thomas and Hannah had purchased in 1890 remained "home" for the rest of their lives. Thomas died there in 1936, two days before their sixtieth wedding anniversary and Hannah lived until 1939, just a few years short of her one-hundredth birthday. During those years, Hannah never had electricity or running water and did her laundry with a washboard. She lived long enough, however, to see her family get a gasoline-powered washing machine.

Bishop Hill: A European Utopia in Illinois

A summer weekday walk through the quiet streets of Bishop Hill lulls one into forgetting the energizing spirit this bustling community possessed at the height of the Janssonist era. On first glance, the deceptively sleepy village camouflages its internationally significant heritage and, like the nineteenth-century theology that gave it birth, forces the visitor to look inward.

Those who seek to understand this utopian experiment must first examine themselves. Only when one begins to appreciate, and perhaps in some ways to share, the intensity of belief and the selfless sacrifice that occurred here can a visitor seriously interact with the Bishop Hill of a bygone era. Present-day visitors must listen with their minds, not their ears, as the staccato rings echo from the once busy but now silent anvils, the soft rhythms of planes that gently smoothed maple boards, or the droning hum of the long-unused flax wheels. Then, perhaps, you may also detect the melodious intonations of Swedish colonists inviting you to pause and learn more. A newcomer soon realizes that lingering is not difficult in a community where time moves so slowly that the town clock has only an hour hand.

If Betsy Lindstrum's Missouri Puzzle quilt could be renamed Swedish Puzzle, it might bring the Bishop Hill experience into sharper focus. Certainly any understanding of the Swedish colony must begin with an examination of the Janssonists' theological labyrinth. Like Betsy's quilt, it mixed broad expanses of idealism with intellectually narrow passageways. Without a doubt, Erik Jansson was an enigma to even his closest adherents.

Similar to scores of other "huddled masses yearning to breathe free," the Swedish religious dissenters sought refuge on a distant shore. Jansson's pietistical leanings rapidly had led him from evangelical lay preaching within the Lutheran state church to proclaiming a perfectionist doctrine that eventually ran afoul of both church and state. Accusations of adultery and heresy had led to imprisonment and the loss of some adherents. His faithful followers pooled their resources, established a communal society, and emigrated to America.

After an ocean voyage, the first band of Janssonist pioneers used the Erie Canal and Great Lakes to reach Chicago. From there they walked 160 miles west to begin their Utopia on the Prairie in 1846. Despite a high death rate the first winter, a subsequent cholera epidemic, and the murder of the charismatic leader in 1850, the colony survived. New recruits continued to arrive, factorylike craft shops produced income-generating goods, and farmers tilled 12,000 acres of land. The hard-working colonists met their own needs and sold linen, furniture, wagons, brooms, and farm produce. Fifteen years after the colony was founded, it disbanded and distributed the assets to its members. A lessening of the religious fervor following Jansson's death and accusations of financial mismanagement against the trustees were primary factors in its demise.

In death as in life, Jansson remains a puzzle. While parts of his ideology are as understandable as the wide yellow sashing on Betsy's

[Figure 18]
The Bishop Hill Colony Church

The church provided one-room apartments under the sanctuary, which occupied the entire upper floor. The church and several other colony buildings are maintained as state historic sites by the Illinois Historic Preservation Agency.

Photo courtesy: Illinois Historic Preservation Agency

quilt, other portions are as difficult to negotiate as following a line through a puzzle block on this quilt. The complexity of both preclude any easy solutions.[24]

Today no one knows why Betsy Britta Ersdotter became a Janssonist or what reasons, other than religion, helped her decide to leave Sweden. In fact, little is known about her beyond the basic facts. She was born August 5, 1827, at Elfkarhed, Alfta, Helsingland, and died on the family farm one mile northeast of Bishop Hill on December 27, 1887. She left Sweden in 1846 with three sisters, and the quartet arrived in Bishop Hill in 1847. One sister and one brother remained in Sweden.

Betsy married Jonas Linholm on July 9, 1848, as one of four couples united in a mass marriage ceremony, one of several held that year. Her husband died of cholera the following year. According to the 1850 census, she was living in the Big Brick, the colony's main housing unit, which was the largest building west of Chicago when it was completed in 1848. It contained ninety-six apartments and the colony's main dining room that could seat more than one thousand people. On June 1, 1851, she married Eric Lindstrum who had arrived in Bishop Hill on July 8, 1850, from Ostrand, Westmanland. She signed the colony charter in 1854. During the colony period, Eric was a carpenter and cabinetmaker; he became a farmer after the colony dissolved. According to the 1877 county history, Betsy's husband owned 280 acres of land valued at $14,000. Eric and Betsy were the parents of four sons—one deceased—and two daughters.[25]

Betsy's quilt has a pieced cotton top, a thick cotton batting, and a cotton back that is brought to the front to create a binding. All the work is by hand, including the wide parallel lines and in-the-ditch quilting (4 stitches per inch). Look at it carefully and see the complexity of life for the Janssonist immigrants in

a strange new world and question the concept of the "simple lifestyle" of the idyllic past.

The followers of Erik Jansson represent a very small part of Swedish immigration to nineteenth-century Illinois. They were not the only Swedish dissenters. A sizable Swedish Methodist church developed in Illinois and throughout the Midwest. Despite the attention focused on Bishop Hill, most Swedish immigrants were Lutheran. Augustana College in nearby Rock Island is a testimony of their adherence to the theology of the Swedish state church. The economic dislocation that disrupted European life in both rural and urban areas during the nineteenth century did not respect religion. It pushed Swedes of all persuasions to seek a better life in the New World.

The Last Great Influx: Eastern and Southern Europeans

Massive migrations of southern and eastern Europeans passed through Ellis Island's cavernous waiting rooms in the late nineteenth and early twentieth centuries. The sheer volume of the "new immigration" permanently transformed the ethnic composition, political alliances, and cultural heritage of metropolitan Chicago and a host of downstate cities, towns, and rural areas. Thousands of disadvantaged Italians, Poles, Serbs, Croats, Russians, Ukrainians, Czechs, and many smaller national groups traded an impoverished life in a European village for an inadequate quality of life in an American slum.

American enterprise needed cheap, easily exploitable, unskilled labor; and immigrant peasants needed the money. Many of them were single men who intended to earn enough to bring over their families or to return to their native village as rich

men. Despite deplorable living and working conditions, hopes ran high; and for many, the Lady of Liberty did indeed lift her torch beside a golden door.

Peasants from southern and eastern Europe entered the coal fields in LaSalle, Macoupin, and Franklin counties or found a grueling job working eighty-four hours a week in an unsafe and unhealthy urban factory. The outbreak of World War I halted the influx, and the immigration quotas of the 1920s imposed permanent restrictions.[26]

If discouragement was ever in the minds of these immigrants, it was not reflected on the quilt registration forms completed for the Project by their descendants. Most working-class ethnic parents dreamed of a middle-class life for their children. Indeed, many of the sons and daughters of Germans, Slavs, Ukrainians, or Lithuanians became home-owning blue collar workers, and their well-educated grandchildren entered a wide variety of professions.

Although most non-English-speaking immigrants found comfort, security, and ethnic identity in their church or synagogue, the educational system finally acquainted their children and grandchildren with American culture. Those who brought no quilting traditions with them from the Old World eventually adopted this American craft and inevitably used the contemporary patterns and color schemes currently popular with their "American" neighbors. The experience of Goldie Stanisha is typical.

Although Goldie was too young to remember traveling from the old country to America, many of her family and friends must have felt as if their immigration journey was indeed a trip around the world. She was born at Lokve, Croatia, in 1902, the daughter of Anton and Anna Kayfes Stanisha. Her father soon left, perhaps because of poverty and dislike of the dictatorial rule Croatia endured under the Austro-Hungarian Empire. His journey took

[Plate 32]
TRIP AROUND THE WORLD
92" x 75"

Goldie Stanisha Malkovich, 1902–1969
Benton, Franklin County, Illinois,
    circa 1935
Collection of Crystal Taylor Glover

him from Croatia's iron-mining area to Minnesota's Mesabi Range where he had relatives. The following year Anton's wife and daughter entered the United States through Ellis Island on their way to Minnesota.

The Stanishas moved frequently within the mining district, but wherever they lived—in Ely, Buhl, or Luchnow—Anna boarded fellow immigrants while Anton worked as a master carpenter. The movement from town to town can be documented by the birthplace of the children who arrived regularly every twenty to thirty months. With the birth of the tenth child in 1920, Anton lost his wife and baby. His younger children were sent to St. James Orphanage in Duluth and the state school in Owatonna.

In October 1920 Goldie eloped to Butte, Montana, with Michael Malkovich, a carpenter who worked for her father. Fearing Anton's anger, the couple remained in Montana for a while, but they returned to Ely, Minnesota, the following year before the birth of their first child, Ann Marie. Shortly thereafter, the young couple moved to Franklin County, Illinois, settling in Benton. Along with many other recent immigrants, Michael took a coal-mining job. Like her mother, Goldie ran a boardinghouse for miners. She also managed to bring four of her younger brothers and sisters to Illinois and raise them along with her three children, Ann Marie, Daniel Leon, and Joseph Florian. During the Great Depression she learned to quilt at the Macabees Lodge in Benton. It was during this time that she completed her Trip Around the World quilt.

The quilt's overall impact depends upon the successful color gradations of very small pieces arranged in a strict angular conformation. When Goldie's daughter Ann Marie gave the quilt to her own daughter, she recalled her mother's distress during its construction period. "Those pieces were so small it drove her up the wall," she reported. Building from the center,

[Figure 19]
Goldie Stanisha Malkovich
Born May 3, 1902, Lokve, Croatia
Died February 8, 1969, Benton, Franklin
   County, Illinois

the ever-enlarging squares radiate farther and farther out and ultimately, like an immigrant's new life in the United States, expands beyond one's comprehension.

It is not easy to choreograph a 4,977-piece textile ballet. Goldie's determination to succeed in this task, as in everything she did, is abundantly evident in the workmanship of her quilt. It is her witness to each generation of her family, while pride in her accomplishment is reflected in the loving care the quilt has received.

The pattern Goldie selected visually summarizes the experiences of many immigrants. The quilt's intense hues eventually blend through shaded edges into the neighboring color. It is not difficult to imagine each color as one of the numerous

ethnic enclaves that existed in Illinois in the early twentieth century. The well-established distinctions that blurred over time are the same whether in Benton or in the urban ghetto that once surrounded Jane Addams's Hull House on Chicago's Halstead Street. A combination of community attitudes and self-imposed restrictions based upon language, cultural ethnicity, and religion, as well as economic and social distinctions, once tended to separate the groups.

For many, the trip around the world from Europe to America and the resulting immigrant experience were not easy. Goldie's admiring granddaughter knows her ancestors "who came over from the old country had to have guts. I wonder sometimes if I could have gotten on a boat and landed in a strange land not understanding the language and not knowing if I would be able to feed myself and my family." Despite the hardships, Goldie always appeared happy. "If Grandma was ever down, I never saw it."

She did, however, experience prejudice, and her son Dan later recalled his dislike of the ethnic slurs he encountered. As is often the case, the third generation finds pride in ethnicity. When Goldie's granddaughter said she was proud to be a "Hunky," her uncle Dan called it "Croat spirit." Dan's son, John Malkovich, achieved an international cinema career without dropping his ethnic surname and, like his grandmother, has made his own trip around the world—through *Empire in the Sun* and *Dangerous Liaisons*—from Benton, Illinois, to China and France.

The lives of Goldie's family and friends were shaped by the immigrant experience. Did it also influence the color choice as she pieced her quilt? Surprisingly vivid colors overshadow the muted palette normally found in Depression-era quilts. It would be interesting to ask her to identify each color as an immigrant group, to explain her reasons for assigning those values.

World War II brought further change to the Prairie State's population. A wave of war brides, many of whom were identified as quiltmakers by the Project, and refugees from the world's trouble spots continually sought solace in the shadow of the Statue of Liberty. Like the ancestors of Anne Marcisz and Goldie Malkovich, these who yearned to breathe free saw the lamp as an eternal beacon of hope.

When Goldie finished her quilt in 1939, a journey across the state would be a miniature trip around the world, for one could easily find numerous ethnic communities that preserved the language, food ways, and customs of the homeland. A sense of loss arose as these cultural identities blurred in the late twentieth century. Goldie's granddaughter wrote: "There is one thing that I really miss. There were all kinds of foreign dialects in Benton when I was growing up. Some people would speak in their mother tongue when they were out on the street. Grandma would not do that. She thought that was being rude to other people. However, she could fall back into a dialect if she wanted to. . . . How I miss that dialect."

Illinois has indeed changed and perhaps a Trip Around the World quilt no longer depicts the characteristics, attitudes, and experiences of contemporary Illinois. What quilt pattern and combination of colors would more accurately define the Illinois that stands on the brink of the twenty-first century?

Our Mariner's Compass has led us through a maze of domestic and foreign-born migrations and settlements. As these families formed communities, they also created a personal and collective heritage that often was associated with a quilt. Some families successfully retain those stories and pass them from generation to generation. Others have only recently preserved their history in quilts. With compass in hand, let us turn our attention toward finding that history which is hidden in the home.

[Plate 33]
JACKSON STAR
86″ x 86″

Leah Millison Thornburgh, 1828–1909
Havana, Mason County, Illinois, 1849
   and 1990
Collection of Alice M. Smith

*H*ISTORY IN THE HOME: LISTENING AS QUILTS TELL THEIR STORIES

The history of every country begins
in the heart of a man or a woman.
—Willa Cather,
O Pioneers! 1913

That which begins in the heart finds many avenues of expression, and history is no exception. For decades quiltmakers have preserved history in a textile-based archive. Unfortunately, the stories within these documents are all too often ignored by researchers who are untrained in the use of nonverbal language. The ability to read artifacts is more than a key to adventure; it is a necessary tool. Historical investigators must learn to use this form of document, for the history that begins in the heart of a woman may be written with a needle rather than a pen.

Stitching Family and Personal History

Leah Thornburgh's textile document clearly chronicles parts of her history, including her birth and marriage dates. While the quilt provides more information than most, it still leaves unanswered questions. Investigation of family records reveals additional facts. She was born

in Belmont County, Ohio, after her parents, James and Dorothy Knight Millison, came to the new state from their native Pennsylvania. Leah married Peter A. Thornburgh, a blacksmith, moved to Mason County, Illinois, and settled southeast of Havana. She gave birth to fourteen children, although not all of them lived to adulthood, and she died in Mason County on November 23, 1909. Peter, who was born at Harpers Ferry, Virginia [now West Virginia], September 14, 1818, died in Mason County in 1879.

Although the stitcher of history does not tell us the quilt was made in Illinois, Leah clearly indicates that she pieced her Jackson Star quilt in 1849. Both facts provide vital information. Quilt patterns and their names were informally transmitted within a family or friendship circle with little need to be officially recorded for future researchers. In an extremely rare example of historical documentation, Leah not only provided the quilt's original name but also attached it to a specific time.

The dates 1844 and 1849 offer a critical tie to the larger historical

[Figure 20]
Leah Millison Thornburgh
Born October 7, 1828, Belmont County, Ohio
Died November 23, 1909, Havana, Mason County, Illinois

context. They coincide with the election and single term of Young Hickory, the nation's eleventh president, James Knox Polk. Old Hickory, his mentor and fellow Tennessean, Andrew Jackson, had served as the seventh president from 1829 to 1837. When he died at the Hermitage, his Nashville home, in 1845, a wave of nostalgic mourning for the hero of the battle of New Orleans swept America.

Both of those Democratic presidents expressed their frontier experiences by pursuing aggressive expansionist policies. Polk, an exponent of Manifest Destiny, extended the nation's western boundary to the Pacific Ocean. During his single term, the United States acquired the Pacific Northwest through negotiations with England, angered Mexico by annexing Texas, and added California and the American Southwest as a result of the Mexican War. It was indeed an age of expansion.[1]

When Peter Thornburgh abandoned Ohio for Illinois in the 1840s

[Figure 21]
"Death of Genl. Andrew Jackson"
Lithograph by N. Currier
New York City, 1845
Private collection

he participated in one of the most massive frontier movements in American history. He became part of that Old America that Morris Birkbeck observed to be "breaking up and moving westward." Frontiersmen equated westward expansion with increased opportunities, not only for themselves but for their posterity as well. Three of Peter's sons moved farther west—one each to Kansas, Oklahoma, and California. Andrew Jackson's long-standing commitment to the West had been important to the American pioneer. America's love affair with national heroes often resulted in attaching their names to places and objects. Naming a quilt pattern in his honor as a wave of manifest destiny carried the Stars and Stripes to the Pacific Coast would have seemed a fitting tribute at the time.

In addition to examining the document's external context, the researcher must also carefully review the internal evidence. A close look reveals an important aspect of the history of quiltmaking in general and of this quilt in particular. Leah Thornburgh did not finish her project.

By 1849 Leah had completed piecing the Jackson Star blocks and appliquéing the descriptive border. One can only speculate why these parts were never set together. Perhaps fourteen pregnancies, child rearing, and housework deprived her of the spare time to return to the quilt. The blocks and border were put away and eventually inherited by Leah's daughter, Mary Jane Thornburgh Eddy.

Mrs. Eddy was the present owner's grandmother. When she died, the pieces, safely stored in the drawer of a chest, passed to her son, Elmer B. Eddy. His wife, Mary A. Chrans Eddy, was not interested in the pieces, and when the chest was placed in a small outbuilding behind the house, the quilt blocks remained in a drawer. A mouse moved in and found all the comforts of home. The Eddys' daughter Alice received the quilt pieces from

her mother before she died in 1978. Alice eventually cleaned and repaired them, purchased modern white cotton/polyester fabric, set the blocks together, attached the border, and with a minimum of quilting, which she primarily placed in the new fabric, put in enough stitches to hold the three layers together.

What factors caused Leah to lay her work aside and subsequently prevented her from completing the quilt? Why did the family save the pieces and pass them down through several generations, and why at long last in 1990—almost 150 years after the quilt was begun—did someone decide to finish it? These are not unusual questions in the history of quilts.

Eleanor Yates Keady's quilt records the history of her husband, Samuel Gilbert Keady (May 4, 1804, County Mayo, Ireland—September 30, 1853, Peoria County, Illinois), and their children. The Keadys were married in Ohio County, Virginia [now West Virginia], on November 4, 1830. Unfortunately, there already is a lapse in the collective memory of the Keady family regarding the significance of the 1855 date and the initials that are quilted into the document. Why? "Because," the owner said, "the quilt was rescued from the attic of my aunt's house after she passed away, and other older members of the family had preceded her. This means that there has been no way to document verbally the history of either the quilt or the many initials stitched into it."

The Keadys' mobility is part of the American story. The two oldest children were born in Ohio County, but the third arrived in adjacent Washington County, Pennsylvania, where Eleanor's brothers Joseph and John lived near Claysville and West Alexander in 1832–1839, according to the death place of their children. The Keadys' fourth

[Plate 34]
TULIP APPLIQUÉ
83″ x 75″

Eleanor Yates Keady, 1808–1881
Dunlap, Peoria County, Illinois, 1855
Collection of Stanley K. Carlson

through ninth children were born in Ohio County, and numbers ten and eleven arrived after the move to Illinois. Their migration route is unknown, but the National Road west from nearby Wheeling would have been convenient.

Son Thomas Keady, born in December 1836, was about twelve years old when the family moved to Illinois. Before his 1918 death in Peoria County, he wrote an extensive memoir of his childhood years in the East.[2] The family apparently lived near West Liberty, a few miles northeast of Wheeling, where they occasionally took goods to market. Since his father was an immigrant, the uncles, aunts, and cousins mentioned in the "Keady Annals" are all members of the Yates family.

As the Keadys' family grew in size, the small log cabin with a one-room addition became increasingly crowded. Thomas Keady recalled:

For several years the project of building a new frame house was before the family. A lot of poplar plank for that purpose was stacked up in the barn and a pile of brick in the lane, while a big oak tree on a high point in the upper woods was set apart for the shingles. But [a] debt had to be paid, money came slow and the new house never got beyond the planning. I believe the rule was to live on the butter and egg money and apply the wheat, wool, and hog money to debt payments.

Joseph Yates (1798–1878) moved to Peoria County in 1846, and, as the story of his nephew Tom Keady continues, other relatives soon followed:

In the fullness of time, Uncle Josie's sold their farm and moved to Illinois. Later on, uncle Johnny [John Yates, 1799–1879] followed to look at the country. When he returned to Virginia he brought a big yellow, pink-eye potato to our house as a sample copy of the four fold and luxurious plenty of the West. The eyes were cut out of that potato to plant and the balance was boiled in the teakettle and pronounced a fine treat. And so vehement was the uncle Johnny laudation of the prairies that the emmigration [sic] fever caught in the Keady family and instead of expanding the house to shelter the expanding tribe of children, the farm was sold, and Westward Ho! turned from a golden dream into a boy delighting reality.

The family made a new quilt after they settled in Illinois. It is dated

1855, but that does not define when it was started and when it was completed. This could have commemorated the Keadys' twenty-fifth wedding anniversary had not Sam Keady died on September 30, 1853. Two daughters were being married and since the quilt includes the initials of the two grooms, *J.F.Y.* for Elizabeth's husband, Joseph Yates, who was also her first cousin, and *R.M.H.* for Robert Morgan Hamilton, who was marrying her older sister, Jane, it could recognize their double wedding on January 1, 1856. Why were Samuel's initials placed on the quilt after his death although the infant son lost in 1849 is omitted? Was the quilt already in process in 1853 before he died but not completed until late 1855 just before the double wedding?

Whatever occasion caused the quilt's creation, it remains today a monogrammed genealogical compendium of the Keadys' ten surviving children, two sons-in-law, and two unidentified individuals. The exquisite quilting (9 stitches per inch) is in grid, stipple, feathering, and grapes and leaves, in addition to the family initials. These small but all important letters are quilted into the various triangles, rectangles, and pots inside the meandering vine border that surrounds the sixteen appliquéd blocks in the center of the quilt. The all-cotton quilt—top, appliqué, batt, back, and handmade straight-cut green print binding—is completely worked by hand. The Keady quilt is a beautiful treasure rich in family heritage that would be even more valuable if the maker(s) would have prepared written information to accompany this heirloom.

Nineteenth-century quiltmakers were not the only ones who thought about recording family history with their needles. Today, a rising interest in genealogy has encouraged quilters to provide extensive family and personal information on a bedcovering. Two

[Figure 22]
Eleanor Yates Keady
Born July 9, 1808, Ohio County, Virginia [now West Virginia]
Died December 2, 1881, Dunlap, Peoria County, Illinois

Mrs. Keady is pictured with her youngest son, Samuel.

recently completed documentary works illustrate a contemporary trend to encapsulate history permanently on fabric. When Bernice Finke decided to record her family on a quilt, she wanted to make it as complete as possible.

After ten years of genealogical research she purchased a Paragon quilt kit and embellished the top with family history names and events. It required one year to complete the embroidery. The family tree quilt is truly a historical document that will convey important family information to her descendants for generations to come. She created it as a wedding present for her only grandson, Ryan Finke.

A genealogical presentation to the Herrin Woman's Club originally sparked her interest. She also knew that an aunt had done some research. "So I began with what she recorded, and through visits and letters to her I tried to learn more. As I got deeper into this, I

found some of her information was wrong and she only recorded the family lines whose members were preachers, missionaries, and saints."

Bernice eventually learned her husband's great-grandfather, Henry C. Finke, was born in 1849 in Nordhemmern, Germany, married Maria Von Behren in 1873, and immediately emigrated to St. Louis. Since completing the quilt, she has received the German church records for the two families going back to 1598. As it is, there are already ninety-eight names stitched into the quilt with dates of births, marriages, and deaths as well as military service and the wars in which they participated.

Nine generations of one branch are outlined on the quilt. The earliest name and date is in this line. Samuel Morris was born in 1746 in Maryland, where he lived until moving his wife and young children to Kentucky in 1810. The 1820 census takers found the family in Shawneetown, Illinois.

There are many reasons Sam Morris might have had for coming to Shawneetown. A decade earlier the Ohio River community was becoming an active commercial center. One 1809 visitor reported the new town's thirty cabins, several taverns, and a log bank gave "more the appearance of business than I have seen this side of Pittsburgh." The federal land office provided an important focal point for western migrants seeking an Illinois farm, and the nearby government-controlled salt springs were another major drawing card.

A new state bank that opened in 1817 survived for seven years before falling victim to the Panic of 1819 and the bad banking practices characteristic of the period. When the bank reopened in 1834, it built the imposing Greek Revival building that remains one of the most outstanding structures in southeastern Illinois. It is maintained as a state historic site by the Illinois Historic Preservation Agency. Whatever part of Shawnee-

[Plate 35]
AMERICAN SAMPLER
92″ x 84″

Bernice Finke, 1926–
Herrin, Williamson County, Illinois,
1986
Collection of Ryan Finke

This was only the second quilt Bernice had made. A polyester batt is between the cotton top and cotton bottom, and it is bound by straight-cut cotton sewn by machine on the front and by hand on the back. The top of cross-stitch embroidery is pieced by machine with the quilting (7 stitches per inch) in feather, grid, and parallel line motifs. It is a modified quilt kit, with the straight grid in the center medallion not following the kit's quilting design.

town's illustrious history attracted Sam Morris, he did not enjoy it for long. The old Revolutionary War veteran died there sometime between 1822 and 1824.[3]

With thirty-five family surnames in addition to that of Morris featured on the quilt, Ryan Finke's history is rich with the stories of Illinois and of the nation. His immigrant ancestors came from Germany, Scotland, Ireland, and Holland; and they lived in New York, New Jersey, Pennsylvania, Maryland, Virginia, West Virginia, Tennessee, Kentucky, Indiana, and Missouri, in addition to Illinois. At the top center of the quilt Bernice embroidered an unattributed quotation she found during her research:

> Hold me not boastful that
> I take pride in what my forefathers
> have achieved. I honour not myself,
> but they who gave a priceless
> heritage on which to build.

Quilting has long been a part of Kathryn Kennedy's life. Although her mother, Louise Ruettiger Kestel, was a busy farmwife, "she made time for the things she enjoyed, and making quilts was one of them" according to Kathryn. "She made quite a number and quilted them on frames she set up in our living room. Sometimes friends quilted with her." Kathryn learned to quilt as a young woman, and in her late teens and early twenties, before she married Arthur M. Kennedy, she made two utilitarian quilts for her hope chest. One was a Dresden Plate pattern and the other an Irish Chain. Her family used them, and "regretfully," she hastily adds, "they are no more." Today she has more than ten quilts.

Since Kathryn saved so many things her mother made and gave to her, it was only natural that she should want to make something special for her daughter, Margaret. She decided it would be a quilt and was eventually inspired to use designs "from my childhood and my

[Plate 36]
YESTERDAYS REMEMBERED
96" x 80"

Kathryn Kestel Kennedy, 1913–
Wilmington, Will County, Illinois, 1980
Collection of the maker

life—in other words from 'Yesterdays Remembered.'" She soon learned it was not an easy task. "I was puzzled on how to get the designs on the blocks. I finally found I could make tissue paper designs by tracing the picture onto the paper through the light of a window, taping it on the white block and then embroidering through the tissue paper." Finding that gift tissue was too fragile, she used the paper that

came with Hanes hosiery because it was stronger and more transparent. Kathryn Kennedy's symbol-filled quilt contains a personal story. She took a popular turn-of-the-century idea and used ninety-nine red embroidered eight-inch blocks to record her memories. She recalled seeing an antique quilt made of white muslin sugar sacks in which each block had "a quaint design of children, flowers, and animals embroidered in red, which I really liked." Using single-strand red floss she embroidered ninety-nine blocks with the same tiny needle. Toward the end she noticed "it had a decided curve." The top and the back are both traditional cotton, although the batting is modern polyester. The commercial bias binding is applied to the front by machine and finished by hand on the back. The blocks are pieced by hand, but the border is put on by machine. The quilting (6 stitches per inch) outlines the embroidery designs, the suns, clouds, and grid in the center, as well as the cable motif used in the border.

Kathryn freely admits that "ideas didn't come easy, and the drawings were another hurdle." She found help in snapshots, newspapers, and friends. The project was often delayed until an idea matured, and then it could still take days to design and embroider a block. The quilt took about four years to complete, and according to Kathryn's account, selecting a name was not easy. "'Yesterdays Remembered' came to me after a lot of thought. It seemed to sum up all the designs, and Margaret and I were pleased with it."

This historically rich family document tells Kathryn's story. It starts with her birth certificate and moves on through the highlights of her long life. She feels some of the most important historical events recorded on her quilt would be the first and second world wars, the Great Depression, Lindbergh's transatlantic flight, her first talking picture show, and the first lunar landing. The most important personal blocks are those depicting her birth certificate, her sister and three brothers, the footprints of her children, her grade school, her mother quilting, her grandmother, her first book, her marriage, Margaret's Christmas letter to Mama, and the marriage certificate of Margaret and William Benoit. It will not require a detective or a cultural translator to explain Kathryn's

twentieth-century life in Illinois to her twenty-first-century family. Her messages are not embroidered in code.

As tedious as the work may have been, she always anticipated the joy of the completed project. As that time drew near, she "could hardly wait to give the quilt to Margaret. We spread it out and stood together looking at the designs, recalling memories, and hugging each other. She told me it is the best inheritance I could have given her." As Kathryn approaches her seventy-ninth birthday, she still finds the joys and sorrows of her life depicted in those ninety-nine red and white blocks. She considers Yesterdays Remembered to be "an expression of love from a mother to her daughter," and the quiltmaker wants each of them "to remember those yesterdays with a grateful heart."

Marking Time: The Rites of Passage

As Americans increasingly value the physical remains of the past, their awareness of the history inherent in those artifacts grows dramatically. Quilts are an important part of this trend. They help us understand the experiences of our life cycle in the context of events common to everyone. All mature humans once experienced birth and puberty; some entered into marriage; and each will eventually die. These are life's primary touchstones where the family and community recognize a transition is taking place and often participate in the event. As traditional activities emerged within a particular culture, certain objects became associated with those rites of passage. Many years later the documentary material culture artifacts remain. Quilts are becoming an important part of the way we mark the periods of our lives.

Birth

A newborn's first prolonged contact with fabric is through clothing and the blanket or quilt with which it is covered. The act of creating and using a baby quilt offers the mother, her family, and her friends an opportunity to join together in celebrating the child's birth. An important aspect of a rite of passage is the sharing of one's life with the community.

Preparation for the birth by cutting, sewing, and quilting, although done entirely by one person, can still involve others who visually and orally participate in the creative process. Once the quilt is completed, it becomes an object of admiration and a conversation piece when used in conjunction with the baby. Although the original purpose of a crib quilt was to provide warmth and security for the infant, it also offered satisfaction to the maker. A mother, grandmother, aunt, or friend could use a quilt to express physically their love and concern for the child and its family. It was also an opportunity for skilled needleworkers to demonstrate their skill to the family and to the community at large.[4]

One ordinarily would not make or give a baby quilt unless there was indeed a baby involved. Therefore, when such an artifact is studied in historical perspective, it becomes an important part of the material culture associated with the birth portion of the rites of passage.

The Illinois Quilt Research Project registrations strongly suggest baby quilts are almost a twentieth-century phenomenon. There are a few earlier ones, and it is possible that many disintegrated through extended use by the large number of children born to many families. Some owners may not have thought about bringing them to be registered along with their regular bed quilts. One must also remember that the child-rearing techniques of our ancestors differed from those of today. In cold, unheated bedrooms infants often slept with their parents or were crowded into a bed with older children. Under such circumstances, there was hardly need for a baby to have its own small quilt.

As the role of children changed during the nineteenth century, so did the way we thought about the material items a family acquired for its offspring. It is interesting to page through early twentieth-century women's magazines and notice the growing interest in children's things, including quilts.[5]

Recent family history studies have heightened our awareness of the evolving role of women and children in middle-class American society during the late nineteenth and early twentieth centuries. As the income of urban, suburban, and small-town businessmen and professionals rose, so did the educational level of their wives; and the family size declined. The proliferation of homemaking publications and a rising circulation indicated a growing interest in an improved lifestyle. The role of children in such families differed greatly from that of the farm and factory family. Even there, however, change was evident by the 1920s. The increase in the number of crib quilts peaked in the 1930s and has begun to grow in popularity again only in the last decade. Most made during the mid-twentieth century are the products of commercial kits and lack the creativity apparent in those being made today.

Although baby quilts come in a wide range of sizes, they are historically about one yard square. Much of the variation in size is due to their being made to fit a specific cradle or bed.[6] Perhaps size was also dictated by the maker's vision of how the child's quilt would eventually be used. Was it to be only a ceremonial covering for publicly displaying the baby during its first few months of life, or was it planned to last through the early years as a sleeping cover for a small bed?

Before the arrival of nursery-

[Plate 37]
NINE PATCH
37" x 30"

Hattie White Curry, 1849–1934
Albany, Whiteside County, Illinois, 1879
Collection of Linda Port

rhyme-character crib quilt kits, each maker was on her own. Many, such as the creator of the 1879 Nine Patch, based the quilt upon an existing adult quilt pattern and simply reduced it to the appropriate size. The top, which is composed of plain and printed cottons within a Nine Patch block set on point, provides an excellent selection of period fabrics. The back is an exceptional bonus because it is a solid piece of printed patchwork. The pattern, but not the color, is identical to the

back of a full-size bedcover registered in the Project that also dates to the late nineteenth century. This is the earliest use of geometrical chintz, or "faux patchwork," discovered in the Illinois Quilt Research Project. The earliest documented pieces date from the mid-nineteenth century.[7]

Although construction of the quilt is by hand, the parallel line quilting was done by a sewing machine. The quilt's present owner also has the cradle in which the quilt was used when Hattie's daughter was a baby.

The homemade straight-cut binding is applied by hand. The very thin batting is actually a piece of muslin.

The quiltmaker, who was born in Garden Plain Township, Whiteside County, was the daughter of Edward and Mary Mathew White. Her father emigrated from England in 1840, and the family still has his two trunks. Each is inscribed with his name, and they are lined with 1840 newspapers from Liverpool, England. On February 17, 1875, their daughter Hattie married Samuel Curry, who was born in Pennsylvania in 1833. Hattie made the Nine Patch baby quilt for the birth of their only child, Mary, who was born February 9, 1879, and died March 3, 1953. Hattie's family still owns Mary's cradle as well as the quilt.

The quilt is badly worn. Intended as a utilitarian object, it was indeed well used. In addition to being placed in a cradle or crib, these objects could also be spread on the floor for children to rest upon. It is also possible that the child was permitted to use it for play after it no longer served its original purpose.

Puberty (Graduation)

Childhood, the period between infancy and puberty, is a period of formal and/or informal education designed to prepare the child for an acceptable adult role. While the specific rites change over time, all primitive and civilized societies have developed public ceremonies that introduce the physically mature person to the group as one who is ready for marriage.

Within our religious and secular society, confirmation and/or grade school graduation mark an advance into puberty and courtship that we term "dating" today. With an increasing emphasis upon education, the rites of passage associated with puberty have been advanced beyond the actual point of physical maturation. Today most families discourage serious thoughts of marriage before high school graduation. For some students, the high school

graduation ceremony symbolizes a terminal point that can be followed by marriage, a career, or further education. No matter what comes next, it is a public recognition of passage into adulthood.[8]

As high school graduation ceremonies slowly increased in community importance during the twentieth century, such material culture objects as invitations, programs, pictures, diplomas, and items of special dress, particularly tassels, became the primary artifacts individuals chose to retain as a physical remembrance of this rite of passage. Recently, quilts have assumed a larger role in more completely

[Plate 38]
SANDY'S LIFE
101" x 85"

Mabel Cullison Wilson, 1910–
Olney, Richland County, Illinois, 1988
Collection of Sandra Kay Wilson Setser

The quilt top is cotton and cotton/polyester; the back is cotton; and the batting is polyester. The binding is handmade straight cut taken from the same fabric as the border and applied by machine on the front and by hand on the back. The construction, both in the blocks and joining the sashing to the blocks, is by hand. It is quilted (8 stitches per inch) in outline and cable motifs.

Blocks one and twenty are the signatures of Sandy, including the outline of her baby footprint, and of the maker. The latter bears the embroidered statement, "Love always from Grandma Mabel Wilson Prov. 3-16."

marking passage of a milestone in one's lifetime.

The quiltmaker, who is Sandy's grandmother, approached her task with the skills of an amateur artist. The retired schoolteacher had studied landscape and still-life painting through the University of Illinois extension courses and at Olney Community College. Mabel was inspired to make the quilt while visiting relatives in Arizona, and she began construction in 1984 when Sandy was a freshman in high school. Sandy's mother helped Mabel search the family album for appropriate pictures.

The quilt was a secret at first, but once Mabel completed the early years she let Sandy select items she wanted stitched into the quilt. One of Sandy's favorite designs is block eighteen, which depicts her senior year in high school, memorable for her role in *Bye, Bye, Birdie* and for the "incredible" opportunity to attend the Orange Bowl with her best friends. Other choice years are eleven, which features her white Persian cat Casper, and year twelve with the details of a special trip the family took with Grandma Wilson to Washington Island, Wisconsin. This is Mabel's favorite block.

When retirement gave Mabel the time to quilt, she was not totally unfamiliar with the craft. Before her marriage, she had helped her mother piece quilts on a sewing machine. Unfortunately, as an active farm wife and schoolteacher, she had no opportunity to continue her work. When she retired she took an appliqué class at Olney Community College and went to work. Each block of Sandy's quilt features some appliqué work.

Marriage

Even if the wedding is not a public ceremony, marriage is traditionally a matter of community concern. Governments require a license to make it an act of public record, with application for one announced in a

[Figure 23]
Evelyn Beyer and William Bodinus on their wedding day, August 22, 1931.

local newspaper whether or not a report of the event is detailed in its social columns. For most couples there is some degree of involvement of the immediate families and close friends, and for others it is indeed a spectacular community-wide celebration. Marriage is a traditional rite of passage that announces to the community two consenting individuals will henceforth be considered a family unit, which may not only legally bear legitimate children but may also file a joint income tax return.

It is not unusual for a quilt to be made or purchased for a wedding gift to the bride and groom. Since most modern brides are much too busy with a career to make their own quilts prior to marriage, it is the only way many young families actually acquire a quilt. These gifts can be very utilitarian, or ornate and too fancy for daily use, or totally commemorative. An increas-

ing number of rite-of-passage quilts have some basic documentation stitched into the fabric. This is generally limited to a short quilted or embroidered statement. Most quilts documenting a marriage discovered by the Illinois Quilt Research Project were made later to celebrate an anniversary.

Winifred Bodinus Seibert created a quilt for her parents' fiftieth wedding anniversary. As they prepared to celebrate their fifty-fifth anniversary, Winifred designed, appliquéd, and embroidered another special quilt top. Her mother, Evelyn, did the quilting.

Winifred began with the wedding photo and "made them look as accurate as possible. They had gone together since high school, and the heart on the tree tried to emphasize young love. The background once again represents our summer home and lake that they truly love. In the scene a young bride and bridegroom—Evelyn Beyer and William Bodinus—hold hands at the base of their family tree." Their son Roland and daughter Winifred are seated on the tree's lower branches. Their children, William and Susan Seibert and Robert and Dawn Bodinus, are on the branches immediately above them. The hair and clothing are accurate depictions of each family member, and the children's clothes are made of scraps from their actual clothing. The other fabric was purchased especially for the quilt.

Winifred was exposed to quilting as a child when she played with her dolls "under the quilting frames as quilts were being made by both my grandmothers, my aunts, and my mother. As I got older, I would sew scraps together and make quilts for my dolls. Through the years I continued to help my grandmother and mother make quilts." Winifred graduated from Chicago's Art Institute and teaches art today. She is interested in the graphic design of quilts and finds it "a great joy to share my talent with my mother in creating these quilts."

[Plate 39]
ANNIVERSARY QUILT
69" x 66"

Evelyn Beyer Bodinus, 1910–
and Winifred Bodinus Seibert, 1933–
Chicago, Cook County, Illinois, 1986
Collection of Evelyn Bodinus

The top and back are cotton/polyester, with polyester batting, quilted (5–7 stitches per inch) in a variety of motifs, including hearts. The visual depiction and the use of names and dates will henceforth identify this quilt as a record of a marriage and a family. When such explicit documentation is not done, it is possible for it to be completely lost over time.

In previous decades some women traditionally recorded their marriages by using portions of their wedding clothing in the design of patchwork quilts (see Plate 89 for a crazy quilt that incorporates wedding clothing). In the absence of any documentation on the quilt, carefully transmitted oral tradition is required to identify the source of these fabrics. However, this line of oral communication can be easily broken when a child fails to assimilate the knowledge accurately or the quilt passes outside the family.

Death

The final public ceremony that officially brings together family and friends marks the end of our mortal existence. Over the years, mementos of the departed frequently included pieces of clothing and locks of hair, which during the nineteenth century were often used in jewelry and wall hangings.

Creating memorials for deceased relatives and friends was a common practice throughout the nineteenth century. The custom of retaining objects associated with deceased family members or creating memorials to them is a practice still followed by many families today. It does, however, involve much less conspicuous display than in former times, and therefore it usually pass-es undetected by the general public. The practice, which was already well established during the Federal and Empire periods of the first half of the century, became more extensive and elaborate during the Victorian era of the late nineteenth century.

By the mid-nineteenth century, photographic studios and local printing facilities offered a wider range of available material culture objects associated with this final rite of passage. While some twentieth-century collectors find such artifacts fascinating, others consider them too morbid to merit consideration. Nevertheless, families have chosen a variety of ways in which to keep the memory of a loved one alive.[9] Some quilts have included pieces of clothing, even from men's suits; but few are so specific as the two embroi-

[Figure 24]
Nineteenth-century mourning objects

The collage illustrates a shadow box in which a floral wreath, created from human hair, surrounds an ornamental silver casket plate (circa 1875); two sampler-type stitched memorials, one on linen (1898), and one on paper (1861); a cabinet photograph of funeral flowers that includes a picture of the deceased (1903); and four pieces of hair jewelry—two locket-type brooches, a bracelet with a picture in the clasp, and a necklace pendant with a watercolor on ivory of a mourning figure on the obverse and plaited hair under glass on the reverse (1825–1875). Private collections.

dered, pieced, and tied bedcoverings Brenda Kirkpatrick made to help her sons remember their father.

When twenty-eight-year-old race car driver Larry Kirkpatrick died four days after a Sprint car accident on July 4, 1976, his sons were seven and nine years old. The statement that his wife Brenda attached to the quilt registration form clearly expresses the maker's motivation. She made each son a quilt because she "wanted the boys to remember 'Dad'—a loving and caring man. He loved the boys and they worshiped the ground he walked on." She wanted "to preserve something for them to remember him by with his other love—a passion for racing." Her narrative introduces the reader to Larry and interprets the symbols she selected:

Larry had a racing style that was all his own—a high rim rider that raced around the track leaving a "rooster tail" of dirt flying. He had a natural talent, and it was beautiful to watch him race. Legend says Larry's only fault was that he had no fear. The tall, sandy-haired, handsome Irishman was one you always knew would walk away from any accident unbent and unyielding to any

human disaster. He was always happy at the race track. Sports commentator Chris Economaki called him the "Smilin' Irishman."

The quilts were fittingly set in the design of a winner's flag because Larry was a winner on the track and in his life. A checkered flag symbolizes the Winner at the End of the Race. The hand-embroidered pictures and decals in each white square are racing symbols.

The cars used on the quilt are the more meaningful or favorite cars driven by Larry. The car called "Hank's Dream" was the first car Larry drove, and he and his father, Ned Kirkpatrick (a former driver), built it together. The orange and blue car, with the number intentionally left off, was Larry's last ride. He had reached his final Checkered Flag. The signature is the actual signature of Larry and he would add a star to autographs for fans.

The quilts were made and given to Rich and Terry the Christmas after Larry's death, maybe as a way to keep him alive another day. The beauty of the sport had felt its ugliest on that dark day—July 8, 1976. Perhaps these quilts made out of love for his sons by their Mother will in some small way help them remember the happy years Larry Ira Kirkpatrick spent with his sons for Memory is the Treasurer and the Guardian of *All Things.*

[Figure 25]
Larry and Brenda Kirkpatrick with their sons, Rich on the left and Terry on the right, in Topeka, Kansas, after a feature win.

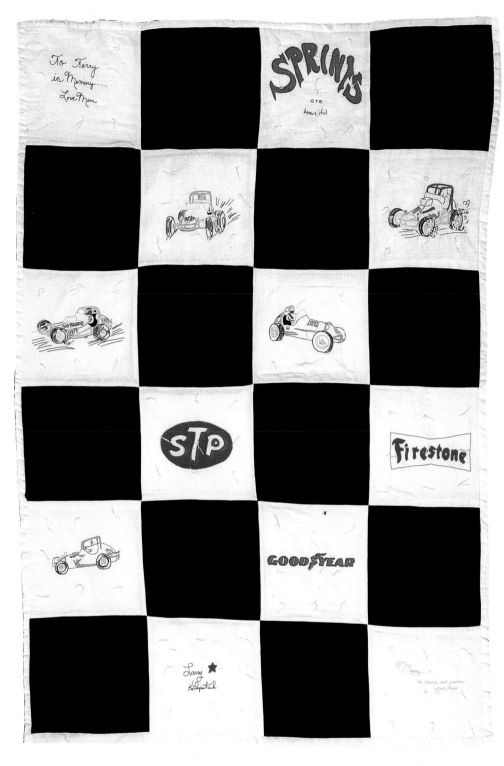

[Plate 40]
MEMORY QUILT
78″ x 53″

Brenda Ray Kirkpatrick, 1947–
Wood River, Madison County, Illinois,
  1976
Collection of Terry Ray Kirkpatrick
Rich has an identical quilt except for the
  name block.

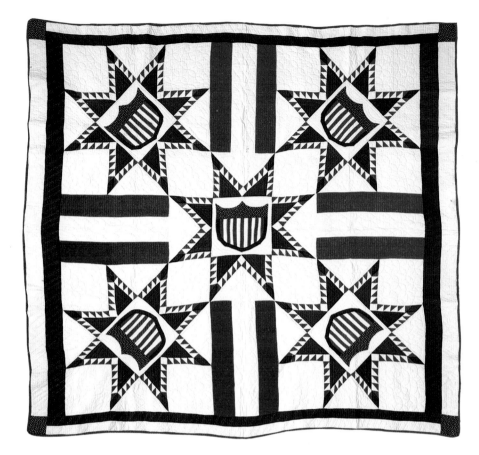

[Plate 41]
G.A.R. FEATHERED STAR
82" x 81"

Maker unknown, dates unknown
Nebo, Pike County, Illinois, 1894
Collection of Lewis M. and the late
    Juanita Grigsby

Some of the sewing on the G.A.R. quilt is by machine, although most of the work on the entire quilt is by hand. It is an all-cotton quilt, including the batting and the handmade straight-cut binding. The quilting (4 stitches per inch) is in the diagonal double and parallel lines, hearts, strings of leaves, and orange peel quilting motifs.

Quilts with Stories to Tell

Each everyday object in a home has a story to tell. In fact, if you thoughtfully look at any piece, you will soon discover not one but many overlapping stories. Begin an artifact adventure with such simple questions as who made it, when was it made, what does it say about the period of its creation, where was it made, why was it made, who used it, how was it used, how and why was it acquired, of what is it made, is it utilitarian or ornamental or symbolic, and what associational value does it have? How does it fit with the context of the period, of your family, and of Illinois history? If a quilt or any other object can answer one or more of these questions, there surely is a story in the making. Personal and family stories

are not the only tales to be found in a quilt. The Project registration forms contain a number of accounts relating to national, state, and local history, and sometimes, as in the case of the G.A.R. quilt, the stories overlap.

American Symbolism

Many quilts are filled with subtle symbolic meaning for the maker and/or the owner. There is, however, very little that is tenuous about the Pike County G.A.R. Feathered Star quilt. The visual aspect of the patriotic story is immediately apparent. From the bold, eye-grabbing red sashing that frames the large white arrows that focus the four directions upon the unified center, to the nostalgically patriotic American shield, the

meaning is obvious. Five giant multi-pieced shield-bearing feathered stars symmetrically "form a more perfect union" preserved by the sacrifices of the surviving veterans and their fallen comrades.

When a group of ten thousand people, including many Illinois Civil War veterans and their families, gathered at Nebo, Illinois, in 1894 to celebrate the preservation of their indivisible Union, they were carrying on a tradition that originated in the Prairie State at the end of the conflict. Much of the credit is due Governor Richard J. Oglesby. The first G.A.R. charter was issued to his Decatur post on April 6, 1866. John M. Palmer, another Republican general who succeeded Oglesby in the governor's office, was the first

[Figure 26]
G.A.R. Reunion, Nebo, Pike County,
Illinois, circa 1895
Collection of Lewis M. Grigsby

state commander. It soon became an important organization in the Northeast and the Midwest. By 1890 there were 7,500 posts with over 400,000 members and an auxiliary organization that undoubtedly played an important community role by making fundraising quilts.

General John A. Logan of Carbondale served as the first national commander. He initiated a pension movement for disabled veterans and instituted the annual spring Memorial Day celebration when he spoke at the first "Decoration Day" observance on April 7, 1867. The next year the date was moved to May 30.[10]

According to family tradition, the Grigsby family acquired the quilt in 1894 when the present owner's great-grandfather, A. C. Matthews, purchased it during a Grand Army of the Republic reunion at Nebo, Illinois.[11]

Asa Carrington Matthews was born in Perry Township, Pike County, in 1833. The Illinois College graduate was admitted to the bar at Pittsfield in 1857. When the Civil War began, he enlisted in the Ninety-Ninth Illinois Infantry

Division and was unanimously elected captain. During the 1863 siege and surrender of Vicksburg, he served as captain, major, and lieutenant colonel.

After the end of the conflict, Matthews returned to his home and law practice. The ardent Republican eventually entered politics, served three terms in the Illinois General Assembly, and was elected speaker of the house during his last term. He was a presidential elector when James G. Blaine lost the election of 1880 and again in 1904 when Theodore Roosevelt won the office. President Benjamin Harrison appointed him comptroller of the treasury.

Matthews served as president of the association that erected the state's monument on the Vicksburg battlefield and, at the time of his death on June 14, 1908, he was the immediate past president of the Illinois G.A.R. It is not surprising that in 1894 Colonel Matthews chose to demonstrate his patriotism and support for the organization by purchasing this remarkable symbol-rich quilt.

The patriotic red, white, and blue of the G.A.R. Feathered Star was still very much in style in the 1970s when the United States planned a nationwide extravaganza to celebrate the country's two hundredth anniversary.[12] The symbol was still a star, but the celebration logo was different from the Feathered Star symbol Colonel Matthews purchased on his quilt in 1894.

The big celebration was coming closer, and Lela Terril had not even purchased the kit for the Bicentennial quilt she had thought about doing. She had seen the ad for it in a farm magazine, but it was expensive. Then one afternoon while she was watching the afternoon movie on WCIA-TV Channel 3 from nearby Champaign/Urbana, she received the random call the station made each afternoon. Yes, she replied, she was watching the movie, and yes, she did know the correct title of the picture. When Lela's check for $315 arrived a few days later, she took one look and called it luck. Her family didn't care what it was; they were just happy she won.

She paid her church pledge, took the family out to dinner, hunted up the farm magazine with the Bicentennial quilt kit ad, and on August 4,

[Plate 42]
BICENTENNIAL
100″ x 82″

Lela Fitzgerald Terril, 1922–
Atwood, Piatt County, Illinois, 1978
Collection of the maker

1975, she wrote a check for $29.95 with the notation "Quilt Kit." This was her splurge.

[Figure 27]
Bicentennial
Quilt kit instruction sheet
Collection of Lela Fitzgerald Terril

The Bicentennial quilt, which was not completed until 1978, two years after the celebration, has a cotton/polyester blend top, a cotton back, and a polyester batt. The applied binding is wide white commercial bias tape that is machine-stitched on the front and sewn by hand on the back. The appliqué is by hand, and the border is joined to the quilt top by machine. The quilting (5 stitches per inch) is in outline and star. Lela joins her friends around the quilting frame one day a week at her church. She enjoys piecing as well as quilting, and she has made about forty quilts.

Labor History

Continuing waves of immigrants from Europe throughout the nineteenth century virtually assured a glutted labor market. Soon after the Civil War, protests about low wages and the twelve-hour day were disorganized and ineffective, but the Panic of 1873, which temporarily ended the nation's postwar industrial prosperity, brought on America's first serious strikes. Governor Shelby M. Cullom requested military support from President Rutherford B. Hayes to break the 1877 railroad strike.

By the 1880s Chicago had emerged as a center for labor radicalism, and the May 4, 1886, Haymarket Riot turned public sentiment more strongly against organized labor. A few years later, the Panic of 1893 brought on a strike against the Pullman Palace Car Company. When the American Railway Union joined the strike, the nation's rail network was paralyzed. Legal action was taken against Eugene V. Debs, head of the union, and the use of federal troops once again broke the strike. The state entered the twentieth century with the management versus labor issue unresolved.[13]

Peaceable assembly in support of a controversial cause was as much an issue in the late nineteenth century as it is in the late twentieth century. Despite the introduction of radio and television, the mass rally is still an effective psychological tool. Today large cardboard signs attract the attention of nonparticipants. In the nineteenth century the traditional manner of showing sympathy and solidarity was to wear a lapel ribbon, which generally carried a message and identified the place and date of the rally. Dedicated partisans often saved them as souvenirs of the cause they supported. As an isolated, but symbolically important textile, they often found their way into the fantastic collages so popu-

[Plate 43]
CRAZY QUILT
91″ x 74″

Sarah Walker Marshall Lindsay,
  1844–1924
Galesburg, Knox County, Illinois, 1898
Collection of the Illinois Historic Preservation Agency–Division of Historic Sites

[Figure 28]
Carl Sandburg State Historic Site,
    Galesburg, Illinois
The Sandburg home is maintained by
the Illinois Historic Preservation Agency.
Photo Courtesy: Illinois Historic Preser-
vation Agency

lar then—the crazy quilt. That is certainly what Mrs. Sarah Walker Marshall Lindsay did for her son, William A. Marshall.

The incorporation of this documentary labor history material into the quilt resulted in its preservation, but the reason for the quilt's eventual presentation to an Illinois state historic site is quite another story. After serving in the Civil War, George Campbell Marshall left his native New Hampshire, moved to Chicago, married, and began rearing a family. William, the youngest of the Marshalls' five children, was born there January 19, 1875, one year before his father's death. Shortly thereafter, his mother remarried, and the family moved to Galesburg.

There, on October 7, 1892, Marshall joined the International Typographical Union. When his mother made the crazy quilt for him in the

late 1890s, she used the ribbons he saved from the many labor events he had attended. The quiltmaker, who was born in the British Isles, used silks and cottons, some of which have metallic threads, on the top, with cotton alone for the back. There is no batting, and it is not quilted. Scallops are attached to three borders, and all the work is done by hand. Years later a Marshall descendant donated the quilt to the Carl Sandburg State Historic Site in Galesburg. Sandburg, who was born in the Knox County town in 1878, was a milk carrier from October 1892 to the summer of 1894; and the Marshall family was on his route.

Both young men eventually left Galesburg to seek their fortunes elsewhere, but each retained an interest in the cause of labor. In 1907 Marshall moved to Portland, Oregon, where he worked at two local

newspapers before being named editor of the *Oregon Labor Press* in 1913. He was instrumental in helping the Oregon legislature pass a workmen's compensation law in 1913.[14] Sandburg went into journalism, worked as an organizer for the Wisconsin Social-Democratic party, and became an internationally famous Pulitzer Prize-winning poet, author, and Lincoln scholar. In his 1916 work *I Am the People, the Mob,* Sandburg wrote:

> I am the people—the mob—the
>   crowd—the mass.
> Do you know that all the great
>   work of the world is done
>   through me?[15]

Thus one family's brief brush with greatness created an opportunity to save an ordinary household object, a quilt, and a piece of Illinois labor history.

Political History

Before moving to Kentucky in 1797, Virginia-born Henry Clay had studied law in Williamsburg with George Wythe. There he entered politics and enjoyed a long and distinguished national career. He served as Speaker of the House of Representatives in 1823–1825 during his 1811 to 1825 career in that body; and ran unsuccessfully for the presidency in 1824, 1832, and 1844. During his first race, he advocated his "American System," which included a protective tariff to support home industry and federal support for internal improvements such as canals and roads to facilitate the movement of agricultural products and manufactured goods to distant markets. It was during his tariff speech in the House on March 30–31, 1824, that he clearly enunciated his support for the tariff that was soon condensed into the political slogan "Agriculture and Industry."[16]

In his lengthy presentation Clay clearly identified agriculture as the nation's

greatest interest. It ought ever be predominant. . . . Can we do nothing to invigorate it? . . . We have seen, that an exclusive dependence upon the foreign market must lead to still severer distress, to impoverishment, to ruin. We must then change somewhat our course. We must give a new direction to some portion of our industry. We must speedily adopt a genuine American policy. Still cherishing a foreign market, let us create also a home market, to give further scope to the consumption of the produce of American industry.

The creation of a home market is not only necessary to procure for our agriculture a just reward for its labors, but it is indispensable to obtain a supply of our necessary wants. If we cannot sell, we cannot buy.[17]

Although the researcher may assume the quilt originated in a Whig home, there is no evidence to support such a statement. The grandmother of the present owner acquired it as a gift from a friend in Bloomington in the 1920s. The quilt is badly worn, but the inscription "Beauty of the Forest" is still visible in a cartouche located at the lower center. The small floral wreath is supported by two stuffed-work horses, and the whole is surmounted by an American eagle with a shield and seven arrows in one claw. The American shield bears the ink inscription "Agriculture—Industry."[18] While the quilt's excessive wear detracts from its visual impact, it does not lessen its historical significance as a memento of Henry Clay's political career and his unsuccessful attempts to win the presidency.

[Plate 44]
BEAUTY OF THE FOREST
84" x 83"

Maker unknown, dates unknown
Place unknown, circa 1840
Collection of Leonard F. Spreen

The center of each quadrant of this quilt features four feathered stars surrounded by a green, red, and orange floral wreath composed of appliquéd flowers and stuffed birds. The four medallions are divided by quilted and stuffed feather motifs in whitework. The quilting (10 stitches per inch) is also worked in grid and parallel lines that cover the entire quilt. An appliquéd floral border completes the design.

Economic History

The American Civil War confirmed national dominance within the preserved Union, strengthened the northern industrial complex, and created new political issues. One important controversy between the two major parties involved the national currency.

The previously solvent national treasury did not have the necessary resources to meet the Civil War's immediate demand for military goods and services, and so carefully regulated issues of paper money expanded the nation's credit and met the financial crisis. In the aftermath of war, deflation replaced inflation as the government tried to withdraw the "greenbacks" from circulation. Fueled by the rich western mining strikes of the postwar era, the nation's gold reserve increased and a satisfactory per capita dollar supply temporarily prolonged national reliance upon the gold standard.

By the 1890s a decline in gold production, coupled with an increasing population, led to loud demands for a new economic policy. An increase in the nation's silver output generated support for bimetalism. As the United States approached the critical 1896 presidential election, most Republicans had no difficulty holding tightly to the gold standard and they nominated Ohio congressman William McKinley, an avowed exponent of sound money and a protective tariff. Fewer and fewer Democrats, however, seemed willing to continue supporting the progold stance of Grover Cleveland, the incumbent Democratic president.

Illinois governor John Peter Altgeld (1893–1897) supported free silver and opposed President Cleveland on the monetary issue. When the Democrats met in Chicago in July 1896, Altgeld dominated the platform committee, and the document it produced repudiated Cleveland's policies. The presidential nomina-

[Plate 45]
ONE PATCH (POSTAGE STAMP)
70" x 68"

Mary Dean Ray, 1820–1912
Macomb, McDonough County, Illinois, 1898
Collection of Laura F. O'Harra

tion went to Illinois-born William Jennings Bryan who eloquently declared American labor should not be crucified upon a cross of gold. The American voter was offered a choice in 1896, and the paraphernalia makers provided ribbons and buttons for every occasion.[19]

Like many other western Illinois Republicans, D. E. Ray attended a Republican rally in support of McKinley on October 8, 1896. He procured a ribbon that he probably wore on his coat lapel as he proudly marched in a parade for "Sound Money and the Nation's Honor."

Despite the fact the ribbon con-

tains the word *Macomb,* there is no indication the rally was held there. Ray may have represented Macomb in a parade at a different location. The Macomb *Daily Journal* for September and October 1896 is filled with political news, but does not mention a local event on October 8. The city's major Republican rally occurred on September 28, a "cold and raw" day, but the afternoon and evening events were well attended. The crowd of two thousand at the afternoon session opened the meeting "by singing the Republican battle cry" which was "Marching Through Georgia." The "evening parade was

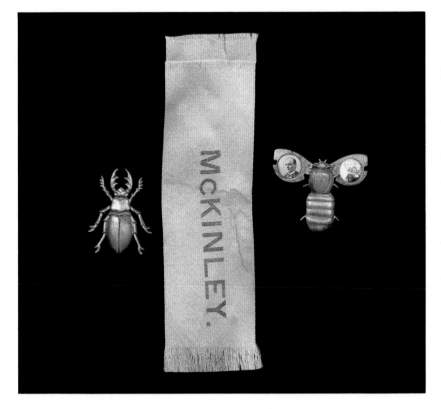

[Plate 46]
Republican items from the William
   McKinley 1896 presidential campaign
Private collection

The 1896 Republican presidential campaign focused on the gold question, and many of the party's political items emphasized that issue. The gold McKinley lapel ribbon is between two "gold bugs." An inanimate stickpin is on the left and a mechanical bug is on the right. The wings, which feature small pictures of the presidential candidate, William McKinley of Ohio, and his running mate, Garret A. Hobart, of New Jersey, automatically extend and reveal the pictures when a small lever is pressed.

exceptionally good, and the pyrotechnical display added considerably to the scene."

If D. E. Ray attended a political rally, he probably made it to the local polling place to join a majority of his fellow Illinoisans in supporting McKinley. The statewide Republican presidential vote was 607,148 to 464,523 for Bryan, while McKinley carried McDonough County with 4,036 votes to 3,678 ballots cast for his Democratic opponent.[20]

Two years after the election, Ray's mother incorporated this textile souvenir as one small piece in a colorful collage of silk squares. Working entirely by hand, Mrs. Ray used the English piecing method, and the individual paper supports remain in place under the top pieces, which are stitched to a silk foundation. Below that is a thin cotton batting above a piece of plain white cotton, which is covered by a printed silk back. Mrs. Ray's five-layer quilt is edged with a wide piece of lace. The small but col-

orful work was placed on the bed for show before guests arrived. If the eye of any visitor carefully scanned the intentionally displayed decorative quilt, that person would surely notice the bright gold ribbon that would forever let the world know a Republican once marched for Sound Money in October 1896.

It would be the work of a researcher rather than a guest, however, to look carefully at the back of the quilt to learn that Mrs. Ray documented the gift for her son that she completed on her seventy-eighth birthday. A century later, many viewers might see it as a puzzling piece of history. What Mrs. Ray's friends and neighbors accepted as common knowledge is enigmatic today. What is Sound Money, and why would anyone want to march for it? How many people understand the symbolism inherent in the *gold* fabric? In a nation dependent upon plastic credit cards, coins with low metallic value, and paper money to-

tally devoid of silver, much less gold, backing, it is easy to ignore the small memento of one of the nation's great issue-oriented presidential campaigns. Fortunately, an elderly housewife in west-central Illinois took the time to make a quilt in 1898. Her thoughtful use of one small ribbon assures us that history does indeed surround us in our homes every day of our lives.

Any interested individual could use the obvious 1896 clue, consult a history textbook, and begin solving this mystery. But what about the many other less obvious clues hidden in our textile archives? Devoid of documentary evidence, interesting stories languish while awaiting a sleuth who can reconstruct their original historical context. Have you read any good quilts lately?

Temperance

The intemperate use of rum and whiskey by many Americans became a national concern in the nineteenth century as more and more citizens, especially women, joined the proactive crusade. The American Temperance Union, which held its first national convention in 1836, and the Washingtonian Temperance Society, formed in 1840 by reformed alcoholics, were the first national organizations. Through the efforts of Neal Dow, the state of Maine passed the first prohibition law in 1846 and became a model for the twelve additional states that joined the movement before the Civil War.

There was little demand for the poor-quality beer brewed in early nineteenth-century America. Then a wave of German immigration following an unsuccessful revolution in 1848 introduced lager beer and improved brewing techniques. The use of machinemade glass bottles enabled individuals to purchase the drink in smaller quantities than the previously used sixteen-gallon kegs, and per capita beer consumption rose from two gallons before the Civil War to eighteen gallons in the 1980s. The diversified glassware shown in late nineteenth-century trade catalogs, such as cordials, wines, champagnes, and decanters, as well as glasses for ale and whiskey, indicates a widespread use of alcohol by middle-class families despite the temperance movement.[21]

The continued use of whiskey, combined with an escalating consumption of beer, fueled the post-Civil War temperance movement. Frances Willard became the leading Illinois activist associated with this nationwide crusade. She graduated from Northwestern Female College in 1859, settled in Evanston, and began teaching at the Evanston College for Ladies. She served as president of the school from 1871 to 1874 before being elected secretary of the

[Plate 47]
WHEEL SPOKES
85" x 73"

Women's Christian Temperance Union
Harvard, McHenry County, Illinois,
    1889
Collection of the Greater Harvard Area
    Historical Society

Illinois Women's Christian Temperance Union. In 1879 she became president of the national W.C.T.U. and held that office until 1898. By the early twentieth century, the state organization claimed 475 local groups in 91 of the state's 102 counties. She was also active in the women's suffrage movement and helped organize the Prohibition party.[22]

One of the state's many W.C.T.U.

circles was in Harvard, Illinois, a few miles northwest of Miss Willard's Evanston home. After the group organized in 1883, a need for money arose, and, as usual, someone suggested the women work together and make a quilt.[23] The project was laid out in forty-two eleven-inch-square red muslin blocks joined by a narrow piece of white muslin sashing, and the entire quilt was framed by a narrow white border. Each block was to have fourteen white appliquéd spokes radiating from a white hub that would resemble a wheel.

A two-part program helped raise the needed funds. First, the privilege of having a name placed on a spoke or on the hub cost the participant ten cents. Subscriptions totaled 639 names, each neatly written on the quilt in India ink by Mrs. J. H. Binnie. Second, additional money was generated by the quilt when C. E. Hunt purchased it at auction. His great-granddaughter later gave it to the Harvard Museum. Block two contains the history of the quilt and names the state and national W.C.T.U. officers. Eleven members worked together to piece, appliqué, and quilt the fundraiser. A sheet separates the red and white top from the solid red back. The quilting (8 stitches per inch) outlines the spokes and the blocks.

Names on the quilt reveal a preponderance of Anglo-Saxons, with a sprinkling of Germans and a conspicuous absence of any "new immigrants" from eastern and southern Europe. The prohibitionist impulse was often as much ethnically motivated as it was a social reform movement.

The crusade helped women become politically active, leading to the suffrage movement and the Nineteenth Amendment. The work of the W.C.T.U. also heightened public awareness of the dangers of alcoholism. Despite the failure of national prohibition in the 1920s, the medical and social study of addiction has increased and the per capita consumption of whiskey in America is now much less than it was before the Revolution. Frances Willard and the many dedicated W.C.T.U. members of her era laid a solid foundation but did not live to see the national alcohol awareness programs being developed today. The Wheel Spokes quilt made in Harvard is a piece of our past that heightens our awareness of their important contribution.

Military History

The August 1896 discovery of gold in the Alaskan Klondike helped solve the financial woes of incoming president William McKinley. However, another crisis was approaching. An increasingly tenuous relationship with the sugar-rich and militarily strategic Hawaiian Islands led the 1896 Republican party platform to call for U.S. control of the island kingdom. While nothing was said then about nearby Cuba or the distant Philippines, all three areas soon became focal points of U.S. foreign policy.

The Spanish-American War was our debut as an international military power, and we embarked upon an era of controversial colonialism. The impetus to war came on February 15, 1898, when two unexplained explosions sank the battleship *Maine* in Havana harbor, and 260 American sailors died. Accusations against Spain ran rampant, and a wave of indignation swept the country. Illinois governor John Tanner received

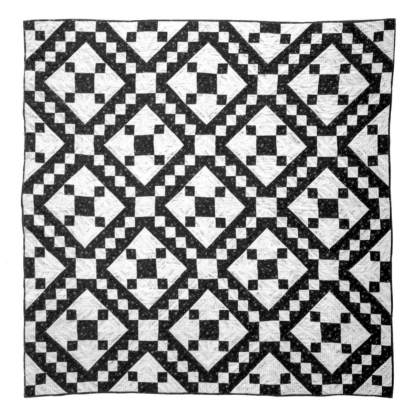

[Plate 48]
ECCENTRIC NINE PATCH
86" x 86"

Maker unknown, dates unknown
Lyndon, Whiteside County, Illinois, 1898
Collection of the Lyndon Historical Society

Apparently a patriotic spirit moved a group in Lyndon, Illinois, to raise money to benefit the deceased sailors' families. Typically, a raffle quilt became the fundraising device. The quilters selected a red and pink cotton print, combined it with plain white cotton, and created an Eccentric Nine Patch block. These were then set on point and joined by sashing pieced in a pattern similar to that found in Jacob's Ladder. The white areas on the top of the quilt contain the 260 names of the men who lost their lives on the *Maine*. The quilt is pieced by hand, filled with a cotton batt, and edged with a straight-cut binding stitched by machine. The quilting (8 stitches per inch) is in parallel lines.

authority from the state legislature to place the state's resources at the disposal of President McKinley.

Congress declared war against Spain on April 11, 1898. Commodore George Dewey flexed the navy's muscles in Manila Bay; Rear Admiral William Sampson blockaded Cuba; and Lieutenant Colonel Teddy Roosevelt's Rough Riders invaded the island. Wake Island was occupied on July 4, and a July 7 joint congressional resolution annexed Hawaii. According to the Treaty of Paris, signed December 10, 1898, Spain relinquished its four-hundred-year hold on Cuba, ceded Guam and Puerto Rico to the United States as indemnity for the war, and ceded the Philippines for a $20 million payment. Illinois sent ten regiments, mostly National Guard units, but only one saw active duty in Cuba; and it suffered more from yellow fever than from shrapnel.[24] The conflict was long remembered as "a splendid little war."[25]

Each year millions of American tourists visit Hawaii, our fiftieth state. Most are unaware of the 260 men who died aboard the *Maine* and their relationship to the acquisition of America's Pacific paradise. The incident has not been forgotten in Lyndon, Illinois, however. There a quilt keeps the memory of these men alive.

Almost ninety years later, another overseas military event occasioned the creation of a very different kind of quilt. This one was meant to express an attitude rather than to memorialize a tragedy or to raise money. In the years between the two events, American soldiers fought in two world wars, the Korean War, and maintained military posts around the globe. However, the controversial nature of the Vietnam conflict generated ardent support and vehement protest.

Although the quiltmaker had no family member involved in the war, she did have friends who partici-

[Plate 49]
ARMISTICE: MOM, I'M HOME (SOLDIERS)
62" x 63"

Carlene Rae Buck, 1947–
Buffalo Grove, Lake County, Illinois, 1987
Collection of the maker

[Figure 29]
The Oklahoma Banner or the Tin Man pattern from an early-twentieth-century newspaper clipping pasted into a quilt pattern scrap book. This design is the basic component of Carlene Buck's Armistice quilt.

Thank God you're home.

Dear God,
please don't let this happen again.

[Plate 50]
ARMISTICE: MOM, I'M HOME (MOM)

pated in the conflict. She made the quilt for the Vietnam veterans and those of other American wars. It also helped her own acceptance of the tragic conflict. The quilt, which is copied from an older pattern known as Tin Man, or the Oklahoma Banner, was completed in the nine weeks between Labor Day and Armistice Day (Veterans Day), which, Carlene notes, is approximately the time it takes to complete a soldier's basic training.

The quilt is filled with symbolism and requires a keen eye and the maker's interpretation to fully understand the message. Each soldier is different—some appear slender, others heavier, and six are even more varied. Three are missing limbs; one is mentally affected; one is scarred; one is bedfast; and another has not returned. The soldiers are depicted in red, with the blue surrounding them symbolizing home. Each returning soldier is at the door with arms outstretched for acceptance. The khaki ground of the quilt represents military uniforms. The red and blue binding symbolizes military service ribbons. A scar in the fabric across the quilt reminds viewers of the disfigurement war brings to the human family. The use of Japanese fabric in one of the blocks recalls World War II. Mom, the single figure on the back side of the quilt, stands for family, friends, the American people, and the quiltmaker. The overall unifying theme is the red, white, and blue of patriotism.

In addition to providing a rather complete interpretation on the Project registration form, Carlene also appended a separate page:

ARMISTICE—the war is over. Peace has finally come. Most of the men and women have come home, but they will never be the same. The physical differences tug at our hearts. Can we also feel the pain of troubled hearts and minds? War forever scars the human family. On the front each calls out, "Mom, I'm home!" The back asks us how will we respond?

Thank God, you're home!
Give him a hug?
I've been worried sick about you.
All the neighbors have been asking about you.
We're so proud of you.
Did you hear about Durward and Dennis?
How long can you stay?
I never thought this day would come.
I've prayed for you every day.
I made your favorite, pecan pie.

What we really mean: *Please God, never let there be another war.*

Business History

The Illinois Quilt Research Project found the Nine Patch to be a commonly used Illinois design. It appears in virtually every decade from the mid-nineteenth century to the present time, and it is one of the many patterns that can be used in both good and everyday quilts. The diamond set of the pieced blocks, the use of printed cotton for the plain blocks, and the addition of a contrasting blue print in the border set this quilt above the ordinary, but most collectors would still not consider it heirloom quality.

The outstanding feature of Lucy Hanner's quilt is not found on the front but in the labeled sacking material used to piece the back. This is the first factor that makes an ordinary early-twentieth-century Nine Patch quilt a significant historical document. The second important detail is found in the name on the sacking. Lucy used those stamped with the Hanner label, which came from the quiltmaker's family store in Griggsville. Small black letters clearly identify "Hanner & Son Griggsville" as the source of the coarse fabric. A business letterhead still owned by the family identifies the Hanners as suppliers of "Staple and Fancy Groceries Bakery Goods and Confectionery."

The present quilt owner, a family member, is unaware of any other existing Hanner-labeled sacks. Perhaps this is the only remaining textile document recalling this Illinois business operation. During the early twentieth century, stenciled wooden boxes and cloth sacks were the most widely used shipping containers. They supplanted the cooper-made barrels of the earlier period and would in turn be replaced by the paper bags that hold most feed, salt, and bulk lawn supplies today.

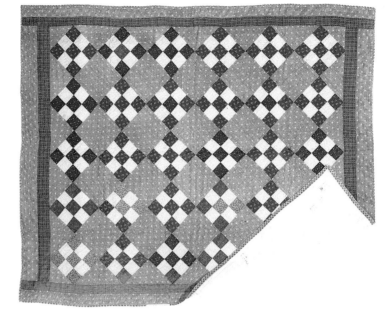

[Plate 51]
NINE PATCH
84" x 68"

Lucy Ann Ash Hanner, 1865–1944
Griggsville, Pike County, Illinois,
   circa 1915
Collection of Dorothy Hanner

The quilt top, which is pieced both by hand and by machine, is composed of inexpensive mass-produced cotton prints that are commonly found in any number of surviving utilitarian quilts. The batting is a woven wool blanket with some color, perhaps several different pieces of blanket, and the back is of common coarse cotton sacking fabric. The edges are bound by handmade straight-cut cotton print applied by hand on both the front and the back. It is quilted (6 stitches per inch) in diagonal parallel lines.

[Figure 30]
William Hanner with his delivery wagon
Griggsville, Illinois, circa 1915
Collection of Dorothy Hanner

A family photograph shows Lucy's husband, store-owner William Hanner (1862–1948), with his horse-drawn grocery delivery wagon in front of their store. The picture was probably taken about the same time the quilt was made.

Urban History

Some quilts tell their own stories. When Susan Auerback designed a quilt for her daughter Lisa, she graphically depicted traditional Chicago landmarks that require little interpretation. Look carefully between the wind of the Windy City on the top and Lake Michigan on the bottom and you will discover Marshall Field's clock, the Field Museum, Buckingham Fountain, Art Institute, Chicago Historical Society, Lincoln Park Zoo, Shedd Aquarium, Adler Planetarium, Picasso sculpture, Sears Tower, Museum of Science and Industry, Hancock Building, the Cultural Center, and the Water Tower that survived the 1871 Chicago fire.

The original intent was to picture the things around Chicago that Lisa loved. During the designing process a problem developed: Lisa's list of favorites grew so long there was not enough room. Thus quilting in the border itemizes additional highlights that are not illustrated. The list includes theaters, architectural landmarks, statuary, and museums.

Susan, the granddaughter of Russian immigrants, is a native Chicagoan. She learned to quilt on her own in the 1970s and has made many quilts. Her deft needlework is readily apparent. The appliqué and embroidered top successfully presents a personal, comprehensive collage of the maker's hometown, her daughter's favorite places, and the nation's Second City. Although numerous contemporary pictorial quilts were registered, very few exhibited the degree of creativity achieved by Susan Auerback.

[Plate 52]
THE CHICAGO QUILT
93" x 79"

Susan Auerback, 1944–
Riverwoods, Lake County, Illinois,
 1977–1982
Private collection

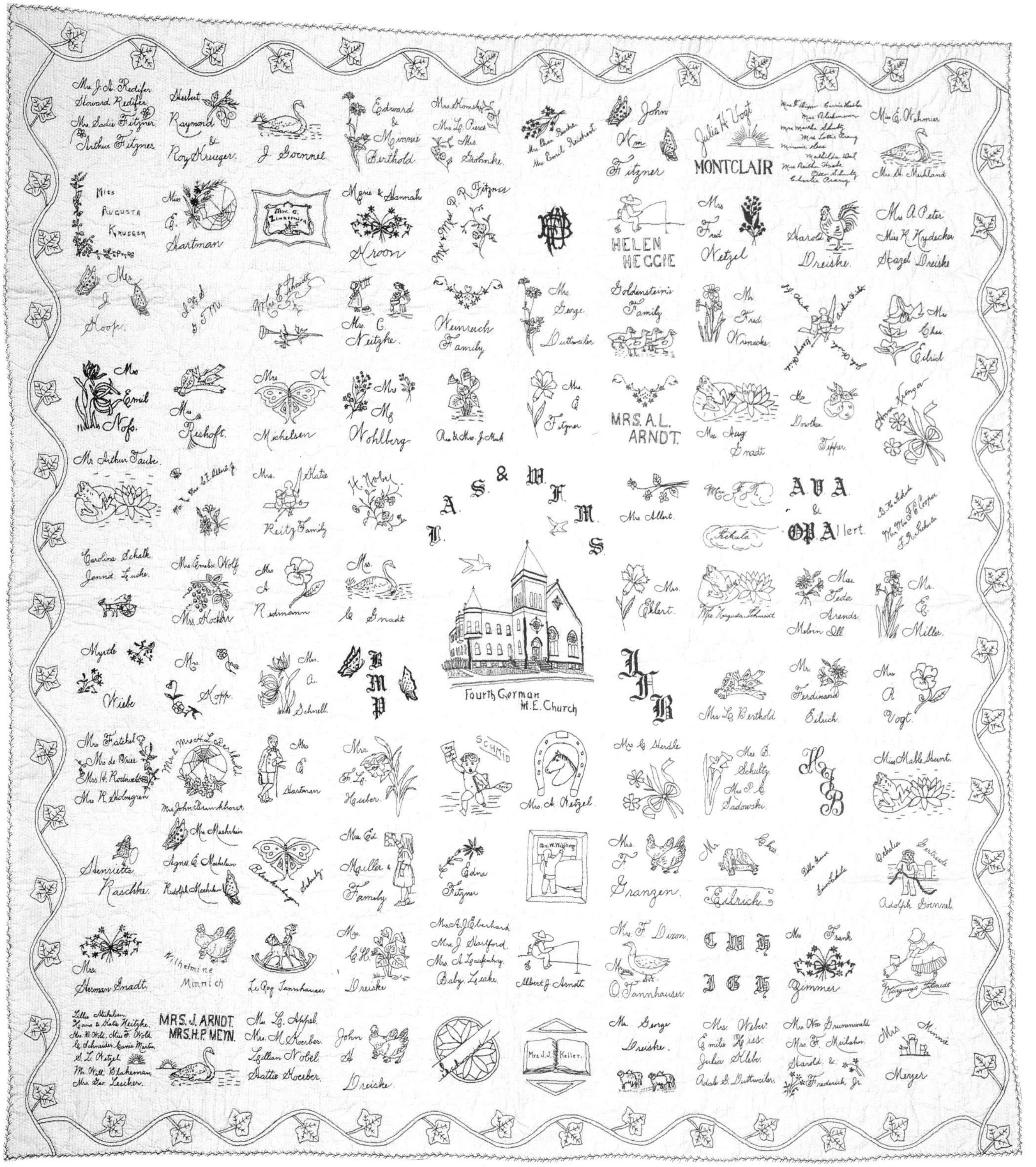

Church History

Chicago's Fourth German Methodist Episcopal Church was organized as the Reuben Street Mission in 1868. When the city changed the address, it became the Ashland Avenue Church. The congregation completed the basement for worship in 1869, and the sanctuary was finished before it was taken off the mission list in 1873. In 1900, when the surrounding community became largely Jewish, the congregation moved west and relocated on Augusta Street near Robey. At that time the name was changed from Ashland Avenue Methodist Episcopal to Fourth German Methodist

[Plate 53]
CHURCH HISTORY AND FRIENDSHIP QUILT
79" x 73"

Members of the Fourth German
  Methodist Church
Chicago, Cook County, Illinois,
  circa 1900–1910
Collection of Ann S. Wall

There are 83 different designs on the 106 blocks that comprise the top of the Fourth German Methodist quilt. All are embroidered in Turkey red on white, a combination typical of early twentieth-century embroidered penny block-type quilts.[26] All the blocks have names or initials, and they are joined to each other by machine stitching. There is no sashing. The top, back, and filling are cotton. The handmade straight-cut binding is applied by machine and by hand, with the quilting (7 stitches per inch) in outline, clamshell, and in-the-ditch motifs.

Episcopal Church. The congregation remained there until 1923 when they sold the building to Polish Baptists. Fourth Church combined with St. John's and a mission started by Centennial Methodist Episcopal Church and in March 1924 dedicated a new sanctuary at the corner of Troy Street and Belle Prairie Avenue.

When Mina F. Eckstein typed a three-page congregational history in 1937, she noted "our German services have been discontinued and we have become part of Chicago's great melting pot." She praised the Ladies Aid, organized in 1886. "As one looks through their minutes, all written in the German language, of course, this saint and that dear sweet old lady comes to mind, and we think of them wistfully and lovingly. Truly what a wonderful heritage they have left us, their untiring efforts, their sacrifices, their little deeds of love and kindness." It was probably the members of this organization who made the quilt that the congregation gave to the Schmids.

Unfortunately, no document tells us why the quilt was made for Joseph A. and Wilhelmina Anna Meyn Schmid, but it is easy to notice their initials, which are boldly embroidered above the church in the center of the quilt. The Schmids emigrated from Frankfurt, Germany. He was a custom shoemaker who did well financially until his partner absconded with their money. He worked for years to pay off his debts. Would this have been a fundraiser to help the family?

There is no doubt that the family easily settled into a German neighborhood where the newspaper was in the mother tongue and everyone used German in the stores and in

church. The children, who learned English in school, often acted as interpreters for their parents. The Schmid girls received a grade school education and went to work at age fourteen. They helped their brother achieve a better education so he could become a Presbyterian minister. The family was much loved by this congregation, but would that alone justify giving the Schmids such a quilt? It obviously became a family treasure and was never used on a bed.

Anabel Simons, whose father married one of the Schmid daughters, found this quilt in her stepmother's home after the woman's death. She had never seen it and never knew her step-grandparents or the congregation. All too often, later generations are left with unanswered questions. Some heirs would eagerly ask questions if they knew about an object's existence, and some owners would willingly share information if they thought anyone cared. Missed opportunities are a permanent loss for tomorrow as well as for today.

If Willa Cather could read the stories collected by the Illinois Quilt Research Project, she would surely realize history may begin in the heart of a man or a woman, but it is frequently preserved in the form of artifacts such as quilts. Over the past 150 years many stories of Illinois—of its people and its places—have been written by quilters. That history has been saved for us by determined families and tenacious collectors who realized the day was coming when someone would listen to what quilts could tell us about ourselves and our past.

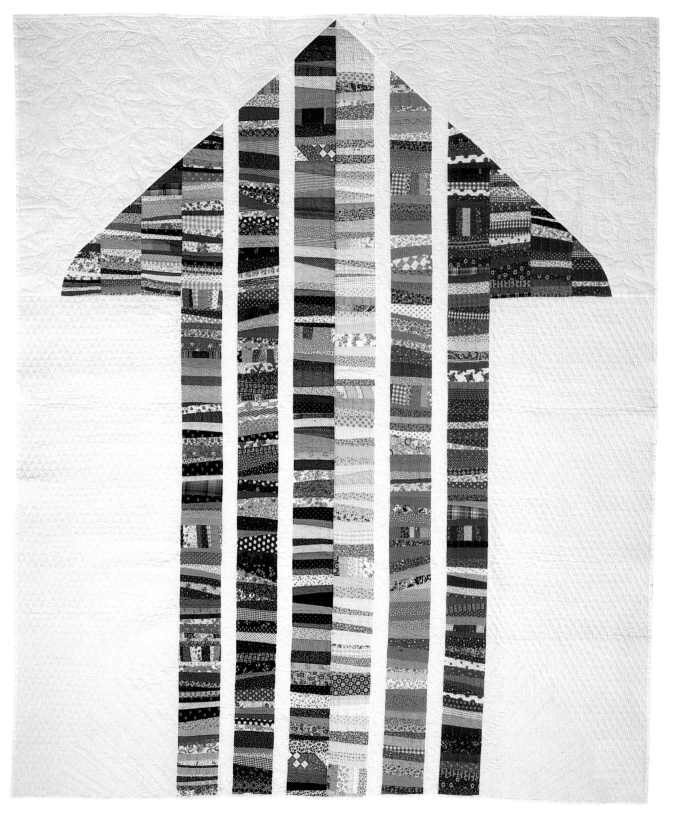

[Plate 54]
RAINBOW DIRECTION
89″ x 76″

Charlene Prasse Koelling, 1937–
Petersburg, Menard County, Illinois,
    1987–1989
Collection of the maker

An EXPLOSIVE CONCEPT: NONTRADITIONAL QUILTS AND QUILTERS

My heart leaps up when I behold
A rainbow in the sky:
So was it when my life began;
So is it now I am a man;
So be it when I shall grow old,
Or let me die!
—William Wordsworth,
"The Rainbow," 1802

Hearts of all ages, races, nationalities, and genders respond with creative joy to Wordsworth's rainbow concept. For those who view life in the context of yesterday, it is relief after a storm; to those reaching for tomorrow, it is hope; to all, it is beauty. Rainbows, like poets, help others live their lives. Can anything less be said of quilts?

At each registration day as the Illinois Quilt Research Project moved around the state, the variety of quilts seemed endless. In their totality they seemed to encompass the entire spectrum, in color, pattern, age, type, and technique, as well as material culture history. Like a rainbow, these quilts offer a spectacular cross section of the state's past and present. Creativity knows no boundaries; imagination is not confined by time or region. Our only limitations are self-imposed.

The Quilt Research Project clearly revealed that Illinois quilters are representative of the general population. Most seem content with the

world as it is; some dare to vary the pattern slightly; and a few are much more adventuresome. They are unwilling to be totally controlled by traditional constraints and, like many of their neighbors, are learning about themselves by seeing things in a changed perspective.

The Illinois Project discovered the many intonations one may use in giving expression to the simple five-letter word *quilt.* Excellent examples of individual achievement are sprinkled throughout this chapter. Placement elsewhere, as an illustration of Illinois quilt history, does not imply any lesser degree of creativity or imagination. In this chapter, the brief focus on the explosive context of Illinois quilting is designed to highlight the use of nontraditional design elements and quilting materials and to open a discussion of age and gender roles in quilting.

Over the decades Illinois quilters have repeatedly plucked their pieces from life's spectrum without de-

pleting an endless supply of creative energy. Using bits of success and failure, joy and sadness, courage and fear, each has created distinctive rainbows, set out in new directions, and given posterity a rich heritage.

Exploring the Possibilities: Nontraditional Quilts

Charlene Koelling, creator and quilter, has no trouble finding a personal rainbow. Despite a constant struggle with physical problems, she fills her life with brightness, color, and laughter. According to the maker, the upward pointing arrow

is a symbol of my fighting to get up, be up, stay up, and keep on in the right direction. The radiating quilting lines are the sun, the hanging diamonds are raindrops, and in between the rainbow colors are vines with leaves going up through the color and spreading throughout the top corners of the quilt. My husband, a botanist, drew the vines, leaves, and tendrils. I got into all kinds of contortions as I quilted all the small turns and curlicues. The vines and leaves symbolize the achievements and accomplishments of my life, sometimes coming from unexpected directions.

The fabrics represent five decades, the 1930s through the 1980s, and were a joy to collect. Some are from my late mother-in-law, Lula Koelling, who was a quilter, from clothes sewing remnants, pieces left from other quilts, and some given to me by friends who wanted to be a part of this, too. Oranges and purples had to be purchased more than other colors, as no one seemed to have liked them much. There was a great deal of pleasure in washing, ironing, cutting irregular strips, deciding on placement of darks next to lights, prints and solids, checks and stripes, width of the individual strips, and in some areas deciding to have the strips go in the opposite direction. I included some Seminole piecing also. I cut the strips about twice as wide as I wanted the finished strip. This gave me more freedom to play with the pieces of fabric. What was cut off is destined for another quilt.

Although the quilt is basically cotton, there are some cotton/polyester pieces in the top. The batting is a light polyester, and the back fabric is brought to the front for the binding. It is hand quilted, but the piecing is by machine; the quilting (8 stitches per inch) creates interesting motifs. Without a doubt the quilt is a conversation piece. Family and friends enjoy finding "their fabric" in the quilt just as they must surely take pleasure in seeing a part of Char's fine qualities reflected in their own lives.

Almost a century and a half separate Char Koelling's colorful, simple, straightforward Rainbow Direction from Polly Wheelock's much more complex version of the heavenly spectrum. Despite a difference in time, color intensity, and spatial arrangement, both quilts exhibit a degree of originality that links them conceptually. Unfortunately, age, dirt, and light have dulled the original impact that Polly's intricately pieced Stars and Rainbows must have possessed when it left the quilting frame.[1]

Polly Wheelock, who was born in Connecticut in 1785, arrived in northern Illinois at mid-nineteenth century. It is possible that she brought this quilt with her in 1850 when she accompanied Almena and John Clifford from upstate New York to LaSalle County. It is equally plausible that she brought the scraps with her and completed the quilt after the family settled in Serena Township. The quilt, which descended in the Clifford family before being donated to the LaSalle County Historical Society, is attributed to Polly, but where it was made is uncertain. Nevertheless, it remains a tribute to the

creativity that can be found in each generation.

Looking at the quilt today raises questions about the maker's motivation and personal vision. One can only imagine the thoughts that crossed the minds, but probably not the lips, of Polly's nineteenth-century friends and neighbors. Without question, Polly Wheelock set a brisk creative pace for the innovative Illinois quilters who followed her. In their own ways Char and Polly clearly demonstrate what a creative mind can accomplish with a stack of scraps and a desire to capture a rainbow.

Undoubtedly, Mary Goudy was inspired by reading about similar string quilts in a publication or seeing one that was owned by a friend. The construction technique is certainly not original to Mary's work, but this in no way diminishes her claim to Illinois quilting fame. No other work like it appeared at a quilt registration day, and surely very few must have been produced in the state.

The maker's imagination is vividly expressed in the motifs she chose for the blocks and the fabric she selected for use. While the designs are those commonly found in late Victorian handicraft items, there is, nevertheless, always an element of personal vision involved in the act of designing and creating.

This decorative bedcover stands as a unique example of Illinois folk art in the string quilt category. It is, without doubt, a highly nontraditional work.

[Plate 55]
STARS AND RAINBOWS
89" x 73"

Polly Wheelock, 1785–date unknown
Plattsburgh, New York, or Serena Township, LaSalle County, Illinois, circa 1850
Collection of the LaSalle County Historical Society

Despite the complicated image conveyed by the unusual set, a close inspection reveals a great deal that is also traditional. The quilter has successfully integrated a number of Nine Patch blocks into a medley of stars. This is easily overlooked because four large rainbowlike arcs, created by hundreds of tiny diamond scraps, visually frame two colorful pathways that intersect in the middle of the quilt. This dominating X ties together a radiating center sunburst with the Lone Star blocks in each of the four corners. The all-cotton quilt is entirely pieced by hand; the batting is probably wool, and the binding is the back brought to the front and stitched by hand. The quilting (5–6 stitches per inch) is in parallel lines, grid, and *Xes*.

MADE FROM TINY FRILLS OF SILK

[Figure 31]
String Quilt Pattern
Ladies' Home Journal, September 1899, p. 27

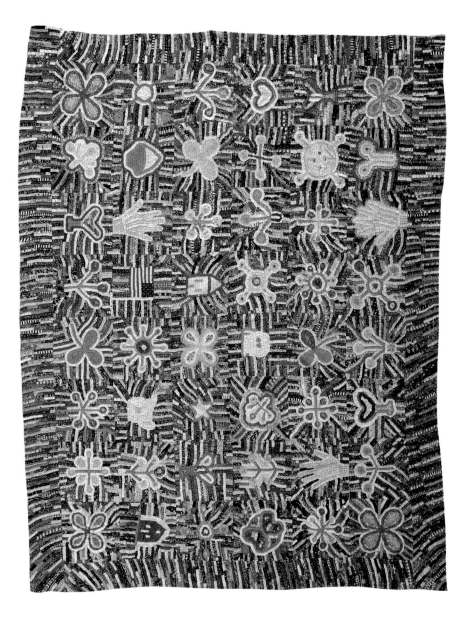

A rainbow in the sky is fleeting; in a flower garden it is temporary; but in a quilt it is forever. Billie Hansberger found her rainbow in acrylic paint tubes, selected a bouquet of beautiful flowers from a Gurney's seed catalog, and preserved them on a quilt. The project discovered very few painted quilts. However, in the hands of an artist, painting rather than appliquéing the flowers heightens realism and offers the quiltmaker the rainbow's entire spectrum.

[Plate 56]
STRING QUILT
83" x 67"

Mary E. Goudy, 1842–1931
Olney, Richland County, Illinois,
   circa 1898
Collection of Joe G. and Elizabeth Weiler

Although Mary was born in Miamisburg, Ohio, she spent most of her life in Richland County. The mother of nine children was in her fifties when she made the quilt. It consists of forty-eight blocks to which one-quarter-inch-wide strips of various colored fabrics are attached by a running stitch down the center of each thin strip. The pieces are gathered to give a slightly ruffled look, and the cut edges are not turned and stitched. The strips are stitched to a foundation fabric, and the individual blocks are sewn together by hand.

The pencil sketches visible on the backside of a few blocks are probably discarded patterns. They are almost identical to blocks that are in the quilt. The design was obviously redrawn on the side now covered by the string strips. This evidence seems to indicate that a design was drawn, outlined with string to create the desired image, and the rest of the block was filled with additional string strips. There is no backing, and the edge has never been bound. Most of the fabrics are cotton; there is no batting, and the work is all by hand. There is no quilting on this "quilt." When viewed from a distance, the work has the look of a hooked rug dating from the same era.

[Plate 57]
PAINTED FLOWERS
103" x 94"

Alice ("Billie") Grant Hansberger, 1920–
Cuba, Fulton County, Illinois, 1984
Collection of the maker

Billie Hansberger got the idea when she was in a painting class where the students discussed quilts; it's a fairly safe bet that Polly Wheelock was not in a painting class when her quilt idea began to germinate. Only the circumstances change with time; the ability to see the usual in an unusual way is timeless.

The only nontraditional element in Billie's quilt is the use of acrylic paint to achieve the design element. The top consists of white cotton/polyester blocks set together with printed blue cotton sashing surrounded by multiple-pieced borders of the same fabrics. The batting is polyester. The binding is back brought to front and hand stitched. It is machine pieced and quilted (9 stitches per inch) in parallel lines, cable, and grid patterns.

One look at Ned's Schoolhouse can leave the viewer saying, "Wow, why didn't I think of that?" That's a good question. It seems rather simple, but simple ideas are often the most difficult to accept, because they are simple. When a burst of creativity occurs, it is often difficult to remember all the ideas, until there is time to act upon them.

The traditional Schoolhouse pattern has enjoyed a long period of popularity and normally is presented in a simple, straightforward manner. An ordinary quiltmaker might consider using a nontradi-tional color, block size, or set, but when creative individuals give their imagination full rein, they may see things in an entirely different light. In this instance it might be more accurate to say, under a different sky.[2]

Not content to sew row after row of traditional red muslin school-houses with light-colored windows and doors on a white ground, this quiltmaker selected polished cotton in a subdued palette, placed the buildings under a night sky, and provided each structure with the soft glow of an evening light. Mary Ann also restricted her houses to the border and filled the center of the quilt with a geometric grid. While these intersecting lines appear to be multilane streets bisecting the city, they certainly are not expressways; each corner has a traffic light. A cotton backing covers the cotton batting, and the edges are turned in and finished without a binding. Construction is by machine, and the outline and star designs are quilted in black thread (4 stitches per inch).

When Mary Ann designed a quilt to honor a ten-year friendship, she saw the past in a delightfully contemporary perspective. Her dramatic presentation makes this Schoolhouse quilt explosively memorable.

[Plate 58]
NED'S SCHOOLHOUSE
72" x 71"

Mary Ann DeWitte-Chatterton, 1943–
Morrison, Whiteside County, Illinois,
    1987
Collection of the maker

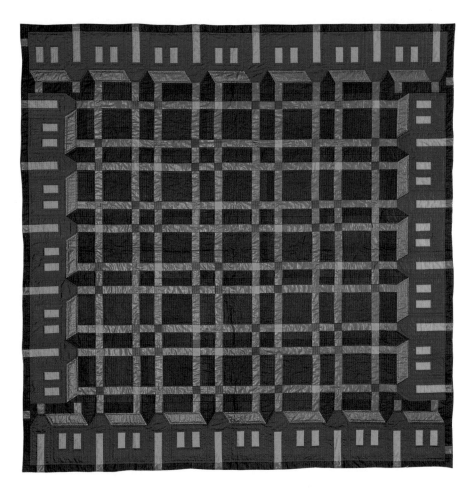

Nineteenth-century quilts are not limited to nonrepresentational pieced works. Many include recognizable objects ranging from the generic to things near and dear to the quilter and/or her friends and family. These are usually limited to flowers, birds, animals, and objects commonly found around the house. They can be appliquéd, embroidered, or quilted into the work. Today, a limited number of daring rule-breakers adventurously use textiles to recreate works of art originally produced in another medium to depict actual scenes, to display historic and contemporary photographic images, and to create original art. Once a barrier is breached, the field is wide open to individual interpretation. Doing something daring in quilting is not as unique as it was fifty years ago, but it is still difficult to do it well.

Without a doubt, this quilt is one of a kind. Within the massive pool of more than fifteen thousand quilts viewed by the registration day workers, the Fairy stands out as truly unforgettable. After the many Drunkard's Paths, Grandmother's Flower Gardens, and Dresden Plates have merged together, there is always the sweet glow of remembrance when someone mentions the Fairy quilt. No further description is needed. It stands alone.

Young, talented Ruby Lanning worked briefly for a Chicago art company. Her stay in the city was shortened by her parents' fear that life there was not safe for a girl from Belvidere; so she returned home, married, moved to Rockford, and became the mother of three children.

In the 1930s Mrs. Lundgren decided to make quilts for her children and asked each to select a pattern. One son chose an oriental scene he found on a *Saturday Evening Post* cover. His mother initially laughed but eventually decided to give it a

[Plate 59]
FAIRY
97" x 76"

Ruby M. Lanning Lundgren, 1885–1951
Rockford, Winnebago County, Illinois, 1936
Private collection

try and successfully completed the quilt. Her other son also chose an oriental scene, but her daughter selected the fairy.

The source of inspiration was a full-color page from *Printer's Inc.,* Volume 3, Number 6, Winter Fashions Number 1925, from Filene's Sons Company of Boston. The signature of artist Harold Gaze, 1924, is easily found. The gossamer-winged female seems to have flown into this scene after escaping from a Maxfield Parrish illustration.

After reviewing the mass of traditionally pieced and appliquéd quilts made in the 1930s, we found the

Fairy to be a truly radical concept because it turned to an advertising illustration for inspiration. The design is a derivative enlargement, rather than an original design. Few quilts registered by the Project rise to the level achieved by Ruby Lanning Lundgren.

The present owner recalls watching Mrs. Lundgren superimpose a grid over the original picture and use basting thread to create an identical grid on the cloth top so she could accurately enlarge the pattern. The appliquéd, embroidered, and tinted design is positioned on a cotton wholecloth ground framed by three narrow solid-color cotton borders. Neatly worked quilting (9 stitches per inch) in grid and echo hold the three layers together. Cotton batting was used between the top and the solid-colored cotton back. The edges are turned in. All appliqué and piece work are by hand.

In 1936 Mrs. Lundgren entered one of her sons' quilts in the third National Quilt Contest held in conjunction with the Eastern States Exposition in Massachusetts. It attracted 372 quilts from 39 states.[3] The Lundgren quilt featured a Japanese woman tending a white parrot in a black wire cage. The program lists it under "Four Specials," and it probably received one of the ribbons awarded for "quilts which merit special commendation." The judges recognized the White Parrot quilt as a "brilliant production, well

[Figure 32]
Ruby M. Lanning Lundgren
Born June 22, 1885, Belvidere, Boone
   County, Illinois
Died March 1, 1951, Rockford,
   Winnebago County, Illinois

[Plate 60]
The original fairy that inspired the quilt design appeared as a magazine advertisement in 1925.

executed, realistic and striking." Without question, the same superlatives apply to the Fairy.

Pat Denaxas, a Chicago-area native, has been quilting for approximately twelve years. Before becoming a self-taught quilter, she enjoyed landscape painting. She became intrigued by a friend's antique quilt collection and started making her own replicas as an alternative to purchasing the more expensive originals. She began by copying simple traditional patterns from photographs of antique quilts. Pat is not a full-time quilter; for the past twenty years she has been an ice-skating instructor for the Northbrook Park District.

Because she did not have much time to devote to quilting, she soon became dissatisfied with copying older designs and began creating larger original, primarily pictorial, quilts. Her first totally original work was the Wizard of Oz, a pieced representation of Dorothy and the other characters from the story.

Garden Nouveau was inspired by an ongoing interest in art nouveau and the decorative elements of that period in the early twentieth century. The quilt, based upon a stained-glass window called "Spring," was a first-place winner at the 1987 American Quilt Society Show at Paducah, Kentucky, and a Best of Show winner at the 1990 Illinois State Fair. Pat used books from the local library to research art nouveau designs, to establish the setting accurately, and to create the many small motifs. She incorporated elements from various illustrations, frontispieces, book bindings, and the decorative letters of the period.

Unlike most appliqué, which is often applied to a solid fabric piece, Garden Nouveau is applied to a background composed of small pieced squares of pink and peach cotton fabrics. Some of the fabrics used in the quilt are English Liberties used right side up, and in the dress of the woman they are placed wrong side out to produce a muted look.

Like most of her works, this quilt uses embroidery effectively. The quilting (8 stitches per inch) is done in parallel lines, chevrons, in-the-ditch, leaf, and echo motifs. The quilting threads match the various colored backgrounds. The straight-cut binding is applied by machine and by hand. Pat has made approximately twenty quilts, with her special interest being appliqué and reverse appliqué. Both techniques are featured in Garden Nouveau.

Starlight, Starbright, another quilt she designed, received an honorable mention in the 1991 Houston show and was a state winner in a contest sponsored by *Good Housekeeping* and the Lands End company. Her current project, Greek to Me, is a pieced and appliquéd quilt depicting the gods and goddesses of ancient Greece. No matter what name she may use, it is safe to predict that it will be well thought out, intricately designed, and painstakingly executed.

[Plate 61]
GARDEN NOUVEAU
91″ x 71″

Pat Pikul Denaxas, 1943–
Mount Prospect, Cook County, Illinois,
    1987
Collection of the maker

A number of quilts made during the last decade represent scenic views of actual places. The Brackebusch quilt depicts the family farm where Scott was reared; his mother made the quilt to commemorate his college graduation. Many members of Scott's family contributed drawings or helped quilt, and their names are stitched into a corner of the quilt.

When young Rosalie Bohnenstiehl was watching her grandmother, Louise Bohnenstiehl, piecing and quilting, it would be safe to say she never saw a quilt resembling this one in the frame. Mrs. Bohnenstiehl died in 1985 at age ninety-five. A lifetime quilter who was still working on her blocks in the retirement home, she set a high standard for Rosalie to achieve.

Since Rosalie's mother also was a quilter, it was probably inevitable that Rosalie would also pursue the craft. Appropriately, her first projects were crib quilts for son Scott in 1963 and daughter Pam in 1964. In 1982 Rosalie created a fifteen-block personalized quilt for Pam's high school graduation, and Grandma Melba Hunker helped with the quilting. It was so well received by the family that she began thinking about "doing our farm on a quilt for Scott for college graduation. I had seen a pattern for a pillow top depicting farm fields with different fabric."

Rosalie, however, was interested in more than fields. She knew what she wanted:

> I had to include the creek and big old tree down the hill west from the house, the grain handling system which is way out on the east end of the farmstead. The star on top of our grain leg was a welding project of Scott's in high school ag class. We had to have pets, pasture along the creek, the Old Barn built by my husband's grandfather, the new barn we built since we took over the farm, and the tractor and

> feed wagon which my husband uses two times a day.

She started with gusto but soon hit a roadblock. "Nothing I concocted resembled our house."

She decided to take a break and think about it. Then Scott came home from school for a weekend and asked her to make him a wall hanging. "I couldn't believe my ears! So I got out what I had completed and asked him what he thought of it. He was genuinely enthused." She knew she could not complete it in time for graduation, but since he was planning to go to graduate school she had a reprieve. Back to work she went with requests to aunts, uncles, siblings, and grandparents for drawings to use on the quilt.

The house remained a problem, and she left the project for almost a year. "Finally, I said this is as good as I can do and put one on, although I was never really satisfied with it." By the time she was almost finished, it was bigger than she had planned. It was not "square," and she knew it would "*never* hang right!" She was ashamed that it was "out of kilter" and had decided to tell the family "it didn't work out." She was preparing to burn it when her husband walked in. "I couldn't throw it in the fire with him in the house," she reported.

She looked at the quilt carefully and decided to add "a piece here and shave off some there (I almost cut off the end of a barn), and got it barely passable." It is machine appliquéd and hand quilted. She used

[Plate 62]
FARM SCENE
100" x 90"

Rosalie Bohnenstiehl Brackebusch,
    1940–
Divernon, Sangamon County, Illinois,
    1985–1989
Collection of Scott Brackebusch

hearts as a quilting motif because "I figured they represented all the love my family has for this farm and for the occupation of farming." It is quilted in different colors; thus there are colored outlines on the unbleached muslin back. She finished it the year Scott received his M.A. in Meats from the University of Illinois College of Agriculture, and the family gave her a vote of confidence.

There is nothing like a little success to give a quilter the encouragement to climb another mountain. Rosalie has photographs of her family quilt collection and plans to do a family calendar with a different picture for each month. But that is not all. "I have another son in college now, and I am starting to think of something for him. Most likely it will be the Montgomery County farm where we may retire." Would it be too much to hope there is no house on that farm?

What motivates a person to voluntarily undertake the stress that creative quiltmaking brings? "I guess I appreciate quilts," says Rosalie, "because they were so much a part of Grandma's life and she was so much a part of mine." Undoubtedly, Rosalie and her one-of-a-kind farmstead quilts will be part of the Brackebusch family life for generations to come.

Like most creative individuals, Lula ("Lou") Clark doesn't worry about being different. Instead of merely drawing images of fantasies or farms, Lou used actual photographs, it's obvious she also is not concerned about having planted a family tree upside down. Of course she knows the trunk is usually reserved for the family's founding father and mother with the latest generation dangling in the uppermost branches. It just happens this quiltmaker has a very good reason for reversing the order of things. Her purpose is to explain the family world to her grandchildren, not to demonstrate to Great-grandpa exactly how many

progeny he has and to whom they all belong.

A few years ago Lou saw a wall hanging made with photo negatives on linen. She decided she wanted to make a quilt using all the pictures she could find of her grandchildren's ancestors. Locating all the needed pictures, she had them printed on fabric; making the quilt took three years. Some of the couples seen on the quilt are composites created from two different pictures, or the pair was picked out of a group photo and enlarged. Her sister-in-law, who operates a monogramming service, volunteered to write everyone's name on the quilt. In creating the tree design, Lou carefully calculated how to have everyone arranged in chronological order and yet keep all the faces on the top rather than on the part that normally falls on the side.

The quilt is meant to be viewed from the foot of the bed. The base of the trunk has Lou's two grandchildren, Franz Milner, born March 26, 1985, and Dana Milner, born January 8, 1988. Above them are their parents, Joni Clark Milner, daughter of the quiltmaker, and her husband, Michael Milner. The quilt illustrates six generations. The earliest recorded birth years are in the 1830s and 1840s.

Lou, whose interest in the quilt was furthered by her long-standing involvement with genealogy, has retained all the negatives in case she wishes to make another one. The quilt is made primarily of cotton/polyester with a polyester batting. The straight-cut handmade binding matches the print used on the quilt top. It is stitched by machine on the front and completed by hand on the back. Both the piecing and the appliqué are by machine. The quilting design includes a farm scene, parallel lines, roping, flowers, and fans in the border.

Lou Clark has proven that where there is creativity and technology, there is the possibility of developing a totally new concept in quilt-

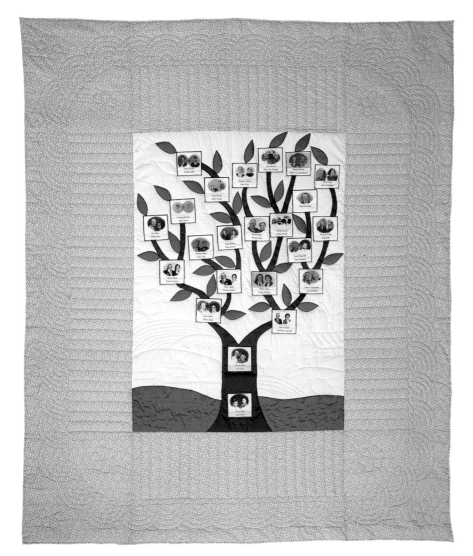

[Plate 63]
THE FAMILY TREE
100" x 87"

Lula Herpstreith Clark, 1935–
Hillsboro, Montgomery County, Illinois,
    1991
Collection of the maker

The transition from representational quilts to those based upon the quilter's personal interpretation can be jarring. What do you see in Grace Stetson's Nine Patch? In what tone and with what character does this quilt speak to you through the mazelike grid, the juxtapositioning of solids and prints, or the contrast of the printed cottons against the solid colors? What was the quilter's intent? What view of her Illinois, her life, her inner world has she invited us to see? Six decades offer a perspective on life. Was this the canvas Grace used to record her story in an era that offered limited opportunities for sixty-year-old housewives in small-town Illinois?

Don't be lulled into believing this or most any other quilt is "just a quilt," a utilitarian object created out of leftover scraps recycled into a second life, the work of a loving, but simple, housewife fulfilling the role assigned to her by society. Far from it. One may wonder what Grace Bumphrey would have become if she had been born in 1978 instead of 1878. Would she have had time to make a quilt? Perhaps her life, like many of ours, would have become a patchwork of many unrecorded expressions and experiences. Had that happened, the scenery along the quilt paths of Illinois would be less colorful.

making. Few photographs have appeared on Illinois quilts, and certainly nothing else in the over fifteen thousand Project registrations has a family tree that looks like this. By reversing the generational arrangement and using photographs, Grandma Clark made it possible for Franz and Dana Milner to study their family heritage "from the bottom up."

Each quilt has a point of view. Even the most casual glance at Lou Clark's ancestors immediately conveys the quilt's purpose. The detail in Rosalie Brackebusch's colorful appliqué makes it obvious to most

viewers that she has captured in fabric the essence of a particular Illinois farmstead. Despite the representational nature of the quilt, it is, nevertheless, not totally accurate in the dimensions of how the images are related to one another. Like many works of art, it is seen through the eye and the abilities of the creator.

[Plate 64]
NINE PATCH
84" x 71"

Grace Bumphrey Stetson, 1878–1949
Neponset, Bureau County, Illinois,
   circa 1940
Collection of Nancy Stetson

If Grace Stetson had a sewing machine,
it never touched this quilt. All the work
is by hand, and it is cotton throughout

the top, back, batt, and binding. It is
quilted in outline and circles within the
squares (8 stitches per inch). Grace was
organized but not inflexible; she tolerated digression without totally dis-
rupting the prescribed decorum. Her
example is worth a second thought; we
are never too old to dream.

The old adage that there is nothing new under the sun certainly applies to quilts. Commercial revivals of traditional patterns can create the stereotype that the past was sterile. The Project discovered, however, that innovation, creativity, and personal vision is not new in Illinois. Contemporary quilter Nancy Green, who prefers to think in terms of line and color, is continuing the proud tradition of her nineteenth- and early twentieth-century counterparts Polly Wheelock and Grace Stetson.

Changed Perspective may push further in bending established tradition than many quilters care to go, but at the same time we must remember that the use of straight and curved lines, as well as a playful use of hues and shades of harmonious and contrasting colors, is a long-standing tradition in quilting. Each generation has produced quilters with the loving hearts and creative hands that touch fabrics and bring forth beauty from a union unrecognized by the casual observer.[4]

For some new quilters like Nancy, the introduction into the field comes from neither a knowledge of quilting nor a family interest in the craft, but rather from an inherited eye for textiles. Her Yugoslavian grandfather, a tailor who migrated to Chicago to join distant relatives after World War I, illustrated the merit of patience and the willingness to tackle complicated procedures, but it was her grandmother who taught her how to do this. An academic career led her further into textiles, and when she "discovered quilts in 1986, something clicked. I liked the idea that my quilts might become heirlooms, whereas all the work, love, and care that went into my clothes was unappreciated when they went out of style."

Her husband, John, likes art quilts because he appreciates their originality. He helped her experiment with the original strips of paper, cutting and taping them until the idea jelled. Changed Perspectives was her first large quilt. Nancy's European background freed her from

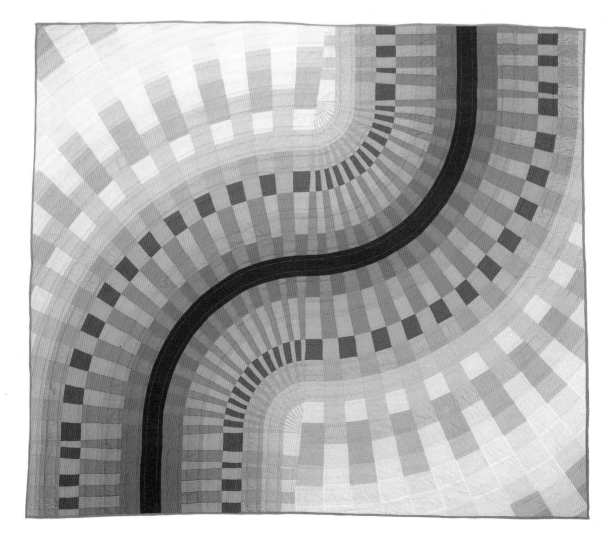

any tie to quilting's traditional format. She wanted to work with her own ideas rather than use an existing pattern. Her major obstacle was creating the curves she so clearly wanted and did not know how to achieve.

"I want to do some sort of quilt with curves. Everything seems to be done in blocks — *not a repetition* — I know I don't want to deal with appliqué. Lauri said to match all the marks for each piece, but I'm afraid of puckering, bulges, etc. Oh well, I'll have to let it percolate," she entered into her quilting diary on April 23, 1987. Now she feels that bending a straight line is a great way to tackle the problem, but she was unaware of it at the time. Despite the initial impression made by the quilt, Nancy claims there are no sewn curves.

The idea did percolate. A couple of weeks later she wrote on May 9, 1987:

> I've been playing around with little strips of paper that I've colored with [horizontal lines made by a] magic marker. Moving them creates different designs — I was cutting them up and down. John suggested cutting them in pie shapes — that's it! They really move now — I can get them to curve. This would be the way to go. I didn't want to fuss with appliqué, etc. I have to make more models and play with it some more, but this is the *direction!*

She later learned that her experimental adventure led her to what others already knew as Seminole piecing.

Fabric selection proved to be more difficult than she expected. On June 5, 1987, Nancy noted that "Joy went with me to Stitches and Stuffing — I'm glad she came along. We went looking all over for gradations of color." Her project came to a temporary standstill when she could not find the desired colors. A short time later, a presentation at a quilt guild meeting inspired her to dye

her own fabrics. Once again the novice sought professional help. No workshops were available. She spent the summer of 1988 teaching herself how to dye fabric.

Nancy's relatively short career in quilting has offered her a changed perspective in three important ways. First, she has learned that working with curves is an ongoing process, and she is only beginning her trek. Second, her adventure offered valuable lessons in creating customized color gradations that will be the foundation for further refinement. Finally, the ongoing process reinforced the value of collaboration, for making the quilt top more than just stitched together pieces of fabrics. John developed an interest in helping her work out the spatial relationships of straight line curves, and she found herself becoming much better acquainted with the Chicago Bears while quilting her way through each football game.

Is it realistic abstraction or abstract realism? Does art imitate life or life imitate art? In truth, it was an innocent experiment that involved neither art nor life! Charlene ("Char") Koelling, who is always willing to try something new, was just having fun when this all began. During the early 1970s she and her husband, Alfred, were attempting to learn more about natural and aniline dyes. While they were dyeing wool fabric for rug hooking, Char did batik and tie-dyed fabrics for skirts, shirts, pillows, and finally miscellaneous pieces of muslin. It was an experiment.

In an attempt to see what could be created with tie-dyeing, she used different kinds of knots and multiple ties of string and rubber bands. The work was accomplished with old Rit and Putnam dyes purchased at an auction. She freely admits that "no thought went into saving something for posterity, I just had fun. Ultimately, I carefully examined what

[Plate 65]
CHANGED PERSPECTIVE
89" x 77"

Nancy Korhorn Green, 1949–
LaGrange, Cook County, Illinois, 1988
Collection of the maker

[Plate 66]
THE FIREWORKS QUILT
82" x 72"

Charlene Prasse Koelling, 1937–
Springfield, Sangamon County,
    Illinois, 1973
Collection of the maker

I had, decided the fabric looked like Fourth of July fireworks, and made a quilt."

What could be more exciting than to create a textile design without any specific goal in mind, and then let the resulting motif in the fabric lead you logically to a quilt? Since the "blocks" were random size, Char's first task was to dye some plain space fillers. Al helped her lay the "blocks" in "rows," and after developing several different patterns, they decided to have an even edge only at the top and to let the blocks protrude irregularly around the other three sides.

A flannel sheet separates the all-cotton top and back. The binding is cotton tie-dyed handmade bias tape, machine stitched on the front and hand sewn on the back. The piecing is by machine. Although Char enjoys quilting, she decided bisecting the explosion patterns in any way would detract, so the quilting (5 stitches per inch) was restricted to the edges of each block.

The quilt has hung on the wall since 1976, and the owners freely admit that "the colors are now definitely less strident than they were originally. We now think more in terms of history and preserving handmade items, but at the time this was made just for fun and done in time for our country's bicentennial." To their guests it may be an issue of art or life, but for Al and Char it daily recalls the celebration's spectacular pyrotechnical fanfare.

Why Not Try It: Nontraditional Quilting Fabrics

Quilts can be made out of the strangest fabrics. Numerous registrations for twentieth-century quilts indicate many pieced tops resulted from scraps acquired from local clothing fabricators. Remnants from seamstresses, dress factories, and millinery shops are not unusual, but swimsuit material and camouflage fabric from a cap factory are two unusual examples recorded by the Project. It probably can truthfully be said that there is not a scrap of some type of material that someone somewhere has not used in making a quilt.

Illinois quilters have successfully combined an off-beat idea and an unlikely fabric with a determined never-say-die spirit to produce some "unusual" quilted bedcoverings. The pristine quality exhibited by these six quilts indicates each maker never intended the quilt would ever be used for anything more than display. In that regard they resemble the show quilts of the past; and like many of those extravagant creations, they are being, and will be, passed from generation to generation within the maker's family.

[Plate 67]
PINEAPPLE
90" x 75"

Fanny Beyer Pershina, 1893–1992
Belvidere, Boone County, Illinois, 1932–1935
Collection of Mary A. Parker

The Project registered numerous Pineapple quilts. Thus when wishing to recall this particular one, something more distinctive than the pattern name was needed to insure instant recall. But all the workers knew what was meant when anyone mentioned "the corset quilt."

Fanny Pershina, originally from Morton, lived in Belvidere during the Great Depression where she acquired corset scraps from a small local company specializing in making women's undergarments. She combined the peach-colored rayon factory scraps with green cotton to create the Pineapple pattern top.

The maker did the piecing, but, because of the thickness of the fabric, she hired a local woman to quilt it on a sewing machine. The pieced blocks are all quilted in-the-ditch, but the solid pink cotton border has a floral motif. A cotton flannel sheet was used for batting, and the binding is straight-cut handmade green cotton stitched by machine. Corset scraps certainly must rank near the top of the list of unusual quilt fabrics.

If Julie Rutt didn't have a magic wand, she certainly had an enchanted needle when she turned her brother's ugly old neckties into an attractive new quilt. Only a few Project registrants brought quilts made from this unlikely fabric.

In the early 1980s, Julie's brother worked for a lumber company and was required to wear a tie. He felt this was unnecessary for that job, and so he scouted the local resale shops and chose to wear ties that ranged from "unusual" to "downright ugly." After several years, he changed jobs, but his tie collection remained in the closet. One Sunday Julie saw a beautiful quilt made out of ties pictured in the Chicago *Tribune*. She thought it would be the perfect Christmas gift, headed for her brother's house, and returned with his prized ties. It was a good start, but she needed more.

In 1985 her family visited friends in Kansas. While shopping in Lawrence, they found a resale shop with a selection of ties second to none. Julie reports, "We had an hour's worth of fun sorting them to make sure the word 'ugly' was stamped all over each tie." Many ties she selected had been there for so long the shop owner reduced the price from twenty-five to twenty cents each and also threw in a couple of extras.

Back in Illinois when Julie began working on the quilt, she noticed a strange thing happening. As she put the ties together, the quilt's design consumed the individual ties, and she found the result surprisingly beautiful. The fans are appliquéd by hand to the thirty machine-pieced blocks. The edges are turned in, and she used a polyester batting. The quilting (4–7 stitches per inch) out-

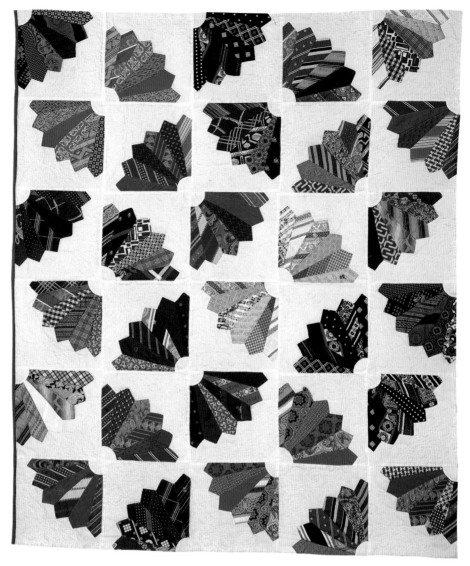

[Plate 68]
GRANDMOTHER'S FAN
88" x 75"

Julie Rutt, 1955–
Lombard, DuPage County, Illinois, 1985
Collection of Michael R. Swanson

lines the ties and creates floral motifs. The other five quilts she has made since taking a class in 1981 are "normal." However, this one is a distinctive reminder of her brother's tie collection and her shopping trip in Kansas.[5]

[Plate 69]
FLOUR SACK LOGO QUILT
83″ x 65″

Elegant synthetic fiber fabrics suitable for men's formal neckwear and for women's undergarments are not the only unusual materials honored by use in a fancy quilt top. More ordinary fabrics, such as cotton flour sacks and everyday blue jeans, also have their individual champions. These innovative quilters decided not to worry about the raised eyebrows, and their attention-grabbing quilts have enjoyed admiration rather than scorn.

When cloth sacks became the commonplace container for household staples such as sugar, salt, and flour, and for livestock feed, it was inevitable that some creative housewives would find a secondary use for this soft, lightweight cotton fabric. For more than a half-century after being introduced in the late 1800s, cotton sacking met a wide variety of fabric needs in America's rural areas.

It is true that those who could afford little else did rely upon bleached sacks to help clothe all family members—father, mother, and children. Cotton sacking enjoyed widespread use for home-made undergarments, as well as for outerwear and various household needs. However, the use of this utilitarian textile was not of necessity limited to impoverished families. Most rural households recycled them for some utilitarian function such as quilting. Sacking could be bleached, washed, dyed, and cut into prescribed shapes and used for piecing or appliqué work the same as any other cotton fabric.

Perhaps there is some truth to the idea that sack quilts were made primarily by families who could afford nothing else. They made them, used them, wore them out, and discarded them. It is also possible there are other scenarios. Some makers may have created an embroidered sack quilt because it became a conversation piece or the sacks provided a usable embroidery pattern

Hannah McDonald Crose, 1862–1947
Iuka, Marion County, Illinois, circa 1900
Collection of Grace E. Turner

The quilt is composed of fifteen different sacks, five in each of the three rows. Two rows face one side of the quilt, and a single row faces the opposite way. While there is extensive embroidery on each logo, every part of every brand is not embroidered. Some words in blue ink remain, because they did not wash out completely. They probably would have disappeared over the years if the quilt had been washed every year. The seams between the sacks which form each "block" are covered with chain stitch embroidery. The quilting (6 stitches per inch) is a double line grid.

Three sacks are from Illinois firms: Kohl and Meyer, Centralia (Marion County); Carnation wheat flour, W. L. Holman, Clay City (Clay County); and Aviston Milling Company, Aviston (Clinton County). The remaining sacks are either unidentified by place or are from out of state.

[Plate 70]
Nine uncut printed cotton feed sacks
Private collections

Barbara Brackman defines *feed sack* as a "midwestern term for the cotton bags in which grain and staple goods" were sold in large numbers during the 1930s and 1940s. Thousands of pieces of this fabric can be found in quilts today.

for someone filling in idle hours during a long winter.

Could the embroidered flour sack quilt have been a fad of only temporary importance? Was it removed from display on a guest bed when the novelty wore off, put away, and forgotten? When it was later discovered by another generation, could it have been misinterpreted as a symbol of past poverty? Unfortunately, many descendants wanting to avoid association with low financial status destroyed these quilts through incorrect assumptions of their socio-economic significance. Were flour sack quilts routinely disposed of or used as packing blankets for family moves? What additional reasons might explain why so few embroidered logo quilts have surfaced? There must have been more made than have appeared. The very scarcity of this quilt genre has thus far accorded them little historical investigation.[6]

It is obvious that Hannah McDonald Crose, who spent hours working on her embroidered flour-sack quilt, regarded it highly enough to use it as a decorative rather than a utilitarian piece and passed it on to her foster son, who also chose not to use it before giving it to his sister. The maker and the family overlooked its humble origins and accorded it heirloom status.

Hannah was born in Romine Township near Iuka on April 7, 1862; she married and lived in Neoga for a time before returning to Iuka around 1900. The quilt probably was made in the early twentieth century. She had no children of her own but reared William Moyer after the death of his mother, and she later gave him the quilt. Before he died, he gave it to his sister, Grace E. Turner.

One Illinois-made sack quilt even reached the White House, although it was very different from Hannah's prized piece. It was a gift to Mrs. Herbert Hoover from Mrs. J. L. Murray of Bloomington, Illinois. Mrs. Murray attributed her "streak of thrift to her pioneer grandmother." A May 1926 *Needlecraft Magazine* article noted Mrs. Hoover's interest in quilts, and her husband's 1928 presidential victory inspired the maker to create a quilt from flour sacks as an inauguration gift. By bleaching and dyeing the sacks, she was able to create a blue and white Irish Chain quilt.[7]

Today the careful observer can examine a quilt and occasionally detect the faint trace of a printed sack logo that did not bleach out entirely. It does not, however, require a trained textile detective to recognize a sack quilt made with embroidered flour company logos. Identification is easy; finding one is difficult. Sack–logo quilts are, indeed, rare in comparison with the more widely available cotton quilts pieced from printed feed sacks, which are often difficult to identify. Chameleon-like, they disguise their humble origins. The loosely woven cottons, printed with stylish motifs in contemporary colors, purposely imitate the currently popular inexpensive fabrics available in local stores. It takes an experienced eye to examine a pieced quilt and correctly identify the scraps that originated as mid-twentieth-century feed sacking.

From the 1930s to the 1950s, these colorful cotton sacks successfully replaced purchased fabrics for a variety of household needs. A problem surfaced when a maker of clothing, curtains, or a quilt found there was not enough matching fabric on hand to complete the project. This was often resolved by exchanging sacks with neighbors and friends. Labels, attached with watersoluble glue, enabled the user to safely remove the company identification without destroying the fabric. Reuse of sacking was so commonplace that the Textile Bag Manufacturers of Chicago issued a Depression-era pamphlet "Sewing with Cotton Bags." Surprisingly, it mentioned only white sacks and omitted any reference to the printed textiles that authorities believe were already available at the time it was printed. Despite the many quilt tops using printed cotton sacking, no period publication mentions this widespread practice.[8]

While denim has a long and honorable history, it is not usually the fabric of choice when one thinks about making a quilt. The word is an Anglicization of the French term *serge de Nîmes,* a twilled woolen cloth long made in France. By the late eighteenth century it was also being woven in cotton. Historically it was a "washable, strong, stout twilled cotton cloth, made of single yarn, and either dyed in the piece or woven with dark brown or dark blue warp and white filling."[9] Through the centuries, its durability made it popular with rural and urban workingmen. Levi Strauss used it to create his jeans for the California gold miners. In the last half of the twentieth century it became a fabric of high fashion.

When Karen Keller was born in California, she entered a world dominated by denim; it was literally everywhere and used for everything. When she taught herself how to quilt, it was natural that she would see this multihued indigo-dyed fabric as inspiration for an explosive quilting concept. Once Upon a Time is a fantastic nocturnal overview of a castellated and turreted fortress reminiscent of the Golden State's Magic Kingdom.

Working with 100 percent used denim blue jeans and the details from those jeans, Karen gave reality to a personal vision. It is pieced and appliquéd by machine. A polyester batting is covered by the cotton/polyester back, which is brought to the front for a binding and is stitched on the front. The quilting motifs (7–8 stitches per inch) include outline, clamshell, diamonds, and feathering.

[Plate 71]
ONCE UPON A TIME
83″ x 70″

Karen L. Keller, 1953–
Chrisman, Edgar County, Illinois, 1986
Collection of the maker

Fair Ribbons As Quilt Fabric

Contests to select the best or the most beautiful are widespread in America today. Historically, this is not a new trend. Derived from the old French term meaning a "holiday or festival" where products were exhibited and buyers and sellers gathered, fairs continue to provide education and entertainment. In medieval Europe the price procured at a market-day fair for an agricultural or household product was often considered the final decision in determining the best and most desirable local commodity in any given category. America's English colonists brought that tradition to the New World.

As American farmers developed an interest in scientific farming, there was an increased desire to obtain the best breeding stock possible. How could that be determined by the marketplace alone when all the good animals were not for sale? Where would a farmer interested in upgrading his herd turn to find the community's best sire from which to select his next bull? A solution was soon found.

During the early nineteenth century, progressive farmers organized local and statewide agricultural societies. Through meetings and publications, members shared their ideas and experimental research to increase yields, develop improved bloodlines, and encourage new production techniques. To reach a wider audience, these societies created the American agricultural fair as a popular educational substitute for the European market festival.

When the Illinois State Agricultural Society organized in 1853, it stressed the need for an agricultural university and for a state fair. Both were viewed as educational opportunities. During the society's meeting at Springfield's

American House in May 1853, members adopted plans for the first state fair. It enjoyed a four-day run at Springfield in October 1854. Until 1893, when a permanent fairgrounds was established in the capital, the fair enjoyed a nomadic existence by meeting in Chicago, Alton, Peoria, Centralia, Freeport, Jacksonville, Decatur, Quincy, DuQuoin, Ottawa, and Olney.[10]

Awarding a blue, red, or white ribbon as a symbol of achievement is a practice of long standing. Ordinarily, an individual or a family accumulated relatively small numbers of these colorful souvenirs. The inability to undertake long trips, except on the railroad, generally precluded exhibiting one's prizewinning livestock, agricultural produce, or household items beyond the

local region. However, with the development of the internal combustion engine and the rapid proliferation of cars and trucks throughout the state's rural areas in the post-World War I era, that restriction was eliminated. For some families the competitive spirit knew no bounds.

Merlyn and Mabel Bowman moved to the family farm in 1945 so their five-year-old son David could grow up in the country. He became

[Plate 72]
SHOW RIBBONS AND SCHOOL
   LETTERS
88″ x 84″

Mabel Stambaugh Bowman, 1912–
Astoria, Fulton County, Illinois, 1983
Collection of Lanny Brian Bowman

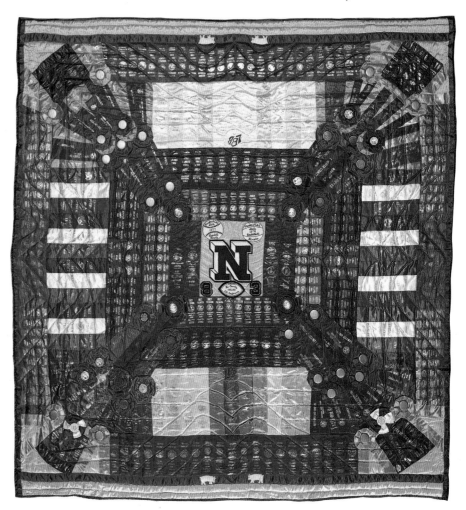

[Figure 33]
Mabel Bowman
Born September 11, 1912, Ipava, Fulton
  County, Illinois
Mabel is shown with three of her four
  grandsons.

a 4–H member and exhibited White Rock chickens, Hampshire hogs, Corriedale sheep, garden produce, and handicraft items at the Fulton County fair, hanging his ribbons on the wall.

In high school David joined the Future Farmers of America, and, as his knowledge and abilities increased, he showed his hogs at Peoria's Heart of Illinois Fair and at the Illinois State Fair in Springfield. When he was ready for college in 1959, his mother suggested preserving the memories associated with his winnings in the form of a quilt. David agreed and helped her lay out the ribbons on a sheet. Between her farm chores that winter, Mabel worked on the ribbon quilt. Despite the fact the Fulton County Fair premium list had no category for it, the quilt was exhibited at the Lewistown fair in 1960 and drew widespread attention.

David graduated from college, continued working with swine, married an Angus cattle exhibitor he met at the state fair, and eventually began his own hog operation at Sciota. His four sons, born between 1964 and 1971, exhibited Hampshire, Chester White, Duroc, and Yorkshire hogs. From the Schuyler County fair in early July through the McDonough, Knox, Warren, Hancock, and Peoria shows to the state fair in early August, the brothers were busy. Every summer the family worked together, and Grandma Bowman sat at ringside holding the ribbons they collected, one at a time.

With Randy and Lanny looking forward to high school graduation in 1982 and 1983, Mabel said, "Get your ribbons together and Grandma will make you a quilt." Each boy created his own design, and again her needle entwined love, memories, and experience with the brightly colored ribbons. The top of the quilt is composed chiefly of synthetic fiber fair ribbons, supplemented by cotton basketballs and high school activity letters, as well as white felt

pigs. The back is a synthetic velvet, and the batting is polyester. The binding is back brought to front. The ribbons were assembled in part by hand and in part by machine. The quilting (5 stitches per inch) is in parallel lines with black thread.

In order to treat all the boys equally, Mabel decided she should continue making the ribbon quilts while she was able to do the work. Jon's was completed in 1984 and Dan's in 1985. The leftovers have gone into wedding gifts for the boys. Mabel Bowman deserves an award of her own, for she has surely set an Illinois record. So far, out of the more than fifty quilts she has completed since learning the technique at the age of six, nine are made of fair ribbons.

Three generations of Bowmans have successfully worked together to accomplish many goals. With needle and thread Mabel Bowman has tied their memories together and created a lasting legacy for her family . . . one stitch at a time.

Blanche Elbert would probably smile and say that entering fair competitions for more than fifty years was something she never thought about; it was simply a way of life. She generally found the difficult and demanding work to be relaxing and rewarding. Competition gave her the opportunity to do what she did best, and she loved it. As the oldest of three children, she acquired skills in the practical arts by helping her mother and her neighbors. She learned the important art of showmanship from her father who bred and exhibited Duroc hogs throughout central Illinois and at the state fair. Her turn came at the 1931 Weston Picnic.

These earliest awards, carefully identified on the first page in her scrapbook, are unmarked strips of narrow ribbon. Although most local fairs that survived the Great Depression began purchasing factory-made ribbons again by the mid-thirties, the Fairbury fair used short pieces of hand-cut ribbon during the entire decade. Blanche knew the value of neatness and quality. Her embroidery and cutwork were without knots or jumps, and the back of each piece was as neat as the front. She was already an expert seamstress when she saved enough money in the 1920s to buy a new Singer treadle sewing machine, which she began using to quilt and to piece.

Food preservation and prepara-

tion were other interests. She loved to cook, whether it was an everyday meal or a banquet, and over the years her yeast breads and cakes won many prizes, as did her jars of canned fruits and vegetables. When she quit exhibiting, at age seventy-eight, she gathered together her well-used booklets, clippings, and handwritten notes, carefully placed them in a kitchen drawer, and appended a simple note: "These are my fair recipes." Her quiet warmth and friendly ways concealed a competitive spirit and an intense pride in her accomplishments.

When she married Elmer Elbert in 1933, Blanche moved her sewing machine, her new cedar chest, her quilts, and a good supply of hand-embroidered household linens into

[Plate 73]
GARDEN PATH
55" x 41"

Blanche Funkhouser Elbert, 1907–1990
Forrest, Livingston County, Illinois, 1936
With Illinois State Fair prizes of Blanche Elbert
Collection of Duane and Rachel Elbert

After her 1933 marriage, Blanche made a number of crib quilts, which she exhibited at the Illinois State Fair. During that decade she kept her ribbons in a scrapbook. She won her first state fair blue ribbon on a quilt in 1937 and her last in 1968. The 1937 prize-winning entry and its ribbon are illustrated, along with the silver cream and sugar set she won in 1968 when her ribbon quilt was chosen Best of Show.

She devoted her final eighteen years of state fair exhibiting to cutwork, embroidery, and clothing construction. She regularly won blue ribbons, and to the end of her long career, she took home several purple rosettes each year. She retired in 1986 after receiving five champion awards at a single state fair. Although still capable of doing skillful needlework, she feared the slow, but irreversible, deterioration of her eyesight would eventually lead to a decline in the quality of her products. She continued to sew for herself but could not be dissuaded from a decision to stop exhibiting while at the peak of her success.

a farm home near Forrest. She kept on taking her handiwork to the local fairs at Fairbury, Pontiac, Melvin, and Farmer City. A third-prize white ribbon on a pair of pajamas gave Blanche her first Illinois State Fair award in 1936. She returned every year until World War II closed the fair after the 1941 season. During these years, the young couple enjoyed an annual August vacation by working at the fair and living in its "tent city."

Her first state fair blue ribbon came on a baby quilt in 1937. During those years she exhibited various quilts identified in the scrapbook as appliquéd, child's, duckies, artistic, bunnies, and sunflower. She also has 1941 Indiana State Fair ribbons for Domestic Arts, and her extensive photographic collection documents the family's visit to that fair. Then World War II closed the Illinois State Fair, and gas rationing limited travel. Her only 1942 ribbons are from Pontiac. When the war ended, ten-year-old Duane joined 4–H and started his own ribbon collection.

Blanche soon returned to county and state fair competition. In addition to preparing her own entries, she and Elmer helped Duane with his sheep, rabbit, grain, vegetable, and flower exhibits. The three worked together in the field and in the dairy barn while following a hectic schedule that every summer took them to fifteen fairs from DuQuoin in the south to Sandwich in the north. The hard work financed Duane's college education. With the exception of Rachel and Duane's wedding in August 1958, and Elmer's sudden death in July 1962, the smoothly functioning team rarely missed a beat.

A fair ribbon quilt was Blanche and Duane's long-standing ambition. By the 1960s they had more than enough ribbons and almost as many ideas. Winning ribbons was easy; deciding how to make the quilt was hard. Ribbons come in different sizes, fabrics, and shades of a single color. Using ribbons from

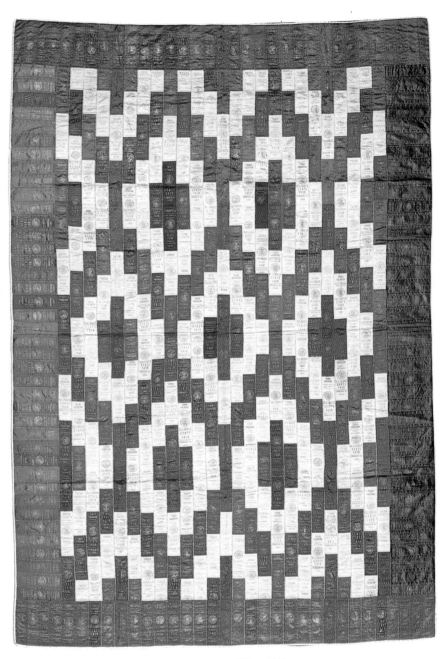

[Plate 74]
STATE FAIR RIBBONS
103" x 73"

Blanche Funkhouser Elbert, 1907–1990
Forrest, Livingston County, Illinois, 1968
Collection of Duane and Rachel Elbert

[Figure 34]
Blanche Olive Funkhouser Elbert
Born December 5, 1907, Weston,
  McLean County, Illinois
Died March 11, 1990, Fairbury,
  Livingston County, Illinois

only one fair would provide uniformity, and what would be better than those from the state fair?

Duane wanted a quilt with a unified pattern and color design. He selected blue, purple, and white. The intent to leave the ribbons as intact as possible inevitably necessitated the rectangular shape of each piece, while the desire to make it easily read from one direction dictated the vertical arrangement. Quite by accident, it assumed an Irish Stitch design. After finally making a decision, they laid out the ribbons and discovered there were not enough blues to complete the border. They returned to the state fair the next year and came home with the much-needed quilt pieces.

Whenever Duane came home during the winter of 1966–67, out came the ribbons. He matched his uniformly cut pieces with the pattern and pinned them; Blanche did the machine stitching. The top is composed completely of synthetic fiber ribbons; the batting is a flannel sheet; and the back is cotton sheeting. The binding is handmade bias-cut synthetic fabric stitched by machine on the front and by hand on the back. The quilting (6 stitches per inch) outlines each ribbon. At last,

in August 1968, Blanche entered it as a pieced quilt at the Illinois State Fair. It won its own blue ribbon in the pieced quilt class and was also selected for the Best of Show award. It was an excellent way to end a quilting career.

A Look at Age and Gender: Nontraditional Quilters

The mere mention of the words *quilt* or *quilter* immediately brings to mind someone we once knew who made a quilt we used or admired. In almost every instance, the image is that of a female. It also is likely that she is in her golden years. Like baking wonderful cookies, quilting is something grandmas naturally do. Although everyone can think of a grandmother who doesn't know how to thread a needle, much less quilt, that doesn't destroy the stereotype.

From the colonial era through the early twentieth century, mothers or grandmothers were responsible for

teaching little girls to sew, and this often included quilting. The primary focus of their childhood was not education for a career outside the home, but preparation for the adult role society then assigned girls. A female child was to be thoroughly prepared to marry, assume command of the household, and raise her own family. Not all, however, intended to become quilters.

In an early-twentieth-century magazine story, Abby Jane pleaded for permission to work a cardboard motto as the other little girls did during recess at school.

"Please, Aunt Mitty!" "Not till you have finished piecing that quilt," returned Miss Mitty sternly. "Why, when I was your age I had pieced a whole bedspread and made a shirt for my father—all by hand—and you couldn't have told any two of them stitches apart, either. I guess machine-work wouldn't have been thought much of those days!" . . . "I wish just once, I might have something like other little girls. I'd get up early every day to work on the patchwork," she added tremulously. "Abby Jane, when I've said a thing you know 'tain't a bit of use saying another word about it. Have you done your stint today?"

"No'm," faltered Abby. "Then you can just sit down and 'tend to it. When it's done you may go into the spare-room and take the pins out of the bedspread," returned Aunt Mitty. "If you can't remember that duty comes before pleasure it's my duty to learn you," she added solemnly.[11]

One is left to wonder if Abby Jane ever voluntarily worked on a quilt again.

The emphasis was clearly on conforming to prescribed standards of behavior. During the nineteenth century and well into the twentieth, very few women refused. However, those who did break with tradition left their mark upon history. There were also those who unwillingly adhered to society's requirements but were not motivated to learn their lessons well. Some never mastered sewing a straight seam; many never became adept at darning stockings; and others apparently could not put in ten quilting stitches to the inch.

Some Project respondents report being taught the art of sewing as a young girl. A few also indicate they learned to piece and quilt as a child, but for the most part those who quilted in their youth generally did it during the teen years, usually during the last few years before their marriage. At least one woman working during the 1950s reported completing a quilt as a 4–H project during her early college years.

Inferences drawn from reading quilt registration forms suggest that a woman often learned quilting techniques as a child, then married, and reared a family. While devoting her waking hours to tasks that had to be done for the family, there was no time for pleasure sewing. The ability to use the quilting skills learned several decades earlier did not come until the children were old enough to assume important household responsibilities. This sometimes happened about the time the quilts a woman brought

into the marriage were beginning to deteriorate. Then she could reactivate her quilting skills, begin making new bedcovers for her household, and provide some items for when her children married. Many used the spare time of their mature years, perhaps from age fifty to eighty, as prime-time quilting.

Girls generally began doing straight stitching as soon as they could learn to thread and hold a needle. Mary Mabel ("Mame")

Firoved was obviously one of those many little girls who were required to sit patiently and sew simple little cotton and wool squares together. She was five years old when she pieced this uncomplicated top.

Mame was born near Kirkwood, Illinois, on November 11, 1869, the daughter of James Polk and Martha Woods Firoved. Her grandfather, Simon Firoved, was obviously an ardent Democrat who named his son after the eleventh president. Indeed, James P. became a prominent Warren County Democrat and served several

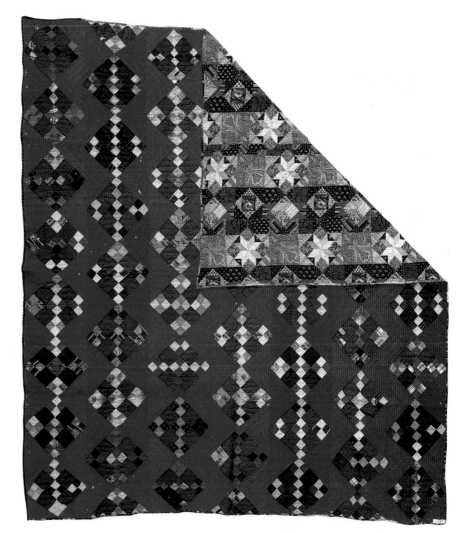

[Plate 75]
FOUR PATCH
84" x 61"

Mary Mabel Firoved Munch, 1869–1955
Kirkwood, Warren County, Illinois, 1874
Collection of Sarabelle O'Daniel

terms in the Illinois state legislature. Mame's Prussian great-great-grandfather, Johan Feirerabend, had disembarked at Philadelphia on December 24, 1778, fought in the Revolutionary War, and then settled at Hogestown near Carlisle, Cumberland County, Pennsylvania. In 1853 the family migrated to Dayton, Ohio, moved on to Bloomington, Illinois, and in 1856 settled permanently in Warren County.

Many small children can learn to sew a simple seam, but few can master the art of quilting at age five. As a young child, Mame probably needed some guidance in correctly piecing the Four Patch pattern set as a Nine Patch in a Streak of Lightning set. Her mother stored the completed top until her daughter was in her early teens. Sometime in the early 1880s the two women did the quilting using a woolen batt and a popular cotton printed patchwork, or "cheaters cloth," for the backing. The straight-cut handmade binding is made from the printed patchwork fabric, and all of the work is done by hand. The quilting (6 stitches per inch) includes parallel lines that follow the vertical zigzag and parallel horizontal lines across the blocks.

Mame married a druggist, John A. Munch. Ralph, their only child, died at the age of twelve. The couple was already living in Mount Vernon, Washington, when her father died in 1904. Mame occasionally returned to Illinois and visited her cousin, the mother of Sarabelle O'Daniel, the present owner. On those visits she told Sarabelle about making the quilt and her interest in keeping it in the family. On July 8, 1940, seventy-year-old Mame Munch placed her treasured childhood quilt in a box, wrapped it in brown paper, took it to the Mount Vernon, Washington, Post Office, paid $1.05, received insurance receipt Number 38, and sent the quilt by parcel post back to Warren County, Illinois.

The Illinois Quilt Research Project forms sometimes indicate that children helped work on quilts. Very few, however, credit the entire quilt to a child. This one is an exception. Katherine Schleisinger was born January 11, 1858, at Mendota, the daughter of German Lutheran immigrants. She made her Tulip Vase Appliqué quilt when she was twelve years old. While some family traditions are open to question, this quilt possesses enough nineteenth-century naïveté to make the story believable. It expresses the simplistic attempt of a school-age child to imitate a currently fashionable adult style.

Katherine selected the proper pre–1870 period colors. She correctly used the stereotypical tulip and symmetrically arranged three flowers in each of the red vases. She filled the voids with a strange single-stalk, multiple-leaved flower that doubles as an arrow. However, her one-sided orientation of these units creates a visual conflict with the quilt's symmetrically arranged vases. Furthermore, the additional top and bottom rows damage the unity of the central design by inserting an obviously dominant vertical line.

If the *how* and *what* of quilting are changing—quilt types, techniques, and concepts are in an explosive period—then there is also a transition in *who* is involved in the various parts of the quilting process. It is interesting to note on the forms that men often lurk in the background; they help with design, cut pieces, and may even quilt. A few even do it all, from beginning to end. Unfortunately, none of the few quilts made entirely by a man that were registered in the Project were Illi-

nois products. As gender roles blur, there are fewer and fewer barriers to anyone doing the things he or she would like to do. Look for more husband–wife quilting teams in the future than have been seen in the past.

It will come as no surprise that within the 15,808 quilts registered in the Project, there were no Illinois-made quilts completely produced, pieced, and quilted by a boy. There were, however, several that were pieced by a boy, and Donald Wood's Pink Pinwheel is one of the best.

[Plate 76]
TULIP VASE APPLIQUÉ
82″ x 70″

Katherine Schleisinger Kaiser, 1858–
    1936
Mendota, LaSalle County, Illinois,
    circa 1870
Collection of Arlene Kaiser Carter

The whole is neatly framed by the typical floral border, but this one meanders much less intricately than those appliquéd by the older and more experienced technicians of an earlier decade. On the undulating line Katherine has abstractly appliquéd red and yellow tulips without any encumbering stems or leaves. For the most part, the colors alternate.

Katherine not only had access to a sewing machine, but her skill in appliquéing by machine probably indicates the family had owned the device long enough for the daughter to have acquired above average skill in using it. It is, however, hand quilted (7–8 stitches per inch) around the appliqués and in double lines of stars. The top, back, and batt are of cotton, as is the handmade binding. Katherine married, provided a home for three sons, made more quilts, and lived in La Salle County until she died there February 1, 1936.

[Plate 77]
PINK PINWHEEL
80″ x 64″

Donald Ray Wood, 1958–
Edgington, Rock Island County, Illinois,
    1966
Collection of the maker

[Plate 78]
TULIP QUILT
75" x 59"

Charles Westfall, 1890–1944
Danville, Vermilion County, Illinois,
    circa 1930
Collection of Charles A. Miller

Westfall created the designs, which his wife embroidered. The blue flower pot, green leaves, and yellow tulips are created by an unusual embroidery technique, an outline stitch and long satin stitches that produce a wavy effect. Mrs. Westfall used six-strand embroidery floss to give the finished product a built-up appearance. The top, back, and batting are all cotton. The straight-cut binding is stitched by machine. The blocks and sashing are put together by machine. The floral blocks are quilted with a grid design, and the pink sashing is stitched with a Greek key motif. The quilting (8 stitches per inch) is neatly done. The present owner, Charles Miller, indicated that the Westfalls worked together on the assembly and quilting.

Donald's hand-pieced cotton top covers a cotton batt and a cotton back. It is nicely quilted (12 stitches per inch) with daisy and outline motifs and feathers on the border. The work was completed by Don's grandmother, Elsie Wood, who also documented the quilt by using white embroidery thread to write on the back, "Donnie Ray Wood age 8 1966." Pink Pinwheel is to date Don's first and only quilt. Perhaps the world will have to wait until this college graduate with an engineering degree retires before he has the time to piece any more quilts for his wife and daughter.

In an electronic media age where a violent male image is constantly available for emulation, it may seem strange to think of quiet little boys sewing patches together. A century ago it was not at all unusual. In previous generations, young boys were generally under their mother's tutelage until they shed the skirts of childhood and acquired their first long pants at age five or six. During that time, they often learned the same skills as their sisters. For instance, as little boys, both Calvin Coolidge and Dwight D. Eisenhower helped their mothers piece quilts.[12]

Men, as well as boys, have played a role in the history of quilting in Illinois. Charles Westfall was born in Germany on February 20, 1890. He emigrated to America and lived in Danville. Mr. Westfall was a typesetter, and he liked to help his wife make quilts. The present owner, a nephew, has two of the four quilts he believes the Westfalls made together.

Over the years men have become increasingly active participants in the quiltmaking process. Robert and Audrey Maurice of Decatur are one of several modern husband–wife quilting teams. In fact, they have quilted with two other couples on a regular basis since 1972. Quilting was a part of Audrey's early life. She learned the basics from her mother, who is still quilting although she is more than ninety years old. Her work won two blue ribbons at the Illinois State Fair.

In 1950, two years after their marriage, Audrey was at work on an Endless Chain quilt when Bob suggested it would go faster if he cut the pieces and she did the sewing. According to Audrey, "He cut out a stack of quilt pieces and soon found there was more to cutting blocks than he thought. He then marked each piece and recut the stack. From then on he knew accuracy was the key ingredient to a successful quilt top." The quilt was used on their bed for fifteen years. Although they did not make another quilt until 1961–1962, since then they have worked on a quilt almost constantly.

Bob decided he wanted a yellow Double Wedding Ring quilt, and during the 1960s when all-cotton yard goods was not plentiful, he shopped two years for the right kind of yellow fabric. His quilt won

[Figure 35]
Bob and Audrey Maurice at work on a quilt

[Plate 79]
BROKEN STAR
94" x 94"

Robert, 1926–, and Audrey Pschirrer
    Maurice, 1928–
Decatur, Macon County, Illinois,
    1983–1984
Collection of the makers

The Maurices' color-coordinated Broken Star quilt is pieced of carefully chosen cotton fabrics. The entire top, back, and homemade double bias-cut binding are of cotton, but the batting is polyester. Audrey stitched the small pieces by hand but used a machine on the larger seams. The binding is machine stitched on the front and hand sewn on the back. The hand quilting (7 stitches per inch) outlines the small pieces one-quarter inch inside the seam; and the large pieces have a flower and leaves motif inside a circle grid.[13]

Bob is a retired vocational education teacher who has switched from crafts to quilting but still enjoys gardening and square dancing. His wife admits he has a good eye for color and design and claims he is always ready to go to a quilt show. He has been a willing helper to the Decatur Quilters Guild and has quilted in the group's Quilt-a-thon. Bob and Audrey are typical late-twentieth-century senior citizens whose retirement years are filled with many shared interests, including quilts. In the early 1920s a *Capper's Weekly* columnist wrote, "Everybody quilts but father (and the rest of his gender)." That statement was not completely true then and is certainly less so today. Modern Illinois quilters are busily bridging the gender gap.[14]

second place in Viewer's Choice at Rockome Garden about 1970. Ever since, the Maurices have alternated selecting the pattern and choosing the fabric. For the first decade, Bob was Audrey's assistant. With the birth of the couple's second grandchild in 1972, Bob decided to make his new grandson a Ship of Dreams crib quilt. It was the first one he helped quilt. Today he drafts blocks, cuts out pieces, marks sewing lines, helps baste, and quilts. Although he does not sew pieces together, he excels at ripping out.

As we move out of the mainstream, we can more easily appreciate the diversity of quilters past and present. It is possible to look at an Illinois quilt today and no longer be surprised to learn that a man, as well as a woman or a child, may have played a role in its creation. The individuals who travel our state's quilt paths are as varied as those who use our highways.

Illinois enjoys a modern network of expressways that facilitates rapid automobile movement from one part of the state to another. Travelers along those routes have ready access to the nation's fast-food franchises, shopping malls, and an array of entertainment opportunities. It is, however, on the slower-paced two-lane backcountry roads that motorists find the one-of-a-kind restaurants, the courthouse squares, and the ordinary to awesome landscapes available in this diverse state.

The same can be said of the Illinois quiltscape. The mass-manufactured, paint-by-number, follow-the-dots quilt kits are the superhighways that can help you complete a quilt in a hurry. There are none of those in this chapter. Nontraditional quilts and quilters shun the superhighways. They can be found most easily along the state's meandering quilt paths. Travel these off-beat roads for real adventure, and enjoy the distinctive creations of quilters whose hearts leaped up when they beheld their rainbow in the sky.

[Plate 80]
SASSAFRAS LEAF
81″ x 81″

Hannah Johnson Haines, 1822–1903
Jay County, Indiana, and Moline, Rock
   Island County, Illinois, 1852–1869
Collection of the Rock Island County
   Historical Society

Hannah used pennies and thread spools
to mark the multiple-size orange-peel
quilting motifs (12–16 stitches per inch).
The border is in triple-line quilting. The
use of a very thin cotton batting facilitated the small stitching. The edges of
the appliquéd cotton patches are not
turned under but are attached to the
white backing by a finely worked buttonhole stitch. The back and front are
cotton, and the binding is red piping fas-
tened on the edge with a narrow strip of
fabric that is hand stitched to the edge of
the backside.

QUILT PATTERNS: FROM SHARING TO SELLING

Our young ladies of the present generation know little of the mysteries of "Irish chain," "rising star," "block work," or "Job's trouble," and would be as likely to mistake a set of quilting frames for clothes poles as for anything else. It was different in our younger days.

—T. S. Arthur,
"The Quilting Party,"
Godey's Lady's Book, December 1849

The first quilts created in the new state of Illinois probably came from a shared folk tradition. Since quilters often worked from memory, some quilts appear to stem from standard genres; but even a casual inspection immediately reveals they are not exact copies. Indeed, many of them, such as Polly Wheelock's Stars and Rainbows (Plate 55), are highly individualistic.

Sharing a Tradition

Patterns arrived anonymously in Illinois in the form of completed utilitarian or decorative bedcoverings. The carefully packed trunks of the ever-flowing streams of pioneers carried a rich textile tradition to the newly opened West. When a proud owner displayed these prized possessions to friends and neighbors, they became the models from which more quilts could be produced. Other patterns entered Illinois as sketches on scraps of paper or indelibly etched on the minds of would-be quiltmakers. Illinois' earliest settlers established an enduring tradition of sharing patterns as well as the labor of piecing and quilting. Sharing was a long-standing American folk tradition.

When Hannah Johnson Haines designed and started to appliqué her Sassafras Leaf masterpiece in Jay County, Indiana, she tried to imitate a quilt she had seen in Ohio while visiting relatives. Family tradition indicates that her father, Enoch Matson Johnson, gathered sassafras and oak leaves to be used as patterns for part of the appliqué motif. Her sister Louisa helped cut the pieces.

Hannah's quilt was not complete when she married Daniel Haines on June 6, 1857, in Jay County.[1] When the newlyweds relocated and established their new home near Moline, her long-term project came with her. There she continued her work with the assistance of a mute neighbor, Mary Henry, who also was a fine needlewoman. Other neigh-

[Figure 36]
Hannah Johnson Haines
Born May 31, 1822, Ohio
Died date unknown, 1903, Rock Island
County, Illinois

125

[Plate 81]
BLAZING STAR
99" x 79"

Sara Anne Morey, 1846–1919
New Canton, Pike County, Illinois,
 circa 1860
Collection of Mary Dell Borrowman

The quilt was found in a walnut dresser at the owner's grandparents' home. Utilizing typical midcentury colors, it is made entirely of cotton materials, including the handmade straight-cut binding. The maker assembled the top entirely by hand and quilted it (5–8 stitches per inch) in outline, parallel lines, fans, feathering, wreaths, and echo lines around the appliqué.

bors helped, until one found Hannah and Mary busily removing the stitches of other quilters. Daniel suggested that Hannah and Mary spare themselves the trouble and do the work alone.[2] It would be interesting to see the model Hannah used and to compare the details of the two quilts. What unique features would differentiate Hannah's product from the original?

Sharing remained the primary medium of pattern introduction, instruction, and exchange throughout the nineteenth century, although the media increasingly implemented the process of spreading designs. Even though individualism was the keynote to early quilt design, there are also many similarities in quilts from that period. Using red and green in the middle of the nineteenth century was quite common, as was the use of flowers and leaves, urns or flower pots, and wide borders. One could look forever and never find another quilt exactly like Hannah's Sassafras Leaf, but several will appear to be quite similar.[3]

Quiltmakers could also acquire patterns by observing the exhibits at the local agricultural fairs.[4] Textile exhibits were a part of the first American fair held at Pittsfield, Massachusetts, in 1810; and home-industry items, such as textiles, became a permanent part of midwestern premium lists.[5] When Illinois held its first state fair at Springfield in October 1854, prizes were awarded for the best entries in the box-work,[6] woolen, silk, calico, worsted, and whiteworked quilts. The following year the premium committee pared the categories to "Best Silk Quilt" and "Best Calico Quilt, Patchwork or Otherwise." Perhaps there were not enough entries the previous year to justify retaining six classes for quilts. In addition, a "discretionary premium" was awarded in 1855 to an "Exquisite white knit quilt," entered by the inmates of the blind asylum at Jacksonville.[7]

The 1859 Champaign County Fair premium list included competitive quilt categories similar to those of the state fair. Prizes were awarded for calico patchwork quilts, for the "Best White Quilt (solid work)," and for the best calico comfort.[8] The proceedings of the county societies published by the state agricultural organization in 1855 indicated the fledgling groups supported competitive classes in quilts at an early date.

The first fair in Edgar County, in October 1854, had classes for the best white quilt, quilted patchwork, and an "unquilted quilt." There was a "pretty good variety of beautiful workmanship" among the "domestic manufactures," which included quilts, at the LaSalle County Fair in 1854. The second annual Randolph County Fair was held on a private farm in October 1853. The "specimens of ladies work, clothing, quilts, blankets, etc." were exhibited in the barn. Surely they were not less worthy than the work of the Winnebago County women whose "domestic articles [were] displayed in the court house" and which "showed ingenuity and industry. To the ladies especially belong great praise."[9] Such nineteenth-century exhibitions offered quilt-oriented visitors the same benefits a fair does today; it was an opportunity to view a design and imitate it.

Although the premium categories define the types of quilts popular in Illinois at midcentury, they do not reveal the pattern names of the patchwork quilts exhibited in each competitive class. There is little opportunity to document quilt-pattern names prior to their publication by the news media later in the century. Even then, creating a reference file is complicated by the use of the same name for more than one pattern or by giving a pattern multiple names. In 1835 when *Godey's* publicized what twentieth-century quiltmakers now universally know as Grandmother's Flower Garden, the pattern was referred to as "the hexagon, or six-sided; this is also

[Plate 82]
WHITEWORK WHOLECLOTH QUILT
  (closeup of center medallion)
106″ x 103″

Maker unknown, dates unknown
Peoria County, Illinois, circa 1860
Collection of Mrs. Valeria Reed

The all-cotton quilt is composed of two very different grades of the primary fabric. The front has an exceptionally fine texture, and the back is a coarse weave that is more suitable for stuffed work. The cotton batting has plant debris. There is no binding. The turned-in edges are held in place by quilting stitches. It is all hand work. The quilting stitches (8–11 per inch) illustrate the work of several participants at the quilting frame. The overall quilting is done in outline, stippling, bow knots, floral swags, stars, and gridwork, in addition to the center medallion.

called honey-comb patch-work."[10]

Leah Thornburgh's Jackson Star (Plate 31) and the anonymous Beauty of the Forest (Plate 44) are rare examples of nineteenth-century pattern names that were preserved by placing them directly on the quilts themselves. Since the author of the 1849 short story "The Quilting Party" mentioned Irish Chain, Rising Star, and Job's Trouble, it is obvious that nineteenth-century quiltmakers knew specific patterns by name and that readers would easily have recognized the author's terminology.[11] Quilt pattern nomenclature developed informally and was regionally based. There would be little standardization or widespread dissemination of pattern names until the turn of the twentieth century.[12]

Godey's Takes the First Step: The Hexagon

In the nineteenth century, patterns were developed, promoted, and exchanged within a community and disseminated through travel and letter writing. The twentieth century ushered in a different system of distributing and acquiring patterns. The emergence of professional designers and a national mass-media system that popularized and standardized quiltmaking established our current practice. Over time the system of patterns spreading slowly switched from the bottom up arrangement of the nineteenth century to the top down format popularized in the twentieth century. When *Godey's* took that first step in 1835, it opened the door to dramatic change.[13]

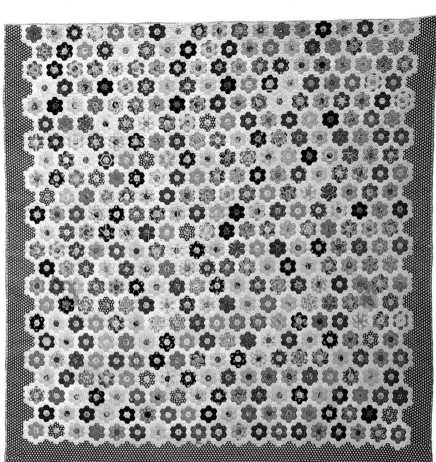

Godey's instructions for making a Hexagon quilt followed the English piecing method:

To make it properly you must first cut out a piece of pasteboard of the size you intend to make the patches, and of a hexagon or six-sided form. Then lay this model on your calico, and cut your patches of the same shape, allowing them a little larger all round for turning in at the edges.

Of course the patches must be all exactly of the same size. Get some stiff papers (old copy-books or letters will do) and cut them also into hexagons precisely the size of the pasteboard model. Prepare as many of these papers as you have patches. Baste or tack a patch upon every

[Plate 83]
HEXAGON
96" x 95"

Rachel Engard Saulnier, 1776–1866
Philadelphia, Philadelphia County,
    Pennsylvania, circa 1835
Collection of James A. O'Daniel

Perhaps Rachel Saulnier followed the advice of *Godey's Lady's Book* to make the rings in her Hexagon quilt the same color. In addition, she carefully positioned patterned-fabric hexagons to subtly create designed configurations. She also "Put a border all round, of handsome calico, all of the same sort," as directed by the *Godey's* article. Her outline quilting (4 stitches per inch) conforms to the recommendation that quilting "follow the shape of the hexagons." Rachel's quilt is cotton throughout, including the batting and the handmade straight-cut print binding. All the work is by hand.[14]

paper, turning down the edge of the calico over the wrong side.

Sew together neatly over the edge, six of these patches, so as to form a ring. Then sew together six more in the same manner, and so on till you have enough. Let each ring consist of the same sort of calico, or at least of the same colour. For instance, one ring may be blue, another pink and a third yellow, &c. The papers must be left in, to keep the patches in shape till the whole is completed.[15]

Unfortunately, we do not know what pattern name Rachel used for her quilt. A century later the pattern achieved coast-to-coast popularity as Grandmother's Flower Garden. However, in the 1830s that name was totally unknown. Researchers have learned that the pattern's roots lie buried in the obscurity of English quilting history. The oldest documented British template quilt is dated to 1770. Sixty years later England was so preoccupied with the hexagon that it became "the most typical of the country's work."[16] Despite the long-standing acceptance of the Hexagon in the United States, the pattern did not reach its peak of popularity on this side of the Atlantic until the 1930s. Its broad acceptance across America, as well as in Illinois, led Marie Shirer to state that "there is possibly no other design that has so completely captured the hearts of quiltmakers."[17]

Mosaic quilts surrounded by black borders became popular in the third quarter of the nineteenth century.[18] During the 1850s, *Godey's* printed revisions of several template patchwork articles originally published in *The Family Friend,* a British periodical first issued in 1849. The Box, or Tumbling Block, was one of eleven presented in April 1850. An additional twelve, copied from the same source, appeared in March 1851, and *Godey's* printed another dozen in December 1851. Two other American publications, *Graham's Magazine*

[Plate 84]
MOSAIC QUILT (HEXAGON SIDE)
62" x 61"

Maker unknown, dates unknown
Bloomington, McLean County, Illinois,
  circa 1870
Collection of the McLean County
  Historical Society

Although the central medallion quilt was out of fashion by the mid-nineteenth century, it is possible to see its remnants in this center block that is embroidered "R. Smith 1853 Bloomington." It is rare for a nineteenth-century Illinois-made quilt to be documented on the textile to a specific place of origin. R. Smith is unidentified, and the 1853 date probably commemorates a birth, death, or wedding. In general,

however, the medallion-style quilt had been replaced by midcentury by the repeating block format used by patterns such as Blazing Star (Plate 82).

In keeping with period fashion, the fabric of choice is silk,[21] with some pieces made with a satin weave. This quilt was probably intended for decorative display rather than for use on a bed. The pink silk border surrounding the mosaic is perhaps the same silk used on the wholecloth side. The border's feather quilting motif (12–14 stitches per inch) is embellished with decorative embroidery stitching. The batting is wool. See Plate 85.

[Plate 85]
MOSAIC QUILT (WHOLECLOTH
    SIDE)
62" x 61"

Maker unknown, dates unknown
Bloomington, McLean County, Illinois,
    circa 1870
Collection of the McLean County
    Historical Society

The wholecloth side is composed of twelve-inch-wide silk strips. It features a quilted center feather medallion and an undulating feather border. The stitches in these motifs are not visible on the mosaic side. It is possible that a hexagon quilt top was placed over a slightly older wholecloth quilt. The border is put on by machine, but all the other work is by hand.

and *Peterson's Magazine,* both used a European source for a "New Pattern for Patchwork in Silk," which each modified and printed in January 1857.[19]

Virginia Gunn, who has researched the early publications thoroughly, believes that when Ellen Lindsay's article on patchwork appeared in the February 1857 issue of *Godey's,* she became the first American to write about quilts. Although pieced quilting was temporarily out of fashion, *Godey's* indicated the magazine intended "to suit all tastes and all classes" as it continued to publish occasional patchwork patterns. Lindsay's work was copied in Florence Hartley's *The Ladies' Hand Book of Fancy Ornamental Work* in 1859. During the 1860s and 1870s, the major magazines gave little attention to quilts. The few articles that did appear primarily repeated the previously published template designs, which were now termed "mosaic patchwork." Post-Civil War women's magazines recommended mosaic-type quilts for the Moorish and Turkish decorative arts styles popular in the last quarter of the nineteenth century.[20]

The hexagon block has endured well. Succeeding generations repeatedly revived the shape, and each time it took on a slightly different look. It was not, however, the only pattern used for template quilting.

Template quilting, or the English piecing method, was never as popular in the United States as it was in England, despite the occasional attempts of *Godey's* to make American quilters aware of English patterns.[22] An unquilted top in the Illinois State Museum collection offers an excellent opportunity to examine closely the underside of an English-pieced quilt with its paper templates still intact.

This unknown quiltmaker followed the advice *Godey's* printed in 1835 to cut the templates from the stiff paper commonly used for letter writing and for creating school exercise books. However, many of the templates were also cut from the much softer newspapers. Perhaps newsprint was more plentiful than letters and no-longer-needed copy books. In the days before the development of inexpensive wood pulp, the recycling of rag paper was quite common. Surprisingly, in the early nineteenth century, textiles were generally less expensive and more available than paper. The 1863 and 1864 dates on the newspapers establish a time frame for the quilt top.[24]

[Plate 86]
HEXAGON STAR
85" x 69"

Maker unknown, dates unknown
Town unknown, Jo Daviess County,
   Illinois, circa 1870
Collection of the Illinois State Museum

Fabrics in the hand-pieced top include many of those found in late-nineteenth century crazy quilts—cottons and silks in various weaves including velvet and satin. Template quilts retained some faithful adherents despite the crazy quilt fad. Post-Civil War women's magazines recommended mosaic-type quilts for the Moorish and Turkish styles popular in the last quarter of the nineteenth century.[23]

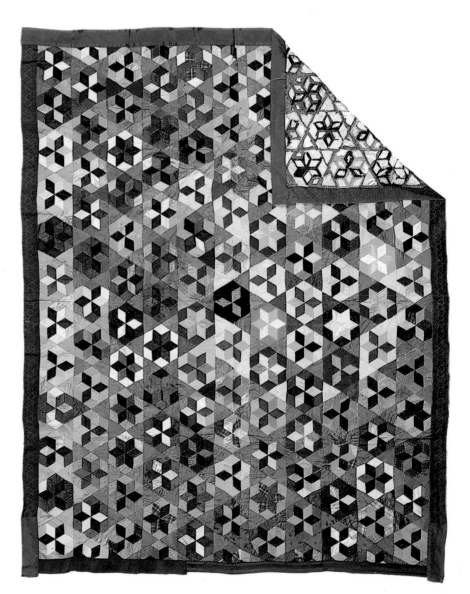

Charm quilts are as popular today as they were in the late nineteenth century. The challenge to accumulate hundreds of different pieces of cloth has, over the years, led to a variety of gathering techniques. In 1902 Miss Jenny Miller decided it was necessary to reach beyond her normal exchange with nearby relatives and friends. Through the requests column of the March *American Woman Magazine,* she announced that she would "be glad to receive from every reader a piece of calico, any color, 6 x 4 inches, for my charm quilt, and will return the favor in any way I can, Miss Jenny Miller, RFD Box 56, Rockton, Ill." Today, much of the exchange process is facilitated by contacting other scrap collectors through the local quilt guilds and at regional and national meetings.[25]

Creating charm quilts is related to the Victorian fascination with endless variety. Collecting buttons for a string, charms for a bracelet, or scraps for a quilt became part of a cultural pattern. Theoretically, in each quilt there would be 999 patches, and 999 different fabrics. Ella Skidmore is not the only quilter who did not achieve the ideal. Since it is basically a type of scrap quilt, there is no reliance on the repeated use of white and no focus on a predominant color. However, in contemporary charm quilts there often is a reliance upon geometrical groupings of shades within a color. The patches in charm quilts may be hexagons, but they may also be diamonds, split diamonds, squares, split squares, triangles, rectangles, tumblers, or clamshells. As Cuesta Benberry illustrated in her January and February 1988 *Quilter's Newsletter Magazine* articles, modern quilters have created many interesting, intricate, and challenging charm quilt patterns.

Charm quilts are excellent textile encyclopedias. They generally can be dated by the use of specific fabrics, colors, and designs appropriate to the late nineteenth century. Brown tones often dominate those from the 1870s and 1880s, while quilts made closer to 1900 include many lighter-colored shirting prints and an increased reliance on blues. The charm quilt fad ebbed in the early twentieth century, enjoyed a slight resurgence in the 1930s, and began a strong revival in the 1980s.[26]

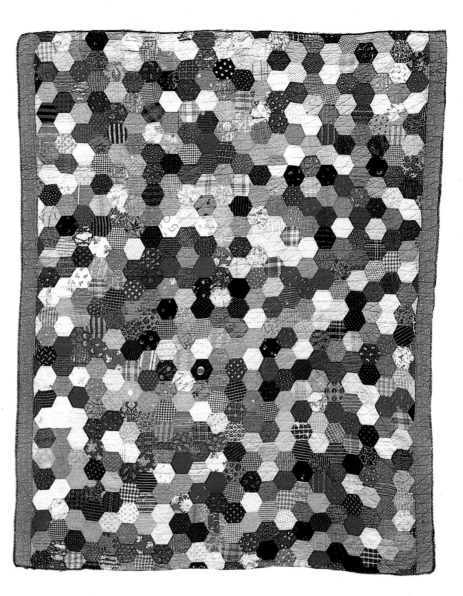

[Plate 87]
VARIEGATED HEXAGON
84" x 68"

Ella Overpeck Skidmore, 1863–1953
Newman, Douglas County, Illinois,
    circa 1900
Collection of Freida Clapp

Ella's hexagon charm quilt, of approximately five hundred pieces, is made entirely of cotton, including the batting, and handmade, straight-cut very narrow black and white binding that is sewn by machine and finished by hand. The quilting (5 stitches per inch) is in the hanging diamonds motif.

Grandmother's Flower Garden returned hexagons to favor during the Great Depression when the quilt pattern suddenly achieved unrivaled heights of popularity. At the Project quilt registration days, it appeared with greater regularity than any other pattern.

The Colonial Revival of the early twentieth century returned the hexagon shape to favor but placed it within the Depression-era palette and removed the paper templates. By this time the quilt pattern was popularized as Grandmother's Flower Garden. Mass-media pattern manufacturers recognized the familiar Hexagon as an old pattern. In fact, *Aunt Jane's* 1914 catalog carried it as the Honeycomb pattern, which was one of its original names. Innovative distributors soon capitalized on its antiquity and began creating a suitable Colonial Revival image by using *Grandmother* in its name.

Colonial Revival decor required a "colonial" quilt, and to satisfy its growing popularity, numerous companies offered the pattern to their customers. Different names were used, however. In 1931 *The Farmer's Wife* catalog illustrated it as the Bride's Bouquet design that was "similar to Endless Chain, the effect depending on the arrangement of colors. The 'Bouquets' are set together with white pieces." Endless Chain was described as "one of the oldest of old patterns."[27]

In a world shattered by the Great Depression, a sense of family heritage and a fond remembrance of the past offered emotional stability. *Grandma Dexter's* 1932 catalog assured its readers, "In the Colonial homes of our grandmothers, the patchwork quilt held a high place in the esteem of all women. This branch of needlework is again enjoying considerable vogue among our present day generation. There is a keen renewed interest in this old and useful art." Grandma offered a wide variety of stamped quilt-patch

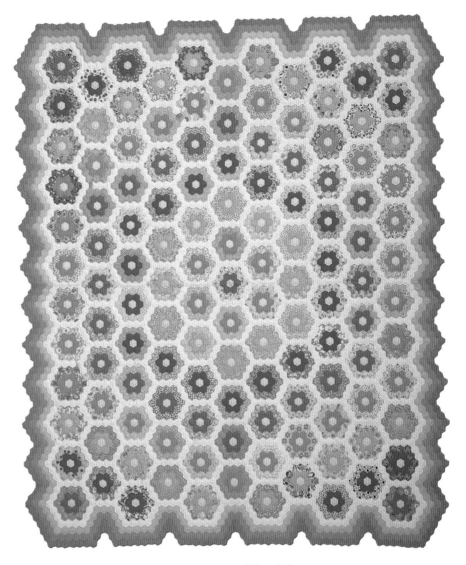

[Plate 88]
GRANDMOTHER'S FLOWER GARDEN
88" x 74"

Nettie Bell Redkey Baker, 1875–1961
Byron, Ogle County, Illinois, circa 1930
Collection of Mrs. James A. Ring

The Trip Around the World color arrangement and the gradation of color in the border are both outstanding features of this Depression-era hexagon quilt. The solid pink backing, the patchwork front, and the batting are all cotton. The edges are tucked in and stitched. The quilting (8 stitches per inch) is in concentric rings radiating outward from around the center hexagon.

blocks through the Elgin, Illinois, Virginia Snow Studios. Two dozen twelve-inch blocks were recommended for a completed Grandmother's Flower Garden quilt. The blocks sold for thirty cents a dozen in bleached cambric, sixty cents in either Indian Head and the "best quality quilting cloth," and "Extra fine quality white sateen" cost seventy-five cents a dozen.

Stearns and Foster's 1938 *Blue Book of Quilts* carried a Flower Garden color illustration. Its list of patterns contained "Hexagon pieced, including Flower Garden (illustrated), Mosaic and Honeycomb." For thirty-five cents, a quilter obviously received instructions for piecing the hexagons into three different patterns. However, if the order included a coupon from a batting wrapper, patterns cost only twenty cents each or six for one dollar. Grandmother's Flower Garden was also available through *Successful Farming*.[28]

Magazines Regenerate Quilting

Various mid-nineteenth-century media tastemakers indicated that the traditional pieced and appliqué forms of quilting were definitely going out of fashion. In 1849 T. S. Arthur used a short story in the nation's most prominent women's periodical to deplore a loss of youthful attention to the art of quilting. He was not alone in noting a declining interest in patchwork quilts. Other commentators observed that quilting was passé but did not, however, regret the loss.[29]

One popular trendsetter for the upper and middle classes boldly declared in 1850:

Patch-work quilts of old calico are only seen in inferior chambers; but they are well worth making for ser-

vants' beds. The custom of buying new calico, to cut into various ingenious figures, for what was called handsome patch-work, has become obsolete. Quilts are now made entirely of the same sort of dark calico or furniture chintz; the breadths being run together in straight seams, stuffed with cotton, lined with plain white or buff-dyed thick muslin, and quilted simply in diamonds, shells, or waves. For a large double bed, a quilt or any other cover should be three yards long, and about three yards wide.[30]

The writer of the "Household" column in the Chicago, Illinois, *Prairie Farmer,* who was in all probability a woman, was equally adamant in her opposition to making pieced quilts:

A friend sometime since sent us a pattern of a "pieced quilt," which is certainly very pretty to look at. ". . . What is the use of tearing cloth into pieces merely to sew them together again?" It cannot be for the sake of fitting it to an irregular shape, in the manner of garments; nor for the sake of combining different colors since they may be had already combined better than can be done in this way. We do not see any use in it, and so do not wish to be accessory to so useless a waste of time, and often health and mental vigor. There is enough to be done by women, both useful and ornamental, without spending weeks, and months, and even years—as we have known done—in piece work; which after all does not equal in beauty such as can be had for a fiftieth part of the cost.[31]

Despite these assertions, there is ample evidence in quilt collections today that the craft remained alive throughout the nineteenth century. There was, however, an easier way to acquire attractive bedcoverings.

A major reason for the decline in quilting among the middle and upper classes, particularly in the urban areas, was the widespread availability of manufactured substitutes.

By the 1850s the national arbiters of taste looked favorably upon those modern conveniences. *Godey's* "Centre-Table Gossip" asserts:

Marseilles quilts are most in vogue; they range from $3 to $10 in price, though they may be found more costly still, and are either plain white, or white tinted with buff, blue, pink, brown, or green. . . . White counterpanes are the most serviceable, unless each room is furnished *en suite,* as is now so much the fashion, that is, the curtains, counterpane, and carpet harmonizing in shade; but nothing could be less agreeable than a mixture of inharmonious tints.[32]

These machinemade "quilts" really were woven bedspreads that imitated the all-white stuffed and corded quilts of Provence, France. The bedcoverings were originally exported through the port of Marseilles. During the colonial period, a few reached North America by way of England.[33]

The article noted several other choices available to the affluent mid-nineteenth-century American housewife who did not have the time, talent, or inclination to make her own quilts. For those who could not afford the Marseilles product, there were the so-called "white English quilts," which cost less, looked as nice, and were easier to wash.[34] There were also additional options:

For summer wear, dimity spreads are both cheap and convenient, costing from a dollar to a dollar and half, and washed with as little trouble as a sheet, being almost as light. . . . Blankets range from three to thirty dollars a pair, the best French blankets costing that extravagant amount. A good pair of fine wide English blankets ranges from six to ten dollars, according to the width; they are the warmest and most comfortable of all bedcovers, and, if well taken care of, will last two generations.[35]

By the middle of the century, American and European looms produced more and more Marseilles spreads, which were thinner and lighter in weight than the original French quilts from which they were copied.[36]

Not all such substitutes for quilts were imported from France or England or shipped west from New England factories. Henry Weiss established the Charleston Woolen Mills at Charleston, Illinois, in 1863. An extensive inventory was made of his factory when he died in 1869. In addition to machinery, supplies, and raw materials, the probate inventory included the finished goods on hand at the mill.[37] Included were:

39	5# Coverlids	@ $3.50 ea.
6	4# Coverlids	2.80
15	Extra long Coverlids	5.25
12	All Wool Com. Coverlids	6.50
11	All Wool Fancy Coverlids	7.00
10	1/2 & 1/2 Fancy Coverlids	5.25
13	White Counterpanes	3.00
1	White Common Counterpane	2.75
1	1/2 Wool Colored Coverlid	4.87
13	Cradel [sic] Coverlids	.80

As manufactured bedcoverings became more abundant and less expensive, there was a declining emphasis on quilting. Trendy mid-nineteenth-century housewives obviously found it socially advantageous to display their artistic abilities by tastefully selecting modern machinemade household goods rather than by relying upon the old-fashioned merits of handwork. Quilting did not, however, die out entirely.

Without a doubt, individualism persisted in a period during which quilters enjoyed little media support. The continual reuse of familiar examples, supplemented by distinctively personal arrangement and color preferences, remained the primary method of design. Change came slowly. There was little media encouragement of quilting between Godey's first printed instructions for using a quilt pattern in 1835 and regeneration of the craft in the late nineteenth century.

An Ohio publication, Farm and Fireside, opened its "Our Household" column to quilters' comments. In 1886 it offered a quilt pattern blitz. The emphasis was primarily on pieced patterns illustrated without any specific written instructions. It was probably assumed that those who wished to use the patterns already knew how to construct them. Since Godey's clearly indicated such crafts were no longer fashionable in urban households, it is not surprising that the resurgence of interest should begin in periodicals targeted for rural audiences, where the practice remained alive and well. Most rural and small town quiltmakers probably cared little for the dictates of fashion in the bedroom.

Early in 1886, Farm and Fireside's "Our Household" column announced:

Quilt Patterns. As we promised, we present our readers with ten new patterns for quilt or patchwork. We have eleven more patterns many of them very original and very much more handsome than these, which will appear in our next issue. Be sure and renew your subscription in time to insure getting the February 1st issue. Tell your friends about the paper, these quilt patterns and its good qualities generally, and get their subscription.

It would seem the motivation was to increase subscriptions as much as to serve readers. Some well-known patterns, including Honeycomb, T, Hour Glass, Basket, Bear's Paw, Aunt Sukey's, and Feathered Star, were illustrated.[38]

There was also opportunity for readers to share patterns. For example, "Guinevere" of East Saginaw, Michigan, a faithful Household reader, noticed "Miriam's request for flower patterns suitable for small blocks," and wished "to let her know that I have a number of pretty sprays, and will send her a half dozen of them, if she will send me two or three stamps for time and postage."[39]

An interesting research project recently revealed that the late-nineteenth-century quilt revival actually began in the pages of inexpensive pulp-wood, formula-production magazines that learned to profit from mail-order advertising rather than depending upon literary or educational merit to attract subscribers. Those cheap story-papers carried advertisements from the Ladies Art Company as well as other quilt pattern suppliers. The patchwork slump of the 1870s and 1880s was about to end.[40]

Eventually even the Ladies' Home Journal joined the proquilting bandwagon. "The decree has gone forth that a revival of patchwork quilts is at hand," the Journal announced in 1894. "The vagaries of fashion are unaccountable and no one can tell in what direction they will lead next. Of late months everything which could be recognized as old-fashioned is the new fashion."[41] In response to a growing interest, the media began rehabilitating a popular traditional craft. Patchwork quilting had survived a major crisis. Like the phoenix, the craft would eventually rise from the ashes, but that would be in the early twentieth century after it had passed through the crazy quilt fad.

Crazy Quilts

This somewhat different "quilt" category usually attracts a host of dedicated admirers as well as a core of equally adamant detractors. The latter group often cites an excessive use of color, a disorganized asymmetrical arrangement, and busy designs reminiscent of late Victorian home interiors. Crazy quilts are clearly offensive to individuals who prefer less crowded confusion and a much more controlled environment. Although the detractors willingly consider the makers totally irrational, if not actually demented, the commonly used term for this type of quilt is probably derived from another source. It relates much more closely to Webster's first definition of *crazy,* which is "full of cracks or flaws," since the design is fragmented into many irregular shapes similar to the surface of crazed ceramics.[42]

Crazy quilts were an American grass-roots response to new decorative arts themes, changing commercial and industrial conditions, a fascination with novelty, and the media hype of the late-nineteenth century.[43] This nationwide, middle-class mania provided a socially acceptable creative activity with which women could fill the expanding leisure time available to them.[44] During the post–Civil War period, domestic cotton prices rose, while the cost of silk declined. Because of newly discovered dyes, brightly colored silk became more plentiful. American production and advertising was on the rise at the same time imports from the Orient were expanding.[45] For those who like crazy quilts, it was, indeed, a fortunate conjunction: middle-class home-

[Plate 89]
CRAZY QUILT
73" x 68"

Belle Edna Gray English, 1864–1925
Elmwood, Peoria County, Illinois,
   1885–1887
Collection of Elwyn C. and Bernice
   Rodgers

Although Belle incorporates several Japanese motifs, she also uses Kate Greenaway's children. *Harper's Bazar* printed the English illustrator's drawings in 1879, 1881, and 1882. A page of Greenaway-type designs also appeared in *Godey's,* although the illustrator was not credited.[49] In a letter to *Farm and Fireside,* "Alice" shared her thoughts on making crazy quilts. She believed the objective was to "get as much variety as possible" and advocated making "no two blocks alike." She "found many 'cute' designs to embroider in outline on the blocks, in little children's books— Kate Greenaway figures for instance."[50] These bonneted young ladies are considered the forerunner of the Sunbonnet Babies.

The lavishly embroidered silk quilt was made to commemorate the wedding of Belle Edna Gray and Daniel K. English (1862–1894) in Elmwood, Illinois, on February 19, 1883. It incorporates the elastic shirt sleeve band the groom wore at their wedding, and the back of the quilt is made from the wedding dress. The dates of the quilt's construction, 1885 to 1887, are embroidered on the border. The outline of the hand of the present owner's mother, Edna May English, has her initials. The significance of other designs and the other initials are not known to the present owners.

makers sought an acceptable means of self-expression; they had the financial ability to purchase extravagant textiles; and American manufacturers provided quilt patterns, embroidery transfers, and ready-to-use appliqués.

Japonica, one of the major ornamental motifs of the late Victorian era, can be found in wallpaper, textiles, ceramics, and furniture as well as in crazy quilts.[46] Until the 1870s, Americans knew very little about Japan. Commodore Matthew C. Perry sailed into Tokyo Bay in 1853, and early the following year the Japanese government reluctantly signed a treaty opening selective ports to American trade. Commercial contact with the previously isolated kingdom remained minimal until the Japanese participated in the 1876 Philadelphia Centennial celebration. Popular intrigue with that nation's exhibit made its artistic contributions an overnight sensation. It was "filled in every part with a rich and valuable display, the variety and beauty of which were one of the great surprises of the Exhibition."[47] American manufacturers carefully noted the popular interest.

During the 1880s decorative elements considered to be Japanese spread over the land and provocatively influenced American quiltmaking. Translated into the small-town American vernacular, this included asymmetrical arrangements, an increased use of red as a major color, and the incorporation of such embroidered motifs as spider webs, flowers, fans, and birds, particularly cranes and owls. In 1882 *Harper's Bazar* published a "mosaic patchwork of odd bits," which the magazine termed Japanese Patch. It was copied from the pavement design in a piece of Japanese needlework. A year later *Peterson's Magazine* presented "Birds from Japanese Designs: In Painting or Embroidery." It was not long before mail-order advertisers offered these motifs to quiltmakers.[48] It appears as though Mrs. Belle English read every article on crazy quilts ever published by *Harper's Bazar,* for her quilt is a classic example of using every popular motif available.

Another Japanese-associated element found in Belle's bedcovering, as in other nineteenth-century crazy quilts, is the fan motif. It is prominently displayed in the Michael Bradley quilt. Many makers considered the incorporation of an embroidered or pieced oriental fan into the decorated cover a necessity. *Harper's Bazar* featured a page of "Japanese Fan Designs for Embroidery for its readers to duplicate."[51]

[Plate 90]
CRAZY QUILT
75" x 70"

Friends of Michael Bradley
Geneseo, Henry County, Illinois, 1893
Collection of Mrs. J. Allan Bradley

Like many nineteenth-century crazy quilts, Michael Bradley's bedcovering is a potpourri of exotic and exciting materials. It includes the usual assortment of plush, satin, taffeta, brocade, and fake fur on the top. There is no back, but the foundation is composed of several different cotton and polished cotton pieces in various shades of brown. The velvet binding is attached with embroidery stitches, and the basting thread has not been removed from the binding.

The entire richly embroidered top contains numerous commemorative ribbons from the 1880s and 1890s. These include an undated Geneseo Fire Battalion badge, a cigar band, a memorial for President James A. Garfield (assassinated in 1881), a veteran's reunion of the Sixty-first Regiment Pennsylvania Volunteers (1862–1884), an 1891 church fair, an 1891 Geneseo St. Patrick's Day celebration, and a ribbon commemorating General John M. Palmer's selection as a U. S. senator from Illinois on the 150th ballot of the state legislature on March 12, 1891.[52]

Rosemary C. Gately considers Maryland crazy quilts to be "Beautifully designed, masterfully pieced and embroidered . . . [and] made by women for commemorative purposes."[53] The description aptly characterizes the quilt made for Michael Bradley of Geneseo, Illinois. Commemorative and souvenir ribbons, as well as American flags, are frequently found stitched into crazy quilts; and they abound in the Bradley quilt. The use of such material culture artifacts helps local history researchers document events of the era, indicates the special interests of the quilt owner, and often identifies that individual as a man. Gately found that crazy quilts were often made as gifts for a fiancé or a highly regarded friend. Many crazy quilts are personalized, and thus they are less anonymous than most quilts. Since they were really decorative rather than functional, there is a better than average chance they have been passed from generation to generation, and thus the family knows the name of the maker and the original owner.[54]

The careful examination of a crazy quilt will probably reveal that it is not pieced in the ordinary sense of sewing two or more bits of cloth together with a straight seam. Most examples from the earlier period consist of rich fabrics layered one over another and stitched to a foundation. The technique was an already well-established practice, having been used extensively on the Log Cabin-type quilts that became popular in the 1870s.[55]

Although most crazy quilts appear to be the individual creations of each maker, the numerous advertisements in periodicals clearly indicate that prepackaged quilt-making materials were available for the first time. A veritable jigsaw of precut quilt blocks could be pieced together and attached to a marked foundation.[56] Fabric kits were not the only help available. Punched embroidery patterns that used white powder to indicate a line that would

be replaced by paint before it was smudged and hot transfer patterns were widely advertised and offered as pattern kits. As coins jingled in the hands of potential buyers, the manufacturers obviously perked up their ears and responded to the call.[57]

Two recent industrial advancements facilitated the addition of decorative motifs to crazy quilt tops. Iron-on patterns developed in England in 1875 and an "embroidery sewing machine," which could produce factory-made embroidery appliqués, was patented by a Connecticut inventor in 1878.[58] This explains why so many of the oriental and Kate Greenaway figures look very much alike. It also means that acquiring the crazy quilts that do not follow a specific media-input formula creates a more individualistic collection.

Perhaps the use of commonly grown North American flowers and children's figures were two of the most westernized elements incorporated into what is essentially an oriental-based decorative scheme. The flowers that are important features of many crazy quilts play an important role in late-nineteenth-century society. Victorians used a special "flower language," and it is necessary to know the meaning of each flower used on a quilt to decode the message incorporated into the stitching.[59]

Crazy quilts are really the first kind of quilt to be heavily promoted through the media.[60] They were often made from "commercially produced patterns and fabric scraps." Much of the media input came through articles and advertisements in *Godey's, Peterson's, Harper's Bazar,* and *The Delineator.* The May 1884 issue of *Peterson's* carried eight advertisements for silk patchwork. Similar products were still being offered in the 1890s. Those publications printed illustrated crazy patchwork for household accessories as well as for quilts. Remembering that the era was known as the Gilded Age

[Figure 37]
Crazy Quilt Kit Advertisement

A circa 1880 advertisement clipped from a magazine or newspaper offered fifteen different pieces of silk and twelve skeins of silk embroidery thread for fifty cents to anyone securing three new subscribers. The fabrics could be cut into smaller pieces and used for "crazy pincushions, sofa pillows, quilts., etc."

helps understand why the February 1881 *Godey's* referred to gold thread as the "great feature of the embroidery of the season."[61]

According to Mrs. John A. Logan of Illinois, "Crazy patchwork, to be endurable, must after all, have 'method in its madness,' Distinct artistic skill in the grouping and harmonizing of colors is indispensable to the beauty of the final result. The separate bits, if not decidedly handsome in themselves, may be embroidered, painted, or enlivened with a design in applique." The use of color, exquisite textiles, and fancy embroidery combines to make a fantastic crazy quilt. "The point was to use as many different colors and textures of rich materials as possible . . . and to add an embroiderer's textbook of different stitches." It is easy to see that high-style crazy quilts were not practical, were difficult to clean, and that they really were intended for ornamentation rather than everyday use.[62]

The fad was not a lengthy one. *Arthur's Home Magazine* noted in 1884, "Old patterns, and modifications of old ones, are continually coming to the front in silk quilts, so that when the crazy quilt has had its day there will be plenty of styles to supplant it." Rosemary Connolly Gately appropriately assesses the significance of these "fabric documents which have survived where personal papers have not. . . . They are vivid and idiosyncratic records of the choices women made in the late nineteenth century."[63] Even though the golden age of high-style crazy quilts ended before the new century dawned, the technique continued to be used.

The role of women in American life had changed substantially by 1900. Many urban women who took the time to make a fashionable crazy quilt were really not interested in producing utilitarian bedcoverings. On the other hand, rural and small-town housewives who made quilts to be used on beds, rather than create nonfunctional ornamental throws, often wished to be as stylish as possible while still producing a serviceable product. For most quiltmakers, crazy quilts were out of fashion by 1900. Nevertheless, some women had reduced the formula to the level of practicality and continued to produce randomly pieced quilts. For the most part, however, twentieth-century crazy quilts were generally made in rural areas or by less affluent families. Many upper-middle-class urban women temporarily turned their leisure time to non-quilting activities.

After 1900, wool and cotton scraps increasingly replaced the elegant silks and satin-weave fabrics of the earlier decades. The designs became simpler, and there is evidence

[Plate 91]
DRESDEN PLATE CRAZY QUILT
70" x 69"

Theophelia Emilie Warnke Ebert,
    1883–1936
Roberts, Ford County, Illinois, 1904
Collection of Ida Ebert Tornowski

Felia Ebert's quilt, which is signed and dated in the center block, is typical of the later period. It is made of wool and cotton. The back is black polished cotton; there is no batting. The edges are turned in and machine stitched. It is pieced, appliquéd, and embroidered. Although the large "plates" or "flowers" are pieced by machine, much of the other work is done by hand. It is tied with small knots on the top. The wool yarn decorative embroidery uses blanket, outline, herringbone, and lazy daisy stitches.

Felia's plates have slightly more than the ten to twenty-four petals usually found on a quilt block. It was occasionally used in the nineteenth century before it appeared in the 1898 Ladies Art Catalog as Chrysanthemum, a well-known Japanese flower very popular in textiles at the time. There are many variations of the pattern, and Louise O. Townsend illustrates fifteen versions. Most Dresden Plate quilts seen today are the scrap-bag type from the 1930s when the pattern was illustrated by Nancy Cabot, Virginia Snow, the Kansas City *Star,* and other pattern sellers. It easily lent itself to becoming a friendship quilt since names could be written on each petal and the center of the flower,[65] the area Felia chose to sign her quilt.

in the Project registrations that some were made as fundraisers. The surviving textile documents indicate that, in general, twentieth-century crazy quilt colors lost their former vibrancy, surface decoration was far less elaborate, and wool yarn frequently replaced silk thread in the decorative stitching.[64] Theophelia ("Felia") Warnke Ebert's Dresden Plate is a typical example.

The maker, who was born April 26, 1883, in Posen, Germany, came to the United States with her mother in 1889. For the rest of her life, she lived in the Roberts area, where her fiancé was killed in a runaway horse and buggy accident in 1902. On her twenty-third birthday she married Samuel Ebert, a widower with six children, whose wife had died from complications of childbirth a year earlier. The couple's four offspring made a family of ten children. She died April 25, 1936, the day before the family was scheduled to gather to celebrate the Eberts' thirtieth wedding anniversary and Felia's fifty-third birthday. According to the April 29, 1936, *Roberts Herald,* the pastor of St. Paul's Lutheran Church who conducted her funeral praised her "ideal relation to her step-children and of her step-children to her."

Between 1920 and 1940 some crazy quilts were still being made by rural and urban women. The development of relatively inexpensive, durable synthetic fabrics enabled some makers to return the crazy's top surface to its more colorful origin. Nevertheless, as is easily noticed in Hattie Hall's 1928 example, the pieces and the blocks are larger than the classical 1880s period, and little rhythm is found within the asymmetrical arrangement. It is also quite evident that the decorative embroidery has been reduced to a functional minimum.[66] It is not difficult to see the striking difference in the technical approach to crazy quilts between the 1890s era and the 1920s.

Even a brief investigation of crazy quilts helps one see how the field of quilt history is changing. Look carefully at the footnotes in this section and notice how recent quilt research has helped reshape our image of the crazy quilt. Less than sixty-five years ago, Ruth Finley told her readers that "The oldest pattern known, the 'Crazy Quilt,' was still popular as late as the eighteen-seventies and eighties." This erroneous statement was accepted as fact by an author almost fifty years later: "Most quilt authorities believe that Crazies got started because the colonists had to patch bedcovers so extensively they eventually became hidden under irregular shapes of fabric salvaged from clothing." Neither statement

of supposed fact is footnoted; neither has stood the test of time; neither retains any validity in the light of recent research.[67]

History rests upon documentable evidence; myth is all too often accepted without question and innocently passed on as fact. Quilt history is at last coming of age. Quiltmakers and quilt collectors are seeking accurate information, and historians are becoming more interested in material culture studies. This fortunate blending of interests brings our vision of the past into sharper focus. *Crazed* should always refer to a type of patchwork bedcovering and never define a quilt lover's view of history.

The Quilt Revival Begins

After the crazy quilt phase peaked in the 1880s and began its decline in the 1890s, it became obvious that the strong piecework quilt undercurrent that ebbed and flowed across the nation was on the threshold of a new lease on life. The increasing activity in rural and pulp magazines and the recent emphasis upon the fancywork quilts in the art needlecraft field bore testimony that quilting was not a dying craft. The media input in such magazines as *The Ladies' Home Journal, Delineator, Harper's Bazar, House Beautiful, Woman's Home Companion, Modern Priscilla, Hearth and Home, Farm and Fireside, National Stockman and Farmer, Orange–Judd Farmer,* and *Ohio Farmer* offered more and more quilt patterns for the interested needleworker. Cuesta Benberry aptly referred to this period as "The Twentieth Century's First Quilt Revival."[68]

While there had always been a free exchange of patterns among interested neighbors, by the late nineteenth century an infant industry was arising that would be the wave of the future. Selling patterns, which first emerged through magazines, soon turned into successful business enterprises for a few farsighted entrepreneurs. Commercial pattern production marked an important development in the history of quiltmaking.

The Ladies Art Company of St. Louis, Missouri, began operation in 1889, although there is no evidence to indicate that the firm sold quilt patterns at first. An early catalog was *Diagrams of Quilt, Sofa and Pin Cushion Patterns.* The first known catalogs that included quilt patterns were issued in October and December 1895. Perhaps several were original, but most were traditional nineteenth-century patterns drawn from a variety of periodicals. Originally under the leadership of a German immigrant, H. M. Brockstedt, the company remained in the family and in the late twentieth century became the oldest quilt pattern

[Plate 92]
CRAZY QUILT
83" x 70"

Hattie O. Holliday Hall, 1888–1978
Chicago, Cook County, Illinois, 1928
Collection of Ann C. Saunders

The African-American Holliday family moved from St. Louis, Missouri, to Chicago, Illinois, in the early twentieth century. When Hattie Holliday Hall and her sisters made a crazy quilt in 1928, they were among only a handful of Illinois quiltmakers who still worked in that genre. Hattie, along with Mamie L. Saunders and Charlie Marie Brannon, used satin leftovers from party dresses to create a crazed image that contrasts sharply with the earlier forms. The three sisters made many quilts as fundraisers for their Chicago parish, St. Monica's Roman Catholic mission. Like many twentieth-century crazies, the bedcovering is tied rather than quilted. Both the top and the back are satin. There is no binding, for the back is brought to the front and sewn by hand. All of the work on the quilt is by hand.

[Plate 93]
Hand-colored Ladies Art Company quilt
    patterns
Early twentieth century
Private collection

The quilt patterns sold by the Ladies Art Company were originally produced by the Brockstedt family. The paper patterns were cut by hand and placed in a numbered envelope. Watercolored cards illustrating the completed quilt block were produced by children in the family after they came home from school. By the 1920s, however, the company employed approximately fifty people to produce the patterns and kits and to handle the large volume of mail.[70]

[Plate 94]
TREE OF LIFE
84" x 69"

Ida May Gray, 1887–1977
LaPrairie, Marshall County, Illinois,
    circa 1900
Collection of Mrs. Charles (Dortha)
    Gray

Patterns known as Tree of Life have
existed in appliqué, pieced, and embroidered form for centuries. Variants of this
pieced block pattern were particularly
popular in Illinois around 1900. The
Ladies Art Catalog offered it as Pattern
Number 260 in an eighteen-inch block
as late as 1928.

The asymmetrical block arrangement
with the blocks set on point and separated by wide sashing is not shockingly
unusual for the turn of the century, but it
is only occasionally found in Illinois
quilts at the time. The top, back, and
batt of Ida's quilt are of cotton, and the
white cotton binding is handmade
straight-cut applied by hand on the back
and front. The piecing, gridwork, and
three concentric rings of quilting motifs
(7 stitches per inch) are worked by hand.

business in the nation. Ladies Art
Company was one of the most important national pattern suppliers in
the early years of this century. It remained a strong business contender
until paper and labor shortages during World War II and declining interest in quilting forced it to scale down
its business.[69]

Much research was necessary to
produce such a comprehensive catalog, but the company's offerings
expanded slightly each time a new
edition appeared. The Ladies Art
Company issued catalogs in 1907,
1922, and 1928. By that time the list
had reached 530 patterns. Cuesta

Benberry believes a 1930s edition
raised the total to 544. Today these
catalogs are excellent sources of
pieced and appliqué designs as well
as pattern names. Unfortunately,
important historical documentation was lost when many of the
original names were changed as a
standardized pattern nomenclature
slowly emerged.[71]

The Ladies Art Company sold
much more than patterns. Presewn
quilt blocks and completed quilts
were also available. By 1922 a
stamped quilt top complete with
appliqués sold for five dollars, while
a finished quilt cost twenty-five to

forty-five dollars. The prices for
completed blocks ranged from 35¢
to $1.50 each.[72]

During the Great Depression
some people could still purchase
the completed blocks and finished
quilts available from the St. Louis-
based Ladies Art Company. For
those less fortunate the company
provided patterns for only twenty-
five cents. However, many quilters
could not afford even that amount;
so friends and neighbors returned
to exchanging patterns, as was so
common earlier in the century.

[Plate 95]
FLAGSTONES
81″ x 76″

Millie Mary Albrecht Larson, 1891–1972
Ohio, Bureau County, Illinois, circa 1915
Collection of Irene E. Larson

Millie Albrecht's German Protestant ancestors immigrated from Alsace–Lorraine, and she learned to quilt from her mother. She quilted from necessity as well as for pleasure. Several of her bedcoverings were used to pay people who worked for her. Construction of the all-cotton quilt is by sewing machine, and the handmade straight-cut binding is also applied by machine. The hand quilting (6 stitches per inch) is worked in an overall grid.

The 1928 Ladies Art Company catalog offers Flagstones in a seven-inch size as Pattern Number 514. Judging from the number of Project registrations, it was a very popular pattern in Illinois during the first few decades of the twentieth century.

Aunt Jane's Quilt Designs, an early quilt pattern catalog, carried a nineteenth-century pattern that appears so frequently in quilt collections and current publications that it virtually constitutes a subgroup of its own. Even though no mid-nineteenth-century published sources for Princess Feather have come to light, it became a very popular pattern, and it can be found today in many museum collections and antique shops in Illinois and other states. The most common form is red and green, but occasionally orange will appear as an accent. There are normally four large quadrants, although it may be set with six or twelve smaller blocks. These are often separated by narrow strips of colored cotton sashing. Many early quilters added a swag border.

[Figure 38]
Ladies Art Company advertisement
Circa 1922
Private collection

[Plate 96]
PRINCESS FEATHER
93" x 78"

Rebecca Smith Smith, 1807–1875
Decatur, Macon County, Illinois,
  circa 1860
Collection of Mildred Jacobs Zindel

Rebecca's Princess Feather quilt is all
handwork. Cotton is used throughout,
including the batt. The binding is handmade of straight-cut dark green cotton.
The quilting (8 stitches per inch) is in
grid, parallel lines, and double lines.

The popularity of Princess Feather quilts extended well into the twentieth century, and many variations were developed. It appeared in the 1914 edition of *Aunt Jane's Prize Winning Quilt Designs.* The small catalog indicated that the pattern should be "pieced of red and green oil calico, whipped down on a square of bleached muslin twenty-two and one-half inches square. Nine blocks or squares make the quilt, except the border."[73] When quilters used larger Princess Feather blocks in a quadrant set, the pattern was sometimes combined with an oak leaf positioned in the corner of each block. This created a distinctive four-part center ornament with double-leaf motifs in the middle of each side and a single leaf in the corners.

The familiar plumes were also featured on a Stearns and Foster Mountain Mist batting wrapper. The pattern appeared in a traditional design in 1928 and acquired a more modern center design with bicolored plumes in 1930 and 1931. Thus, what began as a vibrant nineteenth-century red and green complimentary color combination can also be found in the muted pastel red and green of the Depression era.

Hannah Haines traced actual leaves to create her quilt. Where did Rebecca Smith's design originate? The widely used nineteenth-century pattern is derived from the Prince of Wales feathered insignia, which played a major role in the decorative motifs used on Federal period furniture at the turn of the nineteenth century. Perhaps the phrase "the Prince's Feathers" may have been misunderstood in a society greatly dependent upon oral rather than written communication.[74]

Rebecca Smith was born in Rutherford County, Tennessee, and married Andrew Wilson Smith in 1836. They spent their entire married life in the same farmhouse southwest of Decatur, and it was there that she made

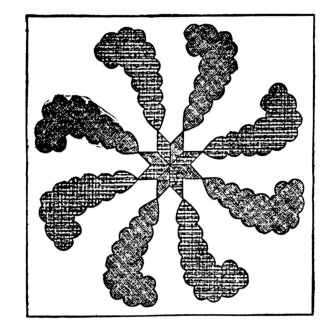

[Figure 39]
Princess Feather Pattern
Aunt Jane's Prize Winning Quilt Designs
Springfield, Ohio, 1914
Private collection

her Princess Feather quilt. Her well-preserved show piece has remained in the family through five generations. Was the pattern part of her Upland South tradition, or did she acquire it in the Decatur area? Unfortunately, we will never know that important bit of cultural history.

The quilt pattern acquisitions of Hannah Johnson Haines, Rachel Engard Saulnier, and Millie Albrecht Larson are as different as the lifelong quilt paths the three quiltmakers followed. Hannah copied a pattern from memory; Rachel might have read about Hexagon quilts in *Godey's;* and perhaps Millie ordered a pattern from the Ladies Art Company. The diversity of their stories clearly documents the changing system of acquiring patterns in the nineteenth century. The informal exchange of the earlier years was increasingly supplemented by commercial production

and distribution. By the turn of the twentieth century, the nation's media breathed new life into an old craft and offered countless design opportunities to a rising generation of quiltmakers. The fortunate reader of the Ladies Art Company catalog, for instance, probably saw more patterns illustrated in that publication than all her quilting ancestors ever saw in their entire lives. Soon even local newspapers would peddle patterns.

Additional changes lay ahead. As the national interest in quilting rose, individual creativity declined. As Cuesta Benberry has shown, Pennsylvania German decorative motifs eventually achieved national prominence.[75] Commercialization encouraged a previously unknown degree of conformity that deprived the craft of distinctive regional and personal expressions. Could a rich heritage survive despite commercial success?

[Plate 97]
WREATH OF ROSES
86" x 75"

Garnet Pearson Pinckly, 1876–1961
Bushnell, McDonough County, Illinois, 1930
Collection of Harriet Pinckly Bricker

Wreath of Roses is one of several well-known designer patterns by Marie Webster. Garnet Pinckly's version of this quilt is all cotton, including the batting and bias tape binding. The appliqués are stitched by hand. There is outline quilting (12 stitches per inch) around each appliqué, and the additional motifs are grids, scrolls, and feather wreaths filled with small orange peel.

𝒯WENTIETH-CENTURY QUILTMAKING TRENDS: COMMERCIALIZING A TRADITION

Today, although there seems to be a marked interest and revival of quilting, yet there is also a feeling of commercialization which tends toward lowering its sincerity and individuality as needle art. Women are depending more and more upon the printed pattern sheet to save time and labor. These, having been used time and time again, often become very tiresome.

—Rose G. Kretsinger,
The Romance of the Patchwork Quilt in America, 1935

Mass-merchandising of quilt patterns did not originate in the twentieth century. There is abundant evidence to indicate that the movement began decades earlier. From *Godey's* presentation of the Hexagon in 1835 through the pieced and crazy quilt designs illustrated in periodicals and offered for sale during the 1880s and 1890s, the quiltmaking public was increasingly offered choices of patterns. Popular response to the magazine articles and pattern-makers' advertisements was obviously encouraging.

The new century did, however, introduce a significant factor, the quilt designer. The major women's magazines raised the once out-of-fashion quilt to new heights of popularity and helped a handful of creative, aggressive businesswomen achieve celebrity status. Mail-order businesses thrived as the railroads and the newly introduced Rural Free Delivery rushed innovative patterns to eagerly awaiting quilters. The rising importance of nationally distributed patterns, highly promoted designers, and mass-produced kits left a permanent commercialized imprint upon America's quilting tradition.

Businesswomen Lead the Quilt Revival

Marie Daugherty Webster (1859–1956)

Marie Webster was already well known to the one-and-one-half-million readers of the *Ladies' Home Journal* when her book *Quilts: Their Story and How to Make Them* appeared in 1915.[1] The daughter and wife of well-established bankers, she was in her early fifties when she submitted her quilt patterns to the *Journal.*[2] The magazine had helped generate the quilt revival, which began before the turn of the century, by illustrating older pieced patterns and by offering the appliqué creations of such leading illustrators as Maxfield Parrish. The editor, Edward Bok, liked Marie's designs, and when he sponsored the Hoosier housewife, he helped make quilt history. Her hometown newspaper, the *Marion Daily Chronicle,* noted Bok found her "unique" quilt designs appealing, and that she had "an artist's eye for color." The January 1911 issue of the *Journal* carried four of her quilts in full color, and nine appliquéd sofa pillows appeared in August of that year. In January 1912 the *Journal* illustrated four more quilts, and the August issue featured baby quilts.[3]

147

[Plate 98]
MAY TULIPS
97" x 80"

Dora Shields Treen, 1859–1942
Evanston, Cook County, Illinois, 1939
    and 1987
Collection of Elizabeth Wyld

Helen Masslich was an avid quilter, and before she died in 1941 she made quilts for three of her children. She was too ill to do so for her fourth child, and so her mother, Dora Treen, made a pair of May Tulip quilt tops. Only one was quilted and finished before Dora died in 1942.

The quilting was completed in the 1980s by Dora's granddaughter, Elizabeth Wyld, with the help of Dora's great-granddaughter, Carolyn Egnor, and her great-great-granddaughter, Elizabeth Klaw. This intergenerational quilt preserves the family heritage and an important part of quilt-design history.

The all-cotton top, appliqué pieces, and minipolka dot lavender backing are bound by cotton handmade bias tape. It is applied by hand. The batting is modern polyester material. The quilting (12 stitches per inch) forms flowers, scrolls, and a grid, in addition to outlining the appliqués.

According to Cuesta Benberry, "Webster became the personification of the new look in quilts. Undeniably she did popularize a trend."[4] When Benberry tried to locate patterns Webster may have used as sources, she determined that a few elements may have been derived from other sources but the designs really were quite original. Webster's work, on the other hand, was widely copied by her competitors without any credit to the designer.

After World War I Marie Webster founded the Practical Patchwork Company. For twenty years she ran a successful mail-order business from her Marion, Indiana, home. Local women prepared tissue paper patterns, boxed quilt-top kits, basted tops, and even completed quilts. Her patterns, kits, and quilts were sold through several retail facilities, including Marshall Field's store in Chicago and the Mary A. McElwain Quilt Shop in Walworth, Wisconsin.[5]

When Elizabeth Wyld completed the Illinois Quilt Research Project registration form, she indicated that McElwain's was the source of her grandmother's kit and included a copy of the shop's small catalog. It identifies May Tulips as the product of a "Marie Webster Design Quilt Kit" and confidently assured customers that "When you have a Quilt or Spread designed by Marie D. Webster . . . you will have something to cherish always." The kit cost $12.50. The large and well-stocked quilt shop in Walworth, Wisconsin, carried at least sixty patterns.[6] McElwain was one of the four judges in the 1933 Sears Century of Progress quilt show who chose the final winner in Chicago.[7]

Marie Webster became a national trendsetter and was well known for her commercial creativity in an age when such characteristics were not expected of women. She revolutionized quiltmaking by returning appliqué quilts to their mid-nineteenth-century prominence, by introducing a pastel palette, and by using strikingly innovative de-

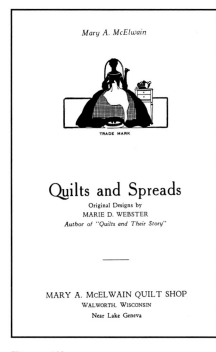

[Figure 40]
Mary McElwain Quilt Shop Booklet
    Cover circa 1940
Collection of Elizabeth Wyld

[Plate 99]
BUTTERFLIES AND BASKETS
82" x 78"

Elizabeth Wells Robertson, 1888–1956
Ravinia, Cook County, Illinois, 1919
Collection of Elizabeth Robertson Beith

sign elements. She left her mark on twentieth-century quilting, and her pioneering work opened the door to other women who would follow in her footsteps.

Elizabeth Wells Robertson (1888–1956)

Elizabeth Robertson began her career as a classroom art teacher in Chicago and by the 1930s became art director of the Chicago public school system. In 1948 her several decades of devotion to an avocation of quilts was capped with the publication of her book *American Quilts.* Robertson's career was contemporary with that of Webster, and she, too, entered the world of commercial design. She soon found the merchandising element too demanding and dropped it to pursue research, writing, teaching, and lecturing.[8]

One of Robertson's circa 1920 brochures, which accompanies the

Illinois Quilt Research Project registration form, proclaims:

> The Elizabeth Robertson Quilts are delightfully original in design and color, having a refreshing modern note not yet observed in any of the unusual contemporary interpretations of the pioneer art of quilt making. . . . Every Elizabeth Robertson quilt is designed and executed by Miss Robertson in her studio home in Ravinia, Illinois.

Her quilts had been exhibited in Washington, D.C., Los Angeles, San Diego, Pittsburgh, and at Chicago's Art Institute (where one was

Butterflies and Baskets is the Project name for Elizabeth's original-design, all-cotton quilt in which the appliqué work is handsewn, but the sashing is stitched by machine. The quilting (8 stitches per inch), completed by a woman in Kentucky, is worked in grid, outline, and parallel line motifs. A printed tape stitched on the front binding identifies it as one of "The Elizabeth Robertson Quilts," while "Copyrighted 1919 Elizabeth Wells Robertson" is embroidered on the quilt.

awarded the Rosenwald first prize in Textiles), as well as in Edinburgh, Scotland, and Leicester and Letchworth, England.

In the brochure's two columns termed "Comments," the reader learns that Robert Harshe, director of the Art Institute, considered her work "one of the most important developments in the entire American Textile field." Dudley Crafts Watson of the same institution said, "Her quilts are very beautiful indeed, the nearest thing to real folk craft that we have in the middle west, or the United States." The *Chicago Daily News* claimed her "fresh adaptation of the old colonial art of quilt making has received much attention at exhibitions both in the country and in England." In the same newspaper Marguerite Williams wrote, "No more stimulating instance of the delights of needlecraft is to be found than in Elizabeth Wells Robertson's quilts. A lively aptitude for designing led her far astray from the precise patterns of our grandmothers to create something in the more adventurous spirit of today."

Wilkinson Art Quilts (circa 1915–1926)

Rosalie and Ona Wilkinson of Ligonier, Indiana, produced quilts commercially from approximately 1915, when they started the mail-order business, to 1926 when the factory burned. The sisters developed a small design and production company that specialized in selling finished wholecloth luxury quilts for as much as $150. They were touted as "prestigious, impressive works of art," and their production was carefully and personally supervised by the sisters themselves. Marked tops were also available.

[Plate 100]
WHOLECLOTH WILKINSON-TYPE
   ART QUILT
76" x 67"

Maker unknown, dates unknown
Town unknown, possibly Illinois,
   circa 1925
Private collection

The firm's catalog advertised the Wilkinsons' "fine artistic ability and keen vision," which made their products "the most beautiful quilts that human hands could make." The quilts were available in cotton sateen, silk, or combinations of the two fabrics. Cotton, wool, or down could be selected for the batting.[9]

The Wilkinson-type quilt registered with the Project is blue cotton sateen on the front and the back, and the handmade bias-cut binding is from the same fabric. The binding is applied by hand. There is a cotton batt. Clamshell, parallel lines, feathering, and scrolls in the border (6 stitches per inch) are quilting design motifs.

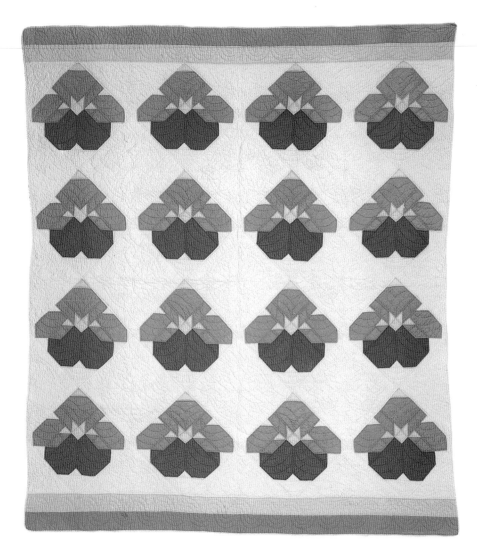

[Plate 101]
PIECED PANSY
83" x 70"

Luzetta Murray Fleming, 1902–
Toulon, Stark County, Illinois, 1930
Collection of the maker

Miss Fleming's all-cotton quilt has hand and machine construction, and the handmade, straight-cut cotton binding is applied by machine on the front and by hand on the back. The primary quilting motifs (10 stitches per inch) are interlocking demilunes on the border, outlines around all of the pansies, and the arc-and-tulip rings on the main portion of the quilt.

Ruby Short McKim (1891–1976)

Ruby McKim was born in Millersburg, Mercer County, Illinois, but spent most of her life in Independence, Missouri.[10] She joined the other early twentieth-century designers in looking to the past for a historical blessing upon the quilting revival. McKim considered quilts, as well as antique period furniture, an important part of the "beauty and tradition bequeathed to us by Colonial forefathers. The American wing of the Metropolitan Museum is not a fad, and neither . . . is quilt making."[11] The graduate of the New York City Parsons School of Fine Arts became, at age nineteen, the art supervisor of the Kansas City school system.[12]

As owner of McKim Studios in the 1920s and 1930s, Ruby McKim acquired a national reputation as an art deco designer. Thomas Woodard and Blanche Greenstein, in a work that focused on quilts of the twentieth century, praised her "fragmented style" for its "unique, zesty appeal."[13] McKim's flower-pattern quilts, such as the Pieced Pansy, Oriental Poppy, and the Beautiful Tulip, imitate the work of machines rather than nature, and harmonize well with the art deco style of the 1930s. She designed her flower blocks with "a jazzy, straight-lined, geo-

[Plate 102]
BEAUTIFUL TULIP
93" x 71"

Myra Haworth Castle, 1871–1942
Ridge Farm, Vermilion County, Illinois,
   1937
Collection of Roberta E. Maudlin

Myra was a devout Quaker who was born and reared in Quaker, Indiana. She then moved to Illinois, where she was living at the time of her death. Late in her life she used a McKim Studios pattern to create what she termed a "summer quilt." The bedcover has a light

cotton batting. Despite McKim's desire to create floral motifs suitable for machine work, Myra's all-cotton quilt is pieced by hand, and the appliquéd stems are also stitched by hand. She did, however, use a sewing machine to stitch one side of the commercial bias tape binding. It is stitched by hand on the back. The quilting (8 stitches per inch) is in the feather border, feather oval, and parallel line motifs.

metric look," so they could be rapidly stitched on a sewing machine rather than laboriously appliquéd by hand. Penny McMorris and Michael Kile contend her designs "remain among the most innovative pieced patterns of all times." Her blocks are not always square; those in the Poppy are rectangular. When she did use a square block, it was often set on point as are those in the Pansy quilt.[14] Her products were not expensive. Around 1930 the Oriental Poppy pattern sold for twenty cents; for $4.50 quilters could buy enough precut poppy pieces to make an entire top.

Ruby McKim was one of the nation's top quilt designers in the early 1930s. Her book *One Hundred and One Patchwork Patterns* was first published in 1931, and her syndicated quilt-pattern column appeared weekly in more than nine hundred newspapers coast to coast. She encouraged readers to use carbon paper to trace her actual-size patterns directly onto the fabric quilt blocks. She was well known for her State Flower and McKim Flower Garden designs. In the early 1930s, the Springfield *Journal* printed her patterns every Sunday.[15]

Serially published patterns could boost newspaper subscriptions. In 1931 the *Illinois State Journal* in Springfield announced that five hundred dollars would be divided among the top three winners in a national quilt contest. A large advertisement provided the details:

Here Is the Complete Plan. *The State Journal* will publish each of these State Flowers Quilt Designs, giving one of them each Sunday. At the close of the series, after you have had time to complete your quilt, there will be an exhibit of these quilts in this city and a committee of impartial judges will choose the best quilt entered. Each of these patterns is worth ten cents. The patterns are given free in this paper and there are no contest fees. Whether you enter the con-

[Plate 103]
FLOWER GARDEN WITH PICKET
    FENCE
91" x 74"

Florence Fretty Hileman, 1902–
Paxton, Ford County, Illinois, circa 1935
Collection of Shirley Hileman Johnson

Mrs. Hileman, who lived with her husband, Edmund, on a farm eight miles southwest of Paxton, entered her McKim-inspired quilt in the Household Science Department of the Ford County Farmer's Institute held at Paxton. She scored a perfect fifty points in the suitability of the article to the purpose, the beauty and quality of design, and the harmony of color and material categories. However, she lost one point in symmetry and accuracy in cutting and three points each in the perfection of stitches and the neatness of finish categories. Her total of ninety-three out of one hundred points earned a third place ribbon.

The top, back, and batting of Florence Hileman's quilt are cotton. There is no binding, as the top is turned to the back and finished by hand. The flower appliqués are turned under and stitched by hand, while the blocks and the fence are joined by machine sewing. The quilting (9 stitches per inch) creates a grid and parallel lines in addition to outlining the appliqués.

test or not, plan to make this beautiful quilt. **Have *The State Journal* Delivered to Your Home Regularly So as Not to Miss a State.**

A fifty-dollar prize was offered for the best local quilt, which would be eligible for the national contest in Washington, D.C.[16]

McKim's popular newspaper patterns were eagerly collected by Depression-era quilters. It is still possible to spot a box of her patterns or a scrapbook filled with McKim clippings at a household auction or at an antique shop. Sometimes a quilt ephemera collector is fortunate enough to find an entire set. One owner possesses all the patterns for McKim's Fruit Basket, which was published serially each Sunday in Springfield's, *Illinois State Journal* between September 23, 1932, and June 11, 1933. The thirty-four-part set consists of thirty-two different fruits and an overview of the completed quilt top, illustrated the first week, with the directions for the pieced basket given the second Sunday.

Ruby's newspaper column started in 1928 when the Kansas City *Star* began its famous quilt pattern column. Her first pattern was the Pine Tree, on September 22. She continued issuing patterns through the *Star,* and seventy-five appeared until her last column ran on July 26, 1930.[17] She went on to a decade-long successful syndicated quilt column of her own.

It was not uncommon for nationally successful mail-order quilt businesses, even those managed by hard-working businesswomen such

The Fruit Basket Quilt

All the riot of color and charming variety of form that are found in nature's abundant fruits are captured and conventionalized for the making of the Fruit Basket Quilt. This drawing shows it in miniature only but when the blocks are made in full size and natural colors all set together as shown, the result is gorgeous.

This quilt combines applique and outline stitch most effectively, yet it is easily made by following the detailed directions that will be furnished to you. The exact pattern for each block will be printed in this paper and all you have to do is to be sure and save each design as it is published and then trace the pattern through carbon paper to your material and work up the block as directed.

There are thirty-two blocks in the entire series with cutting patterns and quilting patterns to complete. When these are set together as shown the blocks will make a top about 66x83 inches. The borders can be varied to make as much larger as desired. Even though you do not plan to make the Fruit Basket Quilt immediately, clip and save each pattern.

The blocks, naming them from left to right beginning at the top are: Malaga Grapes, Lime, Kumquat, Queen Anne Cherries, Blueberries, Currants, Blackberries, Red Cherries, Tangerine, Gooseberries, Strawberries, Lemon, Pineapple, Bananas, Red Raspberries, Pears, Figs, Loganberries, Quince, Delicious Apple, Avocado, Concord Grapes, Persimmon, Pomegranate, Prune Plum, Crab Apple, Oranges, Red Plum, Apricot, Yellow Apple, Grapefruit, Peach.

Note: If you have any special inquiries regarding this quilt or quilt making in general, just write Ruby Short McKim, Quilt Editor, in care of this paper enclosing a self-addressed and stamped envelope and she will answer you personally without charge.

[Figure 41]
McKim Studios Fruit Basket Quilt
  Design
Illinois State Journal, September 23, 1932
Private collection

as McKim, to decline in the 1940s as popular interest in quilting waned. During World War II, Ruby McKim wisely turned her business interest from quilting to dolls and founded the Kimport Doll Company. However, over the years Ruby Short McKim's contribution to quilting has never been forgotten; and, as the *Quilter's Newsletter Magazine* noted in 1984, the popularity of her patterns "never seems to wane."[19]

[Plate 104]
FRUIT BASKET
84" x 63"

Mayme Beaman Bender, 1909–1975
Nokomis, Montgomery County, Illinois,
    circa 1933
Collection of Mary Beth Weeks

It is possible Mayme Bender collected
the Fruit Basket patterns from the
Springfield *Journal.* She certainly followed McKim's directions. Each of the
thirty-two different fruits is in its spec-
ified location, and the recommended
appliqué fruit colors closely follow her
directions. Perhaps Mayme purchased

her fabrics directly from the designer. For
one dollar, McKim offered "enough
beautiful walnut brown in fast color to
piece the thirty-two little baskets" and
sufficient amounts of the required colored cotton "to make all the appliqués
used in the thirty-two blocks."[18]
    Mayme's pieced and appliquéd Fruit
Basket quilt is made entirely of cotton
with cotton binding. It is all handwork
and is quilted (8–9 stitches per inch) in
outline and braid motifs.

Anne Champe Orr (1875–1946)

Anne Orr of Nashville, Tennessee, achieved national recognition from 1919 to 1940 when she served as needlework editor of *Good Housekeeping*.[20] As the daughter of a wealthy family, Anne's early training was in art rather than practical stitching. A neighbor later commented that she suspected one of the nation's premier needlework authorities actually had very little practical quilting experience. It was scarcely a secret that she had a large number of female employees in Tennessee and Kentucky who made the completed quilts and other hand-stitched articles she sold to wealthy customers.[21]

Orr's literary experience began in 1913 with a needlework column in the Nashville-based *Southern Woman's Magazine*. After the publication went out of business in 1918, Mrs. Orr produced crochet patterns for J. P. Coats Thread Company and the Clark Thread Company. It was through her work for *Good Housekeeping* that she attracted a national following and eventually developed a profitable mail-order business.

Her first quilt pattern, an appliqué Mother Goose design, appeared in 1921. During the following years, she introduced an additional thirty-five appliqué quilts, as well as thirty pieced and two wholecloth quilt patterns. Quilts became a regular part of every monthly column in 1928, and her original patterns began in 1929. Much of her early needlework career was devoted to developing graph paper designs for cross-stitch embroidery and filet crochet. Thus, it is not surprising that her most distinctive quilt patterns are composed of one-inch squares of color that imitate these designs. Today, her name is synonymous with the style.[22]

Anne Orr's position with *Good Housekeeping* offered her a national platform from which she could join

[Plate 105]
STAR FLOWER
92" x 76"

Garnet Pearson Pinckly, 1876–1961
Bushnell, McDonough County, Illinois, 1932
Collection of Harriet Pinckly Bricker

Hundreds of small cotton pieces are combined to create this monochromatic quilt top. The batting, top, back, and straight-cut binding are cotton. All the piecing on the top is by hand, and the binding is applied by machine on the front and by hand on the back. The quilting (10 stitches per inch) is in grid, scroll, and floral motifs. The quilting does not match the Orr quilt illustrated in *Good Housekeeping,* January 1935, page 57. That bedcovering has a scalloped edge that is much more typical of an Anne Orr design than the straight edge used by Mrs. Pinckly. The differences indicate the maker used a pattern and did not work from a kit.

[Plate 106]
IRIS APPLIQUÉ
86″ x 72″

Helen Eugenia Ehlin Ranguette,
    1904–1981
Chicago, Cook County, Illinois,
    circa 1940
Collection of Jeanette L. Billstrand

The all-cotton quilt with cotton batting is bound by factory-made cotton bias tape that is applied by machine on the front and finished by hand on the back. The entire top is appliquéd by hand. The quilting (8 stitches per inch) is worked in grid, outline, and interlocking-swirl motifs.

her contemporary, Marie Webster, in promoting a romanticized link between the quilting revival and America's colonial past. "Women of Colonial times made beautiful hand-pieced quilts which they preserved as heirlooms," Orr wrote in her January 1933 column. She praised Storrowton, near West Springfield, Massachusetts, as "an ideal American Colonial community." It was at this "old New England village" that the 1932 Eastern States Exposition quilt contest was held. Orr's national reputation earned her a position on the judging panel there. She was also named one of the four judges for the Sears quilt contest held in conjunction with the 1933 Chicago World's Fair.[23]

Two of Anne Orr's patterns made it into the finals of the Sears contest. An Autumn Leaf quilt, a January 1930 *Good Housekeeping* introduction, won at Kansas City but did not place at Chicago. The pattern, however, was included under the name Autumn Leaves in the *Sears Century of Progress in Quilt Making* book. That pattern was also entered in a preliminary contest by an Illinois quiltmaker (Plate 113). Anne Orr's Lincoln Quilt, touted as a copy of one made by Abraham Lincoln's mother, won the Memphis regional contest and was shown at Chicago. Although Orr published the pattern in January 1933, the quiltmaker acquired the pattern from a friend.[24]

In the same article with the Lincoln Quilt, Orr illustrated a scalloped-edge Iris appliqué quilt. Helen Ranguette of Chicago made a quilt in this pattern before World War II. The iron-on transfer patterns Anne Orr offered for sale in her monthly columns did not include quilting directions, which were sold separately. The quilting motifs Mrs. Ranguette used on the central medallion-type bedcovering do not match those on the quilt illustrated in *Good Housekeeping.* She probably purchased Orr's transfer pattern to make the appliqué flowers and leaves but used her own quilting design. While Orr's prices were never extravagant, this evidence indicates Helen economized by purchasing the pattern rather than the more expensive eight-dollar kit. A quilt made from a prestamped top would have been quilted with the standard pattern.[25]

During the time the Nashville designer served as a *Good Housekeeping* editor, she routinely advertised her patterns in her monthly column. After her 1940 retirement, Orr made some of her better-selling patterns available through the Lockport Cotton Batting Company. Other Anne Orr-type patterns were eventually distributed through Montgomery Ward and Stearns and Foster, but there is no documentation to indicate those patterns were actually her original designs; and no credit was given to her when they were advertised and sold.[26]

In reality, Orr's "squared off" design was based upon a traditional graph paper technique used to convey a color scheme for needlework patterns. Surprisingly, it also possesses a contemporary computer graphic quality. They are distinctive. Nevertheless, these patterns represent only 15 percent of all the quilts she presented in her columns, and very few of them are seen today. It would certainly seem that the tedious hand sewing required to join several thousand small pieces into a completed top would have made these quilts special and worth saving. Her quilts were, however, not the only designs based upon small square pieces.

Similarly sized square pieces were commonly used during the Depression era in quilts known as Postage Stamp or Trip Around the World (Plate 32, "Goldie's Quilt"). While they are not as plentiful as Grandmother's Flower Garden quilts, they are found more frequently than the Anne Orr squared-off designs that were made during the same period. That there are a relatively small number of Orr squared-design quilts in existence may mean only a few were made in comparison to the many other more traditional designs pieced by Illinois quilters during the Great Depression. Why? Perhaps the an-

[Figure 42]
Lockport Batting Company
   advertisement
Circa early 1940s
Private collection

The Lockport flyer features Anne Orr's Cross Stitch Bouquet design and her Lincoln Quilt. However, her name is not mentioned in the ad.
Private collection

swer lies in the theory proposed by Merikay Waldvogel. Comparing Anne Orr's patterns and target audience to that of Laura Wheeler, she convincingly presents the idea that Orr appealed to a modern clientele interested in the new look in quilting while Wheeler attracted a much more traditional audience.[27]

Orr's patterns required a pattern and purchased fabrics. A Postage Stamp quilt could come from the scrap bag, and experienced quilters did not need to subscribe to *Good Housekeeping,* or even to buy a pattern, in order to make a Trip Around the World quilt.

Not every ambitious businesswoman became as successful as Marie Webster, Ruby McKim, and Anne Orr. There were, however, many other designers, promoters, and writers who made important contributions to the quilt revival. Public demand created business opportunities, and any ambitious player could get into the game. It is surprising how many businesswomen developed a profitable operation on the basis of what was essentially a cottage industry. Although the high unemployment rate of the 1930s meant many people were looking for work, a few creative individuals sought investment opportunities. A brief glance at the magazine advertisements of the time provides an idea of how many quilters tried to take advantage of the opportunities available during the craft's strong revival.

Scioto Imhoff Danner (1891–1974)

Mrs. Danner liked to quilt. In the late 1920s she was recently divorced when she discovered that wealthy people would pay twenty-five dollars for a completed quilt. She thought she had struck gold. Encouraged by her mother, she began displaying her quilts at department stores in Kansas and Oklahoma. When she exhibited her quilts at the Innes department store in Wichita, she learned that there was another angle to the quilt business. Those who admired her quilts but could not afford to buy them wanted to purchase the patterns.

Mrs. Danner's "manufacturing" process ultimately became the mimeograph machine. Her patterns sold well at prices that varied from twenty-five cents to two dollars. Shortly after publishing a catalog, she began to acquire a national reputation. However, she soon tired of the work, became ill, and issued no additional catalogs for almost twenty years. After her father's death in 1945, Scioto returned to El Dorado, Kansas, to live with her mother. Requests for quilt patterns arrived continuously; thus she printed updated catalogs in 1954, 1958, and 1969. In 1970 Mrs. Danner sold out to Helen Ericson, a business associate.[28]

Newspaper Quilt Columns

These columns, such as one published by the Kansas City *Star,* made an important contribution to the quilt revival of the 1920s and 1930s. In reality, the columns were paid advertisements, and they regularly appeared in many Illinois papers. Editing a quilt pattern column offered women designers and illustrators employment and a chance eventually to develop their own business. After Ruby McKim of McKim Studios became the first designer to provide patterns for the *Star,* she went on to a national newspaper quilt column career, but her work had opened a door of opportunity for other pattern designers and/or illustrators.[29]

Two Kansas City illustrators followed in McKim's footsteps. Evaline Foland, whose career at the *Star* overlapped McKim's, published her first quilt pattern in March 1929. She was already employed by the newspaper as a fashion illustrator when she began drawing quilt pictures. She left the paper in December 1932 to teach fashion art at a Kansas City school[30] and was followed by Edna Marie Dunn, the most anonymous of the three and also the longest lasting. Born and trained in Chicago, Dunn began her long career with the *Star* in 1922 as a fashion artist. She was not a quilter, and she relied upon her readers for pattern suggestions rather than creating original designs; so she signed almost none of her illustrations. In reality, she administered a huge quilt pattern exchange from the time she took over the column in 1932 until it was discontinued in the 1950s.[31]

Newspaper quilt columnists were not, however, always real people. Famous designers, such as Webster, McKim, and Orr, used their actual names professionally. So did Mrs. Danner, but the lack of a first name produced a more generic effect. Assumed names for quilt promoters proliferated during the 1930s with many a corporate business lurking behind a host of fictitious names. Aunt Jane's quilt pattern catalog appeared in 1914, and she would eventually be followed by the anonymous Grandmas Dexter and Clark who were created to evoke a comfortable image for their respective thread companies.

Laura Wheeler and Alice Brooks were fictional names used by Old Chelsea Station Needlecraft Service to sell quilt patterns through local newspapers. The column first appeared in the early 1930s. That company also provided quilt pattern service for Chicago's well-known midwestern weekly farm magazine, *Prairie Farmer.*

Another name associated with quilts that appeared in many Illinois newspapers during the Great Depression was Nancy Page. The syndicated column was written by Florence LaGanke, a home economist from Cleveland, Ohio. Nancy Cabot was an Illinois-based syndicate originating with the Chicago *Tribune* in 1933 that produced more than two thousand patterns under several names in addition to Nancy's. Barbara Brackman's research reveals Cabot emphasized appliqué and "was one of the first to publish and name the classic designs of the mid-19th century, and [the column] was one of the major sources of modern appliqué patterns that reflect the taste of the 1930s."[32]

Surely one of the most famous fictional pattern purveyors was Aunt Martha. She first entered the marketplace in the early 1930s as a part of Jack and Clara Tillotson's Colonial Readicut Quilt Block Company that soon became Colonial Patterns, Inc. As their original syndicated quilt pattern column did not have a personalized image, a Chicago editor suggested the name Martha to provide a link to Mrs. Washington and colonial times.

Occasionally, Colonial issued a group of patterns in packets and sold them as Aunt Martha's Workbasket. That name was soon attached to a popular monthly needlework publication that appeared during the 1930s and 1940s. When Colonial/Aunt Martha's Studio and *Workbasket* divided in 1949, the Tillotson family retained the publication but rarely printed quilt patterns. *Workbasket* did, however, continue to distribute iron-on transfers that could sometimes be used as

Laura Wheeler Designs

BUTTERFLY   PATTERN 1408

BUTTERFLIES GLORIFY PIECED QUILT

Butterflies—wings spread for flight—make this most stunning "Nature" quilt. And here's the marvel of it—their wings are composed of otherwise useless scraps—colorful ones, set in, in a fan shape. Here's a wonderfully simple 10 inch block to piece! Lovely when done! Pattern 1408 contains complete, simple instructions for cutting, sewing and finishing, together with yardage chart, diagram of quilt to help arrange the blocks for single and double bed size, and a diagram of block which serves as a guide for placing the patches and suggests contrasting materials.

Send 10 cents in stamps or coin (coin preferred) for this pattern to Illinois State Register, Needlecraft Dept., 82 Eighth Avenue, New York, N. Y. Write plainly pattern number, your name and address.

Contents: Merchandise
Postmaster: This parcel may be opened for postal inspection if necessary.

BLOOMINGTON PANTAGRAPH
NEEDLECRAFT DEPARTMENT
82 EIGHTH AVE.   NEW YORK CITY

Return Postage Guaranteed

Laura Wheeler Designs

When you order two or more patterns you may not receive them at the same time as they are mailed in separate wrappers.

[Figure 43]
Laura Wheeler newspaper
    advertisement
Springfield, *Illinois State Journal,* February
    10, 1937.
Laura Wheeler address return on an
    envelope for a pattern ordered
    through the Bloomington *Pantagraph,*
    circa 1950
Private collections

Laura Wheeler advertised quilt patterns in local newspapers. They were ordered through that publication but were then mailed to a New York City address. When the pattern was sent to the customer, the return address indicated the newspaper through which it had been ordered. This system helped the pattern company know which newspapers generated enough business to merit continued advertising in that locality.

[Plate 107]
LOVE IN THE MIST
100″ x 82″

Victorena Stanis, 1923–
Westville, Vermilion County, Illinois,
1968
Collection of the maker

Victorena ("Vic") Stanis acquired an Aunt Martha pattern through the *Workbasket* magazine in the early 1950s but did not use it for many years. When she had time to begin quilting again in the 1960s, it was the second quilt she would make. The top and the back are a cotton/polyester blend, while some of the appliqué pieces are all cotton. The pink petals are reverse appliqué under the blue. The binding is commercial bias tape stitched by machine on top and by hand on the back. The batt is polyester. The quilting (5 stitches per inch) is in flower and feather motifs that supplement the stitches outlining the appliqués.

quilt patterns. Although the patterns are not marked, the company is the only one to use red ink transfer lines on cream paper. Colonial/Aunt Martha's Studio, the Kansas City-based pattern company, occasionally produced Aunt Martha's patterns. In 1974 Aunt Martha's Studio once again became Colonial Patterns, Inc., and it successfully rode the crest of the 1970s quilting wave as it had forty years earlier in the 1930s.[33]

The widespread publicity that quilts received through newspapers often sparked an interest in the past. The link between our colonial past and the quilt revival encouraged a study of quilting history. Slowly, writers probed deeper and moved beyond a search for patterns. Several authors made important contributions to preserving the nation's quilt heritage. In the introduction to her 1915 book *Quilts: Their Story and How to Make Them,* Marie Webster correctly notes that "the quilt is one of the most familiar and necessary articles in our households [but] its story is yet to be told."[34] Her work was the first serious attempt to study the American quilt, and it remained the only book in the field for many years.

Ruth Ebright Finley (1884–1955)

Ruth Finley, who is famous in quilt history as a writer rather than as a designer, was the second American author to produce a quilt book. The Ohio-born writer dropped out of Oberlin College to work for the Cleveland *Press.* She married fellow journalist Emmet Finley in 1910, and ten years later the couple accepted jobs in New York City. They acquired an 1810 home on Long Island, and Ruth became an antique collector at a time when there was a rising emphasis on Americana. Her interest in the Colonial Revival led her to quilt collecting, and an inherent curiosity about the past encouraged her to collect the stories that

came with the antique bedcoverings.[35]

Almost fifteen years after Marie Webster had opened the door, Ruth Finley published her 1929 work, *Old Patchwork Quilts and the Women Who Made Them,* which detailed the origin of quilt names and the migration of patterns.[36] The experienced journalist's work was a valuable contribution to quilt scholarship that is still used today.

Carrie Alma Hackett Hall (1866–1955)

Carrie Hall dedicated an important part of her life to quilts. Her childhood interest in the craft bloomed after World War I when she started collecting quilt patterns. She began the project with all the exuberance familiar to most collectors but eventually realized the task she had set for herself was far more complex than she ever imagined. Carrie filled six scrapbooks with patterns clipped from magazines and newspapers and made approximately one thousand quilt blocks before deciding there was no end in sight. She frequently shared her treasured collection with others. In the 1930s Carrie assumed the title Madam Hall, donned "colonial" attire, packed a suitcase full of her blocks, and became famous for the quilt talks she offered to a variety of audiences.

Carrie Hall eventually donated more than eight hundred of her valuable blocks to the Spencer Museum of Art at the University of Kansas, where the collection has benefited quilt students ever since. In recent years it afforded help to Lawrence resident Barbara Brackman as she prepared her monumental pattern encyclopedia. However, when Hall and fellow author Rose Kretsinger published *The Romance of the Patchwork Quilt in America* in 1935, there was no encyclopedia, and Hall's listing of patterns was the first attempt to provide a standardized list. For many years her small black and white photographs of about eight hundred patterns provided the only visual aid for interested quilt scholars.[37]

Rose Good Kretsinger (1886–1963)

Carrie Hall's co-author, Rose Kretsinger, was both a student and teacher at Chicago's Art Institute in the early twentieth century. While in Chicago, she also worked as a jewelry and fabric designer. Rosie, as she was known, traveled to Europe and by 1915 was living in Emporia, Kansas, as the wife of William S. Kretsinger, a local lawyer. She did not become interested in quilting until the late 1920s; but when that interest developed, she left her mark on the craft.

One of Kretsinger's most lasting contributions was her work as co-author of *The Romance of the Patchwork Quilt* with Carrie Hall. In the 1930s she shared her quilt knowledge with a circle of interested students, and that group has steadily grown larger over the ensuing decades. In her portion of the volume she noted: "In the last few years there has been a sort of universal enthusiasm for quilting, which has prompted the making of many different things in both modernistic and old colonial modes." It was the latter style that most seriously attracted her design attention and enabled her to make a second contribution to America's quilt heritage. She borrowed ideas and motifs from previously published works, such as the Indiana Wreath frontispiece from Webster's book, and updated several intricate nineteenth-century quilts for the Colonial Revival style of the Depression era. The best-known and most outstanding of

these adapted designs is a central medallion wreath, which she named Paradise Garden.[38] It inspired many copies, including one created by Marian Brockschmidt of Springfield.

The original Garden quilt that Kretsinger adapted appeared as Plate 57, a black and white illustration, in Ruth Finley's *Old Patchwork Quilts*. Finley photographed the quilt, which belonged to one of her Long Island neighbors. The owner attributed it to an ancestor, Arsinoe Kelsey Bowen, a minister's wife from Cortland, New York, who completed it in 1857 after working on it for some years. After Finley's book was published, copies of the quilt won several national quilting contests as well as state fair competitions. Hand-colored drafts of the pattern sold for as much as five dollars in Kansas during the 1930s.

After Rose Kretsinger created her version, which she named Paradise Garden, she won several prizes on it and began receiving requests for her pattern. For many years she shared her patterns, but like many others she was eventually forced by the volume of requests to begin selling them. They were priced from $2.00 to $3.50 and were sold through *Farm Journal* and *The Farmer's Wife*. Mary Kretsinger, her daughter, said "her mother never really thought of quilt-making as a 'business' or herself as a 'quilt designer.' . . . My mother enjoyed art and needlework and did it all for fun. She was never competitive." Barbara Brackman's recent attempt to learn more about the maker of this famous 1857 bedcovering, or to locate the original quilt, proved unsuccessful. Kretsinger's adaptation, however, is safely preserved in the

Spencer Museum of Art on the campus of the University of Kansas at Lawrence.

Like many of her contemporary quilt designers, Kretsinger placed her primary emphasis upon the quilt top design rather than on the quilting. She did not do her own quilting and advised others to concentrate on the appliqué work and to find a professional to do the stitching.[39]

Quilt designers, researchers and authors of quilt books, and popular women's and farm-wife-oriented magazines all contributed to an increased interest in quilts and a heightened awareness of our American heritage, but they spread a host of historical and technological myths. It would take much more serious historical research over the next half-century to begin reconstructing a completely accurate quilt history of Illinois and the United States.

Without a doubt, quilting reached a new peak of popularity in the early twentieth century, when the Colonial Revival appliqué designs of Marie Webster and Anne Orr achieved national popularity. These well-known designers favored a return to the central medallion of the nineteenth century and replaced the straight binding with a sculptured edge. Both women emphasized the use of solid-colored cotton fabric that utilized the currently popular pastel shades. The impact of these innovative, enterprising businesswomen upon the quilt paths of Illinois is evident from even a cursory examination of the early twentieth-century quilts registered with the Illinois Quilt Research Project.

[Plate 108]
PARADISE GARDEN
102″ x 102″

Marian Kanke Brockschmidt, 1922–
Springfield, Sangamon County, Illinois,
  1990
Collection of the maker

Mrs. Kretsinger based her 1945 appliqué and stuffed-work design upon an
1857 quilt. Marian Brockschmidt, a well-
known central-Illinois quilter, saw the
Kretsinger masterpiece while attending
the 1978 Kansas Quilt Symposium, and
she eventually found the time to make

her own copy. Like most of her quilts, it
won a prize at the Illinois State Fair.

The cotton top and back of the
Brockschmidt quilt are separated by a
polyester batting. The handmade cotton
bias binding is machine stitched on the
front and hand sewn on the back. The
top is all hand construction. It is quilted
(8 stitches per inch) in diagonal parallel
lines and feather scroll motifs. The top
contains 1,886 appliqué pieces.

[Plate 109]
Sears, Roebuck Century of Progress
   building
Souvenir post card, 1933
Private collection

A Contest Encourages Commercialization

Although the Sears Century of Progress quilt show provided more publicity for the nation's quilters and the craft of quilting than any other single event in the twentieth century, it was not the first national quilt contest. Cuesta Benberry's research indicates that honor goes to the competition held at historic Storrowton, Massachusetts, in 1932. This was a part of the Eastern States Exposition, which sponsored additional national contests in 1933 and 1936. The Fairy quilt (Plate 59) by Ruby Lundgren of Rockford, Illinois, received one of four "special awards" in the 1936 competition. Prior to the Storrowton event, national quilt block competitions had been sponsored by periodicals, including *Comfort Magazine* (Augusta, Maine), 1921–22; *Capper's Weekly* (Topeka, Kansas), 1926; *Michigan Farmer* (Detroit, Michigan), 1926; *Farm and Fireside* (Springfield, Ohio), 1929; and, during the 1920s, a series of monthly quilt block contests sponsored by *Household Journal* of Batavia, Illinois. Several major contests were also sponsored by newspapers, such as the 1931 event hosted by the Springfield, *Illinois State Journal*.[40]

Thirty prize-winning quilts were exhibited in the Sears building on the Century of Progress fairgrounds in Chicago during the summers of 1933 and 1934.

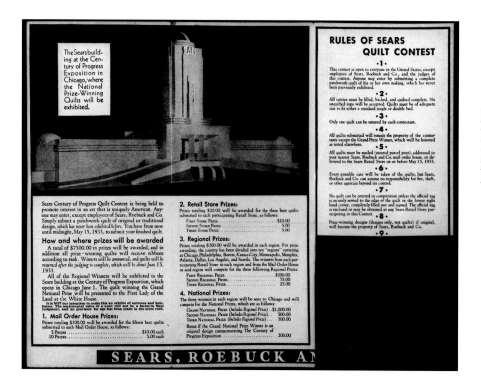

[Figure 44]
Rules for the Sears Century of Progress quilt contest were published in January 1933. All entries had to be taken to a local retail or mail-order store before May 15, 1933.

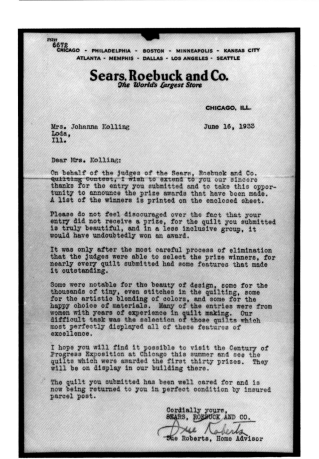

[Figure 45]
In June 1933, after the final winners were selected, Mrs. Kolling, like all other entrants, received a letter of thanks from the contest sponsor.

[Figure 46]
All contest entrants also received a list of the top winners at Chicago and in their region. It is unusual to find a contestant who saved every bit of documentation associated with her prized creation's brush with greatness in America's famous quilt contest.

After the Chicago-based national mail-order company announced its contest in January 1933, its local retail facilities were deluged with almost 25,000 quilts. The three best entries from each Sears, Roebuck store went to one of the ten regional centers. Once again, three quilts were selected from each site and sent to the final competition in Chicago. A panel of four judges picked the grand prize winner and the runners-up. Sears, Roebuck and Company displayed all thirty quilts in its building on the fairgrounds. The exhibit was seen by more than five million of the visitors who flooded the Chicago lakefront in 1933 and 1934 to celebrate the Windy City's one hundredth birthday.[41]

Several Illinois-made quilts registered with the Project were entered in the contest, and a few received green Merit Award ribbons. None, however, made it into the elite group

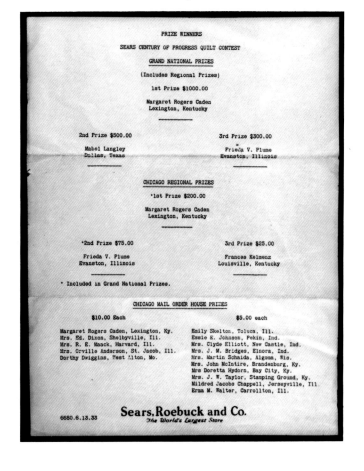

of thirty winners exhibited at the fair. All contestants received the same materials. Most prize winners still have the small green ribbon, but few kept the full set of documentation retained by Mrs. Johanna Kolling of Loda.

There was not much time available between the contest announcement in January and the last day to enter a quilt in May 1933. The rules very clearly discouraged owners from entering antiques; but at a time when experienced quilters actively plied their craft, it is likely many contest entries were newly out of the frame when the owner learned about the contest. The family of Mrs. Kolling believes she completed her prize quilt shortly before the contest was announced.

New York Beauty was, by the 1930s, an old pattern with a recently standardized name. Its popularity rose after Mountain Mist placed the picture prominently on its colorful wrapper in 1931. A brief glance at its picture there will reveal Mrs. Kolling's source of inspiration. The pink and blue colors, the two-part solid-color borders, the eight-pointed pink and blue star at the sashing corners, the white stripe through the middle of the sashing,

[Plate 110]
NEW YORK BEAUTY
88" x 83"

Johanna Foehr Kolling, 1865–1950
Loda, Iroquois County, Illinois,
    circa 1932
Collection of Shirley J. Meece

Mrs. Kolling's New York Beauty is pieced and quilted entirely by hand. She used a sewing machine to attach the commercial bias tape binding on the front, but it is stitched by hand on the back. It is an all-cotton quilt, including the batting. The quilting motifs (9 stitches per inch) include chains and feathering in the border and long feathering, circles, and wreaths with a center grid, in addition to outline stitching around the small pieces.

and the diagonal set match the illustration exactly.

The New York Beauty pattern dates back to the early 1800s and has been known by several different names during its long history. Although New York Beauty may have been its common name in the Northeast, it was also known as Split Rail, Sunrise, Crown of Thorns, Rocky Mountain Road, Great Divide, and Springtime in the Rockies. When Stearns and Foster began using the illustration on its Mountain Mist wrapper, New York Beauty became the commonly accepted pattern name for this "dramatic design which commands respect."[42]

[Plate 111]
Mrs. Kolling won a Merit Award ribbon on the New York Beauty quilt that she entered in the 1933 Sears contest.

[Figure 47]
Johanna Foehr Kolling and her daughter, Mary Kolling Gingerich, who helped her mother complete the quilt.

pieced and appliquéd quilts attracted the eyes of the four judges.[43]

Although this added incentive stirred many women to new heights of creativity, the regional and national judges routinely by-passed such entries. At least one disgusted quilter wrote to complain about wasting her time trying to follow the guidelines. She was especially miffed by the rumor that "One of the judges was overheard to state she could not give three minutes of her time to consider a Century of Progress design."[44]

Sixty-year-old Sarah E. Preble was one Illinois quilter who attempted to win the creativity award

[Plate 112]
FORT DEARBORN
97" x 79"

Sarah Green Preble, 1873–1956
Steger, Will County, Illinois, 1933
Collection of Sally Diegnau

Like so many girls of her generation, Sarah learned at the early age of seven the proper use of a needle and acceptable quilting techniques while working with her mother and other older women. Her 1933 contest entry is constructed entirely by hand and of all-cotton materials. It is quilted (9 stitches per inch) in grid and parallel line motifs with fans in the corners. The center fort scene is embroidered in a running stitch. It is surrounded by pieced multiple borders that graphically depict the protective palisades of the 1804 frontier fortress.

Fort Dearborn, the original settlement that became Chicago, appealed to many amateur quilt designers as an ideal theme to depict a century of progress. Although some quilts may have been completed before the contest was advertised, there was an entire category that had to be designed and made within a very short time span. These were the "theme quilts."

There is little doubt that the grand prize of one thousand dollars was a tremendous lure to America's quilters, who were struggling to survive the nation's greatest financial depression. In addition to the large monetary prizes awarded in Chicago, many modest amounts were distributed to the regional winners. One prize, however, was never awarded. The contest prospectus noted that "if the Grand Prize Winner is an original design commemorating the Century of Progress Exposition," an additional two hundred dollars would go to the lucky quilter. A few theme quilts were exhibited at Chicago, but none received an award. Only the traditional

[Plate 113]
AUTUMN LEAF
90" x 74"

Anna Sandhagen Meyer, 1865–1966
Loda, Iroquois County, Illinois, 1932
Collection of Ruth M. Studley

Autumn Leaf achieved much wider popularity because of the Sears contest. The vast array of Depression-era print cottons used for the numerous leaves usually offers the researcher a good index to the colors and patterns available in the 1930s. Anna Meyer's all-cotton quilt is bound with homemade straight-cut binding that is stitched by machine on the front and sewn by hand on the back. Although the appliqué is by hand, the top is pieced together by machine. The quilting (7 stitches per inch) is in the floral, grid, and parallel line motifs.

in addition to the Grand Prize. Like Mrs. Kolling, she won a green Merit Award ribbon. She created the design, cut the pieces, and sewed them together by hand. It was quilted on a frame made by her husband, Jesse. After winning a green ribbon, the quilt was displayed in a Sears, Roebuck store in Chicago at Halsted and Sixty-third streets. Her granddaughter has preserved the quilt and its Merit Award ribbon.

Sarah's quilt commemorated the log fort that stood on the south bank of the Chicago River near the original Lake Michigan shoreline. The historical site is well marked today at the corner of Michigan Avenue and Wacker Drive. The fort was destroyed during the Fort Dearborn Massacre in June 1812 as the War of 1812 began on the Illinois frontier.

Autumn Leaf was introduced by Anne Orr in *Good Housekeeping* in January 1930. As a modern multi-scrap quilt in an old-fashioned medallion-style format, it appealed to many would-be winners as an ideal way to depict a century of progress in quilting. Anna Meyer entered her recently completed quilt in the Sears contest. Although her entry was not a major winner, two Anne Orr patterns made it to Chicago. Another Autumn Leaf quilt received the top prize at the Kansas City regional contest, and the Lincoln Quilt design placed first at Memphis. However, neither received an award at Chicago. Nevertheless, Autumn Leaf was included among the winning patterns in *Sears Century of Progress in Quilt Making,* where it was called the Autumn Leaves pattern.[45]

Iris, the easy-to-grow and ever-popular "flag" found in many early Illinois flower gardens, appeared in modern dress on the wrapper of Mountain Mist batting as early as 1930. Like most quilts, the appliqué

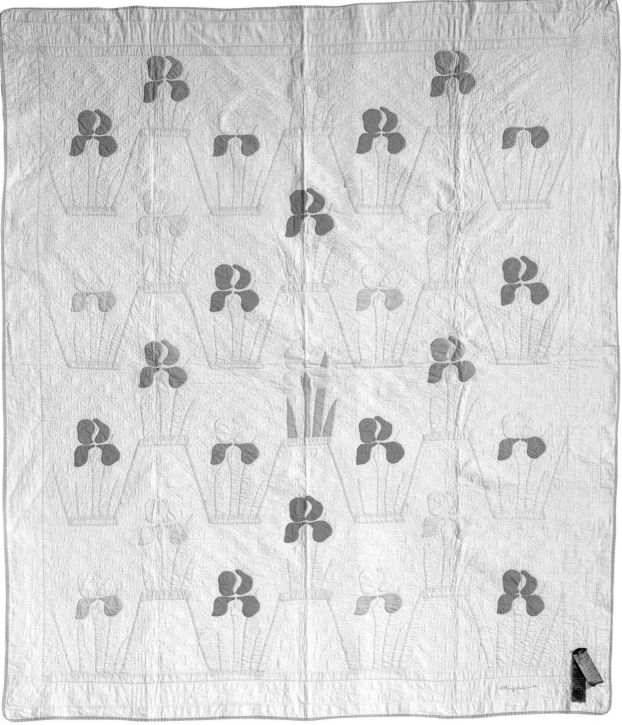

[Plate 114]
IRIS
78″ x 71″

Antoinette Bergeron Betourne, 1913–
Kankakee, Kankakee County, Illinois,
    1933
Collection of the maker

A cotton flannel sheet is used for filling
between the cotton top and cotton back.
The handmade straight-cut green cotton
binding is stitched by machine on the
front and sewn by hand on the back. All
the appliqué work is by hand, but the
border is attached by machine. The
quilting (9 stitches per inch) is in double
grid lines and a diamond and oval chain
in the border. The Iris pattern was available from Stearns and Foster as early as
1930 and remained on their list for many
years.[46]

quilt made by high school student Antoinette Bergeron was meant to be used on a bed. The extent to which they may have been intended for occasional rather than daily use is, of course, different from quilter to quilter.

Despite ample evidence of wear and fading, the Iris appliqué quilt from Kankakee County proudly appeared at the Bourbonnais registration day with the 1933 Sears Merit Award green ribbon attached to a corner. When Miss Bergeron took her new quilt home from the Sears contest, she had little choice regarding its future. During the Great Depression, most newlyweds had little extra money for the necessary bedding, and when the contest was over the beautiful new quilt was used for its intended purpose.

Florence Baxter's Flower Garden quilt, like many others, failed to meet the May 15 deadline. Without a doubt, the Sears proposal encouraged thousands of quilters to enter their very best work in the Century of Progress contest. How many grew tired of the project or were unavoidably delayed and missed the deadline will never be known. However, at least one Project registration fits into this category.

A seed catalog inspired Florence to create her many different lifelike floral appliqués. She was living with her parents when she made this quilt. The present owner, her niece, was about six years old at the time it was in the quilting frame. Since Audrey often visited her grandparents, she remembers sitting with her chin on the quilting frame and watching her aunt create the intricate quilting that embellishes the top. Even a hasty examination will indicate Florence would not be rushed to meet a deadline. Creating a true showpiece was far more important to her than the faint possibility of winning an award.

It is regrettable that Florence Baxter's quilt was not completed in time to be entered in the contest.

However, as striking as the workmanship may be to the eye today, it probably had little chance of displacing the ultimate winners. The four judges—Mary McElwain, a Walworth, Wisconsin, quilt collector, designer, and quilt shop owner; Sue Roberts, Sears, Roebuck home advisor; Beth Burnett of the Chicago Art Institute; and Anne Orr from *Good Housekeeping*—selected traditional patterns and placed primary emphasis upon outstanding quilting.[47]

The Sears contest encouraged what was already a rich and growing American craft tradition. The regional and national winning patterns attracted much attention and were often copied by other quilters in the remaining years of the decade.[48]

[Plate 115]
FLOWER GARDEN
94" x 72"

Florence Baxter, 1904–1973 `
Hume, Edgar County, Illinois, 1933–34
Collection of Audrey B. Porter

The workmanship on this all-cotton quilt serves to enhance the design, which is reminiscent of a diamond-shaped Trip Around the World placement, as the rows of flowers surround the yellow daisies in the quilt's center. The edges of the appliquéd flowers are turned under, and the colorful blossoms of cotton fabric are attached with a blanket stitch. The quilt edges are turned in. All the work is by hand. The quilting (12 stitches per inch) creates fleurs-de-lis and grids and outlines the appliqués.

Commercial Quilt Supply Companies

Sears, Roebuck and Company and other profit-oriented companies such as *Capper's Farmer,* Aunt Martha, and the Needlecraft Supply Company of Chicago offered patterns, kits, and textiles to quilters wishing to duplicate the prize-winning entries. Sears offered quilt patterns for sale in its Century of Progress building where the company displayed the contest winners, and a World's Fair visitor from Champaign County purchased the Martha's Vineyard pattern.

When the Colonial Revival increased the popularity of quilting and needlework in the early twentieth century, a wave of commercial

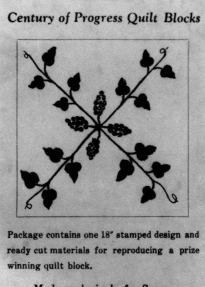

[Figure 48]
Century of Progress Quilt Pattern Box
Collection of the Early American Museum, Mahomet, Illinois

Pattern Number 5779, Martha's Vineyard, was offered by Sears, Roebuck and Company to Century of Progress visitors.

enterprise followed. The companies that eventually provided many Illinois quilters with patterns, kits, and quilting supplies either were already in existence or were firms that originated as a commercial response to the rising demand for needlework kits and sewing supplies.

Stearns and Foster of Cincinnati, Ohio, is one of the oldest and best-known quilt supply companies in the United States. Long known for its Mountain Mist quilt batting, the firm has been in operation since 1846. The company began a mail-order pattern business in the 1920s. For many years thereafter a colorful wrapping on the batting illustrated several designs that could be ordered for ten cents each, while the inside of each wrapper contained a ready-to-use full-size pattern. Since the 1930s the company has issued several editions of *The Mountain Mist Blue Book of Quilts.*[49]

Dancing Daffodils, Stearns and Foster Pattern Number 24, appeared on a Mountain Mist wrapper as early as 1935. In the 1938 *Blue Book,* it is interpreted as a quilt that "captures and records those memorable days in early spring when golden daffodils bloom in bright profusion." The Project quilt closely resembles the full-page, full-color illustration with the exception of the border and flower stems. The *Blue Book* shows a border composed of three shades of green plus a binding. The dark green of the leaves is next to the quilt's center field and is followed by narrow bands of medium and light green. The binding is the dark green. On the Stearns and Foster model, the stems are the darkest shade of green rather than the lightest.

Dancing Daffodils has remained a popular pattern. It also appears in a circa 1950s Stearns and Foster catalog and again in a later undated edition (circa 1970). Despite various claims to the contrary, the latter publication

[Plate 116]
DANCING DAFFODILS
77″ x 61″

Marion Pokorny Jelinek, 1908–
Berwyn, Cook County, Illinois, 1954
Collection of the maker

The top is composed of solid-color cotton appliqués on a cotton ground. The back is cotton, and the batting is a cotton blanket. The edges are turned in and stitched by hand. The hand quilting (7–8 stitches per inch), in motifs that are worked in white cotton thread, are in outline and grid. The maker followed the manufacturer's suggestion to place a spider web motif in the center of each daffodil circle. The arrangement of blossoms and leaves creates an overall design of circles and ovals.

identifies it as "an original MOUNTAIN MIST pattern that glorifies the loveliest of the Spring flowers, with Wadsworth's [sic] poem 'The Daffodils' as its inspiration."[50] Perhaps the writer meant to refer to the 1807 work of William Wordsworth:

> I wandered lonely as a cloud
> That floats on high o'er vales and
>   hills,
> When all at once I saw a crowd,
> A host, of golden daffodils.

Chanticleer, Pattern G, is also illustrated in the company's 1938 catalog. Charlotte Kroepfl's 1964 quilt follows the model quite closely. She does not, however, treat the corners the same way, and she omits one vertical row of five blocks. Over the years, Stearns and Foster has expanded its pattern offerings, but the company continues to sell most of its old favorites. Thus, it was not surprising to find Chanticleer still available in the 1950s and 1970s. The illustrations in all the company booklets show red sashing dividing twenty blocks instead of fifteen; therefore, the Kroepfl quilt is smaller than the suggested 87″ x 72″ size. The most recent catalog proclaims that "Ten cheerful chanticleers and little hens march proudly across this appliqué quilt, with round little chicks just out of their shell on the border to make a delightful child's quilt."

The Canadian immigrant quilter now lives near Bourbonnais, which was the center of French-Canadian Illinois in the nineteenth century.[51] As a girl growing up in Canada, Charlotte learned quilting from her mother and maternal grandmother. While still living there in 1964, she completed this widely advertised Mountain Mist quilt. The brightly colored red roosters readily attract the viewer's attention, and the soft yellow chicks in the border are not easily overlooked; but in this child's quilt art realistically reflects nature by gently camouflaging the hens. They are quilted with white thread on the plain white squares.

[Plate 117]
CHANTICLEER
84″ x 62″

Charlotte M. Kroepfl, 1932–
Quebec City, Quebec, Canada, 1964
Collection of the maker

Cotton is used throughout for the appliqués, sashing, top, back, and batt. The
edges are turned in and sewn by hand.
The appliquéing and piecing on the
top are also handwork. The quilting
(7 stitches per inch) is in outline and
grid.

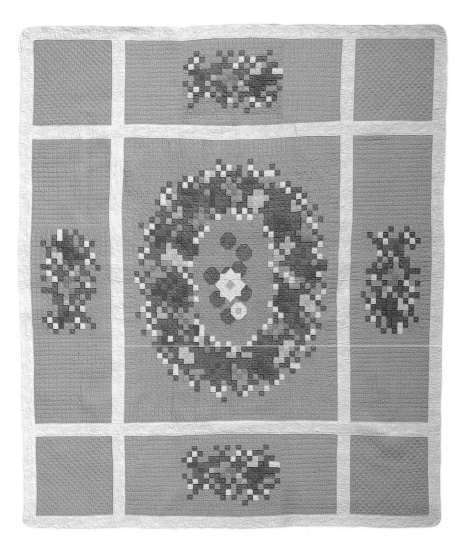

[Plate 118]
CROSS-STITCH GARDEN
90" x 80"

Lydia Volkmann Jannusch, 1883–1979
Kankakee, Kankakee County, Illinois,
   1955
Collection of Kathryn A. Treece

The all-cotton quilt has a solid green
ground, just as it was illustrated in the
1938 Mountain Mist publication. In the
registered quilt, the solid green back is
slightly lighter in color than the green on
the front. The cotton binding is commercial bias tape that is applied by machine
on the front and by hand on the back.
The body of the quilt is constructed by
machine as well as by hand. The quilting
(6 stitches per inch) can be found in outline and grid on the green panels. There
is a floral and leaf motif in the sashing
and in the border. The quilt has never
been washed. Mrs. Jannusch made the
quilt for her granddaughter, the present
owner, who also owns the original 1933
Stearns and Foster pattern.

Cross-Stitch Garden is designed in
the style popularized by Anne Orr.
Stearns and Foster sold patterns
closely resembling quilts associated
with well-known designers. When
Marie Webster introduced her Sunflower pattern in the *Ladies' Home
Journal* in 1911, she emphasized the
vivid colors, the realistic design, and
the spider webs in the quilting. If
one did not look closely, her word
picture could aptly describe the illustration on the 1928 Mountain
Mist wrapper. Closer examination
reveals some obvious differences,
however. The leaves are very different; there are more sunflowers
than on the Webster design; and the
quilting motifs are not the same.

The Cincinnati firm's cross-stitch-
type designs imitate the work of
Anne Orr but do not directly copy
any of her known patterns. Cross-
Stitch Garden is illustrated in full
color in the 1938 *Blue Book,* where
matching quilts are displayed on
twin beds. The same illustration was
used in the 1950s, and a schematic
drawing appeared in the 1970s. The
"quaint garden quilt is abloom in all
weathers and is fascinating and
easy to make," according to the
more recent catalog. Despite the
fact the company had already been
selling the pattern for perhaps four
decades, the copywriter termed the
transfer of the cross-stitch pattern
technique to quilting a "new idea."

Everything about Cross-Stitch
Garden is a tribute to the work of
Anne Orr, the Nashville designer
who introduced the use of cross-
stitch designs to the quilt format and
helped restore the central medallion
concept. She heightened the visual
impact of the medallion by framing it
with sashing. This technique created
four additional design units that defined the portions of the quilt that fall
to the floor and cover the pillows.
The 1940 Mountain Mist batting
wrapper features another cross-
stitch-inspired pattern advertised
as Roses Are Red.

Jack and Jill, another Stearns and Foster cross-stitch-type design, is illustrated in full color in the 1938 catalog. The patterns are for a pair of youth bed quilts. Although the concept is certainly based upon the Anne Orr cross-stitch technique translated into one-inch-square pieces, the publication proudly noted:

> These gay "Jack and Jill" quilts are exclusive Mountain Mist originals designed to win the special favor of the youngest, and often the most discriminating, members of the family. . . . The bright primary colors appeal strongly to most children, though the color plan may be changed if it seems advisable. Since one quilt tells but half the story, complete instructions for the second quilt are included with this pattern, making an ideal set for two children, or a splendid alternate set for one.

The pattern remained one of the company's standard offerings through the ensuing decades and attracted the attention of a Grundy County quilter in the 1970s.

Stearns and Foster may have been the oldest quilt supply firm to capitalize on a growing interest in the craft during the Colonial Revival era, but it certainly was not the only one to profit as the quiltmaking craze spread across Illinois in the 1920s and 1930s. Many of the leading urban department stores responded to the arts and crafts movement of the early twentieth century by adding an Art Needlework department. As the demand for quilt supplies accelerated, those goods joined the embroidery, crochet, and knitting lines already carried by prominent urban retail outlets.

[Plate 119]
JACK AND JILL
80″ x 59″

Leila Mason Vilt, 1916–
Coal City, Grundy County, Illinois, 1979
Collection of the maker

Leila followed the Mountain Mist color key in making her Jack and Jill quilt. She pieced and backed it with all-cotton fabric and used a polyester batt. It is bound by bringing the back to the front and stitching it by hand. All of the cross-stitch-type squares are pieced by hand. The quilting (4 stitches per inch) creates a grid motif by outlining each small piece.

Marshall Field's State Street store in Chicago displayed an array of completed full-size quilts that provided the would-be maker an opportunity to see the finished product firsthand.[52] In the days before-shopping centers and outlet malls, these large-scale, magnificent commercial enterprises attracted customers from an extensive geographical area. It was not unusual for shoppers from the smaller communities of central Illinois to take the train to Chicago for the day. Many could spend most of that time inside Field's, a store that offered an endless assortment of personal and household goods in addition to beautiful needlework.

When a quilt kit was no longer available, the finished model would be removed from display and sold. A quilt pattern of unknown origin, termed Flower Basket Appliqué by the Illinois Quilt Research Project, was put on display at Fields in 1927. The date is embroidered on the back of the quilt. When the pattern was discontinued, the model was purchased by Ms. Ethel Sweet, Field's needlework buyer for forty-three years.

[Plate 120]
FLOWER BASKET APPLIQUÉ
92" x 75"

Maker unknown, dates unknown
Place unknown, 1927
Collection of Carlyn Lovgren
   Whitehand

The Marshall Field's display quilt is made of cotton, and the appliqué and reverse appliqué is worked entirely by hand. The straight-cut binding is applied by machine on the front, but the back is stitched by hand. The quilting (7 stitches per inch) is in grid, parallel lines, ribbons, flowers, and leaves and in outline around the appliqués.

Magazines, such as *Country Gentleman* and other rural-oriented publications, occasionally continued to offer quilt patterns. Mrs. E. M. Murney remitted the required three-cent stamp, and the Old-Fashioned Sunbonnet Girl quilt pattern was shipped to her by the Curtis Publishing Company of Philadelphia. The large-size manila envelope carried the company's personalized National Recovery Administration blue eagle stamp.[53] There were two mimeographed patterns in the packet, and Mrs. Murney used only the Sunbonnet Girl and did not place any Overall Boy blocks into her quilt.

The quilt was begun by Vera Murney in 1932 for her daughter, Patricia. It remained incomplete for several decades until Vera finished the appliquéd blocks with the help of her daughter, Patricia Murney Gieson. Mrs. Murney wanted to present the quilt to two-year-old Amy Schuchard, her oldest great-granddaughter. Amy's mother, Sylvia Gieson Schuchard, marked the quilting design, and Amy's paternal grandmother, Fern Schuchard, did the quilting.

Textiles underwent a dramatic change in the four-decade interval between the time Vera appliquéd her Sunbonnet Girls on cotton squares and the time her family purchased cotton/polyester blend fabric for the alternating plain blue blocks.

Anyone who thinks in terms of one or two types of Sunbonnet Babies has not read Betty J. Hagerman's *A Meeting of the Sunbonnet Children*. Although these faceless individuals hit a peak of popularity in the decades before and after World War I, their roots are in the nineteenth century and their appeal is timeless. The *Country Gentleman's* "old-fashioned" Sunbonnet Girl of the 1930s is only one of countless versions.[54] The magazine's stylish girl, used by Mrs. Murney, has gone modern with a cloche-type bonnet.

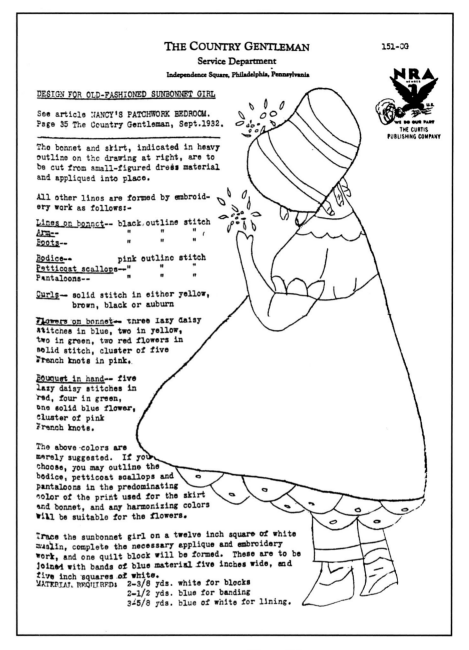

[Figure 49]
Sunbonnet Girl quilt pattern
Country Gentleman, September 1932
Collection of Sylvia Gieson Schuchard

The pattern received by Mrs. Murney was a drawing of the completed appliqué with minimal directions for making the block. No templates were included in the packet. To replicate the Overall Boy, the quilter was instructed to trace the pattern onto "a 9" x 9" block of white material. . . . Then trace the hat, the overalls and the dog on the materials you are using for them and cout [*sic*] out, allowing a ⅜" edge for turning under."

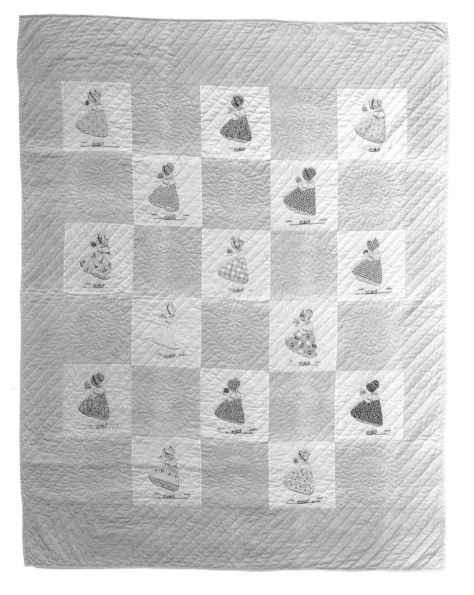

[Plate 121]
OLD-FASHIONED SUNBONNET GIRL
87" x 70"

Vera Snyder Murney, 1890–1980
Sterling, Whiteside County, Illinois,
   1932 and 1975
Collection of Sylvia Gieson Schuchard

Both cotton and cotton/polyester blend
are used on the quilt top, while the back
is a solid blue cotton/polyester blend.
The batting is polyester. The straight-cut
binding is applied by machine with a
zigzag ornamental stitch. The blocks are
put together by machine stitching. The
quilting (6 stitches per inch) outlines the
appliqués, fills the border with diagonal
parallel lines, and decorates the plain
blue blocks with feather wreaths.

She is, in actuality, as up-to-date as a 1920s flapper.

The prototype of the Sunbonnet Babies originated in England in the late nineteenth century. The drawings of Kate Greenaway and her imitators depicted girls wearing sunbonnets, and those figures were often incorporated into the embroidery on crazy quilts (Plate 89). Once the idea caught on, there were many variations. Several early-twentieth-century American illustrators created figures that were easily converted to a format suitable for quilts. Perhaps Marie Webster was the first to use the girls on a quilt top. The group of children's quilts she introduced in her August 1912 *Ladies' Home Journal* article included her "Sunbonnet Lassies" on the Keepsake quilt. The eight faceless girls probably trace their inspiration to a Kate Greenaway design.[56]

Perhaps one of the most familiar images of a Sunbonnet Baby resulted from the artwork of Bertha L. Corbett. She popularized the face-

[Figure 50]
Sunbonnet Babies Quilt Block Designs
Ladies Art Company Catalog, 1928
Private collection

The Ladies Art Company of St. Louis, Missouri, sold a set of "Stamped Outline Embroidery Blocks For Nursery Quilts," which featured the white ruffled-brim bonnet associated with the drawings of Bernhardt Wall. The 1928 catalog offered nine-inch muslin or sateen squares stamped with the Sunbonnet Babies and Overall Boys at work and at play. The blocks were suitable for solid-color embroidery.[55]

[Figure 51]
Title page
Eulalie Osgood Grover, *Sunbonnet Babies, A First Reader*
(New York: Rand, McNally & Company, 1914)

Sunbonnet Babies gained national popularity when they became the main characters in a primary reader written by Eulalie Grover. The illustrations in the original 1902 book and subsequent editions were by Bertha Corbett Melcher. Her faceless girls, gowned in their smocklike dresses, became so famous that by 1914 the textbook characterized her as "the Mother of the Sunbonnet Babies." This simple image was easily converted to a quilt block.

less children in America and soon became known as "the Mother of the Sunbonnet Babies." Her book, *The Sun-Bonnet Babies,* which appeared in 1900, attracted the interest of Eulalie Osgood Grover, a New Hampshire school teacher who was dissatisfied with the primer she was currently using. The collaboration of these two women soon resulted in Rand, McNally's 1902 publication *The Sunbonnet Primer.* It was the first primer issued in four colors. The popular reader went through a number of editions and sold more than one million copies before being replaced by the Dick and Jane series in the 1930s.[57]

As a result of the primer's widespread popularity, a Sunbonnet

mania swept the country, and the much-loved Babies, often referred to as Sunbonnet Sue and Overall Bill, eventually became popular quilt images. As the popularity of the Babies grew, they soon ornamented everything from postcards to ceramics. In many illustrations the girls performed children's daily household activities including washing, ironing, mending, scrubbing, sweeping, and baking. Several years ago Bonnie Leman termed the pattern a classic design of children that are "growing older but never aging."[58] The Illinois Quilt Research Project statistics indicate the faceless children are, indeed, timeless.

[Plate 122]
SUNBONNET BABIES
67" x 60"

Blanche Funkhouser Elbert, 1907–1990
Forrest, Livingston County, Illinois, 1935
    and 1965
Collection of Duane and Rachel Elbert
The book, postcard, and plate are from a
    private collection.

The drawings of Bertha Corbett
Melcher and Bernhardt Wall inspired a
variety of objects in addition to quilts.
Whether printed or stitched, the Babies
appeared with many different bonnet
and body shapes. One or more of the
equally faceless Overall Boys frequently
accompanied the bonneted girls as they
worked and played.

Needlework specialty suppliers, many with origins in the early twentieth century, actively meet the needs of Illinois quilters today. During the decades of the 1940s and 1950s, the

[Plate 123]
TREE OF LIFE
90" x 74"

Norine E. Spiegel Smith, 1912–
Galva, Henry County, Illinois, 1980
Collection of the maker

The quilt top has cotton/polyester blend fabric as well as plain cotton, while the back is cotton. The binding is a commercial bias tape stitched by machine on the back and by hand on the front. Polyester is used as the filler. All the appliqué and embroidery is worked by hand. The quilting (9 stitches per inch), which follows the stamped design of the kit, is in oval feather wreaths, clamshell, grid, and parallel lines. Mrs. Smith purchased the kit from Herrschner's in Chicago. Upon running out of embroidery thread before completing the top, she wrote to the company and received enough matching thread to complete the quilt. Frederick Herrschner, Inc., was founded in Chicago in 1899 and, according to the 1933 catalog, was located at 6610-30 South Ashland Avenue.

[Plate 124]
AMERICAN BEAUTY BOUQUET
95" x 76"

Ferne Irene Cook Carlson, 1901–1982
LaGrange, Cook County, Illinois,
   circa 1955
Collection of Joanne Carlson Mankivsky

The quilt top and appliqués are of cotton fabric, as is the back and the commercial bias tape binding, which is applied by machine and by hand. The appliqués are whipped down by hand. The quilting (5 stitches per inch) outlines the appliqués and follows the feathering, floral, vine, and parallel lines stamped on the top fabric supplied with the kit. The four separate shades of pink, each applied independently, lend an aura of realism to the large roses that dominate the central medallion and provide a border for it. The kit was available from the Lee Ward's firm in Elgin, Illinois, or from the Gold Art Needlework Company of Chicago.

demand for quiltmaking supplies declined, and many department stores eliminated their Art Needlework areas. Companies, such as Herrschner's, Lee Ward's, Paragon, and Bucilla, have continued to furnish Illinois quilters with their craft needs.

Some twentieth-century quilts are unfairly branded as kits because so many appear to be taken from the same mold. As far as the design is concerned, this is true. However, many in this look-alike parade are actually produced from patterns acquired from a company that included directions suggesting preferred colors. Many makers followed this advice and purchased colored fabrics to piece or appliqué the top as close to the suggested model as possible.

When the first quilt "kits" were sold in the early years of this century, all the parts were not prestamped as they are today. The seller merely included the fabric and the stamping materials. Appliqué quilt kits began to enjoy greater popularity once the various parts were already stamped and ready to be cut out for use on the prestamped top. Many quiltmakers have considered the use of kits a controversial matter from the very beginning.[59]

[Plate 125]
EMBROIDERED SAMPLER
97" x 84"

Rosemary Boyle Murfin, 1918–
Decatur, Macon County, Illinois, 1983
Collection of the maker

A polyester batting separates the cotton top from the cotton/polyester blend backing. It is bound by commercial bias tape, which is applied by machine and by hand. The blocks are joined by machine stitching, and the cross-stitch embroidery is by hand. The grid and floral quilting (5–10 stitches per inch) was completed by a woman's group of the Patoka, Illinois, United Methodist Church. Rosemary purchased Paragon Quilt Kit Number 01167. It did not include the thread.

Contemporary Quilt Design Sources

The post-World War II manufacturing boom contributed to a declining social prestige for quilting. The Great Depression was over; the war was won. In the popular image, the machine age had arrived and the era of hand labor was a thing of the past. The postwar cyclical economic, industrial, social, and attitudinal trends appear to be very similar to those of the nineteenth century when factory-produced consumer goods made serious inroads into the quilting craft. However, one hundred years after its first obituaries were written, the art of quilting once again refused to die out. It lived on in the hearts and minds, and especially the thimbled fingers, of those who love it. Nevertheless, quilting did not inspire national economic leadership or increase commercial production during the 1950s and 1960s.

Disillusion with the "system" became increasingly apparent as the 1960s wore on. The millennium had not arrived; society was not perfect; neither prosperity nor peace appeared to be permanent; the environment was at risk; the machine was destroying our Garden of Eden. Filled with a feeling of betrayal, a generation turned toward the handmade values of the past and acquired a newfound respect for those who had never abandoned their heritage. The generations discovered, tolerated, and finally began sharing each other's interests and value systems. A quilting renaissance flowered in the 1970s.

Along with a growing interest in the craft came a rising demand for goods and services. Hope once again glimmered, and slowly the darkness of economic despair that had hovered over quilting businesses for three decades was dispelled. Patterns were rediscovered; designers opened new doors of creativity; existing periodicals offered encouragement and new publications; and magazines and books flooded the marketplace. Museums mounted exhibits; prices of antique quilts zoomed; clubs, classes, and shows proliferated; cash registers hummed; and once again in the twentieth century there was joy in the quilted wallet of corporate America.

During the past twenty years, many new designers have made outstanding contributions to quilting. Jean Ray Laury, Trudy Hughes, Nancy Pearson, and Judy Martin, as well as Jinny Beyer, not only have improvised but have looked at the craft from the perspective of what it could become rather than what it once was.[60] Will this burst of creative energy make a lasting impression on quilting?

It is difficult to compare the impact of today's rising interest in quilting with the earlier quilt revival. The nation's population is larger; communication and transportation are quicker; and the potential marketplace is much greater. Thus it is easy to say that more people may be involved in terms of absolute numbers, but is the percentage greater? The economic impact is also difficult to assess because of inflation, and a comparison of today's economy with that of the Great Depression is misleading. The effects of the Colonial Revival are still felt today. Will the current renaissance have a long-lasting effect also? History will eventually make that judgment.

Jinny Beyer's *The Scraplook* has been a popular inspiration for quilters ever since it was published in 1985. Ms. Beyer is one of several late-twentieth-century designers who have inspired a new wave of Illinois quilters to look at an old craft in a contemporary light. In an earlier work, *Patchwork Patterns,* she simplified the difficult task of drafting geometric patterns. The book's clearly drawn and easily understood illustrations are bound to help even an experienced quilter visualize an old pattern with a new perspective. Chapters based upon four-, nine-, five-, and seven-patch structures, as well as different types of stars and the hexagon, merit a quilt student's serious consideration. Combining distinctive colors and textiles with creative geometric arrangements, such as the use of the hexagon in her well-known Inner City pattern, helped make her name familiar to the new generation of quilters.

After Jinny Beyer created Inner City as an original design, she found similar motifs pictured in two sources. Now she teaches that while it is perhaps impossible to put geometric shapes together in a totally new configuration, original contributions can still be made "in the placement of blocks, the size of units, the type of borders, and the interaction of color and fabric." The basic concept of Inner City is the same principle used in Tumbling Blocks: the creation of "an unusual optical effect if the dark, medium and light pieces are used in a consistent manner."[61] The design template is half a hexagon.

Perhaps one of the sources of Inner City Beyer eventually found, was in the late nineteenth-century

[Figure 52]
Right Angles Patchwork Pattern
Caulfield and Saward, *Dictionary of Needlework* (1882)

The pattern now known as Inner City was illustrated over a century ago as Right Angles Patchwork. An optical illusion is created by using light, medium, and dark pieces of fabric cut in a half-hexagon shape.

[Plate 126]
INNER CITY
85″ x 76″

Leona Lowenstein Pahlmeyer, 1919–
Litchfield, Montgomery County, Illinois,
   1989
Collection of Joan Kasich

According to the quilt owner, Leona is
an active senior citizen, an avid quilter,
and a "neat person" in the eyes of her admiring grandchildren. When she made
Inner City as a gift for her friend, she
used her own scraps and gathered pieces
from others to collect enough cotton and
cotton/polyester materials for the top.
Only the cotton/polyester border and
back were purchased. The batt is polyester, and the cotton/polyester handmade
straight-cut binding is applied by machine and by hand. The construction of
the top uses both techniques. The quilting (5 stitches per inch) outlines the
hexagons and creates a zigzag in the inner border and a square grid in the outer
one.

English publication *Dictionary of Needlework*. In an extended seven-page discussion of Patchwork, the identical pattern is illustrated as Right Angles Patchwork.[62]

Magazines remain an important source of quilt patterns and ideas. While a publication such as *Quilter's Newsletter Magazine* is expected to be filled with pictures, patterns, and inspiration, there are plenty of other sources. Audrey Heidorn's Butterfly emerged from a *Better Homes and Gardens* pattern in the spring of 1977.

More than a half-century ago, Hall and Kretsinger announced, "The whole country is 'quilt-conscious'—the newspapers report every quilt show with glowing headlines. . . . The making of quilts in the home has become astonishingly popular."[63] The same could be said of Illinois and the nation today. Indeed, the twentieth century may appropriately be considered the period in which quilting came into its own. Although the craft certainly suffered a post-revival slump in midcentury, it has come back stronger than ever in the closing decades. Encouraged by newspapers, books, magazines, and the electronic media, sparked by a new wave of quilt designers, and supplied by an increasing number of business enterprises, the contemporary quilting revival has emerged as a vigorous nationwide movement.

Despite the temporary ups and downs of quilting's popularity, the trend within the field has been unchanged over the past eighty to ninety years. The media have created a huge business enterprise by commercializing a craft tradition. This effort has succeeded because the buying public is eager to acquire the product being sold. Whether it is the Colonial Revival of an earlier era or the search for the roots of our heritage today, history, or what the public believes to be history, is a saleable commodity when it is attractively packaged and priced right.

[Plate 127]
BUTTERFLY
106" x 96"

Ruth Perry Heidorn, 1921–
Westchester, Cook County, Illinois, 1977
Collection of Bill and Audrey Heidorn

A variety of solid-color cottons and cotton/polyesters are joined in a type of butterfly sampler quilt. The pieced and appliquéd top uses vivid colors and multiple-size blocks to create an asymmetrical design. The quilting (5 stitches per inch) is in the grid and outline quilting motifs. The batting is polyester, and the handmade bias tape binding is applied by machine and by hand.

Jinny Beyer was on target in 1979 when she noted, "The past ten years have seen a remarkable renewal of interest in our heritage. The renaissance of 'craft art' has been astounding."

More than a decade later, the trend has strengthened and shows no evidence of abating. This is a tribute to the effectiveness of the nation's modern mass communication systems and a compliment to the ability of the American business community to assess accurately what the customer wants. It is also an indication that an increasingly insecure and rootless society is forging a strong material culture link with the heritage of an idyllic, seemingly less stressful, and quite often nonexistent past.

[Plate 128]
DOUBLE WEDDING RING
73″ x 73″

Geretta Bell Smith, 1880–1963
Galesburg, Knox County, Illinois, 1930
Collection of Martha J. Gilson

A CULTURE AT RISK: OUR INCOMPLETE PAST

My whole life is in that quilt. It scares me sometimes when I look at it. All my joys and all my sorrows are stitched into those little pieces. When I was proud of the boys and when I was downright provoked and angry with them. When the girls annoyed me or when they gave me a warm feeling around my heart. And John too. He was stitched into that quilt and all the thirty years we were married. Sometimes I loved him and sometimes I sat there hating him as I pieced the patches together. So they are all in that quilt, my hopes and fears, my joys and sorrows, my loves and hates. I tremble sometimes when I remember what that quilt knows about me.

— An anonymous Ohio great-grandmother
Marguerite Ickis, *The Standard Book of
Quilt Making and Collecting*, 1935

Although America's Dust Bowl classic *The Grapes of Wrath* appeared more than fifty years ago, its poignant characterization of the link between people and their possessions remains valid today. As his family packed a jalopy to head for California, Tom Joad surveyed the discarded belongings and sadly asked, "How can we live without our lives? How will we know it's us without our past?"[1]

John Steinbeck's eloquent passage expresses our human need for the things of history. The Illinois Quilt Research Project responded to that felt need. Its work demonstrated that individual, family, and community stories are an extremely valuable part of our total history. May we assume that the Joads took their family quilts to California? After all, extreme need has transformed many a keepsake quilt from a luxury into a necessity. Surely the family ex-

perienced many a cold night in the mountains and on the desert as they made their way to the Golden West. Any quilt that survived such a journey carried with it the collective memory of the family's past and the events of that famous Dust Bowl migration.

While thousands of migrants struggled to reach California, Geretta Bell Smith of Galesburg, Illinois, carefully pieced a Double Wedding Ring quilt. She meticulously planned, cut, and stitched each ring so that a red and gold unit appears uniformly on opposite sides of the blue ovals. It is a technique rarely seen in the many Depression-era examples made from this pattern in Illinois. That distinctive design element, combined with the solid blue ovals and the scalloped edges created by the natural curve of the pattern, makes an unforgettable visual impression.[2]

The all-cotton quilt is bound by white commercial bias tape applied by machine and by hand. The quilting (8 stitches per inch) creates curved lines through the piecing, a grid bisected by diagonal lines in the white centers and overlapping leaves in the blue ovals. All the piecing is by hand. As is often the case in scrap quilts, some of the fabrics predate 1930. Although Geretta Smith may have felt the effects of financial distress during the Great Depression, her Wedding Ring quilt clearly indicates she maintained a lifestyle significantly different from Dust Bowl migrants.

Sixty years after it came out of the frame, the Double Wedding Ring quilt retains the vibrancy its maker surely intended to create. Time has soothed the heartache of loss and unhappiness; beauty has dispelled the dark clouds of worry and uncertainty. Did Geretta Smith plan this part of her legacy also?

For most present-day Illinois residents, the Great Depression is merely a part of the state's historical past. Personal memory is dimming, and each year fewer and fewer people remain who can share their first-hand experiences with the present generation. As those personal links slip away, we slowly realize the power of the surviving objects. In the absence of people, it is through these things of the past that a family preserves its collective memory of a bygone era. "How will we know it's us without our past?" is not a meaningless question. As quilts increasingly possess the power to remind us of our heritage, they become more and more important. Perhaps Geretta's hopes and fears, joys and sorrows, loves and hates are in this quilt. What lessons can be learned today from the work she did yesterday?

Steinbeck's story is fictitious, but it conveys the harsh realities of a historical period. From the power within that epic, each new generation of readers acquires a feeling of rapport with the 1930s. The Joads' fictional trauma is not confined to the pages of a book; millions of real people shared their experiences in many different ways. Geretta Smith is real; her story is real; her quilt is real. The more than fifteen thousand other quilts registered by the Illinois Research Project are real also. If we can learn from fiction, what may we learn from reality?

A preliminary analysis of the findings suggests three significant areas worthy of further investigation. First, the Project created a significant body of information for future study. Second, it identified a serious lack of awareness, knowledge, and sometimes even interest by owners in the heritage their quilts preserved. A third focus emerges from a study of the registration forms. Because the Project board chose not to establish a cutoff date, the research material has created an excellent overview of contemporary Illinois quilters.

A Collection of Textile Documents

The chronological sweep of the quilt documents collected spans the two-hundred-year history of Illinois, from the creation of the Old Northwest in 1787 to the present day. Several quilts date to the 1790s, and many more were made in the 1990s. It is understandable that while none of the former were stitched in Illinois, most of the latter originated in the state.

A surprisingly small minority—approximately 15 percent—of the registered quilts span the entire nineteenth century. Eleven percent have been dated between 1876 and 1900, leaving a scant 4 percent for the period 1790 to 1875. Most of the quilts in that early period were not made in Illinois. The data clearly indicate that the earliest surviving quilts either came to the state with migrating families or have been brought into Illinois more recently. The later arrival of older quilts is attributable to heirlooms coming in the moving vans of a highly mobile population and a heightened interest in developing private documentary quilt collections that are not limited to Illinois-made bedcoverings.

A deep indigo blue-and-white post-Civil War Sawtooth quilt can still be found in Adams County, not far from the place where it was made. As a textile document, it is representative of the time in which Harriett Logue pieced it. Unfortunately, there are not many like it in the data bank. Only 3 percent of the quilts registered were made between 1851 and 1875. For some Illinois quiltmaking families, the postwar decades were a period of economic prosperity, and factory-made bedding was readily available. However, there was sufficient leisure time for at least a few women to create one or more high-quality show quilts as opposed to numerous utilitarian bedcovers.

Although the owner is proud of this family heirloom, she knows little about it. She received it from "a second cousin, but the quilt came from the other side of the family." All attempts to learn more about the maker and the circumstances that led to its making have been unsuccessful. Nevertheless, a great deal of information, such as the type and quality of the fabric and the dye as well as the expertise of the quiltmaker, can be gathered through carefully observing the object.

Log Cabin quilts, according to the findings of the Project, were very popular in Illinois during the last quarter of the nineteenth century. Approximately 8 percent of all the quilts registered were made in this pattern. Since some have been created in the last two decades, not all

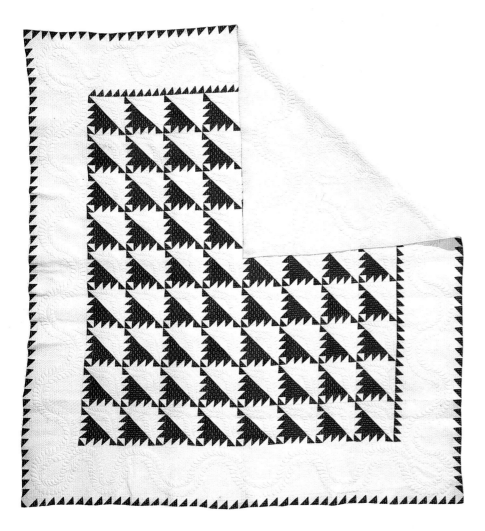

[Plate 129]
SAWTOOTH
88" x 82"

Harriett E. Davis Logue, 1844–1925
Clayton Township, Adams County,
   Illinois, circa 1860–1880
Collection of Isabel Craig Baptist

It appears that Harriett Logue had the time and patience needed to produce a high-quality quilt. This blue-and-white Sawtooth is filled with the type of stuffed work and cording more commonly found a few decades earlier (see Plate 10). The ends of the cords still protrude on the back. Made in a period during which the art of quilting received little attention, and less emphasis, the overall impression conveyed by the quilt is that the maker was looking to the past rather than to the future. The stitches on the all-cotton quilt are made by hand. The back is brought to the front to form the binding. The quilting (10 stitches per inch) creates feathering, diagonal lines, and the stuffed work motifs. The deep indigo blue was frequently combined with white during the post-Civil War era.

date from the last century; but many of them do. None, however, date from the pre-Civil War era when log houses were commonly built in the wooded areas of Illinois.

In 1882, during the era when the pattern was very popular, the English authors Caulfield and Saward included the Log Cabin pattern in their *Dictionary of Needlework,* referring to it as American or Canadian Patchwork, or Loghouse Quilting. They recommended using silk ribbon three-fourths of an inch wide "arranged so as to give the appearance of different kinds of wood formed into a succession of squares."

Seven rows of ribbons would create a twelve-inch block with a light- and a dark-colored side. These could then be arranged to form many different sets in the way Anna Fink created her Barn Raising design.[3]

This contemporary reference does not mention any of the myths about the pattern that seem to have emerged in the twentieth century. Today we know the pattern apparently did not originate in and was not made during the first half of the nineteenth century, the prime log cabin period of American history. Most of the people making Log Cabin quilts probably did not have

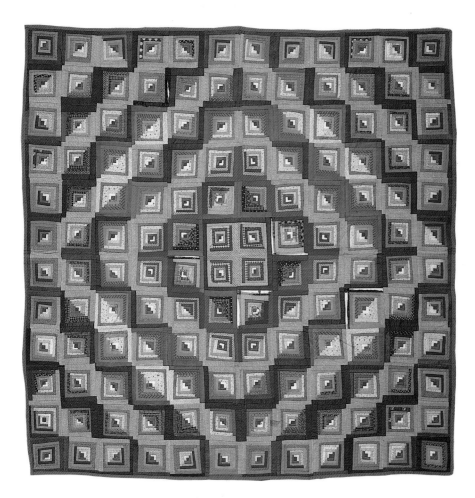

[Plate 130]
LOG CABIN (BARN RAISING SET)
86" x 85"

Anna M. Ehrlicher Fink, 1854–1943
Pekin, Tazewell County, Illinois,
    circa 1870
Collection of Martha Alfs Madarasz and
    Johanna Alfs Bruns

The bedcovering is made of wool, cotton, and silk strips stitched to a plain cotton muslin foundation. The back is an orange and brown cotton print of the 1870 era. The straight-cut cotton binding is applied by machine on the front and by hand on the back. All of the blocks are stitched by hand. There are no quilting stitches, but there is some tacking. The center of each block is a red, white, and blue cotton print that perhaps is a centennial fabric.

any experience living in a log cabin, when fuel for artificial lighting was too precious to keep a lantern in the window to aid a traveler who might "lose his way on the unmarked paths." While the pattern does use up narrow strips of fabric unsuitable for most other quilt pieces, it is not always a scrap quilt made of necessity from leftovers. Many Log Cabin designs required special fabrics to create the desired effect.[4]

Repeating romanticized myths and implying that quaint but undocumentable stories are factual deny the essential search for truth implicit in the research process. Professional quilt researchers seek the facts. The material currently being assembled by the various state quilt projects will go far toward developing a new and a more accurate interpretation of quilt history.[5]

The Johann Georg Ehrlicher family was part of the German immigrant group that settled in the Pekin–Peoria area during the nineteenth century. Along with many of their fellow countrymen, they were members of the Evangelical Synod of North America and attended St. Paul's church. It was there that Anna met John Jacob Fink, a German immigrant who was the teacher in St. Paul's parochial school. In preparation for their 1875 wedding, Anna's mother helped her construct a Log Cabin quilt.

After their marriage, the couple lived in Pekin until they moved to St. Louis in 1884. Because of Professor Fink's failing health, they moved to California in 1912, but he survived only three years. Anna continued living in California until her death in 1943. Before leaving for the West, she placed some of her possessions in storage in St. Louis. When she decided not to return to the Midwest, she gave those goods to her Illinois relatives. The trunks were placed in a farmhouse attic, and the quilt remained there until it was registered with the Illinois Quilt Research Project. The opportunity to compare this quilt with other nineteenth-century Illinois-made Log Cabin quilts will help future researchers determine what is fact and what is fiction about this important pattern.

Baskets appear on quilts in a variety of shapes and sizes, and they have long been one of the favorites of Illinois quilters. Approximately 7 percent of all the quilts registered with the Project are in some form of a basket pattern. The pattern's popularity goes back to the mid-nineteenth century but it seems to have peaked at the turn of the twentieth century and then remained strong for a few decades. This was a time when quiltmaking was becoming more widespread, but the percentage of quilts dating from the 1901 to 1925 period remains at 12 percent—the same as for the previous quarter century. A majority of the basket quilts are pieced, and pieced quilts represent a majority of the quilts brought to the thirty quilt days.[6]

Since most pieced-block quilts in this pattern feature empty baskets, Mary Delbridge's interpretation offers several variations. First, it contains a flower; second, that single large flower—a stylized lily—is typical of folk quilts in that it assumes both a disproportionate size and an assortment of jaunty asymmetrical positions. One can easily imagine the fun the maker had in creating each pieced block. The quilt is made entirely of cotton and features handwork throughout. The quilting (5 stitches per inch) is in outline and crossed parallel lines that create a gridwork.

[Plate 131]
LILY IN A BASKET
79″ x 64″

Mary Carroll Delbridge, 1875–1976
Vera, Fayette County, Illinois, circa 1890
Collection of Mary E. Delbridge

The quarter century between 1926 and 1950 encompassed two of the most memorable events of the twentieth century—the Great Depression and the Second World War. Both affected the production of quilts. The craft expanded beyond all previously known dimensions during the 1930s and suffered a severe cutback during the 1940s. Nevertheless, approximately 35 percent of all the quilts registered in the Project date from this period.

Ocean Waves is a typical pieced scrap quilt pattern that traces its origins to the nineteenth century. Innumerable triangular ocean waves dash against the solid color blocks in Mrs. Stanley's quilt and provide the researcher a field day for examining the fabrics of the late 1930s. Pieced quilts emerged from the Project's statistical summary as by far the most favored kind of quilt made in Illinois. Approximately 71 percent of all the quilts brought to registration days were pieced quilts.

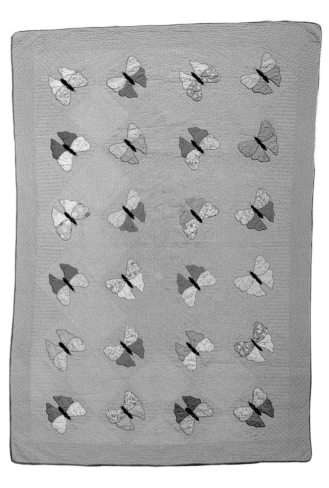

[Plate 133]
BUTTERFLY
97" x 69"

Gladys Kathryn Thornburg-Dinsmore,
 1890–1964
Lawrenceville, Lawrence County,
 Illinois, circa 1950
Collection of Laura Jane Humphrey-
 Drassler

[Plate 132]
OCEAN WAVES
81" x 70"

Luanna Dillman Stanley, 1926–
Ingraham, Clay County, Illinois, 1940
Collection of the maker

Luanna Dillman was about fourteen years old when she made this quilt. Today she is an experienced custom quilter with more than 250 quilts to her credit, and she reports she particularly likes "doing close quilting." Her all-cotton quilt is pieced by machine but quilted by hand. The quilting (8 stitches per inch) is in the parallel lines that follow the Ocean Waves motif. The diagonal arrangement of the blocks is the usual Ocean Wave set. Quilts in this pattern are, however, sometimes found with a straight set.[7]

Appliqué quilts began enjoying a rebirth with the early-twentieth-century introductions of Marie Webster and Anne Orr. By the 1920s and 1930s an increasing number of quilters were using this technique, but it still remained less popular than the tried and true pieced quilt. The Illinois Quilt Research Project statistics indicate that approximately 22 percent of the quilts brought to registration days were either all appliqué or appliqué with some piecework. Gladys Thornburg-Dinsmore's Butterfly quilt is typical of many simple appliqué quilts made during this period.

The pastel palette of the second quarter of the twentieth century is distinctive, and the colors and extensive selection of printed cottons are well preserved in the quilts of that time. Butterflies, which first became prominent motifs on the crazy quilts, went on to assume a pattern all their own. About 2 percent of the registered quilts used one of the many variants.

It is hard to believe that these large, colorful insects might appear threatening to a small child. Yet Laura Drassler reported on her registration form that when she was a little girl, the quilt her grandmother made and gave to her was frightening. She feared that the butterflies would bite her if she sat on them. Thus, she always pulled back a corner of the quilt when she needed to sit on the edge of the bed. She eventually learned that the all-cotton butterflies that decorated an all-cotton quilt were a very gentle variety and never bit her at all. The quilt is constructed by hand and machine, and the simple quilting is worked in outline and parallel lines.

A declining national interest in quilting began with the onset of World War II. By 1940 an influx of money into defense spending generated increased disposable income available for the purchase of consumer goods such as factorymade bedding. Within two years, a rising number of women were going to work outside the home as substitutes for the men who were off to war, while the volunteer hours many other women devoted to the home front war effort lessened the time available for quilting.[8] The annual quilt output declined but did not disappear. It remained strong in many rural areas of central and southern Illinois. The craft was often practiced by older homemakers, small-town women who chose not to work outside the home, and farm women. Several southern Illinois embroidered quilts registered by the Project attest to the popularity of that form of decoration in the lower part of the state.

Embroidery designs were available to southern Illinois quilters from the St. Louis-based Ladies Art Company. Its catalog illustrated many different examples. The tabulation of the Illinois Quilt Research Project forms indicates that only 6.5 percent of all the quilts registered were embroidered. This group earned a very weak third place ranking against pieced and appliquéd quilts. Except for the lavish embroidery used on many nineteenth-century crazy quilts, decorative stitching rarely appears on quilts before the present century. Although popular women's magazines published many different embroidery stitches, they are not usually seen on ordinary quilts.

The Embroidered Daisies quilt Emma made for her church, St. Catherine's Catholic Church in Grand Chain, has come back to her family. Several years ago when the old rectory was torn down, the quilt

[Plate 134]
EMBROIDERED DAISIES
86" x 79"

Emma Elizabeth Erhstein Schoenborn,
   1881–1966
Grand Chain, Pulaski County, Illinois,
   circa 1955
Collection of Carolyn Mayberry

was raffled off as a fundraiser. The winner of the quilt was Emma's daughter, Cecilia Schoenborn Tennis, who recognized it as the work of her mother. She passed it on to her own daughter, the present owner. The all-cotton bedcovering is pieced by machine and by hand. It is quilted (8 stitches per inch) in parallel lines, concentric diamonds with scrolls, and straight line cables. As a quilt document, it is an example of a popular regional quilt form.

[Plate 135]
ENGAGEMENT RING
82″ x 71″

Cherita Page Walker, 1925–
Elizabethtown, Hardin County, Illinois,
    1970
Collection of the maker

Although the top of the quilt is made of cotton, the back is a cotton/polyester blend; a polyester batting has replaced the traditional cotton. It is all hand pieced with hand quilting (6 stitches per inch) outlining the pieces.

Quilting stayed in a severe national slump during the 1950s and 1960s. Those who continued as active quilters made pieced quilts or turned to the factory-assembled kit. Others retained the traditional piecing system but used the newer types of materials coming on the market. Twelve percent of the quilts registered in the Project were made between 1951 and 1975, and once the statistics are analyzed more thoroughly, they will probably indicate that most of the quilts were made near the end of that time when quilting began to experience the renaissance that it is still enjoying.

The most recent period, 1976 to 1991, represents the second largest group of quilts registered with the Project. About one-fourth of all the quilts brought to registration days are the product of this contemporary time frame. Within this 25 percent, many traditional patterns and techniques are still being used. However, there is also a tremendous burst of artistic creativity totally unmatched in any previous period, with some quilters adapting older patterns and presenting them in different ways.

The choice of appliquéd blocks with sashing is not new, nor is the

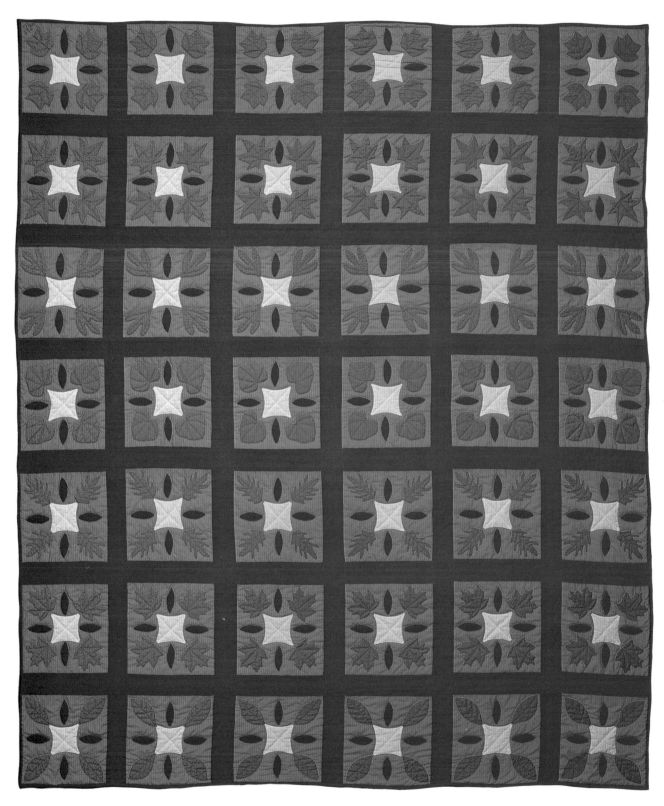

[Plate 136]
LEAVES
108″ x 91″

Dorothy J. Rankin, 1908–
Champaign, Champaign County,
  Illinois, 1976
Collection of the maker

use of natural forms as appliqué patterns. Leaves have long been a popular motif.[9] However, Dorothy's Leaves quilt is an original contemporary interpretation of this old format. The idea was suggested by her son Stanley, who became familiar with leaves while teaching tree identification as a Boy Scout leader. He designed and made the patterns for the quilt, which features leaves from trees commonly found in the Champaign County area—the tulip poplar, sweet gum, sassafras, linden, oak, maple, and elm. The quilt is typical of those quilters who maintain a traditional approach while expressing a contemporary desire to "do your own thing."

The research file developed by the Illinois Quilt Research Project is not balanced chronologically for several reasons. Most of the quilts registered by the Project were made in the twentieth century. The opportunity to register a quilt was voluntary. There was no attempt to interest specific collectors or museums to share their collections from the early period. More quilts were made in the twentieth century, and more have survived. Therefore, it is not surprising that 85 percent of the entire 15,808 quilts registered date from 1901 to 1991. Only 12 percent of the whole date from the century's first quarter; 73 percent fall after 1926; and one-third of all the quilts registered are from 1926 to 1950. The decade of the 1930s was a booming period of quilting in Illinois. The tremendous output stands as a tribute to the work of the media promoters and the heightened social acceptance of quilting as a handicraft, as well as the search for old-time values exemplified by the Colonial Revival.

A Culture at Risk

The optimism of beginners, whether young or old, knows no boundaries. Most new researchers start a project determined to uncover every scrap of information and solve problems others have been unable to unravel. Quilt researchers seek information. They do not invent it. However, no matter how essential a fact may be, it cannot be found if it no longer exists.

The *History from the Heart* authors were not a part of the Illinois Quilt Research Project team when the work began. Nevertheless, they were interested in it and kept abreast of its progress through the Project's newsletter. When offered the opportunity to join the team, they naively accepted the challenge in the belief that the registration forms would contain the same amount of information they provided when registering their quilts. The first review of the data base was shocking. Numerous forms had little information beyond the owner's name and address.

Fortunately, there were also those knowledgeable owners whose small handwriting filled the margin as well as the blanks, and who often attached copies of documents and photographs. A survey made at the end of the project indicated that approximately 56 percent of the quilt owners supplied the valuable historical documentation for their quilts. That means 44 percent of the accumulated research base provides little or no historical background information. The problem is serious. The amount of historical information lost by each family, when multiplied by the number of American households and compounded over time, can devastate the heritage of an entire culture.

These quilts for which the owners could provide no historical context are, nevertheless, a valuable component of the Project. They have been photographed; and researchers know they existed, can place them within basic quantifiable categories, and can answer certain questions through observation. Some of these orphaned textile documents also went through physical analysis, so additional data have been gathered. There is little the Project can do if an owner does not know who made the quilt, where it was made, or when it was made. A basically empty form is especially ironic when the relationship of the maker to the owner is "grandchild" or "great-grandchild." Such replies indicate that our heritage is at risk.

There are understandable reasons why the information is sometimes not available. One frequently encountered problem is associated with those quilts that have passed out of the family and into museum collections. Modern museum record-keeping methods provide opportunities to collect family information from donors. Nevertheless, the donation often comes from an estate in which the descendants have little information that can be shared. However, in the not-too-distant past, museums acquired gifts without even asking for provenance. Artifacts were all too often accepted as art objects collected only for their beauty, or they were viewed as items for a cabinet of curiosities instead of as potential storytellers. Unfortunately, many museums also accepted gifts that they did not want at the time, but the donor could not be turned down. Present-day curators are now struggling to find information about these past acquisitions.

A quilt was delivered to DeKalb's Ellwood House Museum in 1978 after the owner's death. The family had found the quilt in a cedar chest with a note attached: "The old red bird quilt is to be given to Elwood [*sic*] House if they want it. It is in mint condition and is over a hundred years old. It was made by a

cousin of my great grandmother Mrs. Wm. Hall. The date is worked on the quilt." The Hall family arrived in DeKalb County in 1845. All research attempts to learn the identity of the cousin have been unsuccessful. If the donor had made the legal arrangements with the museum prior to her death by establishing a promised gift, completing the necessary paperwork, and providing the information only she knew about the quilt, she could have kept it until she died, and the museum would have an excellent quilt and better information upon which to base its interpretation.

[Plate 137]
Appliqué Sofa Pillow
Elizabeth Roeder, 1872–1963
Forrest, Livingston County, Illinois,
    circa 1935
The Woman's World Service Library,
    The Patchwork Book (Chicago:
    Manning Publishing Company, 1931),
    p. 14.
Private collections

Finding documentation for the relationship between a needlework object and a specific pattern or an inspirational idea is difficult. Project quilts with accompanying documentation are unusual. See Bicentennial, Figure 42; Changed Perspective, Plate 65; and May Tulips, Plate 98. Rarely does a researcher stumble upon the documentation establishing the positive relationship that is visible between the black sateen Grecian Urn pillow and the full-color advertisement. Its perforated pattern cost only twenty cents.

The publication in which the pillow pattern was found is filled with Colonial Revival myth so typical of the period. The advertisement writer indicates we are "indebted to our great-grandmothers for the beauty of patchwork, for it has its origin with them. These colonial forebears were motivated by the strictest economy when they pieced together little odds and ends of gay calicos to make pillows and warm quilts, but love of the quaint designs has perpetuated them and given them an important place in modern homes."

[Plate 138]
WREATH OF ROSES WITH REDBIRDS
91″ x 79″

C.M.W., dates unknown
Town unknown, DeKalb County,
    Illinois, 1859
Collection of the Ellwood House
    Association

Wreath of Roses with Redbirds is an unusual form of a popular nineteenth-century quilt pattern. The one at the Ellwood House Museum in DeKalb is dated 1859. The pattern was one of the most commonly used album quilt designs between 1840 and 1860, and it was popular "from Maine to Florida and from cosmopolitan Baltimore to the edges of the frontier."[10]

The all-cotton quilt, which is constructed entirely by hand, is an important historical document even without a complete provenance. An important period red-on-red print fabric is used for the birds, the flowers, and the sashing; there is an abundant use of reverse appliqué for the eye of each bird and the center of each flower. There also is an extraordinary amount of stuffed work, which includes different stuffed quilting motifs inside each wreath and stuffed appliqué of the birds in the border. It would be interesting to know why one of the birds is white. The quilting (10–11 stitches per inch) is in outline, parallel lines, and the hanging diamond motifs.

One of the Project's many orphans is a Thousand Pyramids quilt. It exemplifies another reason why many forms are empty. The owner purchased the quilt. It is unfortunate that many quilts on the market have lost their identity with their maker and the past. Buyers should always ask for a written provenance when considering a quilt purchase. If the seller is unable to furnish any information, he or she should be encouraged to get such documentation when future quilts are acquired. When buying a quilt at a household auction, request information from the owner or heirs rather than from the auctioneer.

[Plate 139]
THOUSAND PYRAMIDS
79" x 73"

Maker unknown, dates unknown
Place unknown, circa 1876
Collection of Mary A. Sullivan

Here is another quilt that is an important document even though the name of the maker and place it was made have been lost. In addition to being a good source of information about period textiles, it contains examples of several scarce cotton fabrics made specifically for use during the nation's centennial celebration in 1876. Three different centennial textiles are arranged side by side in the center of the close-up illustration. On the left is a brown and red print featuring a bust of Washington in an oval with *1776* under it. Surrounding the portrait are four red shields with the scales of justice and the word *Peace*. The center pyramid features a brown on white textile in which vertical and horizontal rows of the word *Centennial* create an overall grid pattern. On the right is a red-and-blue-on-white cotton featuring a variety of stars and stripes. The quilt is made entirely of cotton, and the piecing is by hand; but when the back is brought to the front to bind the edge, it is stitched by machine. The quilting (5 stitches per inch) is in diagonal lines.[11]

Additional problems with provenance arise when there is no direct connection between the maker and the owner. The quilt is technically a family heirloom, and it was saved for that reason; but the connection is so peripheral that a lack of personal involvement between the maker and owner contributes to a lack of information. The maker of the Hour Glass quilt was the aunt of the present owner's grandmother. Jean Davis supplied most of the information on the form and was able to locate the remaining needed facts when requested to do so, even though it soon will be sixty years since the maker died. The farther an object fades into time, the more difficult it is to locate accurate orally transmitted information.

[Plate 140]
HOUR GLASS
75" x 70"

Josie Steinsultz Fife, 1854–1935
Raleigh, Saline County, Illinois, 1870
Collection of Jean Davis

The Hour Glass quilt has an intriguing story. According to Ms. Davis, the white fabrics came from the tails that her great-great uncle's mother cut off his "dresses when he began to walk. That little boy was a twenty-seven-year-old married man when my grandmother was orphaned (at age five) and went to live with him and his wife." Jean's grandmother's aunt eventually acquired the cut-off dress tails and used them for the white fabric in the pieced blocks. The all-cotton bedcovering is stitched entirely by hand, and the small colored-print triangles illustrate numerous period fabrics. The edge is finished by bringing the back to the front. The quilting (7 stitches per inch) is in outline, parallel lines, leaves, feather wreaths in the pink blocks, chevrons through the triangles, and triple diagonal lines in the border.

The owner and the maker of the unusual China Plate Variant quilt are not far apart in time, but the owner lives far away from her family in Wayne County. The quilt was made by her aunt and given to her by a cousin. For the most part, such gifts are intended as keepsakes because of the relationship between giver and/or maker and the receiver. Although everyone realizes that a quilt will normally last longer than one generation, there is the tendency to believe everyone in the family knows the family heritage associated with the quilt or if they wanted to know, they would ask. Questions about this quilt were answered by a phone call, and the complete heritage information is now supplied on the registration form.

The innovative random placement of the modified Dresden Plates, the unusual addition of leaves and stems, the use of plate sectors to create fans in three corners, and the unlikely placement of the fourth sector along the center edge of a width rather than in the empty corner combine to create a provocative design. Most of the Plates are pieced of older cotton fabrics, but there are also cotton/polyester blends, polished cottons, and heavier fabrics. The back is brought to the front and stitched by hand. Addie Shehorn appliquéd her design on unbleached muslin and used the same fabric for the back. The quilting (5 stitches per inch) outlines the design, and white areas are filled with variable-sized clamshells. Although the maker created parts of the quilt prior to World War II, it was not completed until shortly before her death. She left a memorable legacy and partially documented it. "Made This 1961" and "Made 1961–62" is written on the quilt.

[Plate 141]
CHINA PLATE VARIANT
87" x 72"

Addie Dawson Shehorn, 1889–1962
Fairfield, Wayne County, Illinois,
    circa 1940–1962
Collection of Patricia Arney

There are some quilts in the survey for which the information chain is broken, and researchers will never be able to recapture their stories. It is equally obvious that other incomplete forms can be improved with some follow-up work while the individuals who have the information are still able to answer the questions. With effort, it can be done.

However, for quilt owners and quilt researchers to preserve our heritage, it is necessary that everyone gather all the information available. Support the work whenever you can. Whether you registered your quilt or not, the next generation needs your help now. Learn more about the history behind your quilt. Send that information, along with pictures of the quilt and the quilter, and any supplementary material that will make your registration form more complete to the Early American Museum (P.O. Box 1040, Mahomet, IL 61853; please include an SASE for replies). Although the Project's documentation for each quilt will remain on file at the Illinois State Museum, it would be best to share this written information with those who will care for the object in the future.

An Overview of Illinois Quilters

As the Illinois Quilt Research Project traveled the state's quilt paths, the team members soon grew to appreciate the rich two-hundred-year-old quilting tradition and the contributions made by the women and men who have stitched the Illinois heritage into layers of quilted fabrics. The Project found that Illinois quilters represent a broad spectrum of the state's population. They are young and old, beginners and skilled professionals, foreign-born and native, and they are people who quilt for pleasure, for profit, and for competition. Thus there is little difference between those who quilt today and those who quilted yesterday, with perhaps one great exception. A similar survey of Illinois quilters fifty or one hundred years ago would have found few respondents indicating that they learned the craft by taking a quilting class. The twentieth century has transformed the craft. Not only have the mass media standardized quilt patterns and their distribution, they have also prepackaged quilt instruction.

Red Cake Stand is the rather recent creation of a woman who has made more than six hundred quilts during her lifetime; she is one of the state's oldest and most productive quilters. At age ninety-four Anna ("Annie") Borders enjoys good health and is still living in her own home, doing her own housework, and enjoying sewing and fishing.

She spends most of her waking hours working on a quilt. The hand-pieced Red Cake Stand uses both cotton and cotton/polyester fabrics and has a polyester batting. The

[Plate 142]
CAKE STAND
97" x 97"

Anna Roberts Borders, 1898–
Hillsboro, Montgomery County, Illinois,
   1981
Collection of the maker

[Figure 53]
Anna Roberts Borders
Born March 1, 1898, DeKalb, Kemper
    County, Mississippi

In comparison to Anna Borders, Jackie McFadden is the new kid on the quilter's block, with six quilts to her credit. Although she learned to quilt by trial and error, she comes from a family where quilting was practiced, if not perfected. Her grandmother was on call to assist her in problem-solving situations.

As is true of most quilters, Jackie's Single Irish Chain shows the work of an experienced quiltmaker and is quite different from her first efforts. The cotton top and back is filled with a polyester batting. After six months

of searching, she finally found the red-colored cloth she wanted for the quilt. Construction is by machine, which she prefers to hand piecing. The binding is bias-cut handmade of the same red cotton used for the pieced chain. The quilting (12 stitches per inch) creates feather wreaths, feather scrolls, and a grid-work. She also quilted her family's birthdays and anniversaries into the border of this quilt. The workmanship on it earned her two blue ribbons when she exhibited it at the Fisher Fair and the Champaign County Fair. She also received the champion quilt ribbon at the county fair.

[Plate 143]
SINGLE IRISH CHAIN (close-up of
    quilted documentation)
92" x 77"

Jackie Pannbacker McFadden, 1954–
Gifford, Champaign County, Illinois,
    1988
Collection of the maker

border is added by machine, and Prairie Points make the binding. The quilting (6 stitches per inch) is in outline and crossed parallel lines in the white blocks.

Mrs. Borders came to Hillsboro more than fifty years ago when her husband, a Pullman porter, relocated there because of his work. As a twelve-year-old child, she had learned to quilt from her mother, but Annie really did not begin making quilts as a serious task until she was forty-one years old. She has given a few of her quilts to relatives, kept about twelve for herself, and sold the others. She normally produces one a month, working on the same quilt from start to finish before cutting the pieces for a new one. For more than fifty years, Mrs. Borders has been active in the worship and work at St. James Baptist Church where she was the treasurer for eighteen years and still serves as an usher.

[Figure 54]
Jackie Pannbacker McFadden
Born March 10, 1954, Champaign,
Champaign County, Illinois

It is easy to get the impression that Jackie developed a warm relationship with her quilting grandmother in spite of their living some distance apart. Jackie fondly remembers the day her grandmother's little car pulled into the McFadden driveway with two long poles sticking out the back window. Grandma Kienietz was passing on to another quilting generation the frame her father had made for her mother many years earlier. It worked well for Great-grandmother Miller, and for many additional years it had served their daughter, Opal Jane Miller Meitzler Kienietz. Now it was Jackie's turn to care for the family heritage. Never mind that her house is too small for a full-size frame or that she prefers to use a quilting hoop. Don't worry about the safety of the quilting frame, however. Even though the yellow-painted poles have been retired from service, they—and a Seven Sisters quilt made on the frame—are lovingly treasured ·as a lasting bond between Jackie and her quilt-making grandmother.

Nothing ventured, nothing gained is an adage Marian Kanke Brockschmidt learned from her mother when she was growing up in Nokomis, Illinois, and she took it to heart. Mrs. Kanke was a quilter and a seamstress, and two of her four daughters also became quilters, although they never quilted with her when they were young.[12] Marian learned quilting as an adult through observation and experimentation. Once she began quilting in 1964, she started entering contests and has won far more than she has lost. Competition has been her pursuit ever since.

Marian's Illinois State Fair exhibition career is slowly edging toward the half-century mark. She began entering the textile division in 1948 but did not enter a quilt in competition until 1964. That year she won a blue ribbon for her Cathedral Window. In 1974 she won third prize on a Dresden Rose cross-stitch quilt. However, her career came into its own in 1975 when her State Bird and Flower quilt received a first prize and was selected as Best of

Show at the state fair. Since then she has accumulated twenty-six blue ribbons and received eleven more Best of Show awards. Her ventures are not limited to the Illinois State Fair. She has entered several national shows and has received eleven first prizes and six Viewer's Choice selections.

Marian admits that her housework takes second place to quilting and that Arthur, her tolerant husband of fifty years, has learned to accept a variety of snips and threads on the floor. In fact, to avoid stray pins he never walks barefoot in the house. Claiming her motto is Quilting Forever, Housework Never, she confidently hopes to be remembered "for my quilts and not how I've kept house." If her work remains properly identified, her quilting heritage will endure for many generations. With any luck, the purple ribbons will be firmly attached to her reputation.

Marian's work reminds one of the work of Bertha Stenge, who won many national awards fifty years ago. Unfortunately, none of Stenge's

[Plate 144]
MARY'S BALTIMORE AND BEYOND
90" x 88"

Marian Kanke Brockschmidt, 1922–
Springfield, Sangamon County, Illinois,
    1990
Collection of the maker, who is pictured
    with the quilt

Using patterns from Elly Sienkiewicz's
Spoken Without a Word and *Baltimore
Beauties and Beyond,* Marian spent four
months creating the quilt, which was
made to be a future wedding present for
her young granddaughter. The materials
on the top include synthetic ribbon as
well as cotton; the back is cotton, and
polyester is used for the batting. All the
piecing and appliqué work is by hand.

Handmade bias-cut, solid-red cotton is
used as a binding. It is applied by machine on the front and by hand on the
back. The quilting (7 stitches per inch)
creates florals and straight lines, and it
echoes the swags and outlines the decorative elements. This *tour de force* pattern, designed to test a quiltmaker's
patience and skill, earned its creator a
blue ribbon, a Best of Show, and the *Better Homes and Gardens* Illinois award at the
1991 Illinois State Fair. Making variations
of Baltimore Album quilts is becoming a
habit for Marian Brockschmidt, as she is
currently working on her fourth one.[13]

quilts were registered as a part of the
Project. The famous Chicago quiltmaker came to national prominence in the 1930s and 1940s when
her original designs appeared frequently in national periodicals such
as *Ladies' Home Journal.* In 1939 she
captured first prize at the New York
World's Fair quilt contest. In 1942
Woman's Day Magazine selected her
entry for the Grand Prize in its national contest. She also won prizes
in other national contests and at the
Illinois State Fair. Her quilts were
rarely sold. Today a few are in the
collections of the Art Institute and
the Chicago Historical Society. She
died in 1957.[14]

Competition is a long-standing
tradition among quilters, and a
challenger to the champion is always preparing to take over. Debra
Taft's Chain of Daisies quilt won
second prize at the Illinois State Fair
in 1987 and has since been shown at
Paducah, Kentucky, Woodlawn Plantation, Virginia, Silver Dollar City,
Missouri, and Rockome Gardens at
Arcola, Illinois.

Using a Mountain Mist pattern, a
polyester batt, and cotton for the
top and the back, Debra completed
a quilt that found favor with the
judges at the Illinois State Fair. Although she freely admits not yet
being in the same league with Marian Brockschmidt, she is committed
to improvement and striving for perfection. Her quilting (8 stitches per
inch) creates floral, echo, spider web,
and outline motifs.

Although Debra learned to knit
and crochet as a child, she did not
come from a family of quilters. However, the first time she met her future mother-in-law, Esther Taft was
sitting behind a quilting frame working on a Periwinkle quilt. In agree-
ment with quilting critics of earlier
generations, Debbie's first thought
was Why would anyone cut tiny
pieces of fabric and sew them back
together again? She later received

[Plate 145]
CHAIN OF DAISIES
91″ x 75″

Debra White Taft, 1952–
Rochester, Sangamon County, Illinois,
    1987
Collection of the maker, who is pictured
with her quilt. Debbie was born July 14,
1952, at Springfield in Sangamon
County, Illinois.

the quilt as a wedding gift. A year
after her marriage, Esther asked
Debra to help on a quilt, and she
rapidly became a convert. She soon
became so busy quilting for other
people that she did not have time to
do her own work. By the time she
made a Sunbonnet Sue quilt for her
daughter Andrea, she had gained
enough experience to begin making
smaller stitches.

When she won a third prize at the
Illinois State Fair, she began taking
quilting seriously. That year she saw
a Marian Brockschmidt quilt for the
first time. It received a Best of Show
award, and Debra considered it "perfect." She decided "my goal right
then was to beat her in the State Fair
competition. Then I would know I
had a perfect quilt, too. Each year I
look at what she comes up with and
try harder for the next year. So far my
goal has not been met, but I have
learned a lot."

A quilting sampler class in 1978, offered by Betty Balestri's School of Quilting in Rockford, introduced sixty-year-old Dorothy Clikeman to the world of quilting. Recently widowed she was looking for a worthwhile activity to occupy some of her free time. She entered the Boone County Fair in 1979 and won Best of Show on her first entry.

Dorothy still attends quilting classes. Not only does she continue to learn, she also enjoys socializing with the friends she has made there. Her jackets and wall hangings are based on information gleaned from her classes. One of her main problems is what to make next; there are so many things she would like to do. She is now moving on to scrap quilts and working with pieces of her daughter's old dresses. She likes to do things that catch the eye, and she has favorite colors with which she prefers to work—rose, mauve, and soft green.

[Plate 146]
DOROTHY'S PIECED TULIP
98″ x 82″

Dorothy Stauffer Clikeman, 1918–
Winnebago, Winnebago County,
    Illinois, 1988
Collection of the maker

[Figure 55]
Dorothy Stauffer Clikeman
Born November 6, 1918, Durand,
    Winnebago County, Illinois

Although Dorothy's Pieced Tulip appears to be similar to Zygocactus, it is not exactly the same thing, according to Dorothy. Her quilt was completed in a class at Quilter's Thimble in Freeport from a pattern that had been drafted by Carol Jacobs before Zygocactus was created and published. The all-cotton quilt is pieced by machine and the back is brought to the front over the edge. It has a polyester batt. The quilting (9 stitches per inch) is in cables, hearts, and bell-flowers.

And still they come—one by one, two by two, or in groups. Many new immigrants, such as Doris Langer, arrive without any knowledge of the American bedquilt. Although quilting in one form or another, is practiced almost worldwide, America's particular form of bedcovering can appear "different" to someone from another part of the world. Doris's experience was not entirely unlike that of the Germans who arrived in the nineteenth century and acquired the art of making bedquilts from their English-speaking neighbors.

Doris met her future husband while he was in Germany during the early 1950s. She came to the United States in 1956 to visit some Texas friends; Robert Langer visited her while she was in this country; they were married the following year; and she went to live at Ottawa in Robert's native LaSalle County. Like so many residents of Illinois, her husband was a descendant of German immigrants. Doris met his grandmother, Louise Langer, who was born in LaSalle County in the

[Plate 147]
CLAY'S CHOICE
93" x 80"

Doris Bense Langer, 1930–
Ottawa, LaSalle County, Illinois, 1988
Collection of the maker

[Figure 56]
Doris Bense Langer
Born July 27, 1930, Heilbronn Am
  Neckar, Germany

1870s, the daughter of German immigrants from Tenningen, Baden-Wurttemberg, in the Black Forest.

During the 1960s when Louise Langer was in her nineties, Doris began watching her quilt. It was a totally new craft to Doris, for she had never seen this in Germany. The older woman also shared with her some turn-of-the-century paper templates for piecing a Double Irish Chain quilt. The instructions were written in German script. Doris became interested in the craft and made her first quilt in 1981. She took no classes, read no books, but watched the work being done, and she was ready to begin. Soon she had completed five quilts, which she proudly displayed to a visiting

cousin from Germany. The amazed relative was also unfamiliar with the art but liked what she saw, took photographs of Doris's quilts, returned to Germany, and made duplicates. One never knows where the effects of sharing will end.

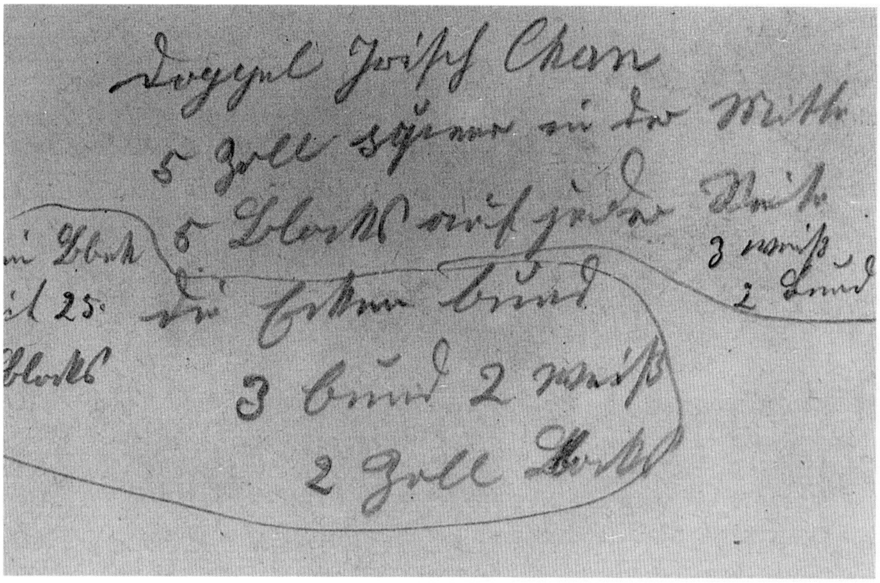

[Figure 57]
German directions on a paper template
  for making a "Doppel Irisch Chain"
Collection of Robert and Doris Bense
  Langer
An English translation is:

"5 inches square in the middle
5 blocks on each side
                          3 white, 2 colored
inside the block
25 blocks   the corners colored
               3 colored and 2 white
               2 inch blocks"

Making Connections

The Illinois Quilt Research Project has explored our state's quilted landscape. Each quilt registration day the board and its volunteer staff marveled at the intricately undulating hills and valleys of stuffed work; admired the gently rolling plains of wholecloth; and savored the seasonal colors in the springtime pastels of the Great Depression, the bright mid-nineteenth-century reds and greens of summer, and the wooded Illinois hillsides glowing in rich 1870s red and brown prints under a warm autumn sun. We crisscrossed the state while exploring. Through exploration we learned; through learning we shared; and through sharing we made connections. We explored far and wide, and we learned a great deal. We learned about the rich heritage that can be gleaned from quilts and the importance of placing them within the context of their existence, and our own lives. We learned what we do not know, what we need to find out, and how much more work needs to be done. We shared technical and historical information with the owners who brought their quilts to registration days, and they in turn enriched us by sharing their personal information with us. We grew to appreciate the value of intergenerational sharing of traditions.

In our highly mobile twentieth-century society, a tightly knit extended family relationship is difficult to maintain. It takes determination like that of Emma Sue Gilkeson Allen, the coordinator of Pieces for the 1989 Elgin Commemorative Quilt Project, to keep traditions alive. Emma, whose Mennonite great-grandmother's Butterfly quilt is illustrated in chapter 2 (Plate 28) obviously carried her rural central Illinois traditions with her to the Chicago suburbs. She explains her connection to quilts, her family, and the past in the Introduction to *Pieces,* the Elgin Project's book:

> The experiencing of quilts creates memories not easily shaken. Thus, some mention should be made of my grandmother, Viola Harnish, and my mother, Mary Gilkeson, who encouraged my interest in quilts. Mom picked up a needle to quilt after all eight of us were out of the nest but Grandma "quilted" all her life. One of my fondest childhood recollections is being tucked in at her house under layers of bedclothes, one being a colorful quilt. These were lovingly made by Grandma and her friends who met regularly to quilt for one another and for their church's relief projects. One of grandma's "crazy quilts" hangs on my dining room wall. A beautiful appliquéd wreath quilt, made by Grandma and my mother as a wedding gift for Chuck and me, is on a guest bed. My children, Ann, Joellen, and Ted, are much the richer because each has one of my mother's quilts made especially for them.
>
> Grandma died in 1988 at the age of ninety but we have the memory that the one thing you always saw when visiting her was a piece of handwork by her favorite chair. Grandpa, who died in 1985, was a Mennonite minister by calling, and a painter and interior decorator by profession. "Work well and willingly with what you have" are words he inscribed in the Bible he gave to Grandma on their wedding day. Grandma, it seems, followed his advice as evidenced by the many beautifully quilted items she made for family and friends.[15]

What experiences will Emma Sue be able to share with her grandchildren who may be geographically and culturally even farther removed from the ancestral Woodford County hearth? How will you preserve your family heritage?

[Plate 148]
Quiltmaking Accessories
Private collections

[Plate 149]
Big 10 Picture Puzzle
   circa 1943
Private collection

The Illinois Quilt Research Project was an educational experience. It increased our awareness of quilts as historical documents; it demonstrated the power of objects; it helped us find our heritage. The quilt paths of Illinois taught us that we cannot live without our past. As we returned to the point of our departure, we share the sentiment of T. S. Eliot:

> We shall not cease from exploration
> And the end of all our exploring
> Will be to arrive where we started
> And know the place for the first
>   time.[16]

The quilts illustrated in this book represent the many stories recorded by the Project. We hope they encourage everyone, whether they participated in the Project or not, to look at quilts in a new way. History is not only the long ago and far away. It is around us every day. It can wrap us in warm memories as easily as a favorite old quilt enfolds the boy pictured on the jigsaw puzzle.

Your quilt can become an important document for you, for your family, and for your community. Take good care of it. Make sure its history is recorded and safely preserved. Without your story, our puzzle will have a missing piece. An incomplete record of the past puts our culture at risk. Your heritage is an important part of a history that is written from the heart.

Five hundred years ago Christopher Columbus, with the aid of a mariner's compass, sailed toward a land that was unfamiliar to most Europeans, and the world was changed forever. The points on Verdilla Zook's Mariner's Compass quilt have served us well as we traveled the quilt paths of Illinois. We hope it has led you into previously unexplored areas and increased your awareness of a unique heritage that surrounds you every day. May you always cherish it.

[Plate 150]
Mariner's Compass, quilt block

Notes

Introduction: Sharing Our Heritage

1. David E. Kyvig and Myron A. Marty, *Nearby History: Exploring the Past Around You* (Nashville, Tennessee: The American Association for State and Local History, 1982), p. 12.

2. *Ibid.,* pp. 1–59. A concise local history research guide is Patricia Mooney Melvin, *Tracing the Quiltmaker* (San Francisco: American Quilt Study Group, 1987).

3. Dorothy Cozart, "Women and Their Quilts As Portrayed by Some American Authors," *Uncoverings,* 1981, pp. 19–33; and Kathryn J. Schilmoeller, "The Role of Quilts in Children's Literature," *Uncoverings,* 1985, pp. 71–84.

4. Kyvig and Marty, *Nearby History,* p. 6.

5. The Kansas Quilt Project report correctly noted an increasing recognition of the legitimacy of the material culture research field by professional historians over the past two decades. Mary W. Madden, "The Kansas Quilt Project: Piecing Together Our Past," *Kansas History,* Spring 1990, p. 2. Much of the work has come from the fields of anthropology, folklore/folklife, and cultural/historical geography. Some recent studies, such as Ricky Clark, ed., *Quilts in Community: Ohio Traditions* (Nashville, Tennessee: Rutledge Hill Press, 1991), included the work of George W. Knepper, Distinguished Professor of History at the University of Akron, and are cited in this volume. As more historians become interested in material culture, their research efforts penetrate deeply into the decorative arts field in general and increasingly into the subject of American quilt history. More than a decade ago a proposal was made to create a quilt section within the Folklore Archive at Southern Illinois University, Edwardsville. See John L. Oldani, "Archiving and the American Quilt: A Position Paper," *Uncoverings,* 1980, pp. 72–76.

6. David J. Russo, *Families and Communities: A New View of American History* (Nashville, Tennessee: The American Association for State and Local History, 1974), p. 191.

7. Ray A. Billington, *Westward Expansion: A History of the American Frontier,* 3rd ed. (New York: Macmillan, 1967), p. 144.

8. For more information about indigo, see Gosta Sandberg, *Indigo Textiles: Technique and History* (Asheville, North Carolina: Lark Books, 1989). This is an English translation of a Swedish work first published in 1986.

9. An excellent study of a quilt collector's motivation and process is Michael Kile, "Looking toward the Future: The Collector," *Quilt Digest,* 1984, pp. 16–25. The viewpoint of another collector is presented in Phyllis Haders, *The Warner Collector's Guide to American Quilts* (New York: Warner Books, 1981), pp. 11–14. The freedom of personal collecting in contrast to that of a nonprofit institution is discussed in Imelda G. De-Graw, "Museum Quilt Collecting," *Uncoverings,* 1981, pp. 105–110.

10. After acquiring enough money to purchase a machine, "Quiltmakers devoted their newfound time to making more quilts, some of which they embellished with visible machine stitching, an indication of the pride they felt in their sewing machines." Suellen Meyer, "Early Influences of the Sewing Machine and Visible Machine Stitching on Nineteenth-Century Quilts," *Uncoverings,* 1989, p. 38. According to Jonathan Holstein, *The Pieced Quilt* (Boston: Little, Brown and Company, 1973), p. 84, about half of the post–Civil War nineteenth-century pieced quilts have some machine stitching, but machine quilting is rare.

11. Harvey Green, *The Light of the Home: An Intimate View of the Lives of Women In Victorian America* (New York: Pantheon Books, 1983), p. 81; Susan Strasser, *Never Done: A History of American Housework* (New York: Pantheon Books, 1982), p. 139; Meyer, "Early Influences of the Sewing Machine," pp. 38–40.

12. Understanding the historical development of textile manufacturing techniques and equipment and the evolution of dyeing are critical to placing quilts into an accurate historical context. Fortunately, several valuable works are available. For an overview see Barbara Brackman, *Dating Antique Quilts: 200 Years of Style, Pattern and Technique* (San Francisco: American Quilt Study Group, 1990). Much more detail is available in Barbara Brackman, *Clues in the Calico: A Guide to Identifying and Dating Antique Quilts* (McLean, Virginia: EPM Publications, 1989). Her preliminary findings were earlier reported in the *Quilter's Newsletter Magazine.* See "Dating Old Quilts, Part One: Green Prints and Dyes," September 1984, pp. 24–25, 45; "Part Two: Cotton Prints up to 1890," October 1984, pp. 26–27; "Part Three: Cotton Prints, 1890–1960," November/December 1984, pp. 16–17; "Part Four: Quilt Dating and Technology," January 1985, pp. 28–29, 45; "Part Five: Color As a Clue in Quilt Dating," February 1985, pp. 22–24; "Part Six: Style and Pattern As Clues," March 1985, pp. 22–25; Barbara Brackman, "Fugitive Dyes in Antique Quilts," *Quilter's Newsletter Magazine,* October 1989, pp. 42–44. Additional help can be found in Diane L. Fagan Affleck, *Just New from the Mills: Printed Cottons in America, Late Nineteenth and Early Twentieth Centuries from the Collection of the Museum of American Textile History* (North Andover, Massachusetts: Museum of American Textile History, 1987); Gail van der Hoof, "Various Aspects of Dating Quilts," in Jeannette Lasansky, ed., *In the Heart of Pennsylvania: Symposium Papers* (Lewisburg, Pennsylvania: Oral Traditions Project), pp. 76–83; Rachel Maines, "Paradigms of Scarcity and Abundance/The Quilt As an Artifact of the Industrial Revolution," in Lasansky, ed., *In the Heart of Pennsylvania,* pp. 84–89; Katherine R. Koob, "Documenting Quilts by Their Fabrics," *Uncoverings,* 1981, pp. 3–9; James N. Liles, "Dyes in American Quilts Made Prior to 1930, with Special Emphasis on Cotton and Linen," *Uncoverings,* 1984, pp. 29–40.

13. One current college textbook notes only that "Elias Howe's invention of the sewing machine in 1846 laid the basis for the ready-to-wear clothing industry and also contributed to the mechanization of shoemaking." Robert A. Devine et. al., *America: Past and Present* (Glenview, Illinois: Scott, Foresman and Company, 1987), p. 372.

14. Kyvig and Marty, *Nearby History,* p. 5.

15. Ruth Haislip Roberson, "Quilted Treasures," in Ruth Haislip Roberson, ed., *North Carolina Quilts* (Chapel Hill: University of North Carolina Press, 1988), pp. 183–197.

16. Marian L. Martinello, *The Search for Emma's Story* (Fort Worth: Texas Christian University Press, 1987), pp. 1–5.

17. If you wish to conduct an oral interview with a relative or friend, a good introduction to the process can be found in Laurel Horton, *The Oral Interview in Quilt Research* (San Francisco: American Quilt Study Group, 1988).

18. Cheryl Kennedy, "Project Perspective," *Illinois Quilt Research Project* [Newsletter], July 1989, pp. 1–2.

19. Sally Peterson, "A Cool Heart and a Watchful Mind: Creating Hmong Paj Ntaub in the Context of Community," in Jeannette Lasansky, ed., *Pieced by Mother: Symposium Papers* (Lewisburg, Pennsylvania: Oral Traditions Project, 1988), pp. 35–45; Lauri Linch with Alice Schmude, "Hmong Needle Treasures," *Quilter's Newsletter Magazine,* October 1984, pp. 18–19, 22; Melissa Ringheim Stoddart, "Cultural Diversity in Minnesota Museums," *Midwest Museums Conference Annual Review* (St. Louis: Midwest Museums Conference, 1992), pp. 33–37.

20. An overview of the projects and the process is available in Barbara Brackman, "Documentation Projects: Uncovering Heritage Quilts," "A Quilt Day," and "Getting Started," *Quilter's Newsletter Magazine,* March 1988, pp. 36–39. General introductions to quilt registration projects can

be found in Jonathan Holstein and John Finley, *Kentucky Quilts, 1800–1900: The Kentucky Quilt Project* (Louisville, Kentucky: The Kentucky Quilt Project, 1982), pp. 81–82; Katy Christopherson, "Documenting Kentucky's Quilts: An Experiment in Research by Committee," *Uncoverings,* 1983, pp. 137–145; Bets Ramsey and Merikay Waldvogel, *The Quilts of Tennessee: Images of Domestic Life Prior to 1930* (Nashville, Tennessee: Rutledge Hill Press, 1986), pp. ix–xi; "The Michigan Quilt Project," in Marsha MacDowell and Ruth D. Fitzgerald, eds., *Michigan Quilts: 150 Years of a Textile Tradition* (East Lansing: Michigan State University Museum, 1987), pp. 165–169; Roberson, ed., *North Carolina Quilts,* pp. xi–xvi; Madden, "The Kansas Quilt Project," *Kansas History,* Spring 1990, pp. 2–4. For detailed instructions on the material needed on a registration form and how to conduct a model quilt registration day, see "Quilt Documentation: A Step-by-Step Guide," in Jeannette Lasansky, *Pieced by Mother: Over 100 Years of Quiltmaking Traditions* (Lewisburg, Pennsylvania: Oral Traditions Project, 1987), pp. 17–23; Jeannette Lasansky, *Quilt Documentation: Planning a Quilt Day* (San Francisco: American Quilt Study Group, 1991); Jonathan Holstein, "Collecting Quilt Data: History from Statistics," *Quilt Digest,* 1984, rev. ed., 1985, pp. 62–69.

21. Lasansky, *In the Heart of Pennsylvania,* p. 42.

22. An excellent study is Gayle R. Davis, "Women in the Quilt Culture: An Analysis of Social Boundaries and Role Satisfaction," *Kansas History,* Spring 1990, pp. 5–12.

23. *Gleason's Drawing Room Pictorial Companion,* October 21, 1854, p. 152.

Chapter 1: Westward, Ho!

1. Ancient maps used an intesecting grid of rhumb lines to indicate bearing winds. The intersections were marked by "wind roses" that were based upon the compass card. A Greek, Timothenes, is believed to have developed the familiar compass design. The tapering points indicate the four main directions and define the intervening degrees. The wind roses can have as many as thirty-two or as few as four points. Mercator's sixteenth-century map introduced meridians and parallels. The wind roses with their radiating rhumb lines disappeared but the decorative element survived in the form of a design pointing to the north on each map using it. Although the layered design is difficult to do well, it has been used since the nineteenth century. However, the common name used for it today does not appear in early quilting literature. Sunburst is one of the most frequently documented names. Judy Mathieson, "Some Published Sources of Design Inspiration for the Quilt Pattern Mariner's Compass — 17th to 20th Century," *Uncoverings,* 1981, pp. 11–17, believes "The difference between a Mariner's Compass quilt pattern and a sun or star pattern is probably only in the mind of the quiltmaker or the viewer of the quilt" (p. 14). Thus it is probable that when Mrs. Zook made her quilt she did not refer to it as a Mariner's Compass. Perhaps Slashed Star or Chips and Whetstones would sound more familiar to her. Bonnie Leman, "Mariner's Compass," *Quilter's Newsletter Magazine,* April 1980, p. 20.

2. The prehistoric, ancient, and medieval types of quilted clothing are presented in Averil Colby, *Quilting* (New York: Charles Scribner's Sons, 1971), pp. 1–19. For information about Early American quilted petticoats, see: Tandy Hersh, "18th Century Quilted Silk Petticoats Worn in America," *Uncoverings,* 1984, pp. 83–98; and Tandy Hersh, "Quilted Petticoats," in Jeannette Lasansky, ed., *Pieced by Mother: Symposium Papers* (Lewisburg, Pennsylvania: Oral Traditions Project, 1988), pp. 5–11. Additional information may be found in Peter Cook, "Art from Necessity: America's Wool Bedquilts," *Early American Life,* October 1991, pp. 55–56. Lynn A. Bonfield, "The Production of Cloth, Clothing and Quilts in 19th Century New England Homes," *Uncoverings,* 1981, p. 85, pointed out that Lydia Maria Child, in her well-known book *The American Frugal Housewife,* asserts eighteenth-century diary references to quilting all refer to making petticoats, unless the entry specifically defines the work in regard to bedquilts.

3. *Miss Leslie's Lady's House-Book: A Manual of Domestic Economy* (Philadelphia: A. Hart, 1850), p. 315. Bonfield, "The Production of Cloth, Clothing and Quilts in 19th Century New England Homes," *Uncoverings,* 1981, p. 83, indicates Child, in *The American Frugal Housewife,* reveals American women were still making quilted petticoats in 1864.

4. Benjamin Harding, *A Tour Through the Western Country, A. D. 1818 and 1819,* (New London: Samuel Green, 1819), p. 5.

5. For more information about the development of early Illinois, see Robert P. Howard, *Illinois: A History of the Prairie State* (Grand Rapids,

Michigan: William B. Eerdman's Publishing Company, 1972), pp. 23–143; Clarence W. Alvord, *The Illinois Country, 1673–1818* (Chicago: A. C. McClurg and Company, 1922); Solon J. Buck, *Illinois in 1818* (Springfield: Illinois Centennial Commission, 1917); Theodore C. Pease, *The Frontier State: 1818–1848* (Chicago: A. C. McClurg and Company, 1922).

6. E. Duane Elbert, *Edward Coles: Freedom's Champion* (Charleston, Illinois: Coles County Historical Series, 1975), pp. 1–16.

7. Kathy Sullivan, "The Legacy of German Quiltmaking in North Carolina," in Jeannette Lasansky, ed., *Bits and Pieces: Textile Traditions* (Lewisburg, Pennsylvania: Oral Traditions Project, 1991), pp. 65–67.

8. The only extant newspaper file for May 1904 in the Illinois State Historical Library is the *Effingham Republican,* which was published weekly. The May 6 issue has a column announcing recent visits by the "Grim Reaper," referring specifically to Spitler among several others. However, the unidentified clipping shared by the quilt owner is a lengthy full obituary headed "THE GRIM REAPER VISITS EFFINGHAM AND TAKES AWAY MANY OF OLDEST RESIDENTS." It was probably published on May 13, which is missing from the file.

9. William H. Perrin, ed., *History of Effingham County, Illinois* (Chicago: O. L. Baskin and Company, 1883), pp. 157, 248.

10. Undated unidentified newspaper clipping.

11. The Irish Chain is not only one of the oldest quilt patterns, it is also distinctive because it has always been known by this name. There are single, double, and triple types. "Irish Chain," *Quilter's Newsletter Magazine,* March 1979, pp. 16–19.

12. In patterns such as Irish Chain, which include large unpieced areas, stuffing is used to create a design that is equal to the primary quilt pattern but at the same time does not distract from or compete with it. Stuffing and cording create a three-dimensional impact that cannot be achieved in any other way. The back of a stuffed quilt is usually made of a coarsely woven fabric that permits the quilter to create a small opening by spreading the threads with a stiletto-type shaft. It is then possible to push the cotton or wool into a cavitylike leaf or grape created by previously quilting around the design to be stuffed. When the work is completed, the opening is closed by pushing the threads together again. Stuffing is an ancient technique that is difficult to do well. Relatively few quilters attempt to do it on the scale used by Ann Spitler. For other Project quilts making an effective use of stuffing, see Beauty of the Forest, Plate 44, and Sawtooth, Plate 129. Susan Burrows Swan, *A Winterthur Guide to American Needlework* (New York: Rutledge Books, 1976), pp. 126–129; Patsy Orlofsky and Myron Orlofsky, *Quilts in America* (New York: McGraw-Hill, 1974), pp. 186–193; Edwin Binney and Gail Binney-Winslow, *Homage to Amanda* (San Francisco: R K Press, 1984), pp. 24, 40.

13. Undated unidentified newspaper clipping.

14. John G. Henderson, *Early History of the "Sangamon Country,"* Typescript (Davenport, Iowa: Day, Egburt, and Fidlar, 1873), p. 15.

15. Arthur C. Boggess, *The Settlement of Illinois, 1778–1830,* (Chicago: Chicago Historical Society, 1908), pp. 120–123.

16. William V. Pooley, *The Settlement of Illinois from 1830 to 1850* (Madison: University of Wisconsin, 1908), pp. 307–329. For a brief overview of the domestic-born population settlement pattern by county based upon the 1850 census, see Douglas K. Meyer, "Folk Housing on the Illinois Frontier," *Pioneer America Society Transactions,* I (1978), pp. 30–42. All population statistics used in this chapter are based on county totals published in the 1860 population census. Joseph C. G. Kennedy, comp., *Population of the United States in 1860* (Washington, DC: Government Printing Office, 1864).

17. James W. Patton, ed., "Letters from North Carolina Emigrants in the Old Northwest, 1830–1834," *Mississippi Valley Historical Review,* September 1960, pp. 266–267, 272–273. The editor retained the original spelling.

18. Boggess, *Settlement of Illinois, 1778–1830,* p. 128.

19. Merikay Waldvogel, "Southern Linsey Quilts of the Nineteenth Century," *Uncoverings,* 1987, pp. 87–106, reports on pieced homespun cotton-woolen, or "linsey" quilts, similar to Sally Mitchell's One Patch, still being made in Tennessee during the late nineteenth century. Her article traces the "long, important, but confusing history of a fabric called linsey-woolsey."

20. Daniel M. Parkinson, "Pioneer Life in Wisconsin," in Lyman C. Draper, ed., *Collections of the State Historical Society of Wisconsin* (Madison: State Historical Society of Wisconsin, 1903), II, pp. 326–327.

21. Pooley, *Settlement of Illinois from 1830 to 1850,* p. 344.

22. Suellen Meyer, "Characteristics of Missouri–German Quilts," *Uncoverings,* 1984, pp. 100–101, indicates the early German women who settled in the Missouri River Valley with their husbands and fathers,

(n.p., Charles T. Branford Company, 1980 reprint of the 1929 edition), p. 32; Bonnie Leman, "Crazy Quilts," *Quilter's Newsletter Magazine,* November 1977, pp. 8–9.

68. Cuesta Benberry, "The 20th Century's First Quilt Revival, Part I: The Interim Period," *Quilter's Newsletter Magazine,* July/August 1979, pp. 20–22; "Part II, The First Quilt Revival," *Quilter's Newsletter Magazine,* September 1979, pp. 25–26; "Part III, The World War I Era," *Quilter's Newsletter Magazine,* October 1979, pp. 10–11, 37.

69. Woodard and Greenstein, *Twentieth Century Quilts,* p. 20.

70. *Ibid.,* p. 20; Cuesta Benberry, "Ladies Art Company: Pioneer in Printed Quilt Patterns," *Nimble Needle Treasures,* Spring 1971, p. 4; Betty J. Hagerman, *A Meeting of the Sunbonnet Children* (Baldwin City, Kansas: Telegraphics, 1979), p. 20.

71. Cuesta Benberry, "An Historic Quilt Document: The Ladies Art Company Catalog," *Quilters' Journal,* Summer 1978, pp. 13–14.

72. Although the Ladies Art Company was an early producer of pre-packed quilt materials, other firms also entered this beginning industry. A number of these companies are presented in Cuesta Benberry, "Quilt Kits— Past and Present, Part II," *Nimble Needle Treasures,* December 1974, p. 1.

73. "The Household Journal," *Aunt Jane's Prize Winning Quilt Designs* (Springfield, Ohio: Central Publishing Co., 1914), p. 2.

74. Jonathan Holstein, *Kentucky Quilts, 1800–1900* (Louisville, Kentucky: The Kentucky Quilt Project, 1982), p. 25; Helen Comstock, *American Furniture, Seventeenth, Eighteenth, and Nineteenth Century Styles* (New York: The Viking Press, 1962), see chairs 424, 425, 428, 429, 436, 441, all of which have the Prince of Wales plumes as a motif.

75. Cuesta Benberry, "The Nationalization of Pennsylvania–Dutch Patterns in the 1940's–1960's," in Jeannette Lasansky, ed., *Bits and Pieces, Textile Traditions* (Lewisburg, Pennsylvania: Oral Traditions Project, 1991), pp. 81–89.

Chapter 6: Twentieth-Century Quiltmaking Trends

1. Marie D. Webster, *Quilts: Their Story and How to Make Them* (New York: Doubleday, Page and Company, 1915).

2. Rosalind Webster Perry, "Marie Webster: Her Story," in Marie Webster, *Quilts: Their Story and How to Make Them* (Santa Barbara, California: Practical Patchwork, 1990), p. 208. The most recently published edition of Webster's book is edited and updated by her granddaughter. It includes additional pictures, footnotes, and a biography.

3. Thomas K. Woodard and Blanche Greenstein, *Twentieth Century Quilts, 1900–1950* (New York: E. P. Dutton, 1988), pp. 11, 20; Cuesta Benberry, "Marie Webster: Indiana's Gift to American Quilts," in *Quilts of Indiana* (Bloomington, Indiana: Indiana University Press, 1990), pp. 88–93; Niloo Imami-Paydar, "Marie Webster Quilts: A Retrospective, March 24–September 30, 1991," (Indianapolis Museum of Art Gallery Guide).

4. Benberry, "Marie Webster," in *Quilts of Indiana,* p. 92.

5. Imami-Paydar, "Webster Retrospective"; Perry, "Marie Webster: Her Story," in Webster, *Quilts* (1990 ed.), p. 209.

6. A small, undated Marie Webster catalog, reprinted with McElwain's name, offered Webster quilts but no patterns. The May Tulips stamped boxed kit was $12.50, a basted top cost $22.50, and a completed quilt was priced at $50.00. Also see Cuesta Benberry, "Quilt Cottage Industries: A Chronicle," *Uncoverings,* 1986, pp. 91–92. Ruth W. Peterson, "Memories of Mary A. McElwain Quilt Shop," *Quilters' Journal,* undated, no. 24, pp. 1–4. It includes a list of quilts prepared by Cuesta Benberry and Edna Ford, and a Mary McElwain bibliography.

7. Woodard and Greenstein, *Twentieth Century Quilts,* p. 24; Merikay Waldvogel, *Soft Covers for Hard Times: Quiltmaking and the Great Depression* (Nashville, Tennessee: Rutledge Hill Press, 1990), p. 46.

8. Elizabeth Wells Robertson, *American Quilts* (New York: Viking, 1948). Woodard and Greenstein, *Twentieth Century Quilts,* p. 12, includes her volume among "Other Important Books," without any further comment. Most quilt bibliographies do not cite her work.

9. *Quilts of Indiana,* pp. 103–104; Woodard and Greenstein, *Twentieth Century Quilts,* p. 26; Thomas K. Woodard and Blanche Greenstein, *Crib Quilts and Other Small Wonders* (New York: E. P. Dutton, 1981), pp. 15–16; Benberry, "Quilt Cottage Industries," 1986, pp. 87–88. Very little information is available in secondary literature on the Wilkinson quilts, and the only reference to primary material is a 1916 catalog mentioned in *Quilts of Indiana,* p. 103. Unfortunately, it is unavailable to other researchers since its location is not identified by depository or private collection.

10. Louise O. Townsend, "Kansas City *Star* Quilt Patterns," *Uncoverings,* 1984, p. 117.

11. Ruby Short McKim, *One Hundred and One Patchwork Patterns* (New York: Dover Publications, 1962, rev. ed. of the original published by McKim Studios in 1931).

12. "Ruby Short McKim: A Memorial," *Quilter's Newsletter Magazine,* December 1976, p. 14; Betty J. Hagerman, *A Meeting of the Sunbonnet Children* (Baldwin City, Kansas: Telegraphics, Inc., 1979), p. 26.

13. Woodard and Greenstein, *Twentieth Century Quilts,* p. 59.

14. Penny McMorris and Michael Kile, *The Art Quilt* (San Francisco: The Quilt Digest Press, 1986), pp. 35–36, 127; "McKim: A Memorial," *Quilter's Newsletter Magazine,* December 1976, p. 14; Marie Shirer, "Lively Iris," *Quilter's Newsletter Magazine,* May 1983, pp. 20–21, is a modern version of McKim's art deco pieced Iris. For a contemporary combination of McKim's Iris, Tulip, Rose, Pansy, and Poppy patterns into a single quilt, see Patricia Marks, letter and photograph, in "Quilting Bee," *Quilter's Newsletter Magazine,* March 1982, p. 40. Barbara Brackman, "Prairie School Quilts," *Quilter's Newsletter Magazine,* March 1982, pp. 14–15, compares McKim's designs to those of Frank Lloyd Wright while pointing out that Tulip and Trumpet Vine are "two of her most 'modern' patterns." An unsigned article "Tulip Quilts," *Quilter's Newsletter Magazine,* May 1978, pp. 16–17, believes Beautiful Tulip was designed circa 1928.

15. McKim's *One Hundred and One Patchwork Patterns* contains full-size drawings of many patterns originally published in her newspaper column.

16. Springfield, Illinois, *Illinois State Journal,* July 15, 1931.

17. Townsend, "Kansas City *Star* Patterns," *Uncoverings,* 1984, pp. 116–117. Other illustrators continued the column until it stopped in 1938.

18. Springfield, Illinois, *Illinois State Journal,* October 14, 1932.

19. Townsend, "Kansas City *Star* Quilt Patterns," *Uncoverings,* 1984, p. 117; Bonnie Leman, "The Needle's Eye," *Quilter's Newsletter Magazine,* May 1983, p. 4.

20. For more about Anne Orr see, "Refining the Tradition: Anne Champe Orr, 1875–1946," in Waldvogel, *Soft Covers,* pp. 24–37; "Anne Orr—She Captured Beauty," *Quilter's Newsletter Magazine,* May 1977, pp. 12–16, 27; Jean Dubois, *Anne Orr Patchwork* (Durango, Colorado: La Plata Press, 1977); Center for the History of American Needlework, *Anne Orr's Charted Designs* (New York: Dover Publications, Inc., 1978).

21. "Anne Orr," *Quilter's Newsletter Magazine,* May 1977, p. 12. "There is a woman in Kentucky with sixty mountain women working under her direction, who will do your quilting. This work is exquisite. Write to Anne Orr for prices," *Good Housekeeping,* January 1932, p. 104.

22. Merikay Waldvogel "The Marketing of Anne Orr's Quilts," *Uncoverings,* 1990, pp. 12–16.

23. Anne Orr, "Quilt Making in Old and New Designs," *Good Housekeeping,* January 1933, p. 56; Cuesta Benberry, "Storrowton Village— Home of the First National Quilt Show," *Quilter's Newsletter Magazine,* September 1987, pp. 36–41.

24. Waldvogel, *Soft Covers,* pp. 32, 44–46; Waldvogel, "The Marketing of Anne Orr's Quilts," *Uncoverings,* 1990, pp. 15–16; Barbara Brackman, "Patterns from the 1933 Chicago World's Fair," *Quilter's Newsletter Magazine,* July–August 1981, pp. 18–20; Barbara Brackman, "Looking Back at the Great Quilt Contest," *Quilter's Newsletter Magazine,* October 1983, pp. 22–24.

25. *Good Housekeeping,* January 1933, pp. 56, 123; Waldvogel, "The Marketing of Anne Orr's Quilts," *Uncoverings,* 1990, p. 18.

26. "Anne Orr," *Quilter's Newsletter Magazine,* May 1977, p. 13; Waldvogel, *Soft Covers,* p. 32.

27. Waldvogel, "The Marketing of Anne Orr's Patterns," *Uncoverings,* 1990, p. 12.

28. Woodard and Greenstein, *Twentieth Century Quilts,* p. 20; Hagerman, *Sunbonnet Children,* p. 25.

29. Townsend, "Kansas City *Star* Patterns," *Uncoverings,* 1984, p. 119.

30. *Ibid.,* pp. 118–120; Louise O. Townsend, "Evaline Foland, Quilt Pattern Illustrator," *Quilter's Newsletter Magazine,* April 1985, pp. 20–22.

31. Townsend, "Kansas City *Star* Quilt Patterns," *Uncoverings,* 1984, pp. 120–124; Louise O. Townsend, "Edna Marie Dunn of Kansas City, Missouri," *Quilter's Newsletter Magazine,* November–December 1978, p. 14.

32. Barbara Brackman, *An Encyclopedia of Pieced Quilt Patterns,* as cited in Woodard and Greenstein, *Twentieth Century Quilts,* pp. 141–145; Barbara Brackman, "Who Was Nancy Cabot?" *Quilter's Newsletter Magazine,* January–February 1991, pp. 22–24; Barbara Brackman, "Who Was Nancy Page?" *Quilter's Newsletter Magazine,* September 1991, pp. 22–27; Hagerman, *Sunbonnet Children,* pp. 29, 34.

33. Brackman, *Encyclopedia of Pieced Quilt Patterns,* as cited in Wood-

ward and Greenstein, *Twentieth Century Quilts,* pp. 141, 146; Barbara Brackman, "Who Was Aunt Martha?" *Quilter's Newsletter Magazine,* June 1991, pp. 42–43.

34. Webster, *Quilts,* p. xxi.

35. Barbara Brackman, "Old Patchwork Quilts and the Woman Who Wrote It: Ruth E. Finley," *Quilter's Newsletter Magazine,* November–December 1988, pp. 36–38.

36. Ruth E. Finley, *Old Patchwork Quilts and the Women Who Made Them* (Philadelphia: J. B. Lippencott Company, 1929), pp. 36–38.

37. Barbara Brackman, "Madam Carrie Hall," *Quilter's Newsletter Magazine,* June 1981, pp. 24–26; Barbara Brackman, "The Hall/Szabronski Collection at the University of Kansas," *Uncoverings,* 1982, pp. 59–74. At the 1978 Kansas Quilt Symposium, Hall's entire collection was exhibited for the participants. Fifty-three of the blocks are illustrated in color in the *Quilter's Newsletter Magazine,* January 1979, pp. 16–17.

38. Carrie A. Hall and Rose G. Kretsinger, *The Romance of the Patchwork Quilt in America* (Caldwell, Idaho: Caxton Printers, 1935), p. 263. Garden became a popular pattern in the 1930s, and many versions of it were made and exhibited. Joyce Gross, "Arsinoe Kelsey Bowen 'Garden Quilt,'" *Quilters' Journal,* undated, no. 31, pp. 11–13. "Evolution of a Quilt Design No. III [The Garden]," *Quilters' Journal,* Summer 1978, p. 9.

39. The most informative and best illustrated piece on Rose Kretsinger, her quilts, and her family is Joyce Gross, "Rose Frances Good Kretsinger," *Quilters' Journal,* undated, no. 31, pp. 2–5. Woodard and Greenstein, *Twentieth Century Quilts,* pp. 20, 25; Waldvogel, *Soft Covers,* p. 10; [Bonnie Leman], "Rose Kretsinger—Appliqué Artist," *Quilter's Newsletter Magazine,* December 1977, pp. 24–25, 29; Bonnie Leman, "Two Masters: Kretsinger & Stenge," *Quilter's Newsletter Magazine,* January 1981, pp. 16–17; Barbara Brackman, "Old Patchwork Quilts and the Woman Who Wrote It," *Quilter's Newsletter Magazine,* November–December 1988, pp. 36–38.

40. Benberry, "Storrowton Village—Home of the First National Quilt Show," *Quilter's Newsletter Magazine,* September 1987, pp. 36–41.

41. See "Sears National Quilt Contest, 1933: Promoting the Tradition," in Waldvogel, *Soft Covers,* pp. 38–47; Woodard and Greenstein, *Twentieth Century Quilts,* 23–25; Barbara Brackman, "Patterns from the 1933 Chicago World's Fair," *Quilter's Newsletter Magazine,* July–August 1981, pp. 18–20; Barbara Brackman, "Looking Back at the Great Quilt Contest," *Quilter's Newsletter Magazine,* October 1983, pp. 22–24.

42. Louise O. Townsend, "New York Beauty," *Quilter's Newsletter Magazine,* April 1981, pp. 10–12; Waldvogel, *Soft Covers,* pp. 20–21.

43. Waldvogel, *Soft Covers,* pp. 40, 42.

44. Ida M. Stow to Sears, Roebuck and Company, June 6, 1933, *Quilter's Journal,* July 1985, p. 13, as cited in Waldvogel, *Soft Covers,* p. 40.

45. Waldvogel, *Soft Covers,* p. 32; Brackman, "Looking Back at the Great Quilt Contest," *Quilter's Newsletter Magazine,* October 1983, pp. 23–24; Brackman, "Patterns from the 1933 Chicago World's Fair," *Quilter's Newsletter Magazine,* July–August 1981, p. 19.

46. Waldvogel, *Soft Covers,* p. 20; Mountain Mist batting wrappers, 1930, 1931; *Mountain Mist 1938 Blue Book,* p. 8.

47. Waldvogel, *Soft Covers,* p. 46; Woodard and Greenstein, *Twentieth Century Quilts,* p. 24.

48. Woodard and Greenstein, *Twentieth Century Quilts,* p. 24; Brackman, "Patterns from the 1933 Chicago World's Fair," *Quilter's Newsletter Magazine,* July–August 1981, pp. 19–20.

49. Brackman, *An Encyclopedia of Pieced Quilt Patterns,* cited in Woodard and Greenstein, *Twentieth Century Quilts,* pp. 144–145.

50. *Quilter's Newsletter Magazine,* April 1976, pp. 12, 26, attributes the pattern's origin to Ralph Meyer of East Sparta, Ohio, on the basis of a letter from a friend who is merely relating the World War I veteran's claim.

51. Charles B. Campbell, "Bourbonnais: Or the Early French Settlements in Kankakee County, Ill.," *Transactions of the Illinois State Historical Society* (Springfield: Illinois State Journal Company, 1906), pp. 65–72.

52. Neil Harris, "Shopping—Chicago Style," in John Zukowsky, *Chicago Architecture 1872–1922: Birth of a Metropolis* (Munich: Prestel-Verlag, 1987), pp. 136–155, is an excellent introduction to State Street department stores with an emphasis on Field's. Also see William R. Leach, "Transformations in a Culture of Consumption: Women and Department Stores, 1890–1925," *The Journal of American History,* September 1984, pp. 319–342; for a special emphasis on a history of the Marshall Field store, see Lloyd Wendt and Herman Kogan, *Give the Lady What She Wants!* (Chicago: Rand, McNally and Company, 1952).

53. Early in 1933, during the first few months of President Franklin D.

Roosevelt's New Deal, Congress created the NRA to encourage economic recovery. It was designed to enlist the support of the country's business sector by securing voluntary agreements to establish realistic production limits, maximum hours, and minimum wages. The unenforceable system eventually proved to be unworkable and was declared unconstitutional by the U.S. Supreme Court in 1935. During its brief existence, the NRA created a large number of colorful "We Do Our Part" stamps that were affixed to boxes and letters. When found today, they are a reminder of the dark days of the Great Depression. Several patriotic quilters found the design ideal for quiltmaking. For their products, see Michael M. Meador, "A Cover for the Nation: Ella Martin's Quilt Comes Home," *Quilter's Newsletter Magazine,* July–August 1989, pp. 16–17; Woodard and Greenstein, *Twentieth Century Quilts,* p. 100.

54. [Betty Hagerman], "Sunbonnets," *Quilter's Newsletter Magazine,* April 1979, pp. 6–8, contains a picture of the author's prize-winning quilt, The Meeting of the Sunbonnet Children, which includes a block with *Country Gentleman's* Old Fashioned Sunbonnet Girl.

55. Hagerman, *Sunbonnet Children,* pp. 17–18.

56. Perry, "Marie Webster: Her Story," in Webster, *Quilts* (1990 edition), pp. 210, 222.

57. Hagerman, *Sunbonnet Children,* pp. 12–16.

58. Bonnie Leman, "The Needle's Eye," *Quilter's Newsletter Magazine,* April 1979, p. 2.

59. Woodard and Greenstein, *Twentieth Century Quilts,* p. 21.

60. [Joyce Gross], "Jinny Beyer, Master Quiltmaker," *Quilters' Journal,* Summer 1978, p. 1. Other well-known names include Georgia Bonesteel, Ami Simms, Liz Porter, Marianne Fons, Virginia Spears, Doreen Speckman, Gayle Pritchard, Sue Benner, Cathy Grafton, Ellen Anne Eddy, Caryl Bryner Fallert, Ann Wasserman, Jan Myers-Newberry, Nancy Crow, and Katie Pasquini-Masopant.

61. Jinny Beyer, *Patchwork Patterns* (McLean, Virginia: EPM Publications, 1979), pp. 175, 128; Jinny Beyer, *The Scraplook: Designs, Fabrics, Colors, and Piecing Techniques for Creating Multi-Fabric Quilts* (McLean, Virginia: EPM Publications, 1985), p. 55. For a similar optical illusion by an Illinois quiltmaker, see Interlocking Arrows, 1978, in Rita Barrow Barber, *Somewhere In Between: Quilts and Quilters of Illinois* (Paducah: American Quilter's Society, 1986), p. 36.

62. Sophia Frances Anne Caulfield and Blanche C. Saward, *The Dictionary of Needlework: An Encyclopaedia of Artistic, Plain, and Fancy Needlework* (London: L. Upcott Gill, 1882), p. 384.

63. Hall and Kretsinger, *The Romance of the Patchwork Quilt,* p. 30.

Chapter 7: A Culture at Risk

1. John Steinbeck, *The Grapes of Wrath* (New York: The Viking Press, 1939), p. 91.

2. Anyone who enjoys Double Wedding Ring quilts will find special pleasure in Bob Bishop's well-written works and the beautiful full-color pictures: Robert Bishop, "Double Wedding Ring Quilts," *The Magazine Antiques,* March 1989, pp. 732–741; Robert Bishop and Carter Houck, *The Romance of Double Wedding Ring Quilts* (New York: E. P. Dutton, 1989); Robert Bishop, "The Double Wedding Ring Quilt," *Quilter's Newsletter Magazine,* April 1989, pp. 35–37. "The Double Wedding Ring Mystery," *Quilter's Newsletter Magazine,* June 1978, p. 9.

3. *Quilter's Newsletter Magazine,* October 1979, pp. 16–17, presents eighteen different sets.

4. Suellen Jackson-Meyer, "Log Cabin," *Quilter's Newsletter Magazine,* October 1979, pp. 12–19; "Log Cabin II," *Quilter's Newsletter Magazine,* November–December 1979, pp. 12–13; Marie Shirer, "Log Cabin: An Update," *Quilter's Newsletter Magazine,* April 1988, pp. 32–35; Carol Anne Wien, *The Great American Log Cabin Quilt Book* (New York: E. P. Dutton, Inc., 1984).

5. Unfortunately, myths have been perpetuated in print and often have been accepted as truth. As accurately pointed out by Barbara Brackman, "Seven Myths about Old Quilts," *Quilter's Newsletter Magazine,* April 1988, pp. 40–42, 57, beginners need to be cautious when using older works. It is best to begin with current literature and work backward when seeking accurate information in the field of quilt history.

6. Bonnie Leman, "Baskets," *Quilter's Newsletter Magazine,* September 1979, pp. 10–11, illustrates thirty different basket blocks.

7. "Ocean Wave," *Quilter's Newsletter Magazine,* May 1980, p. 15.

8. For the role of women on the World War II homefront, see A. A. Hoehling, *Home Front, U.S.A.: The Story of World War II Over Here* (New York: Thomas Y. Crowell Company, 1966); Ronald H. Bailey, *The Home*

Front: U.S.A. (Alexandria, Virginia: Time-Life Books, 1978); Richard Polenberg, ed., *America at War: The Home Front, 1941–1945* (Englewood Cliffs, New Jersey: Prentice-Hall, 1968).

9. Barbara Brackman, "Leaves and Foliage: Nineteenth-Century Album Patterns," *Quilter's Newsletter Magazine,* October 1989, pp. 36–39.

10. Barbara Brackman, "Buds and Blossoms, Nineteenth-Century Album Patterns," *Quilter's Newsletter Magazine,* June 1989, p. 24.

11. Amelia Peck, *American Quilts and Coverlets in The Metropolitan Museum of Art* (New York: Dutton Studio Books, 1990), p. 125; Katy Christopherson, *The Political and Campaign Quilt* (No place: Kentucky Heritage Quilt Society, 1984), pp. 28–29.

12. Marian and her sister, Ruth Neitzel of Indiana, were featured in "The Meetin' Place," *Quilter's Newsletter Magazine,* November–December 1987, pp. 48–49.

13. For more information about Baltimore Album quilts, see: Peck, *American Quilts and Coverlets,* pp. 50–61; Elly Sienkiewicz, "Baltimore Brides Speak Without Words," *Quilter's Newsletter Magazine,* March 1984,
pp. 36–37; Elly Sienkiewicz, "The Numsen Family Quilt: Fancy Flowers from Baltimore," *Quilter's Newsletter Magazine,* January 1990, pp. 12–15; Dixie Haywood, "The Making of a Masterpiece Bride's Quilt," *Quilter's Newsletter Magazine,* June 1983, pp. 40–42; Dena S. Katzenberg, *Baltimore Album Quilts* (Baltimore: Baltimore Museum of Art, 1981); Jeana Kimball, *Reflections of Baltimore* (Bothell, Washington: That Patchwork Place, 1989).

14. Cuesta Benberry, "The Superb Mrs. Stenge," *Nimble Needle Treasures,* Summer 1971, p. 4; "The Woman Who Made 'The Bible' Quilt," a reprint from the *Chicago Tribune,* April 5, 1971, *Nimble Needle Treasures,* Summer 1971, p. 6; Bonnie Leman, "Two Masters: Kretsinger & Stenge," *Quilter's Newsletter Magazine,* January 1981, pp. 16–17; "Bertha Stenge Quilts Found," *Quilters' Journal,* no. 26, undated, p. 15.

15. Gladys J. Peterson, *Pieces: The Story of Elgin in a Quilt* (Chelsea, Michigan: BookCrafters, 1989), p. 11.

16. Thomas Stearns Eliot, "Little Gidding," in *Four Quartets* (New York: Harcourt, Brace & World, Inc., 1943), p. 39.

GLOSSARY

Album quilt: Quilts assembled from various blocks signed by their makers have served as textile autograph albums since the 1840s. True album quilts are signed by more than one maker. For more information about the two types of album quilts, see *Friendship quilt* and *Sampler album quilt* and the subtype, *Baltimore album quilt.*

Alternate set: A design created by placing decorative blocks next to plain fabric blocks. This set can be either straight or on point.

Amish quilt: In the late nineteenth century, a distinctive religious subculture created a unique quilt type. Although this immigrant German sect used patterns available to other quilters, their products stand out because they chose plain (often woolen) fabrics, emphasized black and a limited palette of other colors, and often used black quilting thread. See Plates 25 and 35.

Aniline dye: The first synthetic coloring agent used in textile manufacturing. The development of this coal-tar-based product was the accidental discovery of a British chemist in 1856. Aniline dye was soon used commercially.

Appliqué: A term derived from the French *appliquér,* "to put on." Laid-on pieces of cloth are attached to a background fabric by sewing—using a blind stitch, buttonhole stitch, or other stitches by hand or machine—or by other means. Barbara Brackman, in *Clues in the Calico,* terms this "conventional appliqué" to differentiate it from the other two types. Also see *Cut-out chintz* and *Reverse appliqué.*

Backing: The piece that forms the underside of a quilt.

Back stitch: A sewing stitch sometimes used for stuffed and corded work that creates a line which appears to be continuous. It can also be used to create scrolling lines in embroidery.

Baltimore album quilt: Sampler album quilts reached the highest state of development in and around Baltimore, Maryland, during the 1840s and 1850s. Plate 144 illustrates a contemporary interpretation of a Baltimore sampler album quilt. See *Album quilt* and *Sampler album quilt.*

Bar set: See *Strip set.*

Batting: A vernacular term generally used to describe the middle layer of a three-part quilt. Technically, however, it is only one type of filler. Batting is made of loose non-woven cotton, wool, or synthetic fibers. Prior to the development of polyester batting circa 1960, cotton was the leading quilt filler of the nineteenth century. A well-known firm, Stearns and Foster of Cincinnati, Ohio, introduced commercial cotton batting in 1846. Poorly ginned cotton used during the nineteenth century often contained small pieces of broken seeds, bolls, or stalks. These small lumps of plant debris lead some to believe they are cotton seeds, and the quilt is incorrectly believed to have been made prior to the development of the cotton gin in 1791. Such material was found in a whitework quilt, Plate 82, that was made circa 1860. See *Fillers.*

Binding: A strip of bias- or straight-cut fabric that may add a decorative element as well as cover the raw outer edges of a completed quilt.

Blanket stitch: A decorative interlocking stitch originally used to bind the edges of woolen blankets. On appliqué quilts this stitch is sometimes used to attach the appliqué pieces to a background fabric. The position of the blanket stitch is reversed on the appliqué pieces in Plate 4. The light-colored thread used for nineteenth-century appliqué was often replaced by black thread for the visual impact desired by quiltmakers in the 1920s and 1930s.

Blind stitch: A frequently used appliqué stitch that is hidden in the folded edge of the appliqué piece. No exposed stitches are visible.

Block: A complete single decorative unit that can be joined together with other similar blocks to create a quilt top. Quilt blocks are generally square and can be made in any usable size, but in most quilts the blocks will have uniform dimensions. A block can be pieced, appliquéd, or embroidered, or be a unit of plain or patterned fabric.

Border: The solid, pieced, or appliquéd fabric comprising an outer framework for the central patterned area of a quilt top and to which the binding is stitched; one or more framework(s) surrounding a center medallion of a quilt top.

Broderie Perse: A late-nineteenth-century term meaning Persian embroidery. Since the words *Broderie Perse* were not known or used when these late-eighteenth- and early-nineteenth-century quilts were made, it is inappropriate to apply it to what is more properly termed cut-out chintz appliqué quilts, or chintz-work. See *Cut-out chintz.*

Buttonhole stitch: A more closely spaced variant form of the blanket stitch in which the stems of the stitches touch the adjacent stitches. Plates 2 and 28 illustrate appliqué attached with buttonhole stitching. See *Blanket stitch.*

Calico: An inexpensive medium-weight roller-printed cotton fabric usually identified by its small print. English-made calico was eventually replaced by an American-made product that became a commonly used quiltmaking textile during the nineteenth century. Calico can be plain or printed. It was originally defined by the weave rather than by the type of pattern. Calico often has a colorful, small-scale abstract design. The name was taken from Calicut, India, its original port of origin.

Calimanco: A glazed, satin-weave worsted wool generally used as a clothing textile in the eighteenth century. It was occasionally used for making solid-colored blue, green, or red wholecloth quilts on which quilting stitches created a design of flowers and feathers. These are sometimes erroneously referred to as linsey-woolsey quilts.

Center medallion: See *Medallion set.*

Charm quilt: A single-piece one-patch scrapbag quilt that challenges the maker to cut each piece from a different fabric. The unit may be a square, triangle, hexagon, diamond, or clamshell. There is no unifying design or pattern. See Plate 87.

Cheater cloth: See *Printed patchwork.*

Chintz: A cotton fabric originally imported from India in the seventeenth century. This sometimes-glazed printed "spotted cloth" textile was known as *chita* in India and eventually called chintz in the West. It is generally a large-scale print suitable for upholstery and draperies. In the eighteenth and early-nineteenth centuries, this colorful textile was used for wholecloth quilts, and the attractive individual motifs were cut out and used as appliqués. See *Cut-out chintz* and *Palampore.*

Comforter: A three-layer bedcovering made like a quilt but tied together at spaced intervals by individual pieces of yarn or thread rather than by quilting stitches. Since a comforter is not pieced by a series of small, closely spaced stitches, it is often filled with a heavier, thicker batt. A comforter may appear to be a quilt because the top may be wholecloth, pieced, or appliqué, but it is not a true quilt as there are no quilting stitches. Sometimes a worn nineteenth-century quilt can be found as the filler inside an early twentieth-century comforter. Also known as a comfort or a comfortable in the United States, as a hap in England and parts of Pennsylvania, and as a wagga in Australia. Plate 29 illustrates a comforter tied by an English immigrant. See *Tying.*

Commemorative calico: Many printed calicoes can be dated to the 1876 centennial era and other periods because of the figures, emblems, and words used in the design. See Plate 139.

Corded work: An eighteenth-century technique that was occasionally used by skilled nineteenth-century quiltmakers. The work was usually done on a wholecloth, white cotton top, or on the plain blocks in an alternate set. The needleworker created a motif in which two parallel lines joined two or three layers of fabric together. A piece of cord would then be threaded into the channel from the reverse side to create a raised three-dimensional design on the front. Corded work, which related to Marseilles quilting, was often combined with stuffed work and flat quilting. Plate 129 shows the uncut ends of cords remaining on the back of a quilt.

Cotton/polyester fabric: A modern, partially synthetic fiber textile, may be found in quilts made since the 1960s. More than half of the fiber in this fabric would be cotton, whereas a polyester/cotton blend would be dominated by the synthetic fiber.

Counterpane: An older term used to describe any bedcovering, not necessarily a quilt.

Coverlet: A single- or double-weave bedcovering produced on a loom.

Crazy quilt: A quilt-top design created by overlapping many irregularly shaped scraps. The style became fashionable during the last quarter of the nineteenth century. Fancy fabrics such as satin and brocaded silks and cottons often dominate. The randomly shaped pieces are often joined by elaborate and colorful embroidery stitches, and individual pieces may be decorated with embroidered designs. The pieces are normally stitched onto a background fabric, and the completed top is tacked rather than quilted to the backing. Usually there is no filler. Plates 43, 89, 90, 91, and 92 show a wide range of crazy quilt types.

Cut-out chintz: The most commonly used appliqué technique of the late-eighteenth and early-nineteenth centuries. Quiltmakers cut the large-scale printed motifs from chintz fabrics and appliquéd them to a plain background fabric to create a more open and symmetrically organized design. Most cut-out chintz quilts made before 1840 used the framed medallion set, and the few made after that date are often found in a block set.

Cylinder printing: See *Roller printing.*

Echo quilting: A quilting pattern that follows the outline of an appliqué design and continuously repeats this line with concentric rows of quilting stitches.

Embroidery: In the seventeenth and eighteenth centuries, silk and wool embroidery thread was used to create the primary design motifs on many bedcoverings. The increased use of cut-out chintz appliqué and piece-work relegated embroidery to a supporting role throughout most of the nineteenth century. The use of fancy embroidery stitches on crazy quilts after 1880 renewed an interest in embroidery as a secondary decoration. The introduction of inexpensive colorfast cotton embroidery floss by the turn of the twentieth century greatly expanded its use and contributed to a rise in the number of embroidered quilts. See Plates 36 and 53. In addition to outline and back stitches, the lazy daisy and French knot became twentieth century favorites. See Plate 134.

Embroidered seams: See *Crazy quilt.*

English piecing: A pieced quilt construction technique in which fabric is basted over a paper foundation—often cut in the shape of a hexagon—to temporarily strengthen the fabric and help it retain the desired shape as it is joined with whip stitches to the adjoining pieces. Although the papers were supposed to be removed, many were not. If the top was not backed, it is possible to examine the newspapers, letters, and copybooks that were cut for use as templates. Hexagon and box quilts continued to be made in the twentieth century, but the use of paper templates fell from favor. Plate 86 shows a quilt top backed by paper templates that are still in place.

Fan quilting: A concentric-arc quilting motif frequently used on late-nineteenth- and early-twentieth-century pieced quilts. The motif was so commonly used by church quilting groups that some communities named it after the local congregation that used it extensively. Thus it is not unusual to encounter references to "Methodist Fan" or "Baptist Fan" quilting patterns.

Filler: The middle layer placed between the top and the back of a three-part quilt. Frequently used fillers are cotton, wool, or polyester batting, but flannel blankets, sheets, and well-worn older bedcoverings are also found inside some quilts. See *Batting.*

Flat quilting: A decorative technique used by skilled nineteenth-century quiltmakers to create a dramatic puckered effect on wholecloth quilts and plain-cloth blocks within a quilt. Many bedcovers with extensive flat quilting have only two layers; omitting the batting makes it easier to achieve more stitches per inch when repeatedly penetrating only the top and back layers. Flat quilting is often used with stuffed and corded work. See *Stipple quilting.*

Foundation: The technique of covering a background cloth with overlapping pieces of fabric was originally termed pressed patchwork when the foundation method became popular in the last quarter of the nineteenth century. After basting the first patch to the foundation, the quiltmaker placed a second piece upon the first with the top sides facing each other and then used a running stitch to attach one side of the second piece to the first. The second piece was then turned over and the seam pressed flat. If a back was added and the quilt tied and bound, it is difficult to determine if the center layer is a foundation fabric or a piece of cloth used as a filler. Most late-nineteenth-century Log Cabin, Pineapple, and Crazy quilts were constructed upon a foundation fabric. The Log Cabin quilt in Plate 130 is stitched to a foundation fabric.

Friendship quilt: Friendship album quilts originated along the East Coast around 1840. All the blocks are usually of a single pattern. Most friendship blocks have a white central square that is often signed and sometimes dated. Friendship quilts usually honored a close friend on a special occasion such as a wedding or when a person left a community. Perhaps the 1834 development of an indelible ink suitable for marking textiles was an important factor leading to the first wave of album quiltmaking. See Plates 16, 17, and 19.

Fundraising quilt: There are several ways that a quilt could be used to make money. Some organizations sold the right to place names on a quilt top as the bedcovering was being made. Successful fundraising quilts have several hundred names embroidered or inked upon their surface. When the quilt was completed, an auction or raffle would generate additional money for the designated cause. A few fundraising quilts, such as the Harvard, Illinois, Women's Christian Temperance Union Wheel Spoke quilt, Plate 47, contain additional information about the sponsoring group. Use of the fundraising quilt was popular in the late nineteenth century. All fundraising quilts will not, however, contain names. Any quilt, such as the G.A.R. Feathered Star, Plate 41, may have once been auctioned or raffled, but family tradition, rather than documentation on the quilt itself, must preserve its identification as a fundraising quilt.

Fugitive color: Colors that are subject to fading because of the type of pigment and/or mordant used in the dye, exposure to light, and/or a reaction to the chemical substances in the air.

Gingham: A cotton fabric, originally imported from India, woven with threads of two or more colors that usually create a check or a stripe. Gingham was made in America by the middle of the nineteenth century. Woven gingham is imitated by printing the pattern.

Glaze: The shiny surface on calimanco woolens was a finish produced by pressing the fabric between heated rollers. Cottons could be glazed by using wax, resins, or egg whites. Laundering may remove the finish.

Hanging diamond quilting: A diamond motif used as background fill that is created by evenly spaced criss-crossed diagonal quilting lines. See Plate 54.

Homespun: A hand-loomed fabric usually woven of either wool or linen, or a fabric created by interweaving a wool weft with linen warp threads. Eventually cotton replaced linen for warp. Factory-spun thread was available in the mid-nineteenth century for hand-weaving. Plates 12 and 18 illustrate two different ways in which homespun wool was used in quiltmaking. See *Linsey-woolsey.*

Indigo dye: A natural blue dye produced from the tropical indigo plant. Indigo was an important agricultural staple of South Carolina during the Colonial and Federal periods when it was the only commercially viable American dye crop. It is chemically manufactured today. See Plate 2.

Inlaid work: See *Reverse appliqué.*

Inscriptions: Names, dates, places, dedications, and so forth that may be penned or embroidered onto or quilted into the top or back layer of a quilt. Plate 15 shows a maker's signature.

In-the-ditch quilting: Quilting stitches that are placed directly into a seam line rather than paralleling the seam.

Linsey: A shortened form of linsey-woolsey.

Linsey-woolsey: A hand-loomed textile of the eighteenth and early nineteenth centuries that was often used for wholecloth or pieced quilts. It is made with a linen or cotton warp and a wool weft. It is not unusual for a coarsely woven all-linen or all-wool quilt top to be incorrectly termed a linsey-woolsey wholecloth quilt. These bedcoverings should not be confused with the more finely woven calimanco wholecloth quilts.

Madder: A natural dye originally obtained from the madder plant's roots. It is colorfast and can produce a wide range of colors, including reds, rusts, oranges, and browns, depending upon the mordant. Today the active ingredient, alizarin, is chemically manufactured.

Marseilles quilt: In the eighteenth century, Marseilles, France, was a port famous for exporting a handmade, two-layer quilt filled with closely stitched, stuffed, and corded work. By the late eighteenth century, American merchants were importing machine-made Marseilles-type bedcovers from both France and England. The introduction of the Jacquard loom in the United States after 1830 increased the use of manufactured bedcoverings, and the production of handmade whole-cloth whitework quilts declined drastically. The popularity of machine-made bedcovering increased after the Civil War. By the turn of the twentieth century, the stuffed appearance of the earlier period gave way to a flatter woven look.

Medallion set: A quilt top with a large central block that often has a dominant graphic motif. The medallion is usually surrounded by a series of pieced, appliquéd, or plain fabric borders that create concentric rings. The borders can be of varying widths, which frequently increase in size toward the outer edges.

Motif: An easily recognized dominant feature, such as a floral design.

Mordant: A metallic oxide or mineral used to produce a colorfast textile dye.

Muslin: A seventeenth-century cotton fabric imported to England from India that was made in England by the late eighteenth century. Today the term implies a medium-quality cotton fabric available in an unbleached natural or bleached white color.

Natural dye: A colorant derived from plant, animal, or mineral sources.

Nylon: A synthetic fiber made from dicarboxylic acid that was introduced shortly before World War II.

One-piece quilt: See Wholecloth quilt.

On point set: Square blocks seamed together in a diagonal pattern with one corner pointing down and the opposite corner pointing up; thus a square block appears to be diamond shaped. See Plate 94.

Outline embroidery: A technique for stitching around the shape of a figure or a design rather than filling in the entire motif with another embroidery stitch.

Outline stitch: An embroidery stitch created when each successive stitch partially overlaps the preceeding one. The technique thus creates the illusion of a continuous unbroken line. Also called a stem stitch. At the turn of the twentieth century, it was popular to decorate white cotton quilt blocks with simple graphic elements outlined in Turkey red floss. See Plates 36 and 53.

Palampore: A colorful eighteenth-century wholecloth chintz panel decorated with mordant-painted and resist-dyed floral and/or bird motifs. Palampores were made in India and imported into the West.

Patchwork: In the eighteenth and nineteenth centuries this term was apparently used for what is now known as appliqué, as well as for piecing. Today it is frequently used as a synonym for piece-work.

Percale: A fine-quality cotton cloth originally imported from India but produced in England by the late seventeenth century. By the turn of the twentieth century, shirting fabrics, which frequently appear in pieced quilts, were made of percale.

Pieced work: A quilt construction technique by which small pieces of selected fabrics are stitched together. Pieced work may create blocks that can be seamed together (with-or without sashing) to produce a quilt top; or a top may be composed of larger pieces of fabric as in many Amish-type pieced quilts; or piecing may be the joining of small irregularly shaped pieces, as in a string quilt.

Piping: The insertion of a fabric-covered cord in the binding seam on the top side of the quilt. Generally, when piping is found, it is on quilts made before the Civil War. The green and red appliqué quadrant quilt in Plate 13 has green piping inside a red binding.

Plaid: A pattern created by intersecting stripes in the warp and the weft. A printed pattern on fabric can achieve the same effect.

Poly/cotton fabric: See Cotton/polyester fabric.

Prairie points: Small fabric squares folded into triangular shapes and stitched to the outer edges of a quilt, creating a serrated perimeter for the bedcovering.

Printed patchwork: A printed textile imitating a pieced quilt, also referred to as geometric chintz, faux patchwork, or cheater cloth. Printed patchwork was introduced in the 1830s or 1840s and is still available today. Printed patchwork was used on the back of quilts in Plates 37 and 75.

Quadrant set: A variation of the block set that features four large blocks, or four whole blocks plus two half blocks that will create a rectangular rather than a square quilt. In quadrant-set quilts the blocks are usually appliquéd, and most surviving examples registered by the Project date from the third quarter of the nineteenth century. Quadrant blocks can be seen on quilts in Plates 13, 24, and 44.

Quilt: Utilitarian and/or decorative bedcovering made of three layers—a top, the filler, and backing—or two layers consisting of a top and a back

without a filler, that is stitched together.

Quilting: The act of fastening together two or three layers of materials, usually with a running, back, or machine stitch.

Quilting stitch: A series of closely spaced running stitches, perhaps six to eight per inch, accomplished by skillfully puckering a number of tiny stitches onto the needle before drawing the thread through the quilt.

Rayon: The first manmade fiber, originally known as artificial silk, became available in 1890. A second form, acetate rayon, was introduced in 1919. Fabrics made from these fibers occasionally appear as pieces within a quilt.

Resist printing: One method of creating a textile design prior to the development of roller printing. Resists were often made in blue and white by using printing blocks to impress a dye-resisting agent, such as wax, into a fabric, dyeing the cloth, and then removing the resisting agent from the fabric. This process created white areas that resisted the dye and untreated portions that absorbed the blue dye.

Reverse appliqué: A rarely seen variation of appliqué quilting that was used as a technical highlight within the designs of some eighteenth- and early-nineteenth-century quilts and which has gained popularity with a few late twentieth-century quilters. The technique involves cutting a design into a fabric, placing a textile under the opening, turning under the raw edges to prevent raveling, and blind stitching the two layers together. The completed element, which is similar to a hollow-cut silhouette, thus exposes the background fabric. The eyes of the birds on the quilt in Plate 138 are created by reverse appliqué. In this way the laid-on fabric has been cut to reveal the quilt top under it, creating a colored eye for the bird.

Reversible quilt: Ordinarily one speaks of the top and the back of a quilt, implying that the decorative top is more likely to be visible upon a bed than the plain back. Reversible quilts do not have a designated "top" and a "back," but, like a coin, they have an obverse and a reverse because there are decorative features on both sides of the quilt. Plate 25 shows the use of lengthwise strips on the back of an Amish quilt, and Plate 84 illustrates a wholecloth quilt with a mosaic pattern on the opposite side.

Roller printing: Copper cylinders that contain an engraved pattern are inked and passed over a fabric to create a continuous design. By the late eighteenth century in Scotland, a single roller could print one color. By 1835 multicolored fabrics could be printed by presses with multiple rollers. Each roller printed a separate color. The process greatly accelerated the production of the colorful printed cloth found in nineteenth- and twentieth-century quilts.

Running stitch: A simple stitch created by continuously moving the needle forward through two pieces of fabric. Since there is no backstitching, the thread creates a broken line as it moves from one side of the fabric to the other.

Sacking: For several decades in the twentieth century, quilters bleached the designs from utilitarian commodity and animal feed sacks to recycle the cotton fabric. Plates 51 and 69 show two quilts that clearly indicate the use of sacks in the top and the back.

Sampler album quilt: A type of album quilt in which each block is different. Completed blocks were often signed by each individual creator before they were given to the quiltmaker. Also see *Album quilt, Baltimore album quilt,* and *Friendship quilt.*

Sampler quilt: A quilt top, with each block a different pattern, may be a quiltmaker's catalog to refer to for future pattern selection. Depending upon the period in which the blocks were made, they may be all appliqué, all pieced, or a combination. They usually are not signed because they are the work of one person, and it was not intended to be a friendship quilt. In some quilts the blocks are not all the same size.

Sashing: A strip of fabric separating and framing each square in a block quilt. Sashing can be plain or printed fabric, pieced, or appliquéd.

Sateen: A weave pattern based upon an irregular twill weave in which the weft threads are more visually prominent than the warp threads. Often woven with cotton fibers, polished sateen wholecloth quilts, such as the Wilkinson-type quilt in Plate 100, were popular in the 1920s.

Satin: A weave pattern that creates a shiny-surface fabric. It is produced by using fine weft threads that are covered on the face by slightly heavier warp threads. Although satin is often made of silk, the weave can also be used with cotton and synthetic fibers.

Seminole piecing: Strips of fabric that are seamed together, cut across the seams to create new strips of pieced fabrics, and set together to form a design element. See Plate 54.

Set: The arrangement of the blocks in a quilt top.

Signature quilt: See *Inscriptions.*

Stipple quilting: An all-over filling pattern of closely spaced, randomly meandering quilting stitches used to create a puckered background. A popular nineteenth-century quilting technique.

Stitches per inch: The average number of stitches visible on the top side of the quilt in an inch measurement. Readings are taken in at least three separate places; if the number is not consistent, the counts are averaged.

Straight set: Decorated quilt blocks seamed together side by side in straight rows.

String piecing: The creation of a pieced scrapbag quilt by randomly joining narrow strips of fabric into a unit. A rarely seen variation of a string quilt has thin strips of selvage attached to a foundation. A design is traced upon a background fabric, and appropriately colored cloth strips are stitched in puckered rows to create a visual image. An example is shown in Plate 56.

Strip set: Wholecloth, appliquéd, or pieced fabric strips that are set together in lengthwise bars. This decorative element, which is found on some Amish quilts, can be used for either the front or back side. See Plate 25.

Stuffed work: Stuffing creates a three-dimensional effect on the quilt surface. The extra padding may be placed inside the selected area as the appliqué work or quilting is being completed. It is, however, often added after the quilting is completed by using a stiletto to create a small opening between the warp and weft threads on the back of the quilt, pushing extra padding into the selected quilting motif, and then closing the opening by easing the threads back into alignment. The holes remain on the back of the quilt in Plate 10.

Tacking: See *Tying.*

Template piecing: A nineteenth-century quilt construction method in which fabric shapes are cut slightly larger than similarly shaped paper templates. The textile is placed on the paper, the excess fabric is folded over the edge of the template, and the two pieces are basted into place. The completed template pieces are usually joined together by whip stitches. A quilt made with paper templates is shown in Plate 86. See *English piecing.*

Top: The upper exterior quilt layer, which is usually the most decorative part of the completed bedcovering.

Tow cloth: A coarsely woven linen fabric sometimes used as backing on early-nineteenth-century quilts. See *Homespun.*

Trapunto: Also called Italian quilting. The word was not in use in the United States until the twentieth century. Thus this non-period term should not be used to describe quilting techniques that were referred to as stuffed work and corded work when these techniques were used to decorate nineteenth-century American quilts. See *Stuffed work* and *Corded work.*

Triple line quilting: A nineteenth-century technique in which the quilter outlines seams with three rows of quilting stitches. See Plate 80.

Turkey red: A colorfast dye process originating in the Near East that was introduced into Europe by 1750. The color remained popular after the advent of synthetic dyes, and Turkey red is commonly found in quilts from the mid-nineteenth century to the World War I era. Outline embroidery quilts worked with Turkey red cotton floss were popular at the turn of the twentieth century. Quilts using Turkey red outline embroidery can be seen in Plates 36 and 53.

Tying: Tying and tacking refer to the method of making a comforter when the layers are not held together with quilting stitches. The three layers of a comforter are secured by pulling a short piece of yarn, cord, or heavy thread through the back to the top and knotting each individual tie. The ties are often spaced about six inches apart in a grid pattern.

Warp: The lengthwise threads or yarn on a loom.

Weft: The crosswise threads or yarn that pass over and under the warp threads on a loom.

White work: An all-white, often a wholecloth quilt, that may include cording, stuffing, candlewicking, and/or embroidery in addition to quilting. A typical whitework wholecloth quilt is shown in Plate 82. See *Marseilles quilt.*

Wholecloth: A quilt top of one piece of cloth or several identical panels of plain cloth seamed together and quilted. A wholecloth quilt may be white, any solid color, or a printed fabric. An all-over quilting motif usually creates the only surface pattern, although some examples also contain cording and/or stuffing. Many early-nineteenth-century wholecloth quilts were made of finely woven wool. Two rather different interpretations of wholecloth quilts can be seen in Plates 18 and 82. See *Calimanco, Linsey-woolsey, Marseilles quilt,* and *Whitework.*

Worsted: A long-staple combed wool, tightly spun yarn.

BIBLIOGRAPHY

QUILT AND TEXTILE HISTORY

Books, Booklets, and Pamphlets

Affleck, Diane L. Fagan. *Just New from the Mills: Printed Cottons in America, Late Nineteenth and Early Twentieth Centuries.* North Andover, Massachusetts: Museum of American Textile History, 1987.

Anderson, Suzy McLennan. *Collector's Guide to Quilts.* Radnor, Pennsylvania: Wallace–Homestead Book Company, 1991.

Art Needlework Creations. Elgin, Illinois: Virginia Snow Studio, 1932.

Aunt Jane's Winning Quilt Designs. Springfield, Ohio: Central Publishing Company, 1914.

Bacon, Lenice Ingram. *American Patchwork Quilts,* 1978. Reprint. New York: Bonanza Books, 1980.

Baltimore Museum of Art. *The Great American Cover-up: Counterpanes of the Eighteenth and Nineteenth Centuries.* Introduction by Dena S. Katzenberg. No place: Art Litho Company, 1971.

Barber, Rita Barrow. *Somewhere in Between: Quilts and Quilters of Illinois.* Paducah: The American Quilter's Society, 1986.

Beecher, Catherine E. *A Treatise on Domestic Economy, For the Use of Young Ladies at Home and School.* New York: 1848.

Beyer, Jinny. *Patchwork Patterns.* McLean, Virginia: EPM Publications, 1979.

———. *The Scraplook: Designs, Fabrics, Colors, and Piecing Techniques for Creating Multi-Fabric Quilts.* McLean, Virginia: EPM Publications, 1985.

Binney, Edwin, 3rd, and Gail Binney-Winslow. *Homage to Amanda.* San Francisco: R K Press, 1984.

Bishop, Robert, and Carter Houck. *All Flags Flying: American Patriotic Quilts As Expressions of Liberty.* New York: E. P. Dutton, 1986.

———. *The Romance of Double Wedding Ring Quilts.* New York: E. P. Dutton, 1989.

Bishop, Robert and Elizabeth Safanda. *A Gallery of Amish Quilts: Design Diversity from a Plain People.* New York: E. P. Dutton, 1976.

Bonesteel, Georgia. *Lap Quilting with Georgia Bonesteel.* Birmingham: Oxmoor House, 1982.

Bowman, Doris M. *The Smithsonian Treasury: American Quilts.* Washington, D.C.: Smithsonian Institution Press, 1991.

Brackman, Barbara. *Clues in the Calico: A Guide to Identifying and Dating Antique Quilts.* McLean, Virginia: EPM Publications, 1989.

———. *Dating Antique Quilts: 200 Years of Style, Pattern and Technique.* San Francisco: American Quilt Study Group, 1990.

———. *An Encyclopedia of Pieced Quilt Patterns.* 8 vols. Lawrence, Kansas: Prairie Flower Publishing, 1979–86.

Bullard, Lacy Folmar, and Betty Jo Shiell. *Chintz Quilts: Unfading Glory.* Tallahassee, Florida: Serendipity Publishers, 1983.

Caulfield, Sophia Frances Ann, and Blanche C. Saward. *The Dictionary of Needlework: An Encyclopaedia of Artistic, Plain, and Fancy Needlework.* London: L. Upcott Gill, 1882.

Center for the History of American Needlework. *Anne Orr's Charted Designs.* New York: Dover Publications, 1978.

Child, Maria. *The American Frugal Housewife.* 12th ed. Boston: Carter, Hendee, and Company, 1832.

Christopherson, Katy. *The Political and Campaign Quilt.* No Place: Kentucky Heritage Quilt Society, 1984.

Clark, Ricky, ed. *Quilts in Community: Ohio Traditions.* Nashville, Tennessee: Rutledge Hill Press, 1991.

Clarke, Mary Washington. *Kentucky Quilts and Their Makers.* Lexington: University of Kentucky Press, 1976.

Colby, Averil. *Patchwork Quilts.* New York: Charles Scribner's Sons, 1965.

———. *Quilting.* New York: Charles Scribner's Sons, 1971.

Cooper, Patricia, and Norma Bradley Buferd. *The Quilters: Women and Domestic Art, An Oral History.* Garden City, New York: Anchor Press/Doubleday, 1977.

Davidson, Mildred. *American Quilts from the Art Institute of Chicago.* Chicago: The Art Institute of Chicago, 1966.

Dewhurst, C. Kurt, Betty MacDowell, and Marsha MacDowell. *Artists in Aprons: Folk Art by American Women.* New York: E. P. Dutton, 1979.

Dubois, Jean. *Anne Orr Patchwork.* Durango, Colorado: La Plata Press, 1977.

Duke, Dennis, and Deborah Harding, eds. *America's Glorious Quilts.* New York: Macmillan Publishing Company, 1987.

Edwards, Phoebe. *Anyone Can Quilt.* New York: The Benjamin Company, 1975.

Ferrero, Pat. *Hearts and Hands: The Influence of Women and Quilts on American Society.* San Francisco: The Quilt Digest Press, 1987.

Finley, Ruth E. *Old Patchwork Quilts and the Women Who Made Them,* 1929. Reprint. No Place: Charles T. Branford Company, 1980.

Fox, Sandi. *Wrapped in Glory: Figurative Quilts and Bed Covers, 1700–1900.* New York: Thames and Hudson, 1990.

Goldman, Marilyn, and Marguerite Wiebusch. *Quilts of Indiana: Crossroads of Memories.* Bloomington: Indiana University Press, 1991.

Grandmother Clark's Crocheted Rag Rugs. St. Louis: W. L. Clark, Inc., 1933.

Graeff, Marie Knorr. *Pennsylvania German Quilts.* Plymouth Meeting, Pennsylvania: Mrs. C. Naaman Keyser, 1946.

Granick, Eve Wheatcroft. *The Amish Quilt.* Intercourse, Pennsylvania: Good Books, 1989.

Gutcheon, Beth. *The Perfect Patchwork Primer,* 1973. Reprint. New York: Penquin Books, 1978.

Gutcheon, Jeffrey. *Diamond Patchwork.* New York: E. P. Dutton, 1982.

Haders, Phyllis. *Sunshine and Shadow: The Amish and Their Quilts.* New York: Main Street Press, 1976.

———. *The Warner Collector's Guide to American Quilts.* New York: Main Street Press, 1981.

Hagerman, Betty J. *A Meeting of the Sunbonnet Children.* Baldwin City, Kansas: Telegraphics, 1979.

Hall, Carrie A., and Rose G. Kretsinger, *The Romance of the Patchwork Quilt in America.* New York: Bonanza Books, 1935.

Hechtlinger, Adelaide. *American Quilts, Quilting, and Patchwork: The Complete Book of History, Technique and Design.* New York: Galahad Books, 1974.

Hinson, Delores A. *Quilting Manual.* 1966. Reprint. New York: Dover Publications, Inc., 1970.

Hoffman, Victoria. *Quilts: A Window to the Past.* North Andover, Massachusetts: Museum of American Textile History, 1991.

Holstein, Jonathan. *Abstract Design in American Quilts: A Biography of an Exhibition.* Louisville: The Kentucky Quilt Project, 1991.

———. *Kentucky Quilts, 1800–1900: The Kentucky Quilt Project.* 1982. Reprint. Louisville: The Kentucky Quilt Project, 1992.

———. *The Pieced Quilt: An American Design Tradition.* 1973. Reprint. New York: Little, Brown and Company, 1982.

Horton, Laurel. *The Oral Interview in Quilt Research.* San Francisco: American Quilt Study Group, 1988.

Ickis, Marguerite. *The Standard Book of Quiltmaking and Collecting.* New York: Dover, 1960.

Imami–Paydar, Niloo. *Marie Webster Quilts: A Retrospective.* [Exhibit Gallery Guide]. Indianapolis Museum of Art, 1991.

James, Michael. *The Quiltmaker's Handbook: A Guide to Design and Construction.* Englewood Cliffs, New Jersey: Prentice–Hall, 1978.

———. *The Second Quiltmaker's Handbook: Creative Approaches to Contemporary Quilt Design.* Englewood Cliffs, New Jersey: Prentice–Hall, 1981.

Johnson, Bruce. *A Child's Comfort: Baby and Doll Quilts in American Folk Art.* New York: Harcourt Brace Jovanovich, 1977.

Katzenberg, Dena S. *Baltimore Album Quilts.* Baltimore: Baltimore Museum of Art, 1981.

Kimball, Jeana. *Red and Green: An Appliqué Tradition.* Bothell, Washington: That Patchwork Place, 1990.

———. *Reflections of Baltimore.* Bothell, Washington: That Patchwork Place, 1989.

Kolter, Jane Bentley. *Forgetmenot: A Gallery of Friendship and Album Quilts.* Pittstown, New Jersey: Main Street Press, 1985.

Ladies Art Company. *Quilt Patterns, Patchwork, and Appliqué.* St. Louis: Hub Printing Company, 1928.

Lasansky, Jeannette, ed. *Bits and Pieces: Textile Traditions.* Lewisburg, Pennsylvania: Oral Traditions Project, 1991.

———. *In the Heart of Pennsylvania: 19th and 20th Century Quiltmaking Traditions.* Lewisburg, Pennsylvania: Oral Traditions Project, 1985.

———, ed. *In the Heart of Pennsylvania: Symposium Papers.* Lewisburg, Pennsylvania: Oral Traditions Project, 1986.

———. *Pieced by Mother: Over 100 Years of Quiltmaking Traditions.* Lewisburg, Pennsylvania: Oral Traditions Project, 1987.

———, ed. *Pieced by Mother: Symposium Papers.* Lewisburg, Pennsylvania: Oral Traditions Project, 1988.

———. *Quilt Documentation: Planning a Quilt Day.* San Francisco: American Quilt Study Group, 1991.

Layman, Joseph B., and Laura E. Layman. *The Philosophy of Housekeeping: A Scientific and Practical Manual.* Rev. ed. Hartford: S. M. Betts & Company, 1869.

Leman, Bonnie. *Quick and Easy Quilting.* Denver: M.O.M. Publishing Company, 1972.

Lipsett, Linda Otto. *Remember Me: Women and Their Friendship Quilts.* San Francisco: The Quilt Digest Press, 1985.

———. *To Love and to Cherish: Brides Remembered.* San Francisco: The Quilt Digest Press, 1989.

Lithgow, Marilyn. *Quiltmaking & Quiltmakers.* New York: Funk & Wagnalls, 1974.

MacDowell, Marsha, and Ruth D. Fitzgerald. *Michigan Quilts: 150 Years of a Textile Tradition.* East Lansing: Michigan State University Museums, 1987.

Martin, Nancy J. *Pieces of the Past.* Bothell, Washington: That Patchwork Place, 1986.

———. *Threads of Time.* Bothell, Washington: That Patchwork Place, 1990.

McCloskey, Marsha Reynolds. *Christmas Quilts.* Bothell, Washington: That Patchwork Place, 1985.

———. *Wall Quilts.* Bothell, Washington: That Patchwork Place, 1983.

McKim, Ruby Short. *One Hundred and One Patchwork Patterns,* 1931. Reprint. New York: Dover Publications, 1962.

McMorris, Penny. *Crazy Quilts.* New York: E. P. Dutton, 1984.

McMorris, Penny, and Michael Kile. *The Art Quilt.* Introduction by John Perreault. San Francisco: The Quilt Digest Press, 1986.

Miss Leslie's Lady's House-Book: A Manual of Domestic Economy. Philadelphia: A. Hart, 1850.

Montgomery, Florence M. *Textiles in America 1650–1870.*

New York: W. W. Norton and Company, 1984.

Mooney–Melvin, Patricia. *Tracing the Quiltmaker.* San Francisco: American Quilt Study Group, 1987.

The Mountain Mist Blue Book of Quilts. Cincinnati: Stearns and Foster, 1938.

Nelson, Cyril I., and Carter Houck. *Treasury of American Quilts.* 1982. Rerpint. New York: Crown Publishers, 1984.

Orlofsky, Patsy, and Myron Orlofsky. *Quilts in America.* New York: McGraw Hill Book Company, 1974.

Packard, Clarissa. *Recollections of a Housekeeper.* New York: Harper & Brothers, 1834.

Peck, Amelia. *American Quilts and Coverlets in the Metropolitan Museum of Art.* New York: Dutton Studio Books, 1990.

Pellman, Rachel, and Kenneth Pellman. *The World of Amish Quilts.* Intercourse, Pennsylvania: Good Books, 1984.

Peterson, Gladys J. *Pieces: The Story of Elgin in a Quilt.* Chelsea, Michigan: BookCrafters, 1989.

Pforr, Effie Chalmers. *Award Winning Quilts.* Birmingham: Oxmoor House, 1974.

Pottinger, David. *Quilts from the Indiana Amish.* New York: E. P. Dutton, 1983.

Quilts. St. Paul: The Farmer's Wife, 1931.

Ramsey, Bets, and Merikay Waldvogel. *The Quilts of Tennessee: Images of Domestic Life Prior to 1930.* Nashville, Tennessee: Rutledge Hill Press, 1986.

Regan, Jennifer. *American Quilts: A Sampler of Quilts and Their Stories.* New York: Gallery Books, 1989.

Roberson, Ruth Haislip, ed. *North Carolina Quilts.* Chapel Hill: University of North Carolina Press, 1988.

Robertson, Elizabeth Wells. *American Quilts.* New York: Viking, 1948.

Safford, Carleton, and Robert Bishop. *America's Quilts and Coverlets.* New York: E. P. Dutton, 1980.

Sandberg, Gosta. *Indigo Textiles, Technique and History.* London: A & C Black, 1989, and Asheville, North Carolina: Lark Books, 1989.

Schaffner, Cynthia V. A., and Susan Klein. *Folk Hearts: A Celebration of the Heart Motif in American Folk Art.* New York: Alfred A. Knopf, 1984.

Schlotzhauer, Joyce M. *Curves Unlimited.* McLean, Virginia: EPM Publications, Inc., 1984.

Sienkiewicz, Elly. *Spoken Without a Word.* Washington, D.C.: The Turtle Hill Press, 1983.

Smithsonian Institution. *American Pieced Quilts.* Introduction by Jonathan Holstein. Lausanne, Switzerland: Imprimeries Reunies, 1972.

Swan, Susan Burrows. *Plain and Fancy: American Women and Their Needlework, 1700–1850.* New York: Rutledge Books, 1977.

———. *A Winterthur Guide to American Needlework.* New York: Rutledge Books, 1976.

Tomlonson, Judy Schroeder. *Mennonite Quilts and Pieces.* Intercourse, Pennsylvania: Good Books, 1985.

von Gwinner, Schnuppe. *The History of the Patchwork Quilt Origins, Tradition and Symbols of a Textile Art.* Translated by Dr. Edward Force. West Chester, Pennsylvania: Schiffer Publishing, Ltd., 1988.

Waldvogel, Merikay. *Soft Covers for Hard Times: Quiltmaking and the Great Depression.* Nashville: Rutledge Hill Press, 1990.

Webster, Marie. *Quilts, Their Story and How to Make Them,* 1915. Reprint. Santa Barbara: Practical Patchwork, 1990.

Wentworth, Judy. *Quilts.* London: Studio Editions, Ltd., 1989.

Wien, Carol Anne. *The Great American Log Cabin Quilt Book.* New York: E. P. Dutton, 1984.

Wilson, Erica. *Quilts of America.* Birmingham: Oxmoor House, 1979.

Woodard, Thomas K., and Blanche Greenstein. *Crib Quilts and Other Small Wonders.* New York: E. P. Dutton, 1981.

———. *Twentieth Century Quilts 1900–1950.* New York: E. P. Dutton, 1988.

Periodicals

"A Child's Good-Night Bedquilt." *Ladies' Home Journal* (November 1905): 17.

"Alice in Wonderland Bedquilt." *Ladies' Home Journal* (September 1905): 13.

Allen, Gloria Seaman. "Bed Coverings: Kent County Maryland, 1810–1820." *Uncoverings 1985,* 6 (1986): 9–32.

"Anne Orr—She Captured Beauty." *Quilter's Newsletter Magazine* (June 1973): 12–16, 27.

Benberry, Cuesta. "Charm Quilts." *Quilter's Newsletter Magazine* (March 1980): 14–15.

———. "Charm Quilts Revisited." Part I. *Quilter's Newsletter Magazine* (January 1988): 30–35; Part II. (February 1988): 18–21.

———. "An Historic Quilt Document: The Ladies Art Company Catalog," *Quilters' Journal* (Summer 1978): 13–14.

———. "Ladies Art Company: Pioneer in Printed Quilt Patterns." *Nimble Needle Treasures* (Spring 1971): 4.

———. "Quilt Cottage Industries: A Chronicle." *Uncoverings 1986,* 7 (1987): 83–100.

———. "Quilt Kits—Past and Present, Part II." *Nimble Needle Treasures* (December 1974): 1.

———. "The Superb Mrs. Stenge." *Nimble Needle Treasures* (Summer 1971): 4.

———. "Storrowton Village—Home of the First National Quilt Show." *Quilter's Newsletter Magazine* (September 1987): 36–41.

———. "The Twentieth Century's First Quilt Revival Part I: The Interim Period." *Quilter's Newsletter Magazine* (July/August 1979): 20–22; "Part II: The First Quilt Revival" (September 1979): 25–29; "Part III: The World War I Era" (October 1979): 10–11, 37.

Berry, Michael. "Documenting the 19th Century Quilt." *American Craft* (February/March 1985): 23–27.

"Bertha Stenge, 'The Quilting Queen of Chicago.'" *Quilter's Newsletter Magazine* (October 1971): 4–6.

"Bertha Stenge Quilts Found." *Quilters' Journal* 26 (undated): 15.

Bishop, Robert. "The Double Wedding Ring Mystery." *Quilter's Newsletter Magazine* (June 1978): 9.

———. "The Double Wedding Ring Quilt." *Quilter's Newsletter Magazine* (April 1989): 35–37.

———. "Double Wedding Ring Quilts." *The Magazine Antiques* (March 1989): 732–741.

Bonfield, Lynn A. "Diaries of New England Quilters Before 1860." *Uncoverings 1988,* 9 (1989): 171–197.

———. "The Production of Cloth, Clothing and Quilts in 19th Century New England Homes." *Uncoverings 1981,* 2 (1982): 77–96.

Bowen, Helen. "The Ancient Art of Quilting." *The Magazine Antiques* (March 1923): 113–117.

———. "Corded and Padded Quilting." *The Magazine Antiques* (November 1924): 250–253.

Boynton, Linda. "Recent Changes in Amish Quilting." *Uncoverings 1985,* 6 (1986): 33–46.

Brackman, Barbara. "Baskets and Vases." *Quilter's Newsletter Magazine* (April 1990): 22–25.

———. "Buds and Blossoms, Nineteenth Century Album Patterns." *Quilter's Newsletter Magazine* (June 1989): 24.

———. "A Chronological Index to Pieced Quilt Patterns, 1775–1825." *Uncoverings 1983,* 4 (1984): 99–125.

———. "Dating Old Quilts, Part I, Green Prints and Dyes." *Quilter's Newsletter Magazine* (September 1984): 24–25, 45; "Part II, Cotton Prints Up to 1890" (October 1984): 26–27; "Part III, Cotton Prints, 1890–1960" (November–December 1984): 16–17; "Part IV, Quilt Dating and Technology" (January 1985): 28–29, 45; "Part V, Color As a Clue in Quilt Dating" (February 1985): 22–24; "Part VI, Style and Pattern as Clues" (March 1985): 22–25.

———. "Documentation Projects: Uncovering Heritage Quilts"; "A Quilt Day"; "Getting Started." *Quilter's Newsletter Magazine* (March 1988): 36–39.

———. "Fugitive Dyes in Antique Quilts." *Quilter's Newsletter Magazine* (October 1989): 42–44.

———. "The Flip Side: Looking Backward at Two-Sided Quilts." *Quilter's Newsletter Magazine* (January 1990): 32–34.

———. "The Hall/Szabronski Collection at the University of Kansas." *Uncoverings 1982,* 3 (1983): 59–74.

———. "Leaves and Foliage: Nineteenth-Century Album Patterns." *Quilter's Newsletter Magazine* (October 1989): 36–39.

———. "Looking Back at the Great Quilt Contest." *Quilter's Newsletter Magazine* (October 1983): 22–24.

———. "Madam Carrie Hall." *Quilter's Newsletter Magazine* (June 1981): 24–26.

———. "Midwestern Pattern Sources." *Uncoverings 1980,* 1 (1981): 3–12.

———. "Old Patchwork Quilts and the Woman Who Wrote It: Ruth E. Finley." *Quilter's Newsletter Magazine* (November/December 1988): 36–38.

———. "Out of Control: Patterns That Break the Rules." *Quilt Digest* (1985): 70–77.

———. "Patterns from the 1933 Chicago World's Fair." *Quilter's Newsletter Magazine* (July/August 1981): 18–20.

———. "Prairie School Quilts." *Quilter's Newsletter Magazine* (March 1982): 14–15.

———. "Quilts at Chicago's World's Fair." *Uncoverings 1981,* 2 (1982): 63–76.

———. "Quilts from Feed Sacks." *Quilter's Newsletter Magazine* (October 1985): 36–38.

———. "Quilts on the Kansas Frontier." *Kansas History* (Spring 1990): 13–22.

———. "Seven Myths about Old Quilts." *Quilter's Newsletter Magazine* (April 1988): 40–42, 57.

———. "Signature Quilts: Nineteenth-Century Trends." *Uncoverings 1989,* 10 (1990): 25–37.

———. "Who Was Aunt Martha?" *Quilter's Newsletter Magazine* (June 1991): 42–43.

———. "Who Was Nancy Cabot?" *Quilter's Newsletter Magazine* (January/February, 1991), 22–24.

———. "Who Was Nancy Page?" *Quilter's Newsletter Magazine* (September 1991): 22–27.

Bullard, Lucy Folmer. "The Collector: Once Out of Time." *Quilt Digest* 3 (1985): 8–21.

Christopherson, Katy. "Documenting Kentucky's Quilts: An Experiment in Research by Committee." *Uncoverings 1983,* 4 (1984): 137–145.

———. "A Little Noted Chapter in the 19th Century Craze for Crazy Quilts." *Quilters' Journal* (Spring 1978): 9–11.

Cook, Peter. "Art from Necessity: America's Wool Bedquilts." *Early American Life* (October 1991): 54–57.

Cozart, Dorothy. "A Century of Fundraising Quilts: 1860–1960." *Uncoverings 1984,* 5 (1985): 41–53.

———. "Women and Their Quilts As Portrayed by Some American Authors." *Uncoverings 1981,* 2 (1982): 19–33.

Davis, Gayle R. "Women in the Quilt Culture: An Analysis of Social Boundaries and Role Satisfaction." *Kansas History* (Spring 1990): 5–12.

DeGraw, Imelda G. "Museum Quilt Collecting," *Uncoverings 1981,* 2 (1982): 105–110.

DuBois, Jean. "Commemorative Quilts." *Quilter's Newsletter Magazine* (July 1976): 20–21.

Duncan, Ruby Hinson. "A Meeting of the Sunbonnet Children," Part I. *Quilt World* (March/April 1980): 17–18, 22; Part II. (June 1982): 52–53.

"English Paper Piecing." *Quilter's Newsletter Magazine* (October 1990): 37.

"English Piecing." *Quilter's Newsletter Magazine* (February 1986): 46.

"Evolution of a Quilt Design No. III [The Garden]." *Quilters' Journal* (Summer 1978): 9.

Fallert, Caryl Bryer. "Creative String Piecing." *Quilter's Newsletter Magazine* (September 1987): 24.

Farm and Fireside (November 11, 1882; October 1, 1885; January 15, February 1 and 15, 1886).

Garoutte, Sally. "The Development of Crazy Quilts." *Quilters' Journal* (Fall 1978): 13–15.

———. "Marseilles Quilts and Their Woven Offsprings." *Uncoverings 1982,* 3 (1983): 115–134.

Garside, Frances. "Patchwork Romance." *House Beautiful* (January 10, 1919): 24.

Gately, Rosemary Connolly. "Crazy Quilts in the Collection of the Maryland Historical Society." *The Magazine Antiques* (September 1955): 558–573.

Gleason's Drawing Room Pictorial Companion (October 21, 1854).

Godey's Lady's Book (September and December 1849; August and October 1855; April 1864; and December 1885).

Gordon, Beverly. "Playing at Being Powerless: New England Ladies' Fairs, 1830–1930." *The Massachusetts Review* (1985): 144–160.

"Great American Quilt Classics—Rose of Sharon." *Quilter's Newsletter Magazine* (October 1978): 15.

"Great American Quilt Contest Winners Showcased." *Quilter's Newsletter Magazine* (May 1986): 8–11.

Gross, Joyce. "Arsinoe Kelsey Bowen's 'Garden Quilt,'" *Quilters' Journal*, 31 (undated): 11–13.

———. "Rose Frances Good Kretsinger." *Quilters' Journal*, 31 (undated): 2–5.

Gunn, Virginia. "Crazy Quilts and Outline Quilts: Popular Responses to the Decorative Art/Art Needlework Movement, 1876–1893." *Uncoverings 1984*, 5 (1985): 131–152.

———. "Quilts at Nineteenth Century State and County Fairs: An Ohio Study." *Uncoverings 1988*, 9 (1989): 105–128.

———. "Quilts for Union Soldiers in the Civil War." *Uncoverings 1985*, 6 (1986): 95–121.

———. "Victorian Silk Template Patchwork in American Periodicals, 1850–1875." *Uncoverings 1984*, 5 (1985): 9–25.

Hagerman, Betty. "The Great American Quilt Classics—Sunbonnets." *Quilter's Newsletter Magazine* (April 1979): 6–9.

Harper's Bazar (January 11, 1879; July 23 and August 27, 1881; January 28 and June 3, 1882).

Haywood, Dixie. "The Making of a Masterpiece Bride's Quilt." *Quilter's Newsletter Magazine* (June 1983): 40–42.

Hersh, Tandy. "18th Century Quilted Silk Petticoats Worn in America." *Uncoverings 1984*, 5 (1985): 83–98.

Holstein, Jonathan. "Collecting Quilt Data: History from Statistics." *Quilt Digest* (1984. Rev. ed. 1985): 62–69.

"How I Do Research: Virginia Gunn, Barbara Brackman, Laurel Horton, Joanna Smith." *Uncoverings 1987*, 8 (1988): 157–171.

"Irish Chain." *Quilter's Newsletter Magazine* (March 1979): 16–19.

Jackson-Meyer, Suellen. "Log Cabin." *Quilter's Newsletter Magazine* (October 1979): 12–19.

"Jinny Beyer, Master Quiltmaker." *Quilters' Journal* (Summer 1978): 1.

Jordan, E. H. "A Colonial Quilt Enters the White House." *Needlecraft Magazine* (July 1929): 18, 30.

Kennedy, Cheryl. "Project Perspective." *Illinois Quilt Research Project Newsletter* (July 1989): 1–2.

Keyser, Pat Glynn. "Pieces and Patches." *Quilt World* (July/August 1985): 46–48.

Kile, Michael. "Looking Toward the Future: The Collector." *Quilt Digest* (1984. Rev. ed., 1985): 16–25.

Kirkpatrick, Erma H. "Quilts and Quiltmaking and the *Progressive Farmer*: 1886–1935." *Uncoverings 1985*, 6 (1986): 137–145.

Koob, Katherine R. "Documenting Quilts by Their Fabrics." *Uncoverings 1981*, 2 (1982): 3–9.

Ladies' Home Journal (October 1894).

Leman, Bonnie. "Baskets." *Quilter's Newsletter Magazine* (September 1979): 10–11.

———. "Crazy Quilts." *Quilter's Newsletter Magazine* (November 1977): 8–9.

———. "Mariner's Compass." *Quilter's Newsletter Magazine* (April 1980): 20.

———. "The Needle's Eye." *Quilter's Newsletter Magazine* (April 1979): 2; (May 1983): 4.

———. "Two Masters: Kretsinger and Stenge." *Quilter's Newsletter Magazine* (January 1981): 16–17.

Liles, James N. "Dyes in American Quilts Made Prior to 1930, with Special Emphasis on Cotton and Linen." *Uncoverings 1984*, 5 (1985): 29–40.

Lynch, Lauri, with Alice Schmude. "Hmong Needle Treasures." *Quilter's Newsletter Magazine* (October 1984): 18–19, 22.

Madden, Mary W. "The Kansas Quilt Project: Piecing Together Our Past." *Kansas History* (Spring 1990): 2–4.

———. "Textile Diaries: Kansas Quilt Memories." *Kansas History* (Spring 1990): 45–51.

Mahan, Vista Anne. "Quilts Used As Backdrops in Old Photographs." *Uncoverings 1991*, 12 (1992): 50–82.

Marks, Patricia. "Quilting Bee." *Quilter's Newsletter Magazine* (March 1982): 40.

Mathieson, Judy. "Some Published Sources of Design Inspiration for the Quilt Pattern Mariner's Compass—17th to 20th Century." *Uncoverings 1981*, 2 (1982): 11–17.

McMorris, Penny. "Crazy Quilts." *Quilter's Newsletter Magazine* (September 1984): 28–31.

———. "Quilts." *Quilt Digest* (1986): 67–75.

Meador, Michael M. "A Cover for the Nation: Ella Martin's Quilt Comes Home." *Quilter's Newsletter Magazine* (July/August 1989): 16–17.

Meyer, Suellen, "Characteristics of Missouri–German Quilts." *Uncoverings 1984*, 5 (1985): 99–114.

———. "Early Influences of the Sewing Machine and Visible Machine Stitching on Nineteenth-Century Quilts." *Uncoverings 1989*, 10 (1990): 38–53.

Nickols, Pat L. "Mary A. McElwain: Quilter and Quilt Businesswoman." *Uncoverings 1991*, 12 (1992): 98–117.

———. "String Quilts." *Uncoverings 1982*, 3 (1983): 53–57.

———. "The Use of Cotton Sacks in Quiltmaking." *Uncoverings 1988*, 9 (1989): 57–71.

"Ocean Waves." *Quilter's Newsletter Magazine* (May 1980): 15.

Oldani, John L. "Archiving and the American Quilt: A Position Paper." *Uncoverings 1980*, 1 (1981): 72–76.

Orlofsky, Patsy. "The Collector's Guide for the Care of Quilts in the Home." *Quilt Digest* (1984): 58–69.

Orr, Anne. "Quilt Making in Old and New Designs." *Good Housekeeping* (January 1933): 56, 123.

Penders, Mary Coyne. "Pieces of the Heart." *Quilt Digest* (1987): 20–29.

Peterson, Ruth W. "Memories of Mary A. McElwain's Quilt Shop." *Quilters' Journal* 24 (undated): 1–4.

Phillippi, Barbara K. "Pre-1940 Quilt Tops: Their Status and Fate in Western New York State." *Uncoverings 1990*, 11 (1991): 164–187.

Prairie Farmer (January 1954).

"Quilt Show" [Adapting McKim patterns]. *Quilter's Newsletter Magazine* (April 1990): 32–33.

"QNM Quilt Show" [Great American Quilt Contest]. *Quilter's Newsletter Magazine* (July/August 1987): 46–47.

Richards, Elizabeth, Sherri Martin-Scott, and Kerry Maguire. "Quilts As Material History: Identifying Research Models." *Uncoverings 1990*, 11 (1991): 88–108.

Ritter, Vivian. "Baby Blocks." *Quilter's Newsletter Magazine* (October 1990): 36–39.

Roberson, Ruth Haislip. "The North Carolina Quilt Project: Organization and Orchestration," *Uncoverings 1987,* 8 (1988): 147–155.

Robinson, Edith. "The Best Housekeeper in Banbury." *Ladies' Home Journal* (June 1905): 9.

"Rose Kretsinger—Appliqué Artist." *Quilter's Newsletter Magazine* (December 1977): 24–25, 29.

Rowley, Nancy J. "Red Cross Quilts for the Great War." *Uncoverings 1982,* 3 (1983): 43–51.

"Ruby Short McKim: A Memorial." *Quilter's Newsletter Magazine* (December 1976): 14–15.

Schilmoeller, Kathryn J. "The Role of Quilts in Children's Literature." *Uncoverings 1985,* 6 (1986): 71–84.

Shea, Elizabeth Weyrauch, and Patricia Cox Crews. "Nebraska Quiltmakers: 1870–1940." *Uncoverings 1989,* 10 (1990): 54–68.

Shirer, Marie. "Beyond the Basics: English Paper Piecing." *Quilter's Newsletter Magazine* (October 1987): 54.

——. "Designing Hexagon Quilt Variations." *Quilter's Newsletter Magazine* (October 1987): 48–49, 70.

——. "Grandmother's Flower Garden." *Quilter's Newsletter Magazine* (October 1987): 40–45.

——. "Lively Iris." *Quilter's Newsletter Magazine* (May 1983): 20–21,

——. "Log Cabin: An Update." *Quilter's Newsletter Magazine* (April 1988): 32–35.

Sienkiewicz, Elly. "Baltimore Brides Speak Without Words." *Quilter's Newsletter Magazine* (March 1984): 36–37.

——. "The Numsen Family Quilt: Fancy Flowers from Old Baltimore." *Quilter's Newsletter Magazine* (January 1990): 12–15.

——. "Penwork Plain and Fancy." *Quilter's Newsletter Magazine* (March 1991): 42–43.

Silber, Julie. "The Reiter Quilt: A Family Story in Cloth." *Quilt Digest* (1984. Rev. ed. 1985): 50–55.

Smith, Wilene. "Quilt Blocks?—or—Quilt Patterns?" *Uncoverings 1986,* 7 (1987): 101–114.

——. "Quilt History in Old Periodicals: A New Interpretation." *Uncoverings 1990,* 11 (1991): 188–213.

Stehlik, Jan. "Quilt Patterns and Contests of the *Omaha World–Herald,* 1921–1941." *Uncoverings 1990,* 11 (1991): 88–108.

Stoddard, Ada C. "A Study of Patchwork Old and New." *Quilt World* (April 1976): 24–25.

Stonuey, Joseph F., and Patricia Cox Crews. "The Nebraska Quilt History Project: Interpretations of Selected Parameters." *Uncoverings 1988,* 9 (1989): 171.

Successful Farming (February 1941).

Townsend, Louise O. "Dresden Plate." *Quilter's Newsletter Magazine* (January 1982): 20–22.

——. "Edna Marie Dunn of Kansas City, Missouri." *Quilter's Newsletter Magazine* (November/December 1978): 14.

——. "Evaline Foland, Quilt Pattern Illustrator." *Quilter's Newsletter Magazine* (April 1985): 20–22.

——. "Kansas City *Star* Quilt Patterns." *Uncoverings 1984,* 5 (1985): 115–130.

——. "New York Beauty." *Quilter's Newsletter Magazine* (April 1981): 10–12.

Trechsel, Gail Andrews. "Mourning Quilts in America." *Uncoverings 1989,* 10 (1990): 139–158.

Trifonoff, Karen M. "Amish Culture As Preserved in Quilts." *Journal of Cultural Geography* (Winter 1989): 63–73.

"Tulip Quilts." *Quilter's Newsletter Magazine* (May 1978): 16–17.

Waldvogel, Marikay. "The Marketing of Anne Orr's Quilts." *Uncoverings 1990,* 11 (1991): 7–28.

——. "Southern Linsey Quilts of the Nineteenth Century." *Uncoverings 1987,* 8 (1988): 87–106.

Wilson, Valerie. "Quiltmaking in Counties Antrim and Down: Preliminary Findings from the Ulster Quilt Survey." *Uncoverings 1991,* 12 (1992): 142–175.

"The Woman Who Made 'The Bible' Quilt." *Nimble Needle Treasures* (Summer 1971): 6.

Monographic Chapters in Books

Benberry, Cuesta. "Marie Webster: Indiana's Gift to American Quilts." In Goldman and Wiebusch. *Quilts of Indiana,* 88–93.

——. "The Nationalization of Pennsylvania–Dutch Patterns in the 1940's–1960's." In Lasansky, ed. *Bits and Pieces,* 81–89.

Brackman, Barbara. "Fairs and Expositions: Their Influence on American Quilts." In Lasansky, ed. *Bits and Pieces,* 91–99.

——. "What's in a Name? Quilt Patterns from 1830 to the Present." In Lasansky, ed. *Pieced by Mother: Symposium Papers,* 106–114.

Clark, Ricky. "Mid-19th-Century Album and Friendship Quilts, 1860–1920." In Lasansky, ed. *Pieced by Mother: Symposium Papers,* 76–85.

——. "The Needlework of an American Lady/Social History in Quilts." In Lasansky, ed. *Heart of Pennsylvania: Symposium Papers,* 64–75.

Cozart, Dorothy. "The Role and Look of Fundraising Quilts, 1860–1920." In Lasansky, ed. *Pieced by Mother: Symposium Papers,* 86–95.

Eanes, Ellen Fickling. "Chintz Appliqué Quilts." In Roberson, ed. *North Carolina Quilts,* 37–62.

Gunn, Virginia. "The Display, Care, and Conservation of Old Quilts." In Lasansky, ed. *Heart of Pennsylvania: Symposium Papers,* 90–95.

——. "Dress Fabrics of the Late 19th Century: Their Relationship to Period Quilts." In Lasansky, ed. *Bits and Pieces,* 4–15.

——. "New Thoughts on Care and Conservation." In Lasansky, ed. *Pieced by Mother: Symposium Papers,* 115–119.

——. "Quilts—Crazy Memories." In Duke and Harding, eds. *America's Glorious Quilts,* 152–173.

——. "Template Quilt Construction and Its Offshoots from *Godey's Lady's Book* to Mountain Mist." In Lasansky, ed. *Pieced by Mother: Symposium Papers,* 68–75.

Haders, Phyllis. "Quilts: The Art of the Amish." In Duke and Harding, eds. *America's Glorious Quilts,* 110–131.

Herr, Patricia T. "What Distinguishes a Pennsylvania Quilt." In Lasansky, ed. *Heart of Pennsylvania: Symposium Papers,* 28–37.

Hersh, Tandy. "The Evolution of the Pennsylvania–German Pillowcase." In Lasansky, ed. *Bits and Pieces,* 38–47.

———. "Quilted Petticoats." In Lasansky, ed. *Pieced by Mother: Symposium Papers,* 5–11.

Holstein, Jonathan. "The American Block Quilt." In Lasansky, ed. *Heart of Pennsylvania: Symposium Papers,* 16–27.

Keyser, Alan G. "Beds, Bedding, Bedsteads, and Sleep: Early Pennsylvania–German Traditions." In Lasansky, ed. *Pieced by Mother: Symposium Papers,* 23–33.

Kirkpatrick, Erma Hughes. "Garden Variety Appliqué." In Roberson, ed. *North Carolina Quilts,* 63–96.

———. "Warming Hearts and Raising Funds." In Roberson, ed. *North Carolina Quilts,* 137–157.

Lasansky, Jeannette. "The Colonial Revival." In Lasansky, *Pieced by Mother,* 105–115.

———. "The Colonial Revival and Quilts, 1864–1976." In Lasansky, ed. *Pieced by Mother: Symposium Papers,* 96–107.

———. "Plain and Fancy." In Lasansky, *Pieced by Mother,* 25–59.

———. "Quilt Documentation: A Step-By-Step Guide." In Lasansky, *Pieced by Mother,* 17–23.

———. "Quilts in the Dowry." In Lasansky, *Bits and Pieces,* 48–55.

———. "Stars Forever." In Lasansky, *Pieced by Mother,* 75–83.

———. "Think of Me." In Lasansky, *Pieced by Mother,* 61–73.

———. "The Typical Versus the Unusual: Distortions of Time." In Lasansky, ed. *Heart of Pennsylvania: Symposium Papers,* 56–63.

Long, Pat, and Dennis Duke. "Baby, Crib, and Doll Quilts." In Duke and Harding, eds. *America's Glorious Quilts,* 176–191.

Maines, Rachel. "Paradigms of Scarcity and Abundance/The Quilt as an Artifact of the Industrial Revolution." In Lasansky, ed. *Heart of Pennsylvania: Symposium Papers,* 84–89.

———. "The Tools of the Workbasket Needlework Technology in the Industrial Era." In Lasansky, ed. *Bits and Pieces,* 111–119.

McCarter, Sue Barker. "Crazy Quilts: Quiet Protest." In Roberson, ed. *North Carolina Quilts,* 159–180.

Peterson, Sally. "A Cool Heart and a Watchful Mind: Creating Hmong Paj Ntaub in the Context of Community." In Lasansky, ed. *Pieced by Mother: Symposium Papers,* 35–45.

Roan, Nancy. "Fabrics Used by Pennsylvania–German Farm Families in Southeastern Pennsylvania." In Lasansky, ed. *Bits and Pieces,* 16–25.

Sullivan, Kathy. "The Legacy of German Quiltmaking in North Carolina." In Lasansky, ed. *Bits and Pieces,* 65–67.

Sullivan, Kathlyn Fender. "Pieced and Plentiful." In Roberson, ed. *North Carolina Quilts,* 97–135.

Swan, Susan Burrows. "Quiltmaking Within Women's Needlework Repertoire." In Lasansky, ed. *Heart of Pennsylvania: Symposium Papers,* 8–15.

van der Hoof, Gail. "Various Aspects of Dating Quilts." In Lasansky, ed. *Heart of Pennsylvania: Symposium Papers,* 76–83.

Waldvogel, Merikay. "Making Little Do Something: Reusing Cotton Sacks." In Waldvogel, *Soft Covers,* 62–75.

———. "The Quilt Revival." In Waldvogel, *Soft Covers,* 2–23.

———. "Refining the Tradition: Anne Champe Orr, 1875–1946." In Waldvogel, *Soft Covers,* 24–37.

———. "Sears National Quilt Contest, 1933: Promoting the Tradition." In Waldvogel, *Soft Covers,* 38–47.

HISTORICAL AND GENERAL WORKS

Alvord, Clarence W. *The Illinois Country, 1673–1818.* Chicago: A. C. McClurg and Company, 1922.

Bank, Mirra. *Anonymous Was a Woman.* New York: St. Martin's Press, 1979.

Bailey, Ronald H. *The Home Front: U.S.A.* Alexandria, Virginia: Time–Life Books, 1978.

Bent, Charles, ed. *History of Whiteside County, Illinois.* Morrison, Illinois: no publisher, 1877.

Billington, Ray A. *Westward Expansion: A History of the American Frontier.* 3rd ed. New York: Macmillan, 1967.

Birkbeck, Morris. *Notes on a Journey in America from the Coast of Virginia to the Territory of Illinois.* London: James Ridgway, 1818.

Bishop, Robert, and Patricia Coblentz. *The World of Antiques, Art, and Architecture in Victorian America.* New York: E. P. Dutton, 1979.

Boewe, Charles. *Prairie Albion: An English Settlement in Pioneer Illinois.* Carbondale: Southern Illinois University Press, 1962.

Boggess, Arthur C. *The Settlement of Illinois, 1778–1830.* Chicago: Chicago Historical Society, 1908.

Brant, Sandra, and Elissa Cullman. *Small Folk: A Celebration of Childhood in America.* New York: E. P. Dutton, 1980.

Buck, Solon J. *Illinois in 1818.* Springfield: Illinois Centennial Commission, 1917.

Burgess, Fred W. *Antique Jewelry and Trinkets.* New York: Tudor Publishing Company, 1937.

Burland, Rebecca. *A True Picture of Emigration.* Edited by Milo M. Quaife. Chicago: R. R. Donnelley and Sons, 1936.

Campbell, Charles B. "Bourbonnais: Or the Early French Settlements in Kankakee County, Ill." *Transactions of the Illinois State Historical Society.* Springfield: Illinois State Journal Company, 1906, 65–72.

Complete Poems, Carl Sandburg. New York: Harcourt, Brace and Company, 1916.

Comstock, Helen. *American Furniture: Seventeenth, Eighteenth, and Nineteenth Century Styles.* New York: The Viking Press, 1962.

Cosco, Ethel Reeser. *Christian Reeser: The Story of a Centenarian.* Privately printed, 1952.

Dearing, Mary R. *Veterans in Politics: The Story of the G.A.R.* Baton Rouge: Louisiana State University Press, 1952.

Devine, Robert A., et. al. *America: Past and Present.* Glenview, Illinois: Scott, Foresman and Company, 1987.

Draper, Lyman C., ed. *Collections of the State Historical Society of Wisconsin.* Vol. 2. Madison: State Historical Society of Wisconsin, 1903.

Dyck, Cornelius J., ed. *An Introduction to Mennonite History: A Popular History of the Anabaptists and the Mennonites.* Scottdale, Pennsylvania: Herald Press, 1967.

Earle, Alice Morse. *Home Life in Colonial Days.* New York: Macmillan Company, 1923.

Eaton, Clement. *Henry Clay and the Art of American Politics.* Boston: Little, Brown and Company, 1957.

Elbert, E. Duane. "The American Roots of German Lutheranism in Illinois." *Illinois Historical Journal* (Summer 1985): 97–112.

———. *Edward Coles: Freedom's Champion.* Charleston, Illinois: Coles County Historical Society Series, 1975.

Elmen, Paul. *Wheat Flour Messiah: Eric Jansson of Bishop Hill.* Carbondale: Southern Illinois University Press, 1976.

Fairbanks, Jonathan L., and Elizabeth Bidwell Bates. *American Furniture 1620 to the Present.* New York: Richard Marek Publishers, 1981.

Fischer, Roger A. *Tippecanoe and Trinkets Too: The Material Culture of American Presidential Campaigns, 1828–1984.* Urbana: University of Illinois Press, 1988.

Flower, Margaret. *Victorian Jewelry.* New York: A. S. Barnes and Company, 1951.

Freidel, Frank. *The Splendid Little War.* Boston: Little, Brown and Company, 1958.

Green, Harvey. *The Light of the Home: An Intimate View of the Lives of Women in Victorian America.* New York: Pantheon Books, 1983.

Grover, Eulalie Osgood. *Sunbonnet Babies: A First Reader.* Chicago: Rand, McNally & Company, 1902 and 1914.

Harding, Benjamin. *A Tour Through the Western Country, A. D. 1818 and 1819.* New London, Connecticut, 1819.

Henderson, John G. *Early History of the Sangamon Country.* Davenport, Iowa: Day, Egburt, and Fidlar, 1873.

The History of Henry County, Illinois, Its Tax-Payers and Voters. Chicago: H. F. Kett and Company, 1877.

The History of Menard and Mason Counties, Illinois. Chicago: O. L. Baskin and Company, 1879.

Hoehling, A. A. *Home Front, U.S.A.: The Story of World War II Over Here.* New York: Thomas Y. Crowell Company, 1966.

Hopkins, James F., ed. *The Papers of Henry Clay.* Vol. 3. Lexington: University of Kentucky Press, 1963.

Howard, Robert P. *Illinois: A History of the Prairie State.* Grand Rapids, Michigan: Eerdman's Publishing Company, 1972.

Horwitz, Elinor Lauder. *The Bird, the Banner, and Uncle Sam: Images of America in Folk and Popular Art.* Philadelphia: J. B. Lippincott, 1976.

Illinois Blue Book, 1931–1932. Springfield: Journal Printing Company, 1931.

Illinois Sesquicentennial Edition of the Christian County History. Jacksonville, Illinois: Production Press, 1968.

Jensen, Richard J. *Illinois: A Bicentennial History.* Nashville: The American Association for State and Local History, 1978.

Keiser, John H. *Building for the Centuries: Illinois, 1865 to 1898.* Urbana: University of Illinois Press, 1977.

Kennedy, Joseph C. G., comp. *Population of the United States in 1860.* Washington, D.C.: Government Printing Office, 1864.

Kennicott, John A. *Transactions of the Illinois State Agricultural Society: with the Proceedings of the County Societies, and Kindred Associations.* Springfield: Lanphier and Walker, 1855.

Kett, Joseph F. *Rites of Passage: Adolescence in America, 1790 to the Present.* New York: Basic Books, Inc., 1977.

Kiner, Henry L. *History of Henry County, Illinois.* 2 vols. Chicago: The Pioneer Publishing Company, 1910.

Kyvig, David E., and Myron A. Marty. *Nearby History: Exploring the Past Around You.* Nashville: The American Association for State and Local History, 1982.

Leach, William R. "Transformations in a Culture of Consumption: Women and Department Stores, 1890–1925." *The Journal of American History* (September 1984): 319–342.

Logan, Mary Simmerson Cunningham [Mrs. John A.] *The Home Manual.* Philadelphia: No publisher, 1889.

Lynn, Catherine. *Wallpaper in America from the Seventeenth Century to World War I.* New York: W. W. Norton and Company, 1980.

Madden, Betty I. *Art, Crafts, and Architecture in Early Illinois.* Urbana: University of Illinois Press, 1974.

Martinello, Marian L. *The Search for Emma's Story.* Fort Worth: Texas Christian University Press, 1987.

Massie, M. D. *Past and Present of Pike County, Illinois.* Chicago: S. J. Clarke Publishing Company, 1906.

McCabe, James D. *Illustrated History of the Centennial Exhibition.* Philadelphia: The National Publishing Company, 1976.

McClinton, Katherine Morrison. *Antique Collecting for Everyone.* New York: Bonanza Books, 1951.

———. *Antiques Past and Present.* New York: Clarkson N. Potter, Inc., 1971.

———. *Collecting American Victorian Antiques.* New York: Charles Scribner's Sons, 1966.

Meyer, Douglas K. "Folk Housing on the Illinois Frontier." *Pioneer America Society Transactions* I (1978), 30–42.

Miller, Harold Kenneth, and Irene Hinds Miller. *Our Family.* Privately printed, 1962.

Miller, R. D. *Past and Present of Menard County, Illinois.* Chicago: S. J. Clarke Publishing Company, 1905.

Oliver, William. *Eight Months in Illinois with Information to Immigrants.* Chicago: Walter M. Hill, 1924.

The Past and Present of Rock Island County, Illinois. Chicago: H. F. Kett and Company, 1877.

Patton, James W. "Letters from North Carolina Emigrants in the Old Northwest, 1830–1834." *Mississippi Valley Historical Review* (September 1960): 263–277.

Pease, Theodore C. *The Frontier State: 1818–1848.* Chicago: A. C. McClurg and Company, 1922.

Perrin, William H., ed. *History of Effingham County, Illinois.* Chicago: O. L. Baskin and Company, 1883.

Pooley, William V. *The Settlement of Illinois from 1830 to 1850.* Madison: University of Wisconsin, 1908.

Polenberg, Richard, ed. *America at War: The Home Front, 1941–1945.* Englewood Cliffs, New Jersey: Prentice–Hall, 1968.

Portrait and Biographical Album of Morgan and Scott Counties, Illinois. Chicago: Chapman Brothers, 1889.

Portrait and Biographical Album of Rock Island County, Illinois. Chicago: Biographical Publishing Company, 1885.

Posadas, Barbara. "To Preserve the Home." In Bridges, Roger D., and Rodney O. Davis. *Illinois: Its History and Legacy.* St. Louis: River City Publishers, 1984.

Robinson, Edgar Eugene. *The Presidential Vote, 1896–1932.* Stanford: Stanford University Press, 1934.

Roller, Scott. "Business As Usual: Indiana's Response to the Confederate Invasion of the Summer of 1863." *Indiana Magazine of History* (March 1991): 1–25.

Russo, David J. *Families and Communities: A New View of American History.* Nashville: The American Association for State and Local History, 1974.

Smith, Elsdon C. *American Surnames.* Philadelphia: Chilton Book Company, 1969.

Smith, Willard H. *Mennonites in Illinois.* Scottdale, Pennsylvania: Herald Press, 1983.

Stoddart, Melissa Ringheim. "Cultural Diversity in Minnesota Museums." *Midwest Museums Conference Annual Review* (Midwest Museums Conference, St. Louis, 1992), 33–37.

Strasser, Susan. *Never Done: A History of American Housework.* New York: Pantheon Books, 1982.

The Statistics of the Population of the United States. Washington, D.C.: Government Printing Office, 1872.

Steinbeck, John. *The Grapes of Wrath.* New York: The Viking Press, 1939.

Thomas, Benjamin P. *Lincoln's New Salem.* 1934. Reprint. Springfield: Abraham Lincoln Association, 1947.

Tillson, Christiana Holmes. *A Woman's Story of Pioneer Illinois.* Edited by Milo M. Quaife. Chicago: R.R. Donnelley and Sons, 1919.

Wendt, Lloyd, and Herman Kogan. *Give the Lady What She Wants!* Chicago: Rand, McNally and Company, 1952.

Williams, Susan. *Savory Suppers and Fashionable Feasts: Dining in Victorian America.* New York: Pantheon Books, 1985.

Wood, John, ed. *America and the Daguerreotype.* Iowa City: University of Iowa Press, 1991.

Wyman, Mark. *Immigrants in the Valley: Irish, Germans, and Americans in the Upper Mississippi Country, 1830–1860.* Chicago: Nelson-Hall, 1984.

Zukowsky, John. *Chicago Architecture 1872–1922: Birth of a Metropolis.* Munich: Prestel–Verlag, 1987.

ARCHIVAL COLLECTIONS

Dudley Store Ledger, October 17, 1844–June 15, 1854. Collection of the Coles County Historical Society, Charleston, Illinois.

Henry Weiss Probate, Charleston, Illinois, 1869, Circuit Clerk vault, Coles County Court House, Charleston, Illinois. Photocopy in Cherie Cook. "Henry Weiss," Historical Administration Local History Research File, Department of History, Eastern Illinois University, Charleston, Illinois.

NEWSPAPERS

Albany, Illinois, *Review,* June 25, 1903; May 31, 1906.

Champaign, Illinois, *West Urbana Gazette,* October 12, 1859.

Effingham, Illinois, *Republican,* May [?], 1904.

Freeport, Illinois, *Daily Journal Republican,* November 19, 1983.

Galva, Illinois, *Weekly News,* January 5, 1888; March 24, 1889.

Moline, Illinois, *Dispatch,* March 16, 1986.

Pittsfield, Illinois, *Democrat,* September 12, 1884.

Portland, Oregon, *Oregon Labor Press,* October 4, 1963.

Springfield, Illinois, *Illinois State Journal,* July 15, 1931; October 14, 1932.

Taylorville, Illinois, *Breeze Courier,* November 9, 1931; February 1, 1939.

INDEX